ultimate

recipe collection

TRIDENT
PRESS
INTERNATIONAL

Published by:
TRIDENT PRESS INTERNATIONAL
801 12th Avenue South
Suite 400
Naples, FL 34102 U.S.A.
©Trident Press
Tel: (941) 649 7077
Fax: (941) 649 5832
Email: tridentpress@worldnet.att.net
Website: www.trident-international.com

acknowledgements

Ultimate Cookbook

Packaged by: R&R Publications Marketing Pty Ltd
Brunswick, Victoria, Australia
Creative Director: Paul Sims
Production Manager: Anthony Carroll
Food Photography: Warren Webb,
William Meppem, Andrew Elton,
Quentin Bacon,Gary Smith, Per Ericson,
Paul Grater, Ray Joice, John Stewart,
Ashley Mackevicius, Harm Mol,
Yanto Noerianto,
Andy Payne.
Food Stylists: Stephane Souvlis, Janet Lodge,
Di Kirby, Wendy Berecry, Belinda Clayton,
Rosemary De Santis, Carolyn Fienberg,
Jacqui Hing, Michelle Gorry,
Christine Sheppard, Donna Hay.

Recipe Development: Ellen Argyriou,
Sheryle Eastwood, Kim Freeman,
Lucy Kelly, Donna Hay, Anneka Mitchell,
Penelope Peel, Jody Vassallo,
Belinda Warn, Loukie Werle.
Proof Reader: Samantha Carroll

Includes Index
ISBN 1 582 79113 9
EAN 9 781582 791135

Second Edition Printed October 2002

Printed in Mexico

ntents

introduction

introduction

Welcome to "The Ultimate" cookbook.

We have attempted to give our readers a book chock full of wonderful, tasty, exciting and very easy to prepare and serve recipes.

It has been titled "The Ultimate" as we believe that you will find every type of food you can cook, combined with imaginative ingredients, all of which are designed to make your daily cooking chores an enjoyable experience.

Within these 800 pages you will find brilliant recipes and ideas which will not only inspire you as the cook, but will also satisfy the tastes and demands of those for whom you are cooking.

Recipes covering a wide expanse of cooking tastes from the quick-and-easy meal to a fully catered dinner party are all featured within this book.

The first chapter contains a wonderful collection of appetisers and hors d'oeuvres, suitable for a quite afternoon with a selected bottle of wine, or if the occasion demands, a full selection to start off that casual, or even formal dinner party.

An international flavour with a range of the world's most popular cuisine "Italian" graces the pages of our second chapter. Try such wonderful tastes as those offered in the traditional osso bucco, hearty minestrone soup, spaghetti and meatballs or chicken livers and mushrooms on spaghetti. Do not forget to try the exquisite and delicate tiramisu and a great cassata siciliana.

That great Northern Italian delicacy "risotto" has pride of place in the third chapter, you will find some imaginative additions to the traditional aborio rice, which is the base for great risotto. Plus a selection of great rice dishes which will stand on their own as light meals or snacks. Include a mixed mushroom risotto or a Creole jambalaya in the weekly recipe schedule, you will be glad you did.

One could be accused of repeating the Italian chapter by the inclusion of chapter four "Pasta Perfect", however, we believe that pasta has now reached such a position in our daily meals that it will stand alone as a food source. We have produced recipes using a wide variety of pasta from the common spaghetti, to crests, tagliatelle, tortellini, bows and others, all in great tasty, easy to prepare recipes.

On to chapter five and one of the most interesting, but not well known food sources, "Pulses and Legumes". Pulses are all members of the legume family, one of the world's most important food groups.
A full complement of recipes covering; soups, meat & poultry, seafood, vegetables and pasta, with information on techniques and types of pulses.

Some like it spicy, some like it hot, chapter six covers all bases. We have included the best recipes in our collection from such culturally diverse places as Thailand and Mexico.

It is a proven fact that recipes from these exotic countries give us some of the best gourmet spicy hot foods in the world. If hot and spicy is your forte, you will love this chapter.

On again to chapter seven "Salads hot and cold", where you will find many delightful surprises. Salads need not have a traditional season; simple, easy-to-prepare green salads with a special dressing or mixed vegetable salads make wonderful accompaniments to meats, poultry, fish, omelettes and quiches at any time of the year.

Learn the secrets of successful salads and apply them to your culinary skills, you will be amazed at the results.

No book of this type would be complete without the addition of a "Vegetarian" chapter.

In chapter eight we have attempted to collate the most interesting meat free recipes available from our kitchens. We are sure you will delight in the tasty, imaginative selection we have offered here.

It is a proven fact that the most popular small cake is the "muffin". So easy to make and such fantastic taste sensations from the results. In chapter nine, we present the best-of-the-best muffin recipes. From savoury muffins to sweets, the results will be accepted by family and friends alike. Also included is a selection of quick breads, recipes which will give that afternoon tea that extra lift, when you present them.

To chapter ten and recipes "to die for". Chocolate sensations will really get the taste buds working overtime. Recipes cover such lusciously rich and sumptuous treats as chocolate chip cookies, chocolate meringue cake, the best mud cake, chocolate nougat to black forest gateau and raspberry chocolate truffle cakes. Everything for the choc-o-holic.

We finish this wonderful tour of exquisite delights with our eleventh chapter covering a fantastic selection of ice-creams and frozen desserts. Here we have produced recipes to really touch the heart, from magnificent mango ice cream and brilliant liqueur based ice creams to tasty sorbets and sherbets.

We have tried, and we feel that we have succeeded, in providing you with a fantastic selection of recipes, which we can only describe as "Ultimate".

Good luck, bon appetite!

appetising
hors d'oeuvres

introduction

Fabulous fingerfoods

The modern trend appears to be moving to more casual entertaining. What better way to entertain family and friends than by providing easy-to-eat food. Finger food allows you to prepare a variety of foods to suit just about everyone's taste.

We all remember a special dip or spread from our childhood...and how many times have you been moved to seek the recipe of a superb-tasting morsel from your hosts?

The recipes that follow have been specially created to provide you with many new ideas which we are sure will quickly become part of your entertainment repertoire and long-term family favourites.

Recipes that follow will smooth the way to cooking for informal gatherings, brunches, lunches, cocktail parties, patio parties and buffets. These stylish, economical recipes have been created for the busy cook and all recipes contain ingredients easily found on your supermarket shelves.

Many recipes can be prepared well ahead of time thereby allowing you, the cook, time enough to enjoy the company of your guests.

How to Give a Successful Party

How often have you thought about giving a party and been put off by the idea of the food preparation involved? Serving drinks is one thing, catering for a crowd is another.

This book has all the answers. Here, for the first time, is a complete selection of delectable hors d'oeuvres to entertain your guests, no matter what the occasion — formal or informal, outdoors or indoors, summer or winter.

The recipes are simple to make, use attractive ingredients, and are designed to give you maximum time enjoying the company of your guests. Most can be prepared beforehand, with little or no last-minute time to spend.

The key word is simplicity. Every single recipe in this book is meant to be eaten with fingers only — no forks or knives please! The only other things you as party-giver have to provide are: the occasion, good cheer and plenty of napkins!

As goes for mixing and matching between the sections in this book, let your imagination go and have fun!

easy antipasto

Easy antipasto platter for six
An antipasto platter is fun as a starter to an Italian meal, or to serve when friends drop by.

- **Vegetable Toss**
- **Crostini**
- **Prosciutto with Melon**
- **Creamy Tuna Spread**
- **Salami Platter**
- **Marinated Olives**
- **Eggplant (aubergine) with Dipping Sauce**

Vegetable Toss
Make this dish several hours ahead of time to allow the flavours to develop.

2 tablespoons olive oil
4 zucchini (courgettes), sliced lengthways
1 large head broccoli, cut into florets
2 carrots, peeled
Dressing
2 small red chillies, finely chopped
1 tablespoon each fresh mint and fresh oregano, finely chopped
¹/₂ cup/125mL/4¹/₂fl oz light olive oil
2 tablespoons red wine vinegar
2 tablespoons lemon juice
freshly ground black pepper

1 *Heat oil in a skillet and cook zucchini (courgette) slices until golden on each side. Drain on paper towels and set aside.*
2 *Boil, steam or microwave broccoli until tender. Refresh under cold water. Drain and set aside.*
3 *Slice carrots into long thin strips, using a vegetable peeler. Boil, steam or microwave until just tender. Refresh under cold water. Drain and set aside.*
4 *To make dressing: place chillies, mint, oregano, oil, vinegar and lemon juice in a screwtop jar. Season to taste with pepper. Shake well to combine. Place vegetables in a serving bowl and toss through dressing. Cover and refrigerate until required.*
Serves 6

Crostini
This recipe can be made using any of your favourite breads.

1 loaf Italian bread, cut into 1cm/¹/₂in slices
¹/₃ cup/90g/3oz butter, melted

1 *Lightly brush both sides of bread slices with butter and place on a cookie sheet.*
2 *Bake at 180°C/350°F for 12 minutes, or until golden and crunchy.*
Serves 6

Prosciutto with Melon

1 cantaloupe (rockmelon) or honeydew melon, halved, seeded and peeled
18 slices prosciutto ham

1 *Cut melon into 18 long thin wedges, wrap a slice of prosciutto around each wedge of melon and secure with a wooden pick. Arrange on platter and chill before serving.*
Makes 18

Creamy Tuna Spread
This spread is great served with Crostini or fresh crusty bread.

185g/6oz canned tuna, drained
¹/₂ cup/125g/4¹/₂oz cream cheese
¹/₂ cup/125g/4¹/₂oz mayonnaise
2 tablespoons lemon juice
¹/₂ cup/125g/4¹/₂oz butter, melted
1 teaspoon snipped fresh chives
1 teaspoon chopped fresh thyme

1 *Place tuna, cream cheese, mayonnaise and lemon juice in a food processor or blender and process until smooth. With machine running, add butter, chives and thyme. Transfer mixture to a serving dish and refrigerate for 1 hour or until firm.*
Serves 6

Salami Selection

125g/4¹/₂oz each of any 2 types of sliced Italian salami (such as: alesandre, felino, cotto, felinetti, calabrese, Napoli, Milano and Genoa)
125g/4¹/₂oz each of any 2 types of sliced Italian hams or sausages (such as: pastrami, pancetta, mortadella and pepperoni)

1 *Cut or fold salami, hams and sausages to make your platter look appealing.*
    Serves 6

Marinated Olives

These olives will keep for up to four months in the refrigerator.
375g/12oz black olives, drained
Marinade
¹/₂ cup/125mL/4¹/₂fl oz light olive oil
¹/₄ cup/60mL/2fl oz balsamic vinegar
1 tablespoon fresh tarragon, chopped
2 bay leaves
2 tablespoons fresh basil, chopped
2 teaspoons freshly ground black pepper

1 *Place olives in a large sterilised jar. Mix together oil, vinegar, tarragon, bay leaves, basil and black pepper. Pour over olives to cover. Seal jar and store in refrigerator.*
    Makes a 500mL/1 pint jar

Eggplant (aubergine) with Dipping Sauce

1 eggplant (aubergine), cut in
half lengthwise, then into 5mm/¹/₄in slices
salt
³/₄ cup/185g/6¹/₂oz cornflour (cornstarch)
vegetable oil for cooking
Dipping sauce
1 red capsicum (pepper), seeded, coarsely chopped

¹/₃ cup/100mL/3¹/₂fl oz light cream
¹/₄ cup/60g/2oz butter, chopped
¹/₄ teaspoon chilli powder
freshly ground black pepper
Batter
1 cup/125g/4¹/₂oz flour
1 teaspoon baking powder
³/₄ cup/200mL/7fl oz milk
2 eggs, lightly beaten

1 *Sprinkle eggplant (aubergine) slices with salt and set aside for 30 minutes.*
2 *To make sauce: place red capsicum (pepper) and cream in a food processor or blender and process until smooth. Transfer to a small saucepan and cook over low heat for 5 minutes. Remove from heat and whisk in butter. Season to taste with chilli powder and black pepper. Set aside; keep warm.*
3 *To make batter: Sift flour and baking powder into a small bowl, make a well in the centre and gradually stir in milk and eggs. Mix to form a smooth paste. Set aside.*
4 *Rinse eggplant (aubergine) well under cold running water. Drain and pat dry on paper towels. Toss eggplant in cornflour (cornstarch) and shake to remove excess.*
5 *Heat oil in a skillet. Dip eggplant (aubergine) slices in batter and cook a few at a time until golden brown. Drain on paper towels. Serve eggplant (aubergine) with warm sauce.*
    Serves 6

mushroom melts

cheese snacks

All foods have a greater appeal

if they are attractively presented, and cheese is no exception. Invest in a cheese board, or bring out a handsome platter and surround your cheese (a choice of varieties, or just your favourite cheddar) with cracker biscuits, celery, radishes, or a lovely wreath of fresh fruit. Cheese and fruit are regarded as the perfect dessert combination by many European gourmets — and for health and sheer good eating we might follow their example.

cheese

There are hundreds of distinct varieties of cheese, but no matter how different the finished product, they all started out the same way.

Firm Cheeses

Cheddar cheese is by far the most popular of cheeses. It ranges from mild to full-flavoured; nothing can challenge it for versatility. Equally delicious in salads, savouries, sandwiches, it is a tasty addition to soups and meat dishes, and as a high energy snack with fruit, when served with crackers.

Other varieties of cheeses are:

Swiss (or Gruyère or Emmenthale) – Used for salads, sandwiches, fondue and popular as a dessert cheese.

Edam – A mild close-textured cheese, is relished as a dessert cheese served with fruit or a selection of cracker biscuits.

Gouda (rhyming with "chowder") – Greatly resembles Edam in taste and style.

Provolone – A smooth hard cheese, with a robust smoky, sometimes salty taste. Excellent for hors d'oeuvres, snacks and hearty cheese dishes. A good grating cheese, with character, everyone should make a point of at least sampling Provolone.

Soft Cheeses fall into two classes – ripened and unripened:

Soft Ripened Cheese – Many famous varieties come into this class. Some of them need careful handling on account of their delicate consistency, but they all keep well, if protected from heat and air.

Blue Vein – This cheese has many illustrious predecessors, including France's Roquefort, Italy's Gorgonzola, Denmark's Danablu and England's Stilton. Particularly good for appetisers and savoury spreads and dips, it is delicious with breton crackers.

Feta – A moist, very white cheese made extensively in Greece and the Balkans, traditionally made from sheep or goat's milk. Always delicious but can be a little salty, particularly enjoyable with dark bread and olives.

Mozzarella – A famous Italian cheese, in demand for both table and cooking. Because of its fast-melting properties it is always used in authentic pizza. A mild but exceptionally pleasing flavour with a slightly resilient texture. Great for melts or grilled on toast, also delicious as a topping for meat loaves, casseroles and melted on crumbed cutlets.

Soft Unripened Cheeses

Cottage and *cream cheeses* have a variety of tastes from mild and bland as the American or sharper as the Continental style. These cheeses are best served chilled and have many delicious uses: in salads, spreads and dips, with fruit, as a filling for pancakes and omelettes and, of course, as the principle ingredient in all types of cheesecake. Italian-style *ricotta* is a similar cheese of delicate bland flavour which can be use a in the same manner as cottage and cream cheeses.

Hard Grating Cheeses

Parmesan – An almost rock-hard, dry cheese with a full and deliciously piquant flavour. Adds great flavour to soups, pasta, meat dishes, vegetables, savouries, stuffings, sauces and risottos. Keeps well and does not normally need refrigeration.

Romana – The mildest of the grating cheeses, it makes an exciting difference to many recipes.

Pecorino – The strongest and most pungent of the grating cheeses. Made from ewe's milk in Italy where it derives its name from the Italian name for sheep. In Australia it is normally made from cow's milk. Richer than Parmesan and much more robust in flavour.

apricots
with blue-cheese topping

Photograph page 15

Method:
1 *Cut apricots in half and remove seed (or drain canned apricots well on absorbent paper).*
2 *Place apricots cut side up on serving plate and spread each with a teaspoon of cheese.*
3 *If desired, apricots and cheese may be grilled for about 1 minute or until cheese begins to melt. Serve immediately.*
Makes 24

ingredients

12 fresh apricots or
1 x 850g/28oz can apricot halves
250g/¹/₂ lb soft blue cheese

cheese
and chive croquettes

Photograph opposite

Method:
1 *Place mozzarella cheese, 1 cup/125g/4oz flour, chives, cayenne pepper and eggs in a bowl and mix to combine. Shape mixture into balls, place on a plate lined with plastic food wrap and refrigerate for 30 minutes.*
2 *Combine cornstarch (cornstarch) and remaining flour on a plate. Roll balls in flour mixture and chill for 10 minutes.*
3 *Heat oil in a saucepan (until a cube of bread dropped in browns in 50 seconds) and deep-fry croquettes, in batches, for 4-5 minutes, or until golden. Drain on absorbent kitchen paper and serve.*
Makes 24

ingredients

500g/1 lb grated mozzarella cheese
1¹/₂ cups/185g/6oz flour
4 tablespoons snipped fresh chives
¹/₂ teaspoon cayenne pepper
2 eggs, lightly beaten
¹/₂ cup/60g/2oz cornstarch
vegetable oil for deep-frying

cheese
twisties

Method:

1 Brush the first sheet of pastry lightly with egg and sprinkle with cheese.

2 Brush the second sheet of pastry lightly with egg and place over the cheese.

3 Press the pastry sheets firmly together. Cut the pastry in half and then cut each half into 2cm/1in-wide strips.

4 Pick up each strip of pastry with both hands and twist before placing on a sheet of baking paper on an oven tray.

5 Bake in an oven at 230°C/450°F for 10 minutes or until golden. Serve warm.

Variation: *Use 1 slice of finely chopped bacon and 1 tablespoon of finely chopped pecans to replace the cheese.*

ingredients

2 sheets ready-rolled puff pastry
1 egg
¹/₂ cup cheese, finely grated

Makes 20

cheese
and garlic pita wedges

Method:

1 Split pita bread in half, cut each half into 4 wedges.
2 Combine butter, garlic and basil, brush over cut side of bread wedges, then sprinkle with Parmesan cheese.
3 Place in single layer on oven trays, bake in moderate oven for 10 minutes or until crisp.

Makes 32 wedges

4 white pita bread
125g/4oz butter, melted
3 cloves garlic, crushed
2 tablespoons chopped fresh basil
$^1/_3$ cup grated Parmesan cheese

baby squash
with capsicum (pepper) and cheese filling

Photograph opposite

Method:

1 *Cook squash in boiling water until tender, drain, cool. Scoop out top part of each squash.*
2 *Combine capsicum, cheese, egg, spring onions and cayenne pepper. Spoon into squash.*
3 *Bake in a moderate oven for 10 minutes or until heated through.*
Makes 24

ingredients

**24 yellow baby squash
1 large capsicum (pepper),
finely chopped
1/2 cup tasty cheese (mature Cheddar),
grated
1 egg, lightly beaten
2 spring onions (scallions),
finely chopped
1/4 teaspoon cayenne pepper**

stuffed
celery sticks

Method:

1 *Place all ingredients except celery, in a food processor and process until ingredients are combined and smooth.*
2 *Fill celery sticks with cheese mixture, arrange on a serving platter with slices of carrot as garnish.*
Makes about 25

ingredients

**6 sticks celery,
cut into 2 1/2cm/1 in lengths
100g/3 1/2oz blue-vein cheese, cubed
125g/4 1/2oz cream cheese, cubed
1 teaspoon brandy
freshly ground black pepper**

toasted
cheese snacks

Method:

1 Toast bread, then spread each slice with a little of the mustard. Top with a slice of chicken or chicken roll.
2 Combine cheese, mayonnaise and spring onions in a bowl; mix well. Spread cheese mixture on top of each chicken slice.
3 Cook under a preheated grill for about 3 minutes, or until cheese mixture bubbles. Serves at once with a salad garnish if desired.

Serves 3-6

ingredients

6 slices brown bread
2 teaspoons mild mustard
6 slices cooked chicken or chicken roll
125g/4oz Cheddar cheese, grated
3 tablespoons mayonnaise
2 spring onions, finely chopped

bubbly cheese,
ham and pineapple toasts

Method:

1 Combine cheese and ham in a mixing bowl. Add beaten egg and mix lightly. Set aside.
2 Toast bread slices on one side only under a preheated grill. Turn bread slices over and top each untoasted side with a pineapple ring. Pile cheese mixture on top, spreading it out to cover toast completely.
3 Return toasts to grill until topping is bubbly and golden brown. Serve at once.

Serves 8

ingredients

250g/8oz Cheddar cheese, grated
90g/3oz lean cooked ham, chopped
2 eggs, lightly beaten
8 slices wholewheat bread
8 canned pineapple rings

cheese
puffs

Method:

1 Combine cheese, breadcrumbs, egg yolks, mustard, paprika, salt and pepper. Mix well.
2 Beat egg whites until stiff. Gently fold into the cheese mixture.
3 Shape mixture into small, walnut sized, balls. Roll in extra breadcrumbs.
4 Deep fry, a few at a time, until golden brown, about 30 seconds.

ingredients

4 cups/500g/1 lb grated tasty cheese
1 cup/90g/3oz fresh breadcrumbs
4 eggs, separated
1 teaspoon dry mustard
1 teaspoon paprika
salt and pepper
fresh breadcrumbs, extra
oil for deep frying

tuna
melts

ingredients

1 small onion, finely chopped
2 teaspoons butter
185g/6¹/₄oz can tuna in oil, drained
salt and pepper
¹/₄ teaspoon Tabasco
16 water cracker biscuits
4 sandwich cheese slices
2 sweet gherkins

Method:

1 *Sauté the onions in the butter till soft and golden. Add the drained tuna, salt, pepper and Tabasco. Stir to mix ingredients and to flake the tuna. Allow to cool.*

2 *Place a teaspoonful of mixture on each water cracker biscuit. Cut each cheese slice into strips. Place a few strips over tuna mixture on each biscuit.*

3 *Cut a slice of gherkin and place on top. Set under hot grill until cheese melts and the tuna mixture is covered.*

Serves 4

mushroom
melts

Method:

1 Melt butter in a small pan, add shallots, mushrooms and garlic and sauté a little. Add salt, pepper and lemon juice. Stir in flour and cook 1 minute. Allow to cool.

2 Place a teaspoonful on each water cracker biscuit. Cut each cheese slice into four squares. Place a piece over the mushroom mixture on each cracker.

3 Place under hot grill until cheese melts. Sprinkle with paprika and serve.

Serves 4

ingredients

2 teaspoons butter
2 tablespoons finely chopped shallots
150g/5¹/₂oz mushrooms, chopped
¹/₂ teaspoon crushed garlic
¹/₄ teaspoon each salt and pepper
2 teaspoons lemon juice
2 teaspoons flour
16 water cracker biscuits
4 sandwich cheese slices
paprika

prawn (shrimp) melts

Method:

1 Reserve 16 prawns (shrimp) for garnish and chop the remainder. Mix in lemon juice, salt and pepper.

2 Place a teaspoonful of mixture on each cracker. Cut cheese slice into quarters. Place a piece over prawn (shrimp) mixture then garnish top with a reserved prawn (shrimp).

3 Place under a hot grill until cheese melts and covers the prawn (shrimp) filling; this will fix the prawn (shrimp) garnish in place.

Serves 4

ingredients

250g/9oz small school prawns (shrimp)
2 teaspoons lemon juice
salt and pepper
16 water cracker biscuits
4 sandwich cheese slices

mini spinach
and cheese quiches

Method:

1 Cut pastry into 6cm/2¹/₂in rounds with a pastry cutter and press into shallow patty pans.

2 In a food processor, process the cheese, spinach, onion, egg, cream, parsley, mustard, salt and pepper until all ingredients are finely chopped and well combined.

3 Spoon I tablespoon of mixture into each patty pan.

4 Bake in a hot 210°C/410°F oven for 20 minutes, or until puffed and golden.

5 Remove from pans, place on platter and serve.

Variations: Crab and Ham:
Substitute cheese, spinach and parsley with a 170g/6oz can crab meat, drained and 125g/4¹/₂oz sliced ham.

Cheese and Ham: Substitute spinach leaves with 125g/4¹/₂oz sliced ham.

Makes about 24

ingredients

3 sheets ready-rolled puff pastry
125g/4¹/₂oz tasty cheese
(mature Cheddar), cubed
2 spinach leaves, washed and torn into
large strips, with stems removed
¹/₂ small onion, peeled and halved
I egg
3 tablespoons cream
I tablespoon parsley sprigs,
firmly packed
I tablespoon French mustard
salt & pepper

crocked
cheese

Photograph opposite

ingredients

Method:
1 *Combine all ingredients in a food processor. Blend well. Turn the mixture into a crock or serving bowl. Sprinkle additional poppy seeds on top for garnish.*
2 *Refrigerate until ready to serve. Serve with an assortment of crackers.*
Makes about 1 1/2 cups dip

$^1/_4$ **cup cottage cheese**
$^1/_4$ **cup ricotta cheese**
$^1/_2$ **cup grated Cheddar cheese**
65g/2oz butter
$^1/_2$ **cup shallots, chopped**
30mL/1fl oz beer
1 teaspoon Dijon mustard
1 teaspoon paprika
$^1/_4$ **teaspoon salt**
1-2 teaspoons poppy seeds
1 packet crackers
extra poppy seeds for garnish

sun-dried
tomato and goat's cheese pâté

ingredients

Method:
1 *Combine all ingredients in a food processor and purée.*
2 *Serve with cracked-pepper water crackers.*
Makes about 1 cup of pâté

90g/3oz sun-dried tomatoes, drained and chopped
125g/4$^1/_2$oz goat's cheese
pinch dried thyme
2 teaspoons finely chopped parsley
1 packet cracked-pepper water crackers

honey-glazed spareribs

meat treats

To eat well in the company of friends

and family is one of life's great pleasures. In the rush and dash of workaday life, cooking for fun rather than out of necessity seems an unattainable dream. But, as you'll find in this section beautifully presented easy-to-prepare beef, lamb, pork and chicken finger food is within reach of us all, no matter how little time we have, and regardless of our level of culinary skill.

Nutritive Value of Meat

Lean beef, lamb, pork and chicken are highly nutritious foods with unique features. Low in fat, yet packed full of high-quality protein and essential vitamins and minerals, lean meat is a valuable contributor to a healthy body. One of meat's prime nutritional benefits is as a supplier of the mineral iron, which is indispensable in carrying oxygen around our bodies, via the bloodstream. If you do not get enough iron you may become tired, have poor stamina and even become anaemic.

Lean beef, lamb, pork and chicken are some of the highest iron foods and this so-called "haem iron" is the most easily used by our bodies. The "haem iron" in meat also helps the body maximise the iron in poorer iron ("non-haem") foods, such as vegetables, nuts, legumes and grains.

Purchasing of Meat

Getting the best out of meat buying relies on the correct choice of cuts, the correct purchasing and storage of meat, and the correct cooking methods of the meat selected. Choosing cuts of meat suitable for each dish is nominated in the recipes that follow.

- Only buy the amount of meat which can be stored correctly in the space available.
- Before setting out to purchase a fresh supply of meat, prepare the refrigerator and freezer ready for meat storage. Make the necessary space available, wash meat trays and defrost the refrigerator and freezer if necessary, so that meat will be stored immediately on arriving home.
- Choose meat that is bright in colour, with a fresh (not dry) appearance.
- Keep meat cold whilst carrying home to prevent the growth of food-spoilage bacteria. This may be achieved by using an insulated chiller bag. For larger quantities, if transporting by car, place in a car chiller and store the meat in it as soon as purchased, particularly if departure for home is not immediate.
- If you are unsure about which cuts to buy seek advice from your butcher – trained professionals who are always willing to assist.
- If calculating the quantity of meat to buy for a meal is a problem, allow 125-150g/4 1/2-5 1/2oz of lean boneless meat per person.

Storage of Meat

In the Meat Compartment:

Remove from pre-package (plastic makes meat sweat which shortens shelf life), and arrange in stacks no more than 2-3 layers high. Make sure there is some air space between each piece of meat. Cover top of meat loosely with foil or greaseproof paper to stop surface drying.

In the Refrigerator Cabinet:

Place a stainless steel or plastic rack in a dish deep enough to catch any meat drippage. Unwrap meat and store as for "Meat Compartment", in the coldest part of the refrigerator. This is normally in the bottom of the refrigerator. If meat is to be used on the day of purchase, it can be left in its original wrapping.

Meat kept in the refrigerator for 2-3 days will be more tender than meat cooked on day of purchase.

In the Freezer:

Pack chops and steaks in 2 layers only, with freezer wrap between each layer, so that they separate easily. Pack flat in freezer bags.

Defrost meats in the refrigerator – never at room temperature or in water. Allow 2 days for a large roast, 1 day or less for smaller cuts, according to quantity. Do not remove from package when thawing. Meat may also be defrosted quickly in a microwave oven.

Do not refreeze thawed meat unless cooked first. Frozen meats should be stored at a constant temperature of -15°C/5°F.

Prolonged storage time in the freezer will result in loss of quality.

cocktail
meatballs

Photograph page 29

ingredients

250g/9oz ground beef
I onion, grated
2 tablespoons dried breadcrumbs
1/2 teaspoon salt
I egg
I tablespoon chopped parsley
1/4 teaspoon pepper
1/4 teaspoon oregano
I teaspoon Tabasco sauce
Filling
8 prunes, pitted and chopped
I tablespoon pine nuts,
coarsely chopped

Method:
1 Mix ground beef and all ingredients for meat balls together, knead well with hands until mixture becomes fine in grain. Allow to stand for 15 minutes before rolling.
2 Combine prunes and pine nuts. Wet palms of hands to prevent mixture sticking, take about a tablespoon of mix, roll into a ball then flatten in palm of hand.
3 Place 1/2 teaspoon of filling in centre and remould into a smooth ball. Space around edge of large dinner plate, glaze meat balls with Worcestershire sauce.
4 Cook in microwave on high for 5 minutes. Cover with Glad Foil and stand 1 1/2 minutes.
5 Serve with a spicey plum dipping sauce.
Variations:
Dried apricots or raisins may be used instead of prunes and walnuts, and almonds in place of pine nuts. You can also make the meatballs without the stuffing, but cook 4 minutes only. Serve with tomato sauce.
Yields 16 small meat balls

lamb
and mango skewers

Photograph opposite

ingredients

I kg/2 lb lean lamb, trimmed of visible fat and cut into 2cm/3/4in cubes
3 mangoes, cut into 2cm/3/4in cubes
Hoisin-soy marinade
I tablespoon finely grated fresh ginger
3/4 cup/185mL/6fl oz hoisin sauce
1/4 cup/60mL/2fl oz reduced-salt soy sauce
1/4 cup/60mL/2fl oz rice wine vinegar
1/4 cup/60mL/2fl oz vegetable oil

Method:
1 To make marinade, place ginger, hoisin and soy sauces, vinegar and oil in a bowl and mix to combine. Add lamb, toss to coat, cover and marinate in the refrigerator for at least 4 hours.
2 Thread lamb and mango cubes, alternately, onto oiled skewers. Cook on a preheated hot barbecue for 3-4 minutes each side or until tender.
Serves 8

honey-glazed
spareribs

Method:

1 To make marinade, combine chillies, garlic, spring onions, ginger, vinegar, soy sauce and honey in a non-reactive dish. Add ribs, toss to coat, cover and marinate in the refrigerator for at least 4 hours.

2 Drain ribs and reserve marinade. Cook ribs, basting occasionally with reserved marinade, on a preheated hot barbecue grill for 8-10 minutes or until ribs are tender and golden. Place on a serving platter, cover and keep warm.

3 Place remaining marinade in a saucepan, add onions, parsley, stock and lemon juice and bring to the boil. Reduce heat and simmer for 15 minutes or until sauce reduces by half. Pour mixture into a food processor or blender and process to make a purée. With motor running, pour in hot melted butter and process to combine. Serve sauce with spareribs.

Serves 8

ingredients

2 kg/4 lb pork spareribs, trimmed of excess fat
2 onions, chopped
2 tablespoons fresh parsley, chopped
1 cup/250mL/8fl oz chicken stock
2 tablespoons lemon juice
125g/4oz butter, melted
Honey-soy marinade
4 small fresh red chillies, chopped
4 cloves garlic, chopped
2 spring onions, chopped
1 tablespoon fresh ginger, finely grated
1 1/2 cups/375mL/12fl oz rice-wine vinegar
1/2 cup/125mL/4fl oz reduced-salt soy sauce
1/2 cup/170g/5 1/2oz honey

curried
trim-lamb vol-au-vents

Method:
1 Heat non-stick pan over a high heat. Add lamb and fry for 2 minutes.
2 Add sauce, uncovered, for 10 minutes, stirring occasionally. Spoon into oyster cases.
3 Preheat oven to 180°C/350°F. Cook vol-au-vents for 10 minutes. Serve hot, garnished with sprigs of coriander (cilantro) or a herb of choice.
Makes 24

**200g/7oz trim-lamb eye-of-loin
or fillet, finely chopped
3/4 cup prepared satay sauce
2 x 60g/2oz packets vol-au-vents
(total 24)**

chicken
yakitori

Method:

1 Place chicken in a glass bowl, mix in the soy sauce, honey, garlic and ginger. Cover, place in refrigerator and allow to marinate for several hours or overnight.

2 Thread one or two strips onto each skewer, using a weaving motion. Brush with marinade.

3 Heat grill or barbecue to high. Grease rack or plate with oil and arrange the skewers in a row. Cook for 2½ minutes on each side, brush with marinade as they cook. Serve immediately.

Makes 25 small skewers

ingredients

400g/14oz chicken stir-fry
½ cup soy sauce
¼ cup honey
1 clove garlic, crushed
½ teaspoon ground ginger
small bamboo skewers, soaked

chicken galantine slices

Method:

1. To make filling, place ground chicken and sausage meats, onion, parsley, garlic, egg and black pepper to taste in a bowl and mix to combine.
2. Place each chicken breast fillet, cut side up, on a flat surface between sheets of plastic food wrap and pound lightly to make a flattened rectangle. Lay 3 slices prosciutto or ham over each rectangle. Place one-sixth of the filling lengthwise down the centre, top with a row of 5 prunes and cover with another one-sixth of the filling.
3. Wrap fillets around filling to enclose and tie at 2cm/³⁄₄in intervals with kitchen string. Wrap rolls in lightly buttered aluminium foil and place in a baking dish.
4. Bake for 30 minutes, remove rolls from foil and bake for 15 minutes or until chicken is cooked. Wrap rolls in clean aluminium foil and refrigerate for several hours or until cold. To serve, remove string and cut into 1cm/¹⁄₂in-thick slices.

Makes about 45

ingredients

3 double boneless chicken breast fillets
9 slices prosciutto or lean ham
15 pitted dessert prunes
<u>**Savoury filling**</u>
375g/12oz ground chicken
200g/6¹⁄₂oz sausage meat
1 onion, finely chopped
3-4 tablespoons chopped fresh parsley
2 cloves garlic, crushed
1 egg, lightly beaten
freshly ground black pepper

wellington
bread loaf

Photograph opposite

ingredients

1 Vienna loaf (soft white bread)
30g/1oz butter, melted
250g/8oz liver pâté
125g/4oz button mushrooms, sliced
750g/1 1/2 lb lean ground beef
2 tablespoons snipped fresh chives
2 teaspoons crushed black peppercorns
2 eggs, lightly beaten
1/2 beef stock cube
1 tablespoon tomato
paste (purée)
Red wine and
thyme sauce
30g/1oz butter
2 tablespoons flour
1/2 cup/125mL/4fl oz
beef stock
1/2 cup/125mL/4fl oz
dry red wine
freshly ground black pepper

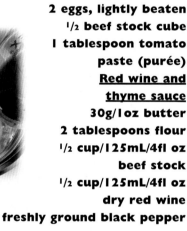

1

2

3

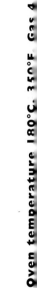

Oven temperature 180°C, 350°F, Gas 4

Method:

1 Cut base from bread loaf and reserve. Scoop bread from centre of loaf leaving a 1cm/1/2in shell. Make bread from centre into crumbs and set aside. Brush inside of bread shell with butter, spread with pâté, then press mushroom slices into pâté.

2 Place 1 cup/60g/2oz reserved breadcrumbs (keep remaining breadcrumbs for another use), beef, chives, black peppercorns, eggs, stock cube and tomato paste (purée) in a bowl and mix to combine.

3 Spoon beef mixture into bread shell, packing down well. Reposition base and wrap loaf in aluminium foil. Place loaf on a baking tray and bake for 1 1/2 hours or until meat mixture is cooked.

4 To make sauce, melt butter in a saucepan over a medium heat. Stir in flour and cook,

stirring, for 1 minute. Remove pan from heat and gradually whisk in stock and wine.

Return pan to heat and cook, stirring constantly, for 4-5 minutes or until sauce boils and thickens. Serve sauce with meatloaf.

Note: Breadcrumbs are easy to make, simply put the bread in a food processor and process to make crumbs; if you do not have a food processor rub the bread through a sieve. It is preferable for the breadcrumbs to be made with stale bread; for this recipe either use a loaf of bread that is a day or two old or scoop out the centre of the loaf as described in the recipe, then spread the bread out on a tray and leave for 2-3 hours to become stale, before making into crumbs.

Serves 8

Method:

1 Wash the zucchini (courgettes) and cut them into 8cm/3in pieces. With a small sharp knife. hollow out the centre by removing all the seeds, being careful not to pierce the skin.

2 Put the zucchini (courgette) pieces in a pot of boiling water and cook them on high heat for 3 minutes. Drain them, run them under cold water and set them aside.

3 In a large frypan melt the butter and sauté the onion and garlic until golden in colour. Do not brown them. Add the meat and cook the mixture over high heat for about 10 minutes or until the meat is completely cooked.

4 Drain on paper towels. Put the meat mixture in a food processor and add all other ingredients. Process until mixture is finely ground.

5 Carefully stuff the zucchini (courgettes) with the filling until firmly packed. Refrigerate them until ready to use. At serving time heat the stuffed pieces for 5-8 minutes in a 180°C/350°F preheated oven. Slice them and serve immediately.

ginger
pork zucchini

ingredients

6 medium zucchini (courgettes)
<u>Gingered pork filling</u>
1 tablespoon butter
2 medium onions, chopped
2 cloves garlic, chopped
350g/12oz ground pork
1/2 teaspoon ground ginger
1/2 teaspoon cayenne
1 tablespoon tomato paste
1 tablespoon dry white wine
1/8 teaspoon salt dash pepper

Makes 36 slices

prosciutto–
wrapped asparagus

Method:
1 Boil, steam or microwave asparagus until just tender. Drain and rinse under cold running water until cool. Drain asparagus again and dry on absorbent kitchen paper.
2 Cut each slice of prosciutto or ham lengthwise into 3 long strips and wrap each strip around an asparagus spear. Cover and refrigerate until required.
Makes about 12

ingredients

**250g/8oz fresh asparagus
spears, trimmed
4 slices prosciutto or lean ham**

beef
carpaccio

Method:

1 *Lightly oil a sheet of greaseproof paper and season it lightly with salt and freshly ground black pepper.*

2 *Arrange 4 slices of beef on this (approximately 5cm apart). Place another oiled piece of greaseproof paper on top, and gently beat the meat (until the it has spread out to at least twice its former size). Repeat with the remaining meat slices.*

3 *Refrigerate until needed. Alternatively, partly freeze the meat (before slicing thinly).*

4 *Place some rocket in the centre of a plate, arrange the beef slices around the rocket, and drizzle with some balsamic vinegar and olive oil.*

5 *Serve (drizzled with balsamic vinegar and extra virgin olive oil) with shavings of Pecorino cheese and black pepper.*

Serves 6

ingredients

**450g/1 lb beef fillet, sliced
into 4mm/$^1/_8$in slices
100g/3$^1/_2$oz rocket, washed
15mL/1 tablespoon balsamic vinegar
45mL/1$^1/_2$fl oz extra-virgin olive oil
Pecorino cheese shavings
freshly ground black pepper
salt**

curried
sausage puffs

Method:

1 To make filling, place sausage meat, carrot, spring onions, chutney, curry powder and black pepper to taste in a bowl and mix to combine. Cover and refrigerate until required.

2 Roll out pastry to 3mm/¹/₈in thick and cut out a 30cm/12in square. Cut pastry square in half. Divide filling into two equal portions then shape each into a thin sausage about 30cm/12in long. Place a sausage on the long edge of each pastry rectangle and roll up. Brush edges with water to seal.

3 Cut each roll into 1cm/¹/₂in-thick slices, place on greased baking trays and bake for 12-15 minutes or until filling is cooked and pastry is golden and puffed.

Note: These savoury puffs can be prepared to the baking stage earlier in the day. Cover with plastic food wrap and store in the refrigerator until required then bake as directed in the recipe.

Makes 48

ingredients

375g/12oz prepared puff pastry
<u>Curried sausage filling</u>
375g/12oz sausage meat
1 small carrot, finely grated
2 spring onions, chopped
1 tablespoon fruit chutney
1 teaspoon curry powder
freshly ground black pepper

italian sausage
and pork roll

Photograph opposite

1

2

3

ingredients

500g/1 lb lean ground pork
250g/8oz Italian sausages,
casings removed
1 onion, chopped
1/2 chicken stock cube
2 slices white bread, crusts removed
2 tablespoons tomato paste (purée)
1 egg, lightly beaten
freshly ground black pepper
250g/8oz ricotta cheese, drained
2 tablespoons chopped fresh basil
4 slices pancetta or bacon, chopped
1 red capsicum (pepper), roasted and sliced
60g/2oz pepperoni sausage, chopped
4 black olives, sliced
4 canned anchovy
fillets, chopped
2 hard-boiled eggs,
quartered
1 tablespoon olive oil
2 tablespoons brown
sugar
1 teaspoon dried
fennel seeds
1/2 teaspoon dried rosemary

Method:

1 *Place pork, sausage meat, onion, stock cube, bread, tomato paste (purée), egg and black pepper to taste in a food processor and process to combine. Press out meat mixture on a large piece of aluminium foil to form a 20x30cm/8x12in rectangle.*

2 *Spread meat with ricotta cheese and sprinkle with basil. Top with pancetta or bacon, red capsicum (pepper), pepperoni, olives, anchovies and hard-boiled eggs then roll up like a Swiss roll and wrap in foil. Place on a baking tray and bake for 40 minutes. Remove foil and drain off juices.*

3 *Place unwrapped roll back on baking tray and brush with oil. Combine sugar, fennel seeds and rosemary, sprinkle over roll and bake for 40 minutes longer or until cooked.*
Note: *Of Italian origin, pancetta is a type of bacon available from the delicatessen section of your supermarket or Italian food shop.*

Serves 6

chicken
satay

Method:

1 Combine water, peanut butter, honey, soy sauce, lemon juice, ginger and onion in a bowl. Stir in sambal oelek, if using, and mix well. Add chicken cubes, cover and marinate for at least 2 hours or overnight.

2 Soak cocktail sticks in cold water for 30 minutes, then drain. Remove chicken from marinade. Thread two pieces of chicken on each cocktail stick and set aside.

3 Pour marinade into a saucepan, bring to the boil, lower heat and simmer for about 10 minutes, or until sauce is reduced and thickened.

4 Cook chicken for about 10 minutes under a moderate grill or over hot coals, until tender. Serve four satay sticks per person, offering dipping sauce separately.

Note: You will need about 36 good-quality wooden cocktail sticks for this recipe.

Serves 8

ingredients

500g/1 lb) chicken breast fillets, cut into 2cm/³/₄in cubes
125mL/4fl oz water
2 tablespoons smooth peanut butter
1 tablespoon honey
1 tablespoon light soy sauce
2 tablespoons lemon juice
1 teaspoon grated fresh ginger
1 onion, finely chopped
1 teaspoon sambal oelek or Tabasco sauce to taste, optional

herb
liver pâté

Method:

1 Melt 60g/2oz of the butter in a frying pan over a low heat, add onion, garlic, thyme and rosemary and cook, stirring, for 6-8 minutes or until onion is very tender.

2 Add livers to pan, increase heat to medium and cook, stirring, until livers are brown on the outside, but still pink in the centre. Set aside to cool.

3 Place liver mixture in a food processor, add remaining butter and black pepper to taste and process until smooth. Spoon mixture into a piping bag fitted with a large star nozzle and pipe rosettes onto melba toasts or rice crackers. Arrange on a serving plate, garnish with olive slices and serve.

Makes about 30

ingredients

185g/6oz butter, softened
1 onion, chopped
2 cloves garlic, chopped
2 tablespoons fresh thyme leaves
1 tablespoon fresh rosemary leaves
750g/1 1/2 lb fresh chicken livers, cleaned and trimmed, coarsely chopped
pinch salt
freshly ground black pepper
75g/2 1/2oz melba toasts or rice crackers
125g/4oz stuffed green olives, sliced

seafood
snacks

bacon-wrapped prawns (shrimp)

seafood snacks

The modern culinary trend is for light,

nutritious, easy-to-prepare meals. The remarkable properties of fish and shellfish fit these criteria well. We have a huge selection of fish available in many different forms: fresh, frozen, canned, smoked, dried and pre-prepared. The recipes that follow use a selection of these, giving you a very wide variation of taste treats.

seafood

Purchasing Seafood

The most important factor in choosing fish is freshness. Fish should not smell "fishy"; this smell is a sure sign of age or improper handling. A fresh fish has a mild odour, firm elastic flesh that springs back when pressed, clear protruding eyes, reddish or pink gills, and scales that are shiny, bright and tight to the skin.

Steaks or fillets should be fresh with a natural sheen, free from yellowing or browning around the edges. Do not buy any fish that has been frozen then defrosted for more than two days. It is always better to purchase frozen fish and defrost them at home when ready to use.

Storing Seafood

General rules to follow:

Wash both the inside and outside in cold running water. Wrap exposed flesh in plastic food wrap, which will prevent fish drying out when exposed to air. Place fish in a shallow tray-type container, ensuring not to put too much weight on bottom layer, so that fish is not squashed. Place fillets skin side up, even if skin has been removed. Keep the fish cool and moist – in ice is best – but do not allow the ice to come in direct contact with the seafood. Instead, place ice underneath and throughout the wrapped seafood.

Create continual drainage by placing the seafood on a perforated tray with a non-perforated tray beneath it to catch the melt-water. The seafood must not rest in its own fluids or melt-water because this can cause the flavour and colour to be leached out and any exposed flesh can go mushy.

Also, don't forget to label seafood with type and date.

Cooking Methods

Steaming: cooks the seafood by steam heat at temperatures greater than 100°C/210°F, retaining the subtle characteristic flavours.

If cooking over direct heat, place the prepared seafood in a single layer on a rack or in a perforated pan over the boiling liquid.

Cover tightly, but take care not to leave too long as the seafood will cook quickly.

Poaching: involves placing the seafood in just enough liquid to cover it, and gently cooking it below boiling point. The poaching liquid should be between 70°C/160°F and 80°C/175°F.

The seafood can be wrapped, placed on a rack, or put directly into the poaching liquid by bringing the liquid to a simmer and gently immersing the seafood. Bring the liquid back to poaching temperature and maintain till cooked.

Wrapping will help hold the flesh together, while a rack or perforated pan will make it easier to remove the seafood.

Boiling: involves cooking in liquid, water or stock, at 100°C/210°F.

Simmering: involves cooking in water or stock that is bubbling gently just below boiling point, between 95°C/203°F and 98°C/308°F. Simmering temperature is between poaching and boiling. There should be enough liquid to cover the seafood completely. As a general guide, it should be four times the volume of the seafood. A classic court bouillon or any other suitable stock can be used instead of salted water.

Place seafood into rapidly boiling water. Never place live crustaceans (except prawns [shrimp]) into boiling liquid as this toughens the flesh and the claws or legs may fall off. Bring the liquid back to boil, then turn the heat down to simmer and cook, covered, for the desired time.

Deep-frying: Deep-frying involves cooking food by fully immersing it in hot oil at 170°C-180°C/340°F-350°F. The temperature is important when deep-frying seafood: if too high the seafood will overcook on the outside, leaving the inside undercooked. If too low, the seafood will absorb more oil and be greasy and pale in colour.

From a health perspective, an oil with a greater proportion of monounsaturated or polyunsaturated fatty acids is recommended for deep-frying seafood.

bacon-wrapped
prawns (shrimp)

Photograph opposite

Method:

1 To make marinade, place oregano, garlic, oil and vinegar in a bowl and whisk to combine. Add prawns (shrimp) and toss to coat. Cover and refrigerate for at least 1 hour or overnight.

2 Drain prawns (shrimp) and reserve marinade. Cut each bacon rasher into three pieces, wrap a piece of bacon around each prawn (shrimp) and secure with a wooden toothpick or cocktail stick.

3 Cook prawns (shrimp) under a preheated medium grill or on the barbecue, turning occasionally and brushing with reserved marinade, for 5 minutes or until bacon is crisp and prawns (shrimp) are cooked.

Makes about 24

ingredients

750g/1 1/2 lb large uncooked prawns (shrimp), shelled and deveined, with tails left intact
8 rashers bacon, rind removed
<u>**Herb marinade**</u>
2 tablespoons chopped fresh oregano
2 cloves garlic, crushed
1/2 cup/125mL/4fl oz olive oil
2 tablespoons white wine vinegar

prawn
(shrimp) boats

Photograph page 53

Method:

1 To make filling, place chives, capers, mustard and sour cream in a bowl and mix to combine. Cover and refrigerate until required.

2 Trim and cut celery into 5cm/2in-long pieces. Spoon or pipe filling into celery boats. Top each boat with a prawn (shrimp) and garnish with lumpfish roe and chives.

Makes about 24

ingredients

6 stalks celery
375g/12oz medium prawns (shrimp), cooked, shelled and deveined
1 tablespoon red lumpfish roe
1 tablespoon snipped fresh chives
<u>**Chive and caper filling**</u>
1 tablespoon snipped fresh chives
1 tablespoon chopped capers
1 tablespoon Dijon mustard
1 1/4 cups/315g /10oz sour cream

stuffed
calamari rings

Method:

1 *Pull tentacles away from head, trim. Remove membrane from tentacles and hood; wash well.*
2 *Pour boiling water over lettuce leaves, drain. Wrap tentacles in lettuce leaves, then in nori sheets. Seal with water.*
3 *Insert tentacle parcels into calamari hoods, secure with a toothpick.*
4 *Combine soy sauce, water and sugar in a saucepan and heat gently. Add calamari parcels, cover, then simmer for about 20 minutes or until tender. Remove, drain and refrigerate until cold. Serve sliced.*

Makes 36

ingredients

4 whole calamari
4 lettuce leaves
4 sheets nori (seaweed)
1/2 cup light soy sauce
1/2 cup water
2 tablespoons sugar

smoked
salmon-potato bites

Method:

1. Wash potatoes, cut in half and place cut side down. Scoop out a cavity in the top.
2. Toss in oil then bake cut side down on oven tray in moderate oven 45 minutes or until tender. Allow to cool slightly.
3. Place some salmon in each cavity, followed by a spoonful of sour cream over each. Top with a wedge of egg, then garnish with dill.

Makes 32

ingredients

16 small pontiac potatoes
¹/₄ cup oil
250g/¹/₂ lb smoked salmon
¹/₂ cup sour cream
3 hard-boiled eggs, sliced
fresh dill for garnish

scallops
with mango salsa

Method:

1 To make salsa, place mango, mint, lemon juice and sesame seeds in a small bowl and mix to combine. Cover and refrigerate until required.

2 Bring a large saucepan of water to the boil. Add scallops and cook for 1 minute or until tender. Using a slotted spoon remove scallops from water and place on a serving platter. Serve warm or chilled, seasoned with black pepper and topped with salsa.

Makes 8

ingredients

16 scallops in half shells
freshly ground black pepper
<u>**Mango salsa**</u>
1 mango, peeled and chopped
1 tablespoon chopped fresh mint
1 tablespoon lemon juice
2 tablespoons sesame seeds, toasted

salmon
curry puffs

Method:

1 Heat oil, add onion, chilli, garlic, coriander (cilantro), ginger, cumin and turmeric. Cook for 2 minutes.

2 Remove pan from heat and stir the lemon juice and salmon into the spice mixture. Let cool.

3 Lightly brush the first sheet of pastry with oil, then layer with a second sheet on top. Brush the second sheet with oil then layer a third sheet.

4 Cut the stack of pastry into 6 short strips. Place a spoonful of the mixture on the bottom right hand corner of each pastry strip. Fold the pastry over the filling to form a triangle, then continue folding to the end of strip, making sure to retain triangular shape.

5 Repeat with remaining pastry and filling. Place triangles on a lightly oiled oven tray, and brush the tops lightly with oil. Bake at 190°C/370°F for 12 minutes or until golden. Serve warm.

Makes 12

ingredients

1 tablespoon canola oil
1 onion, finely chopped
1/2 teaspoon each minced chilli, garlic and coriander (cilantro)
3/4 teaspoon minced ginger
1/4 teaspoon each cumin and turmeric
1 tablespoon lemon juice
210g/7 1/2oz can pink salmon, drained and flaked
6 sheets filo pastry
extra tablespoon canola oil

oysters
marinated with bacon

Method:

1 In a small bowl combine soy sauce, Worcestershire sauce, and honey. Set aside.
2 Wrap a bacon strip around each oyster, then thread two wrapped oysters on each skewer. Place skewers in a foil-lined grill pan. Pour marinade over oysters, cover and leave for 30 minutes.
3 Cook oysters under a preheated grill until bacon is golden. Serve immediately.

Makes 12

ingredients

2 tablespoons soy sauce
1/2 teaspoon Worcestershire sauce
1 tablespoon honey
2 dozen oysters, shells discarded
4 rashers rindless back bacon,
cut into 3cm/1 1/4in-long strips
12 small wooden skewers

seafood
pâté

Method:

1 Coarsely chop trout and prawns (shrimp) and set aside.

2 Melt butter in a saucepan over a medium heat, add spring onions and garlic and cook, stirring, for 1 minute or until onions are soft. Add trout and prawns (shrimp) and cook, stirring, until seafood is just cooked. Add brandy and cook for 1 minute, then stir in dill, cream, lemon juice and chilli sauce. Remove pan from heat and set aside to cool.

3 Transfer mixture to a food processor, season to taste with black pepper and process until smooth. Spoon mixture into a serving dish, cover and refrigerate for at least 6 hours . To serve, garnish pâté with dill sprigs and lemon slices and accompany with melba toasts.

Serves 8

ingredients

500g/1 lb trout fillets, skinned and boned
500g/1 lb uncooked prawns (shrimp), shelled and deveined
90g/3oz butter
4 spring onions, chopped
2 cloves garlic, crushed
2 tablespoons brandy
2 tablespoons chopped fresh dill
1/2 cup/125mL/4fl oz thickened cream (double)
1 tablespoon lemon juice
2 teaspoons chilli sauce
freshly ground black pepper
fresh dill sprigs and lemon slices
melba toasts or cracker biscuits

ratatouille kebabs

veggie treats

With the fruits of the fields, never

have we had it so good. Because of world-wide fast transport, we can now obtain a wide variety of fruits and vegetables all year long. When once we could only indulge in salad vegetables in summer and soup vegetables in winter, now all are available from your nearest fruit and vegetable vendor. The recipes in this chapter have been designed to take advantage of this variety and assist you in expanding your repertoire of fruit and vegetable usage.

vegetarian

Preparation Tips

Over the centuries certain combinations of herbs and foods have become traditional because they work so well together. Many of these complementary pairings are listed below. Try new combinations and make notes on your favourites.

Herbs intensify in flavour when they are dried. If substituting fresh herbs for dried, use three times the suggested amount. The exception is rosemary, which retains its natural strength when dried. Add fresh herbs to dishes at the last moment so the flavour retains its intensity. Dried herbs will need the intensity of heat to release their flavour, therefore they will need to be added earlier into the recipe.

Fruits & Vegetables

Corn: *basil, chervil, chives, coriander (cilantro), marjoram, oregano, parsley, sage, tarragon, thyme.*

Cruciferous vegetables *(i.e. Brussels sprouts, broccoli, cauliflower, cabbage): chives, coriander (cilantro), dill, marjoram, mint, oregano, parsley, sage.*

Fruits: *basil, bay, chervil, chives, dill, marjoram, mint, oregano, parsley, rosemary, sage, tarragon, thyme.*

Gourds *(i.e. cucumber, squash, zucchini [courgettes]): chervil, chives, coriander (cilantro), dill, marjoram, mint, oregano, parsley, tarragon, thyme.*

Leafy Green Vegetables *(i.e. kale, silverbeet [chard], spinach): chives, dill, marjoram, oregano, parsley, thyme.*

Legumes *(i.e. green beans, jicama, shell beans): basil, bay, chervil, chives, cilantro, dill, marjoram, mint, oregano, parsley, rosemary, sage, tarragon, thyme.*

Lettuces: *basil, chervil, chives, coriander (cilantro), dill, marjoram, mint, oregano, parsley, rosemary, tarragon, thyme.*

Mushrooms: *basil, bay, chervil, chives, dill, marjoram, oregano, parsley, tarragon, thyme.*

Onion Family *(i.e. garlic, leek, onion, shallot): basil, bay, chervil, chives, coriander (cilantro), dill, marjoram, oregano, parsley, rosemary, sage, tarragon, thyme.*

Root and Bulb Vegetables *(i.e. beetroot, carrot, celery, fennel): chervil, chives, dill, mint, parsley, rosemary, sage, tarragon, thyme.*

Tomato Family *(i.e. eggplant [aubergine], capsicum [pepper], potato, tomato): basil, bay, chervil, chives, coriander (cilantro), dill, marjoram, mint, oregano, parsley, rosemary, tarragon, thyme.*

Guidelines for Cooking Vegetables

The following general guidelines for cooking vegetables should be considered regardless of the cooking methods used:

- *Vegetables should be cut into uniform shapes and lengths to promote even cooking and provide an attractive finished product on your plate or table.*

- *Do not overcook. You will preserve texture, colour and nutrients if you cook vegetables for as short a time as necessary.*

- *Cook vegetables as close to serving time as possible. If held in containers they will continue to cook.*

- *When necessary, vegetables may be blanched in advance, refreshed in ice water and refrigerated. When required they may be retrieved and reheated as needed.*

- *White and red vegetables may be cooked with a small amount of acid, such as lemon or lime juice, vinegar or white wine to help retain their colour.*

- *It is important, when preparing an assortment of vegetables, to cook each type separately, then combine. Otherwise vegetables will be unevenly cooked.*

- *There is no one standard of doneness for vegetables. Each item should be evaluated on a recipe-by-recipe basis. Generally, however most vegetables are done when they are just tender when pierced with a fork or skewer.*

antipasto

Photograph page 65

ingredients

1 large head cauliflower
750g/26¹/₂oz sweet pickled onions
4 stalks celery
2 medium zucchini (courgettes)
3 large green capsicum (peppers)
3 large red capsicum (peppers)
800g/1³/₄ lb mushrooms
800g/1³/₄ lb plum tomatoes
112g/4oz flat anchovy fillets
350g/12¹/₂oz tin flaked tuna
250mL/9fl oz vegetable oil
750g/26¹/₂oz stuffed green olives
400g/14oz Kalamata olives
800g/1³/₄ lb green beans
250mL/9fl oz tomato sauce
175mL/6fl oz chilli sauce
125mL/4¹/₂fl oz white vinegar

Method:

1 Chop the cauliflower, onions, celery, zucchini (courgettes), capsicum, mushrooms and tomatoes. Drain the liquid from anchovies and tuna.

2 Rinse the anchovies and tuna under hot water. Chop the anchovies and break up the tuna.

3 Combine vegetable oil, cauliflower and onions in a large pan and cook over high heat for 10 minutes, stirring frequently. Add all other ingredients except the anchovies and tuna and vinegar and cook an additional 10 minutes, stirring frequently.

4 Add the anchovies, tuna and vinegar and cook another 10 minutes, stirring frequently. Set aside to cool. Surround with cracker biscuits.

5 Put the antipasto in sterilised jars and store in a refrigerator, it will keep for many weeks.

Makes enough for 20

vegetable
frittata wedges

Photograph opposite

ingredients

2 tablespoons vegetable oil
1 onion, very thinly sliced
1 potato, very thinly sliced
350g/11oz canned asparagus
spears, drained
1 red capsicum (pepper),
cut into long strips
1 zucchini (courgette), cut into
long strips
6 eggs, beaten
freshly ground black pepper
2 tablespoons grated Parmesan cheese

Method:

1 Drizzle oil over the base a 23cm/9in quiche dish, then spread with onions and top with potato slices. Cover dish with aluminium foil and bake for 30 minutes or until potato is tender.

2 Arrange asparagus spears and red capsicum (pepper) and zucchini (courgette) strips like the spokes of a wheel onto top of potato, then pour over eggs and season with black pepper to taste. Scatter with Parmesan cheese.

3 Bake, uncovered, for 15 minutes or until frittata is firm. Cool for 10 minutes, then cut into thin wedges and serve.

Serves 8

herb
savouries

Method:
1 *Remove crusts from bread, butter one side.*
2 *Cut into shapes as desired using a knife or biscuit cutters.*
3 *Sprinkle with combined fresh herbs, press on firmly.*
Makes about 24

12 slices white or wholemeal bread
125g/4oz butter
¹/₃ cup chopped chives
¹/₃ cup chopped parsley
¹/₄ cup thyme leaves
1 tablespoon chopped dill

bruschetta

Method:

1 *Grill ciabatta slices on each side for 2-3 minutes.*
2 *Brush with olive oil, spread with sun-dried tomato paste, then top with bocconcini slices and shredded basil leaves (or whole leaves).*

Serves 6

ingredients

1 ciabatta loaf (cut in 1 ½cm/½in slices)
60mL/2fl oz olive oil
⅓ cup sun-dried tomato paste
180g/6oz bocconcini (each ball sliced into 5 slices)
½ cup basil leaves (sliced, or whole leaves)

chilli bean
corn cups

Method:

1. To make pastry, place butter and cream cheese in a food processor and process to combine. Add flour and cornmeal (polenta) and salt, then process to form a soft dough. Turn dough onto a lightly floured surface and knead until smooth. Divide dough into small balls, press into lightly greased muffins tins and bake for 20 minutes or until golden.

2. Heat oil in a frying pan over a medium heat, add onion and garlic and cook, stirring, for 5 minutes or until onion is tender. Add beef, cumin and chilli powder and stir-fry for 4-5 minutes or until is beef brown.

3. Stir in tomatoes and beans and bring to the boil. Reduce heat and simmer, stirring occasionally, for 1 hour or until most of the liquid evaporates and mixture is quite dry. Season to taste with black pepper and spoon into hot polenta cups. Serve immediately.

Makes 24

ingredients

2 tablespoons vegetable oil
1 large onion, chopped
2 cloves garlic, crushed
250g/8oz lean ground beef
2 teaspoons ground cumin
2 teaspoons chilli powder
440g/14oz canned peeled tomatoes, undrained and mashed
440g/14oz canned red kidney beans, drained and rinsed
freshly ground black pepper
<u>Polenta pastry</u>
185g/6oz butter
185g/6oz cream cheese
2 cups/250g/8oz flour
1 cup/170g/5^1/$_2$oz cornmeal (polenta)
pinch salt

potato skins

Method:

1 Preheat the oven to 180°C/350°F. Wash and dry each potato. Pierce with a fork and place in the preheated oven. Bake for 30 minutes or until the centre is firm but can be easily pierced with a fork.

2 Cool the potato, cut in quarters lengthwise and cut out the centre leaving the skin with 0.5cm/¹/₂in to 110mm/¹/₂in of potato on it.

3 Brush the skins with butter, then sprinkle them with salt and pepper. Bake them at 180°C/350°F for 10 minutes. Top them with chosen topping and bake for another 5-10 minutes until warmed.

Makes 4 pieces per potato

ingredients

baking potatoes
Bacon and mushroom topping
potato pulp
sautéed bacon and mushroom
parsley
Prawn (shrimp) and chives topping
potato pulp
sour cream
chopped fresh chives
prawns (shrimp)
salt and pepper to taste
Chicken and almond Topping
potato pulp
cooked chicken
toasted pine nuts
chopped shallots
sour cream
black pepper

devilled
eggs

ingredients

12 eggs
1 teaspoon dry mustard
1 teaspoon curry powder
2 tablespoons mayonnaise
2 tablespoons thickened (double) cream
snipped fresh chives or dill

Method:

1 *Place eggs in a saucepan, cover with cold water and bring to the boil. Stirring gently will keep the yolks centred. Discontinue stirring, reduce heat and simmer for 10 minutes. Drain eggs, then rinse under cold running water until cool enough to handle.*

2 *Peel eggs and cut in half lengthwise. Remove yolks and place in a bowl. Set whites aside. Add mustard, curry powder, mayonnaise and cream and mash until mixture is well combined and smooth.*

3 *Spoon egg yolk mixture into a piping bag fitted with a small star nozzle and pipe rosettes into reserved egg white shells. Garnish with chives or dill.*

MAKES 24

scotch
eggs

Method:

1 Place sausage meat, parsley and curry powder in a bowl and mix to combine. Divide mixture into four equal portions. Place each portion on a piece of plastic food wrap and press into a 12cm/5in circle.

2 Combine milk and egg in a shallow dish. Dip hard-boiled eggs into milk mixture then roll in flour to coat. Place an egg in the centre of each portion and mould around egg to enclose. Dip wrapped egg in milk mixture, then roll in breadcrumbs to coat.

3 Heat oil in a saucepan until a cube of bread dropped in browns in 50 seconds. Deep-fry eggs, two at a time, for 5-6 minutes or until golden. Drain on absorbent kitchen paper and cool completely. Cut in half to serve.

Makes 8 halves

ingredients

500g/1 lb sausage meat
2 tablespoons chopped fresh parsley
1 teaspoon curry powder
1/2 cup/60mL/2fl oz milk
1 egg, beaten
4 hard-boiled eggs, peeled
1/2 cup/60g/2oz flour
1 cup/125g/4oz dried breadcrumbs
vegetable oil for deep-frying

guacamole

Method:

1 Cut avocados in half, remove seeds and skin. Mash roughly with a fork.
2 Plunge tomatoes into boiling water for 30 seconds, remove. Peel off skin, cut into quarters, remove and discord seeds. Cut tomatoes into small dice.
3 Combine avocado, tomato, onion, chilli, coriander (cilantro) and lemon juice. Serve with corn chips for dipping.

Serves 8

ingredients

3 avocados
2 small tomatoes
1 small onion, very finely chopped
3 red chillies, chopped
2 tablespoons fresh coriander (cilantro), chopped
2 tablespoons lemon juice
2 x 200g/6¹/₂oz) packets corn chips

ratatouille
kebabs

Method:

1 Cook onions in a saucepan of boiling water for 5 minutes. Drain, cool and cut into halves.
2 To make marinade, place garlic, chillies, basil, oregano, oil and wine in a bowl and mix to combine. Add onions, eggplant (aubergine), red capsicum (pepper), zucchini (courgettes), tomatoes and mushrooms, toss to coat and marinate at room temperature for at least 1 hour.
3 Drain vegetables and reserve marinade. Thread vegetables onto lightly oiled skewers and cook on a preheated hot barbecue grill, basting occasionally with marinade, for 4-5 minutes each side, or until cooked.

Serves 8

ingredients

250g/8oz small pickling onions
1 small eggplant (aubergine),
cut into 2cm/³/₄in cubes
1 red capsicum (pepper), seeded and cut
into 2cm/³/₄in squares
4 zucchini (courgettes),
cut into 2cm/³/₄in pieces
250g/8oz cherry tomatoes
250g/8oz button mushrooms
<u>Herb marinade</u>
2 cloves garlic, crushed
2 small fresh red chillies, chopped
2 tablespoons chopped fresh basil
1 tablespoon chopped fresh oregano
¹/₂ cup/125mL/4fl oz olive oil
¹/₃ cup/90mL/3fl oz red wine

1

2

3

spring
roll baskets

Photograph opposite

ingredients

vegetable oil for deep-frying
8 spring roll or wonton wrappers,
each 12.5cm/5in square
2 tablespoons unsalted cashews,
toasted and chopped
<u>**Pork and prawn (shrimp) filling**</u>
1 tablespoon peanut (groundnut) oil
2 teaspoons fresh ginger, finely grated
1 small fresh red chilli, finely chopped
4 spring onions, finely chopped
250g/8oz lean ground pork
125g/4oz uncooked prawns (shrimp),
shelled and deveined
1 tablespoon soy sauce
2 teaspoons fish sauce
2 teaspoons honey
2 teaspoons lemon juice
30g/1oz bean sprouts
1 small carrot, cut into thin strips
1 tablespoon fresh coriander
(cilantro), finely chopped

Method:

1 *Heat vegetable oil in a large saucepan until a cube of bread dropped in browns in 50 seconds. Place 2 spring roll or wonton wrappers, diagonally, one on top of the other, so that the corners are not matching. Shape wrappers around the base of a small ladle, lower into hot oil and cook for 3-4 minutes. During cooking keep wrappers submerged in oil by pushing down with the ladle to form a basket shape. Drain on absorbent kitchen paper. Repeat with remaining wrappers to make four baskets.*

2 *To make filling, heat peanut (groundnut) oil in a frying pan, add ginger, chilli and spring onions and stir-fry for 1 minute. Add pork and stir-fry for 5 minutes or until meat is brown.*

Add prawns (shrimp), soy sauce, fish sauce, honey, lemon juice, bean sprouts, carrot and coriander (cilantro) and stir-fry for 4-5 minutes longer or until prawns (shrimp) change colour.

3 *To serve, spoon filling into baskets and sprinkle with cashews.*
Note: *Wonton or spring roll wrappers are available frozen from Asian food shops and some supermarkets.*
Serves 4

pork and apple
cabbage rolls

Photograph opposite

1

2

3

ingredients

2 tablespoons vegetable oil
I onion, finely grated
2 rashers bacon, chopped
I green apple, peeled, cored and grated
I teaspoon caraway seeds
500g/I lb lean ground pork
125g/4oz brown rice, cooked
I egg, lightly beaten
freshly ground
black pepper
8 large cabbage leaves
60g/2oz butter
I ¹/₂ tablespoons
paprika
I ¹/₂ tablespoons flour
I tablespoon tomato
paste (purée)
¹/₂ cup/125mL/4fl oz red wine
I ¹/₂ cups/375mL/12fl oz chicken stock
¹/₂ cup/125g/4oz sour cream

Method:

1 *Heat oil in a frying pan over a medium heat, add onion and bacon and cook, stirring, for 3-4 minutes or until onion is soft. Stir in apple and caraway seeds and cook for 2 minutes longer. Remove pan from heat and set aside to cool.*

2 *Place pork, rice, egg, black pepper to taste and onion mixture in a bowl and mix to combine.*

3 *Boil, steam or microwave cabbage leaves until soft. Refresh under cold running water, pat dry with absorbent kitchen paper and trim stalks.*

4 *Divide meat mixture between cabbage leaves and roll up, tucking in sides. Secure with wooden toothpicks or cocktail sticks.*

5 *Melt 30g/1oz butter in a frying pan, add rolls and cook, turning several times, until lightly browned. Transfer rolls to a shallow ovenproof dish.*

6 *Melt remaining butter in pan over a medium heat, stir in paprika and flour and cook for 2 minutes. Stir in tomato paste (purée), wine and stock and bring to the boil. Reduce heat and simmer, stirring, for 5 minutes. Remove pan from heat and whisk in sour cream. Pour sauce over rolls, cover and bake for 1 hour.*
Note: *These rolls are also delicious when made using ground lamb instead of the pork. This recipe is a good way to use up leftover cooked rice and spinach or silverbeet (chard) leaves can be used instead of cabbage.*

Serves 4

chilli
cheese dip

ingredients

90g/3oz green chillies, seeded, chopped
1 red chilli, seeded, chopped
90g/3oz mature cheddar cheese
1/8 tspn Worchestershire sauce
1/4 tspn tabasco sauce
2 spring onions, chopped
salt
pepper

Method:

1 Combine all ingredients in a food processor. Blend until light and fluffy. If the mixture is too thick, thin with some milk.
2 Cover and refrigerate for at least 1 hour before serving.

Serves 8

taramosalata

ingredients

250g/1/2 lb potatoes
6 slices white bread
100g/31/2oz can tarama or 60g/2oz fresh
1 onion, finely grated
freshly ground black pepper
1/2 cup olive oil
1/2 cup lemon juice
4 slices pita bread

Method:

1 Peel and chop potatoes, cook in boiling water until tender, then drain and let cool.
2 Remove crusts from bread, combine in a bowl with 1 cup water then stand 2 minutes. Strain and press out excess water.
3 Place potatoes, bread, tarama, onion and pepper in a blender or processor, blend until smooth.
4 With blender running, gradually pour in combined olive oil and lemon juice, blend until combined.
5 Split pita bread in half, cut each half into wedges, and serve with taramosalata.

Serves 8

spicy
prawn (shrimp) dip

Method:

1 *Combine all ingredients except prawns (shrimp) in a blender or food processor. Blend well.*
2 *Stir the drained prawns (shrimp) in by hand. Chill until ready to serve. Serve with an assortment of crackers.*
Makes about 2 cups dip

ingredients

225g/8oz cream cheese
85mL/3oz mayonnaise
125mL/4¹/₂fl oz seafood cocktail sauce
1 tablespoon lemon juice
3 tablespoons shallots, chopped
1 tablespoon parsley, chopped
120g/4¹/₂oz small prawns (shrimp)
assorted crackers

fish
pâté

Method:

1 *Place fish fillets, shallot, lemon peel, wine and stock cube into a frypan. Simmer gently for 5 minutes or until fish is just tender.*
2 *Drain fish fillets, reserving liquid. Remove and discard any bones from fillets.*
3 *In a food processor, place boned fish, reserved liquid, butter, salt, cayenne pepper, cream and lemon juice. Purée until smooth.*
4 *Spoon into a serving bowl or individual moulds. Refrigerate for several hours.*
5 *Serve with crispbread.*
Makes about 750g of pâté

ingredients

500g/18oz fish fillets, skinned
1 shallot, finely chopped
2 strips lemon peel, finely chopped
125mL/4¹/₂fl oz dry white wine
1 chicken stock cube
60g/2oz butter
salt and cayenne pepper
85mL/3fl oz cream
2 teaspoons lemon juice
1 packet crispbread

italian

al dente

introduction

Italian cuisine

Food is a passion in Italy, where even a modest meal can be spectacular. Both light-hearted and imaginative, this cuisine is celebrated for its ability to turn the simplest, freshest staples into feasts for both the eye and the palate. Italians like nothing better than to get together, eat, drink, tell jokes, sing and discuss the merits of their food – all of which is rich, robust, rustic and abundant. Italian food is just right for today's casual lifestyle and preference for a healthy diet that curbs cholesterol and enjoys a bit of fibre. It offers choices for every need – especially when the budget is limited.

If you imagine Italian food to consist only of pizza, pasta and tomato sauce, this cookbook will be a revelation because it's loaded with wonderful food ideas from first course – antipasti – to sweet and heavenly desserts – la Dolci. In between, you'll find recipes for vegetable dishes filled with the sun-drenched flavours, scents and colours of the Mediterranean. You'll also enjoy classic Italian treatments to main courses that feature, among others, poultry, succulent seafoods, tender lamb and veal. Last but not least, there is a choice of four superb menus to suit almost any entertaining occasion. These are filled with ideas as easy for the cook to prepare as they are enjoyable to eat in the true Italian style.

Italian cooking

In the minds of some people, Italian cooking is synonymous with pasta. It is true that pasta is very popular in Italy, but so too is rice, which grows in Italy's north. Soups are also very popular, varying from region to region, and from season to season. Meats, fish, crustaceans and shellfish together with vegetables – either cooked or served as salads – make up the secondo piatto (second course). Fresh fruit and a variety of cheeses complete the meal, which is then finished off with a strong cup of coffee.

Eating habits

Traditionally, the main meal in Italy is lunch. With most offices, shops and schools closed between 1.00 pm and 4.00 pm, and with some public offices closing for the day at 2.00 pm, lunch in an Italian household is on the table any time from 1.00 pm onwards. For those who have only a one-hour break, lunch is still a very important meal. Whether at home, in the restaurant around the corner from the office, or at the mensa (the factory refectory), lunch comprises the primo piatto (first course) of soup, rice or pasta, the secondo piatto (second course) of meat or fish, together with cheeses, vegetables or salad and, finally, fruit. The evening meal, any time after 8.00 pm, is usually a lighter version of lunch. However, the pasta is often replaced by a light soup containing very small pasta-shapes cooked for only a few minutes, and a frittata might replace the meat dish. For the evening meal, the emphasis is on easily digestible foods: vegetables, salads, cheeses and fruit. Bread (but not butter) is part of every meal.

Italians prefer to have a very light breakfast: a cappuccino or a short black coffee, and perhaps a small cake from the local coffee-bar on the way to work. Caffé latte and biscotti, a thick slice of homemade cake, or bread and butter with jam, make up the more homely Italian breakfast.

Snacks are readily available from a myriad of coffee-bars, pizzerie, Italianised McDonald's, the family fridge and, of course, from the household biscuit tin.

Italian glossary

When browsing through a book about Italian food or working through a menu or recipe, a term sometimes crops up which is unfamiliar unclear. This list of words and phrases commonly used around an Italian kitchen may help make your reading more rewarding and enjoyable.

Affumicato	Smoked
Agio e ogio	Garlic and oil, as a dressing
Al dente	To the tooth, a texture with some bite to it
Al forno/alla fornaia	In the oven; baked or roasted
Antipasto	The very first course of a meal; starter
Arrosto	Roasted, baked
Asciutto	Dry, as in pasta asciutto
Bollito	Boiled, particularly boiled meat
Cacciatora	Hunter's style
Caldo	Hot
Casalinga	Homemade
Condito	Dressed, as in a salad
Contorno	Vegetable dish, garnish
Cotto	Cooked
Crudo	Raw, uncooked
Cucina	Kitchen
Diavola	Devilled, or with a spicy sauce
Dolce	Sweets, dessert
Farcito	Stuffed
Fritto misto	Mixed fry
Freddo	Cold
Fresco	Fresh, cool
Fritto	Fried
Grasso	Fat
Integrale	Wholemeal
Il primo	The meal course between antipasto and the main course, consisting of soup, pasta, risotto or polenta
Il secondo	The main course of a meal
Magro	Thin, lean
Paglia e fieno	Straw and hay, meaning green and white
Pelato	Peeled
Petto	Breast, e.g. breast of chicken
Piatto	Plate
Ragu	Rich meat sauce
Ripieno	Stuffed
Rotolo	Roll, as in a Swiss roll
Rustico	Rustic
Saor	Soused, as with fish
Secco	Dry
Soffritto	A mixture of chopped vegetables fried in butter or oil and used as a flavour base for soups, sauces and stews
Sugo	Sauce, usually for pasta
Tavola	Table
Tritato	Minced, finely chopped
Verde	Green
Verdure	Vegetables

cheese

Gorgonzola, mascarpone, Parmesan, pecorino – the list of Italy's splendid cheeses is virtually endless. Different regions have developed unique cheese styles over the centuries, and whether you're cooking with an Italian cheese, adding one to a cooked dish, or assembling a cheese platter, you're dealing with some of the world's best.

The cheeses of Italy originated in the dairies and kitchens of farmers. Now, each region has at least one cheese that is characteristic of it, and this is reflected in that region's cooking. It would be difficult to create authentic Italian dishes without having the appropriate cheese available and we are lucky that most cheese counters offer a range of both imported and locally made cheeses to choose from. Price is not always an indication of which is best, so it is a good idea to taste-test before buying.

Bel Paese

Meaning 'beautiful country', Bel Paese is a commercial variation of a mild, semi-soft, creamy cheese made from cow's milk. Originating from the Lombardy region, it melts easily and is perfect for cooking. Bel Paese can be used in place of mozzarella and fontina.

Caciocavallo

Harking from southern Italy and Sicily it is made from cow's milk and is sometimes mixed with goat's milk. The name means 'cheese on horseback', which refers to the way the cheeses are strung together in pairs and hung to mature over poles, as if astride a horse. When fresh, it is soft and sweet and eaten as a table cheese. When aged, it becomes spicy and tangy and should be used for grating. If unavailable, use provolone which is the more widely known member of the same family of cheeses.

Dolcelatte

One of the Gorgonzola cheeses, its name means 'sweet milk'.

Fontina

A semi-hard cow's milk cheese with a sweet and nutty flavour. Although classified as a table cheese, it is most commonly used in fonduta, a traditional dish from the region of Piemont. If fontina is unavailable, use gruyère for a fondue, or Bel Paese or matured mozzarella for other dishes.

Gorgonzola

Made from cow's milk, it has a soft, creamy texture and a buttery flavour. Its character-istic blue mould is produced by introducing a harmless penicillin bacteria to the cheese. There are several kinds of Gorgonzola, with Dolcelatte being the best known. Meaning 'sweet milk', it is the creamiest and sweetest variety. Dolce verde is more piquant and is stronger in flavour and smell. You can use any other creamy, mild blue-vein cheese, or blend some cream with a sharper, crumbly blue-vein in place of Gorgonzola.

Grana

A collective name used to describe matured, hard cheeses from northern and central Italy, these cheeses have a close grain ideal for grating. Parmesan and grana padano are the most well-known in this group of cheeses. Grana padano is made from cow's milk from areas outside those designated for reggiano production. Because of a shorter maturing time it is less flavoursome and moister than Parmesan. Wherever possible, grana cheeses should be bought in a piece to be freshly grated as required.

Mascarpone

A fresh cheese made from cream, Mascarpone is unsalted, buttery and rich with a fat content of 90 percent. It is used mostly as a dessert, either alone or as an ingredient. If it is unavailable, mix one part thick sour cream to three parts thickened (double) cream or beat 250g/8oz ricotta cheese with 250mL/8fl oz pure (single) cream until smooth and thick.

wine

Italian wines:

The climate and soil of Italy are perfect for wine production and every region produces wine. In fact, Italy produces more wine than any other country in the world.

Aperitifs:

Campari

This is a strong alcohol which is usually served with soda water.

Vermouth

A fortified wine. The French also have a vermouth but you will find that the Italian one is much sweeter.

White Wines:

Frascati

Ideal for serving with fish and chicken. It is a light, dry straw-coloured wine that ranges from dry to sweet. The sweet frascati is known as Canellino and makes a good accompaniment to beans and gnocchi. Dry frascati is the best known of this group of wines.

Verdicchio

A young, light, fresh, fruity semi-dry wine.

Red Wines:

Lambrusco

A light, dry, slightly sparkling wine, good to serve with meat meals.

Barbera

This robust red wine complements the full flavour of Italian food.

Chianti

Available as either red or white wine. As a young wine, chianti is wonderfully fragrant and fruity; as it ages it becomes even better. This is the wine that is found in the straw-covered bottles so often associated with Italy.

Dessert Wines:

Marsala

This fortified, full-flavoured sweet wine is named after a town on the island of Sicily. It is used mainly for cooking and dessert, however some varieties are also drunk as aperitifs.

Vin Santo

A dessert wine from Tuscany. It is made from grapes that are dried in the shade for several months. They are then pressed and the wine aged for four to five years in small oak casks. The casks are stored under the roof, thereby exposing the wine to variations in temperature, which adds to the unique flavour.

Sparkling Wines:

Asti Spumanti

The best known sweet Italian sparkling wine that makes a perfect finish to a meal. It is made in vast quantities and exported all over the world.

Liqueurs:

Galliano

A rich yellow liqueur flavoured with herbs.

Sambuca

A clear anise-flavoured liqueur.

Amaretto

A rich toffee-coloured liqueur that tastes of almonds.

Frangelico

A delicious liqueur made from hazelnuts, berries, almonds, orange flowers and cinnamon.

mixed bean soup

soups
&
starters

From classic favourites like Minestrone

to more luxurious dishes like Butterflied Prawns
with Garlic, Chilli and Parsley, you are sure
to be inspired to try the delicious soup and
starter ideas on the following pages.

roasted
eggplant soup

Photograph opposite

ingredients

1 kg/2 lb eggplant (aubergines), halved
4 red peppers, halved
1 teaspoon olive oil
2 cloves garlic, crushed
4 tomatoes, peeled and chopped
3 cups/750mL/1 ¼ pt vegetable stock
2 teaspoons crushed black peppercorns

roasted eggplant soup

Method:

1 *Place eggplant (aubergines) and red peppers, skin side up under a preheated hot grill and cook for 10 minutes or until flesh is soft and skins are blackened. Peel away blackened skin and roughly chop flesh.*

2 *Heat oil in a large saucepan over a medium heat. Add garlic and tomatoes and cook, stirring, for 2 minutes. Add eggplant (aubergines), red peppers, stock and black pepper, bring to simmer and leave for 4 minutes. Remove pan from heat and set aside to cool slightly.*

3 *Place vegetables and stock in batches in food processor or blender and process until smooth. Return mixture to a clean pan, bring to simmer over a medium heat and simmer for 3-5 minutes or until heated through.*

Note: *This soup can be made the day before and reheated when required.*

Serves 6

91

minestrone

Method:

1 Heat butter and add garlic, onion, bacon and bones. Sauté 4-5 minutes.
2 Add all other ingredients except pasta and bring to the boil. Allow to simmer covered for approximately 90 minutes.
3 Remove and discard bacon bones.
4 Stir in both pastas and cook until al dente.
   Note: To serve, sprinkle with a generous helping of Parmesan and a good crusty loaf of your favourite bread.
   Serves 4

ingredients

2 tablespoons/60g/2oz butter
2 cloves garlic, crushed
2 small onions, finely chopped
4 rashers bacon, chopped
250g/8oz bacon bones
150g/4^1/$_2$oz red kidney beans
100g/3^1/$_2$oz haricot beans, soaked overnight
^{1}/$_2$ small cabbage, roughly chopped
100g/3^1/$_2$oz spinach, washed and chopped
3 medium-sized potatoes, peeled and chopped
2 medium-sized carrots, peeled and diced
150g/4^1/$_2$oz fresh (or frozen) peas, shelled
I stalk celery, chopped
2 tablespoons parsley, finely chopped
2 litres/3^1/$_2$pt chicken stock
salt to taste
100g/3^1/$_2$oz tomato and cheese tortellini
50g/2oz pasta of your choice
fresh Parmesan cheese

tomato
and basil bruschetta

Method:

1 Combine oil and garlic. Brush bread slices liberally with oil mixture and place on an oiled baking tray. Bake for 10 minutes or until bread is golden. Set aside to cool.

2 Place tomatoes, basil or parsley and black pepper to taste in a bowl and mix to combine. Just prior to serving, top toasted bread slices with tomato mixture.

Note: For a light meal, top bruschetta with a little grated Parmesan or mozzarella cheese and grill until cheese melts. Serve with a salad.

Serves 6

ingredients

¹/₂ cup/125mL/4fl oz olive oil
2 cloves garlic, crushed
1 French bread stick, sliced diagonally
3 tomatoes, finely chopped
3 tablespoons chopped fresh basil
or parsley
freshly ground black pepper

tuna and beans

Method:

1 Place tuna, beans and onion in a bowl and mix gently so that tuna remains in chunks.
2 Place oil, vinegar, garlic and mustard in a screwtop jar and shake well to combine.
3 Pour dressing over tuna mixture and toss gently. Stand at room temperature for 1 hour. Sprinkle with parsley and serve.

Serves 6

ingredients

375g/12oz can tuna in oil, drained
440g/14oz can red kidney beans, drained
$^1/_2$ red onion, diced
60mL/2fl oz olive oil
1 tablespoon wine vinegar
1 small clove garlic, crushed
1 teaspoon French mustard
chopped fresh parsley to serve

capsicums
(peppers) roasted in garlic

Method:

1 Preheat oven to 180°C/350°F/Gas 4. Place red capsicum (pepper) in a bowl. Combine oil, garlic, red chilli and oregano, pour over capsicum and toss to coat.
2 Layer capsicum (pepper), skin side up, in a baking dish, cover with aluminium foil and bake for 30 minutes. Uncover and bake for 20-30 minutes longer or until capsicum (pepper) blackens slightly.

Note: When available, use a mixture of red, green and yellow capsicum (peppers). Store, covered with olive oil, in a clean glass jar for up to 3 weeks. The capsicums (peppers) taste best served at room temperature.

Serves 6

ingredients

3 red capsicums (peppers),
cut lengthwise into eighths
1$^1/_2$ tablespoons olive oil
5 cloves garlic, finely chopped
1 fresh red chilli, cut into slivers
$^1/_2$ teaspoon dried oregano

Oven temperature 180°C, 350°F, Gas 4

eggplant
antipasto

Method:

1 Sprinkle eggplant with salt and stand for 15-20 minutes. Rinse under cold water and pat dry with absorbent paper.

2 Brush eggplant lightly with olive oil. Place under a preheated grill for 4-5 minutes each side or until cooked through.

3 Divide eggplant into four portions of three or four slices, overlapping in a shallow ovenproof dish. Top with mozzarella and grill for 4-5 minutes or until cheese melts.

4 Transfer eggplant to four plates. Top with capers and serve with an arrangement of gherkins, tomatoes, ham, bread, lettuce and chutney.

Serves 4

ingredients

2 eggplant, cut into 2 cm slices
salt
olive oil
150g sliced mozzarella cheese
1 tablespoon capers
2 tomatoes, sliced
12 slices leg ham or prosciutto, rolled
4 slices rye or wholemeal bread
4 lettuce leaves
4 tablespoons chutney or relish

butterflied
prawns with garlic, chilli and parsley

Method:
1 Cut prawns down the back and remove vein.
2 Combine oil, lemon juice, garlic, chilli and parsley in a bowl. Add prawns, mix well, and leave to marinate for 2-3 hours.
3 Heat oil in a large pan, coat prawns with flour, and cook quickly in oil for 2-3 minutes. Drain on absorbent paper.
4 Serve with lemon wedges and parsley.

Serves 4

ingredients

1kg/2¹/₄ lb (approx. 20) green prawns, heads and shells removed, tails left on
2 tablespoons olive oil
1 tablespoon lemon juice
2 cloves garlic, crushed
2 red chillies, seeded and finely chopped
2 tablespoons parsley, chopped
¹/₂ cup/60g/2oz flour
oil (for frying)
lemon (to garnish)

mixed
bean soup

Photograph page 9

Method:

1 Place red kidney and cannellini beans in a bowl. Cover with cold water and set aside to soak overnight. Drain.

2 Heat oil in a saucepan over a medium heat, add bacon, onion and garlic and cook, stirring, for 5 minutes · or until onion is tender. Add celery, carrots and potatoes and cook for 1 minute longer.

3 Stir in stock, tomatoes, cabbage, pasta or rice, red kidney and cannellini beans, herbs and black pepper to taste and bring to the boil. Boil for 10 minutes, then reduce heat and simmer, stirring occasionally, for 1 hour or until beans are tender. Sprinkle with Parmesan cheese and serve.

Note: This minestrone-style soup is delicious served with hot crusty bread.

Extra vegetables of your choice may be added – it is a good way to use up odds and ends.

Serves 4

ingredients

90g/3oz dried red kidney beans
90g/3oz dried cannellini beans
2 tablespoons olive oil
60g/2oz bacon, chopped
1 onion, chopped
1 clove garlic, crushed
3 stalks celery, sliced
2 carrots, chopped
2 potatoes, chopped
6 cups/1¹/₂ litres/2¹/₂pt chicken or vegetable stock
440g/14oz canned tomatoes, undrained and mashed
¹/₄ cabbage, finely shredded
60g/2oz small pasta shapes or rice
1 teaspoon dried mixed herbs
freshly ground black pepper
grated Parmesan cheese

fresh
basil carpaccio

Method:

1 *To make dressing, place basil, oil, lemon juice, capers and garlic in a bowl. Mix well to combine.*
2 *Arrange beef slices on a serving plate and season with black pepper. Pour dressing over and sprinkle with onion. Cover and marinate for 10 minutes.*

Serves 4

ingredients

500g/1lb eye fillet, very thinly sliced
1 onion, finely sliced
freshly ground black pepper
<u>Basil Dressing</u>
10 fresh basil leaves, chopped
4 tablespoons olive oil
3 tablespoons lemon juice
2 tablespoons capers, chopped
2 cloves garlic, finely chopped

chargrilled
vegetables with pesto

Method:

1 *Prepare vegetables for grilling.*
2 *Grease and heat a chargrill pan. Brush vegetable slices with a little olive oil and chargrill until golden brown and vegetables are cooked.*
3 *Serve with pesto or basil aïoli.*

Serves 4

ingredients

1 capsicum (pepper), cut into pieces
1 eggplant (aubergine), cut into slices
2 red onions, quartered
2 zucchini/courgette, sliced lengthwise
1 small sweet potato, thinly sliced

pasta
&
rice

spinach and ricotta cannelloni

Few things are more delicious than a

creamy risotto or a dish of gnocchi. The best results require a little patience, but they are worth every minute. When you see these dishes, you'll understand why the Italians love them so.

spaghetti
with meatballs

Photograph opposite

ingredients

500g/1 lb lean ground beef
2 tablespoons chopped fresh parsley
60g/2oz salami, very finely chopped
60g/2oz grated Parmesan cheese
3 tablespoons tomato purée
1 egg, beaten
15g/¹/₂oz butter
1 onion, very finely chopped
2 teaspoons dried basil
1 teaspoon dried oregano
440g/14oz can tomatoes, chopped
125mL/4fl oz beef stock
125mL/4fl oz white wine
1 teaspoon caster sugar
250g/8oz spaghetti

spaghetti with meatballs

Method:

1 *Combine beef, parsley, salami, Parmesan cheese and 1 tablespoon tomato purée in a bowl, mix in enough egg to bind. Form mixture into small balls, cook in a nonstick frying pan for 10-12 minutes until cooked, then set aside.*

2 *Melt butter in a large frying pan over moderate heat. Add onion, basil and oregano and cook for 2 minutes. Stir in tomatoes, remaining tomato purée, beef stock, wine and sugar. Simmer mixture for 30 minutes, stirring occasionally, until thick.*

3 *Cook spaghetti in boiling salted water until just tender, drain. Stir meatballs into the tomato sauce, warm through, stirring occasionally. Serve on a bed of spaghetti.*

Kitchen Tip: *To cut down on preparation time make the meatballs in advance and freeze them in the tomato sauce in a covered container for up to 3 months. Simply reheat over a gentle heat when required and serve with spaghetti.*

Serves 4

saffron
and chicken risotto

Method:

1 Place stock and wine in a saucepan and bring to the boil over a medium heat. Reduce heat and keep warm.

2 Heat oil in a saucepan over a medium heat, add chicken and cook, stirring, for 5 minutes or until chicken is tender. Remove chicken from pan and set aside.

3 Add butter and leeks to same pan and cook over a low heat, stirring, for 8 minutes or until leeks are golden and caramelised.

4 Add rice and saffron to pan and cook over a medium heat, stirring constantly, for 3 minutes or until rice becomes translucent. Pour 1 cup/250 mL/8 fl oz hot stock mixture into rice mixture and cook, stirring constantly, until liquid is absorbed. Continue cooking in this way until all the stock is used and rice is tender.

5 Stir chicken, Parmesan cheese and black pepper to taste into rice mixture and cook for 2 minutes longer. Serve immediately.

Note: Arborio rice is traditionally used for making risottos, as it absorbs liquid without

ingredients

chicken
4 cups/1 litre/1³/₄pt vegetable stock
1 cup/250mL/8fl oz dry white wine
1 tablespoon vegetable oil
2 boneless chicken breast fillets, sliced
45g/¹/₂oz butter
3 leeks, sliced
2 cups/440g/14oz arborio or
risotto rice
pinch saffron threads
60g/2oz grated Parmesan cheese
freshly ground black pepper

becoming soft. If Arborio rice is unavailable, substitute with any short grain rice. A risotto made in the traditional way, where liquid is added a little at a time as the rice cooks, will take 20-30 minutes to cook.

Serves 4

chicken
livers and mushrooms on spaghetti

Method:

1 To make tomato sauce, heat oil and butter in a frypan, and cook onion until soft. Add garlic and mushrooms and cook for 2-3 minutes longer. Combine tomatoes and sugar and add to mushrooms. Cook over a low heat for 10 minutes. Stir in stock and simmer for 30 minutes longer or until sauce reduces and thickens. Season to taste with black pepper.

2 To make chicken liver sauce, melt butter in a saucepan and cook chicken livers and thyme over a medium heat until brown. Increase heat, stir in Marsala and cook for 1-2 minutes. Stir in parsley.

3 Cook spaghetti in boiling water in a large saucepan until al dente. Drain and fold through oil.

4 Arrange half spaghetti on a warm serving platter, top with half chicken liver mixture, then half Tomato Sauce. Sprinkle over half Parmesan cheese, then repeat layers. Serve immediately.

Note: This recipe is a variation of a sauce created for the great singer Caruso.

Serves 4

ingredients

500g/1 lb fresh spaghetti, or
400g/13oz dried spaghetti
1 tablespoon vegetable oil
90g/3oz grated fresh Parmesan cheese
Tomato sauce
1 tablespoon vegetable oil
30g/1oz butter
1 onion, finely diced
2 cloves garlic, crushed
12 small button mushrooms, halved
440g/14oz canned Italian peeled tomatoes,
undrained and mashed
1 teaspoon sugar
300mL/9¹/₂fl oz chicken stock
ground black pepper
Chicken liver sauce
30g/1oz butter
250g/8oz chicken livers, trimmed and sliced
1 teaspoon finely chopped fresh thyme,
or ¹/₄ teaspoon dried thyme
90mL/3fl oz Marsala
1 tablespoon finely chopped fresh parsley

rice
with mozzarella and herbs

Method:

1 Place water in a large saucepan and bring to the boil. Add rice and cook, covered, for 15-20 minutes or until the rice is just tender. Stir occasionally during cooking to prevent sticking.

2 Drain, then return rice to same pan. Stir in butter and chopped herbs then fold through mozzarella and Parmesan cheeses and season to taste with black pepper. Transfer to a warm serving dish and serve immediately.

Note: Much simpler than a risotto, this dish relies on the quality of the fresh herbs and mozzarella used.

Serves 4

ingredients

4 litres/7pt water
315g/10oz Arborio rice
90g/3oz butter, cut into small pieces
2 tablespoons fresh mixed herbs, chopped
250g/8oz grated mozzarella cheese
60g/2oz grated fresh Parmesan cheese
freshly ground black pepper

seafood
lasagne

Method:

1 Preheat oven to 180°C/350°F/Gas 4. Heat the oil in a large frying pan, add the leek and cook until tender. Stir in the tomatoes and tomato purée. Cook until mixture boils then simmer uncovered until sauce is slightly thickened. Stir in the prawn and fish pieces, cover and cook over low heat for about 5 minutes.

2 Cook the lasagne in a saucepan of boiling water until al dente. Place lasagne in a large bowl of cool water until ready to use.

3 Spoon one third of the sauce into the bottom of a 5cm/2in-deep casserole dish. Drain lasagne sheets and arrange a single layer over the seafood sauce. Spoon another third of the sauce over the lasagne, and top with another layer of lasagne.

4 Spread the remaining third of sauce over lasagne and top with mozzarella cheese. Bake in oven for 40 minutes.

Serves 4

ingredients

2 tablespoons olive oil
1 leek, white part only, finely chopped
440g/14oz chopped canned tomatoes
2 tablespoons tomato purée
500g/1 lb uncooked prawns, shelled
and deveined, cut into small pieces
250g/8oz boneless white fish fillets,
cut into small pieces
15 sheets spinach lasagne
125g/4oz mozzarella cheese,
thinly sliced

Oven temperature 180°C, 350°F, Gas 4

linguine
with prawns and scallops in a roasted tomato sauce

Photograph opposite

linguine with prawns and scallops in a roasted tomato sauce

ingredients

400g/14oz linguine
1kg/2¹/₂ lb tomatoes
salt and pepper
80mL/3oz olive oil
200g/7oz scallops
200g/7oz green prawns, peeled
150g calamari, cut into rings
200g/7oz firm white fish pieces
3 garlic cloves, crushed
2 brown onions, diced
1 tablespoon tomato paste (optional)
80mL/3oz water
¹/₃ cup/20g/²/₃oz parsley, chopped
Parmesan cheese

Method:

1 Cook the linguine in salted boiling water until al dente and set aside.

2 To roast the tomatoes: preheat the oven to 180°C/350°F/Gas 4. Cut the tomatoes in half and place on a baking tray. Drizzle with a little olive oil, sprinkle with a little salt and pepper, and roast in the oven for 20-25 minutes until tomatoes are well roasted.

3 Place roasted tomatoes in a food processor and process for a few seconds, but do not over-process. (The mixture should still have texture.)

4 Heat half the oil in a pan. Sauté the scallops and the prawns for 2 minutes until just cooked, and remove from the pan. Add the calamari and cook for 2 minutes, before removing from the pan. Adding a little more oil if needed, sauté the fish for a few minutes until just cooked, and remove from the pan.

5 Heat the remaining oil, and sauté the garlic and onion for a few minutes until cooked. Add the tomato mixture, tomato paste and water, and simmer (for 10 minutes). Carefully add the seafood to the sauce, season with salt and pepper, and mix through the chopped parsley.

6 Serve with the linguine and Parmesan cheese.
Serves 4

mixed mushroom
risotto

Method:

1 In a pan, heat the butter, add the mushrooms, and cook for a few minutes. Remove from the heat and set aside.

2 Heat the oil in a large heavy-based saucepan, add the garlic and leek, and cook for 5-6 minutes until cooked. Meanwhile, place stock in a saucepan and simmer gently.

3 Add the rice to the garlic and leek mixture and stir for one minute (to coat the rice). Add the white wine and cook until liquid is absorbed. Start adding the stock, a ladle at a time, stirring continuously, until liquid has been absorbed. Continue adding stock (a ladle at a time), until all stock is used and rice is cooked.

4 Stir in mushrooms, lemon rind, cheese and parsley, serve immediately.

Serves 6-8

ingredients

2 tablespoons butter
500g/1 lb mixed mushrooms (oyster, shiitake, flat, enoki, Swiss), sliced
40mL/1 ¹/₂fl oz olive oil
2 cloves garlic, minced
1 leek, finely sliced
1 litre/1³/₄pt chicken stock
2 cups arborio rice
¹/₂ cup/120mL/4fl oz white wine
rind of 1 lemon, finely grated
¹/₂ cup/60g/2oz each pecorino and Parmesan cheese, grated
2 tablespoons parsley, chopped

spinach,
green pea & ricotta gnocchi

Method:

1 Steam or microwave spinach until tender. Drain and squeeze to remove excess liquid. Set aside.

2 Boil, steam or microwave peas until tender. Drain and combine with spinach. Chop mixture finely.

3 Place spinach mixture and ricotta in a saucepan. Season to taste with black pepper and nutmeg. Add 15g/¹/₂oz butter and cook over a very low heat, stirring frequently until butter melts and all excess liquid evaporates. Remove from heat. Beat in eggs, then add the breadcrumbs, flour and half the Parmesan cheese. The mixture should be firm enough to hold its shape, but soft enough to create a light-textured gnocchi.

4 Using well-floured hands, take heaped spoons of mixture and roll lightly into small oval balls. Bring a large saucepan of water to the boil, then reduce heat. Drop gnocchi in a few at a time and cook for 4-5 minutes or until they rise to the surface. Remove from pan and drain. Cover and keep warm.

5 Melt remaining butter in a saucepan and cook until lightly browned. Pour butter over gnocchi, sprinkle with remaining Parmesan cheese and serve.

Serves 4

ingredients

220g/7oz fresh spinach leaves, or
200g/6¹/₂oz frozen spinach,
thawed and drained
220g/7oz shelled fresh or
frozen green peas
220g/7oz ricotta cheese, drained
freshly ground black pepper
ground nutmeg
60g/2oz butter
2 eggs, lightly beaten
3 tablespoons dried breadcrumbs
5 tablespoons plain flour
90g/3oz fresh Parmesan cheese, grated

spinach
and ricotta cannelloni

Photograph page 101

ingredients

250g/8oz instant (no precooking required) cannelloni tubes
440g/14oz canned tomatoes, drained and chopped
1 clove garlic, crushed
125g/4oz grated mozzarella cheese
2 tablespoons grated Parmesan cheese
Spinach filling
1/2 bunch/250g/8oz English spinach, shredded
1/2 cup/125mL/4fl oz water
250g/8oz ricotta cheese, drained
2 tablespoons grated Parmesan cheese
1 egg, beaten
1/4 teaspoon ground nutmeg
freshly ground black pepper

Method:

1 *To make filling, place spinach and water in a saucepan, cover with a tight fitting lid and cook over a medium heat, shaking pan occasionally, for 4-5 minutes or until spinach wilts. Drain well, squeezing out excess water and set aside to cool.*

2 *Finely chop spinach and place in a bowl. Add ricotta cheese, Parmesan cheese, egg, nutmeg and black pepper to taste and mix to combine. Spoon mixture into cannelloni tubes and arrange tubes side-by-side in a lightly greased ovenproof dish.*

3 *Combine tomatoes and garlic in a bowl and spoon over cannelloni. Sprinkle with mozzarella cheese and Parmesan cheese and bake for 30-35 minutes or until cannelloni is tender and top is golden.*

Note: *Cottage cheese may be used in place of the ricotta cheese if you wish. If using cottage cheese, push through a sieve to achieve a smoother texture. Serve cannelloni with an Italian salad and herb or garlic bread.*

Serves 4

Oven temperature 180°C, 350°F, Gas 4

pappardelle
with peas and bacon

Method:

1 *Melt butter in a large frypan and cook onion, garlic and chilli for 6-8 minutes. Add bacon and cook for 5 minutes longer. Stir in peas, mint and 2 teaspoons parsley. Season to taste with black pepper. Set aside and keep warm.*

2 *Cook pappardelle in boiling water in a large saucepan until al dente. Drain, then add to pea mixture, toss lightly to coat and remove from heat. Combine eggs, cream, pecorino and remaining parsley and stir into pasta mixture. Serve as soon as eggs begin to set and cling to pasta- this will take only a few seconds. The sauce should be slightly runny.*

Serves 4

ingredients

60g/2 oz butter
1 onion, sliced
1 clove garlic, crushed
pinch chilli flakes, or to taste
3 bacon rashers, chopped
90g/3 oz shelled peas, blanched
1 teaspoon mint, finely chopped
1 tablespoon fresh parsley, finely chopped
freshly ground black pepper
500g/1 lb fresh pappardelle
2 eggs, lightly beaten
90 mL/3fl oz cream (single)
1 tablespoon pecorino cheese, grated

chicken with ricotta, rocket &
roasted red capsicum (peppers)

poultry

Today, alongside the standard

commercially raised poultry, the eager
Italian cook can also find quails and
spatchcock that have been commercially
grown. However, for the Italian who enjoys
poultry, nothing beats the taste of wildlife.

chicken
with anchovy sauce

Photograph opposite

chicken with anchovy sauce

ingredients

1 1/2kg/3 lb chicken, jointed
freshly ground black pepper
1 1/2 tablespoons olive oil
1 small onion, finely chopped
1 clove garlic, finely chopped
125mL/4fl oz dry white wine
1 1/2 tablespoons white wine vinegar
125 mL/4fl oz chicken stock
1/2 teaspoon dried oregano
1 bay leaf
1 tablespoon slivered black olives
3 flat anchovy fillets, rinsed in cold water,
dried and chopped
2 tablespoons chopped parsley

Method:

1 *Wash chicken under cold running water, then pat dry with absorbent kitchen paper. Season to taste with black pepper.*

2 *Heat oil in a heavy-based frypan and cook chicken a few pieces at a time, until brown on both sides. Remove from pan and set aside. Drain off pan juices and discard.*

3 *Add onion and garlic to pan and cook, stirring constantly, for 5 minutes or until lightly browned. Stir in wine and vinegar, bring to the boil and simmer until reduced to 3 tablespoons.*

4 *Pour in chicken stock and boil stirring constantly, for 2 minutes. Return chicken to the pan, add oregano and bay leaf. Bring to the boil, cover and simmer for 30 minutes or until tender.*

5 *Remove chicken pieces from pan and set aside to keep warm. Remove and discard bay leaf. Bring stock to the boil and boil until slightly thickened. Stir in olives, anchovies and parsley and cook for 1 minute longer, then spoon over chicken.*

Serves 4

spatchcock
with ricotta and herbs

Method:

1 To make stuffing, place all ingredients in a bowl and mix well. Divide into four portions. Gently ease skin from breast of each bird and fill pocket with stuffing.

2 Brush birds with oil and top with a sprig of rosemary and a sprinkle of black pepper. Place on a roasting rack in a baking dish and cook at 220°C/425°F/Gas 7 for 30 minutes. Reduce heat to 180°C/350°F/Gas 4 and cook, basting with pan juices, for 20 minutes longer or until birds are tender.

3 Remove birds and set aside to keep warm. Place baking dish over a hot plate and bring juices to the boil, pour over birds and serve.

Serves 4

ingredients

4 x 500g/1 lb spatchcocks, cleaned and dried
2 tablespoons olive oil
4 fresh rosemary sprigs
375mL/12fl oz dry white wine
Freshly ground black pepper
<u>Stuffing</u>
155g/5oz ricotta cheese
60g/2oz finely grated fontina cheese
60g/2oz gorgonzola cheese, crumbled
4 slices mortadella, finely chopped
2 tablespoons fresh parsley, finely chopped
1 tablespoon fresh marjoram, finely chopped
1 tablespoon fresh sage, finely chopped
30g/1oz butter, melted

Oven temperature 180°C, 350°F, Gas 4

chicken
with ricotta, rocket & roasted red capsicum (peppers)

Photograph also page 115

Method:

1 *Preheat the oven to 200°C/400°C/Gas 6.*
2 *Combine ricotta, rocket, pine nuts, capsicum (pepper), and pepper & salt in a small bowl and mix together until smooth.*
3 *Place 1-2 tablespoons of ricotta mixture under the skin of each chicken breast. Lightly grease a baking dish. Place the chicken breasts in the dish, sprinkle with pepper and salt, place 1 teaspoon butter on each breast, pour stock around the chicken and bake for 20-25 minutes.*
4 *Serve chicken with pan-juices and a rocket salad.*

Serves 4

ingredients

**200g/7oz fresh ricotta
1 cup rocket, roughly chopped
¹/₄ cup/45g/1¹/₂oz pine nuts, toasted
¹/₂ red capsicum (pepper), roasted
and finely chopped
freshly ground pepper and salt
4 chicken breasts (200g/7oz each),
with skin on
1 tablespoon butter
250mL/9fl oz chicken stock**

119

duck
with vinegar

Method:

1 Heat oil in a frypan and cook duck, skin side down, over a low heat until skin is golden. Turn and cook on other side.

2 Add vinegar, black pepper to taste, cinnamon and blueberries. Cover and cook over a low heat for 15 minutes, or until duck is tender.

3 To prepare flowers, gradually sift flour into water and mix with a fork until batter is smooth. If necessary add more water. Pour 2^1/$_2$cm/1in oil into a frypan and heat until very hot. Dip flowers into the batter and cook a few at a time in oil until golden.

4 To serve, arrange duck and flowers on serving plate and spoon blueberry sauce over duck.
Note: Blueberries are used in this recipe, but any other berry fruit may be substituted.
Serves 4

ingredients

2 tablespoons sunflower oil
4 duck breasts, with skin on
3 tablespoons balsamic vinegar
freshly ground black pepper
^{1}/$_4$ teaspoon ground cinnamon
4 tablespoons fresh blueberries
<u>Zucchini (courgette) flowers</u>
90g/3oz flour
250 mL/8fl oz water
oil for cooking
12 zucchini (courgette) flowers

chicken marsala

chicken
marsala

ingredients

4 large chicken breast fillets, pounded
seasoned flour
30g/1oz butter
2 tablespoons olive oil
185mL/6fl oz dry marsala
4 tablespoons chicken stock
30g/1oz butter, softened
freshly ground black pepper

Method:

1 Coat chicken in flour and shake off excess. Heat butter and oil in a frypan, until butter is foaming. Add chicken and cook for 3 minutes each side.

2 Stir in marsala, bring to the boil and simmer for 15 minutes, or until chicken is cooked. Remove chicken and set aside to keep warm. Add stock, bring to the boil and cook for 2 minutes. Whisk in softened butter and season to taste with black pepper. To serve, spoon sauce over chicken.
Serves 4

quail with rice
and olives

Method:

1 Heat oil and butter in a frypan and cook onions and garlic over a low heat for 3 minutes, or until onions soften.

2 Add quail to pan and cook over a high heat until brown on all sides. Add sage, rosemary and black pepper to taste.

3 Stir in Marsala, bring to the boil and simmer for 20 minutes or until quail is cooked.

4 To prepare rice, place rice, butter, mortadella and olives in a saucepan and heat gently, stirring, until butter is melted. Mix in Parmesan cheese and basil. To serve, arrange rice on serving plate, top with quail and spoon a little of the pan juices over.

Serves 4

ingredients

1 tablespoon olive oil
30g/1oz butter
2 onions, chopped
2 cloves garlic, crushed
8 quail, cleaned
5 fresh sage leaves
3 teaspoons chopped fresh rosemary
freshly ground black pepper
300mL/9¹/₂fl oz dry Marsala
Olive rice
375g/12oz rice, cooked
60g/2oz butter, chopped
6 slices mortadella, chopped
90g/3oz pitted black olives, chopped
3 tablespoons grated
fresh Parmesan cheese
3 tablespoons chopped fresh basil

seafood

tuna in piquant tomato sauce

Italy is surrounded on most sides by sea,

and you'll be surrounded on all sides by people clamouring for more of these tasty, easy Italian seafood dishes!

garlic
and rosemary mackerel

Method:
1 *Heat oil and butter in a large frypan and cook garlic for 1 minute. Add cutlets and cook for 3-4 minutes each side or until browned.*
2 *Pour lemon juice over and sprinkle with rosemary. Season to taste with black pepper. Cover and simmer for 5-8 minutes or until flesh flakes when tested with a fork.*

ingredients

1 tablespoon olive oil
30g/1oz butter
2 cloves garlic, crushed
4 large mackeral cutlets, or thick fillets
3 tablespoons lemon juice
2 teaspoons fresh rosemary, 1/2 teaspoon dry rosemary leaves
freshly ground black pepper

spicy scallops
and mushrooms

Method:

1 Melt butter in a large frypan and cook mushrooms, spring onions (shallots) and garlic for 4-5 minutes. Remove from pan and set aside. Add scallops to pan and cook for 2-3 minutes or until tender. Remove from pan and set aside.

2 Stir in wine, chilli and parsley and cook over a high heat until reduced by half. Return mushroom mixture and scallops to pan, toss to combine.

Note: Scallops, mushrooms and garlic are a wonderful combination in this quick dish.

Serves 4

ingredients

45g/1¹/₂oz butter
500g/1 lb button mushrooms
6 spring onions (shallots), chopped
2 cloves garlic, crushed
500g/1 lb scallops, cleaned
60mL/2fl oz dry white wine
1 red chilli, seeded and finely sliced
3 tablespoons chopped fresh parsley

sardine
fritters

Method:

1 Coat sardines in flour, dip in egg mixture, then coat with breadcrumbs.

2 To make minted chilli butter, place butter, mint, spring onions, garlic and chilli in a bowl and mix well. Place butter on a piece of plastic food wrap and roll into a log shape. Refrigerate until required.

3 Heat oil and one-third minted chilli butter in a large frypan and cook sardines for 1-2 minutes each side or until golden. Serve sardines topped with a slice of minted chilli butter.

Serves 4

ingredients

12 fresh sardine filets
4 tablespoons plain flour
1 egg, blended with 2 tablespoons milk
125g dried breadcrumbs
oil for cooking
125g/4oz butter, softened
3 tablespoons finely chopped fresh mint
2 spring onions, finely chopped
1 clove garlic, crushed
1/4 teaspoon chopped red chilli
freshly ground black pepper

Oven temperature 180°C, 350°F, Gas 4

tuna
in piquant tomato sauce

Photograph also on page 123

Method:
1 *Heat oil in a frypan and cook tuna for 2-3 minutes each side. Transfer to an ovenproof dish and reserve juices.*
2 *To make sauce, cook onion and garlic in pan for 4-5 minutes or until tender. Add reserved pan juices, tomatoes, tomato juice, capers, anchovies and oregano. Season to taste with black pepper. Bring to the boil and pour over tuna. Cover and bake at 180°C/350°F/Gas 4 for 20-30 minutes, or until tuna flakes when tested.*

Serves 4

ingredients

1 tablespoon olive oil
4 fresh tuna cutlets
<u>Sauce</u>
1 onion, chopped
2 cloves garlic, crushed
440g/14oz canned Italian peeled tomatoes, undrained and mashed
125mL/4fl oz tomato juice
2 tablespoons capers, chopped
4 anchovy fillets, chopped
¹/₂ teaspoon dried oregano
freshly ground black pepper

lemony
prawn kebabs

Method:

1 To make marinade, place oil, lemon juice, garlic, chilli and sage in a bowl. Season to taste with black pepper and mix to combine. Add prawns and mushrooms and toss to coat with marinade. Set aside to marinate for 1 hour.

2 Thread prawns, mushrooms and green capsicum (peppers) alternately onto eight oiled wooden skewers. Grill kebabs for 8-10 minutes or until cooked, turning and basting with marinade during cooking.

Note: These are delightful on the barbecue.

Serves 4

ingredients

750g/1 1/2 lb large uncooked prawns, peeled and deveined
16 button mushrooms, stalks removed
2 green capsicums (peppers), seeded and cut into 16 pieces
Marinade
60mL/2fl oz olive oil
2 tablespoons lemon juice
2 cloves garlic, crushed
1 small red chilli, seeded and finely chopped
1 tablespoon chopped fresh sage
freshly ground black pepper

cheesy
stuffed squid

Method:

1 To make stuffing, combine breadcrumbs, parsley, ricotta cheese, Parmesan cheese, oregano, garlic, cayenne and egg. Divide mixture into four equal portions and spoon into squid hoods. Secure ends with a toothpick or skewer.

2 Heat oil in a frypan and cook squid for 3-4 minutes each side or until brown. Add garlic, tomatoes, rosemary, wine, sugar and black pepper to taste. Reduce heat and simmer for 20-30 minutes or until squid is tender. To serve, remove skewers, slice squid and accompany with sauce.

Serves 4

ingredients

4 small squid hoods, cleaned
2 tablespoons olive oil
I clove garlic, crushed
440g/14oz canned Italian peeled tomatoes, undrained and mashed
¹/₂ teaspoon dried rosemary
60mL/2fl oz dry white wine
¹/₂ teaspoon sugar
freshly ground black pepper
Stuffing
45g/1¹/₂oz breadcrumbs, made from stale bread
4 tablespoons chopped fresh parsley
125g/4oz ricotta cheese
3 tablespoons/60g/2oz Parmesan cheese
¹/₂ teaspoon dried oregano
I clove garlic, crushed
pinch cayenne pepper
I egg, lightly beaten

chargrilled lamb with mint pesto
and creamy potatoes

Italian cuisine has an extraordinary

*number of different ways of cooking meat.
Italian cooks use herbs and spices to bring
out and enhance the flavour of the meat.*

rack of veal

with thyme on roasted garlic mashed potato

Photograph opposite

rack of veal with thyme on roasted garlic mashed potato

ingredients

750g/26oz potatoes, peeled and chopped
120mL/4oz olive oil
1 tablespoon capers, chopped
2 tablespoons roasted garlic purée
salt
freshly ground black pepper
2 tablespoons olive oil
1kg/2pt rack of veal (8 points)
2 tablespoons thyme leaves
300mL/10fl oz white wine
300mL/10fl oz veal or chicken stock

Method:

1 Preheat the oven to 180°C/350°F/Gas 4.

2 Boil the potatoes until soft. Drain, then mash (or purée), and add the olive oil, chopped capers and half the roasted garlic. Mix well, season with salt and pepper (to taste), and set aside until ready to serve.

3 Heat olive oil in a pan, and brown the veal on both sides until well sealed. This will take approximately 5 minutes. Remove the veal from the pan, and place on a rack in a baking dish. Rub the veal with remaining roasted garlic and 1 tablespoon of thyme leaves. Season with salt and pepper, add half the wine and stock to the baking dish.

4 Roast in the oven for 20 minutes or until veal is cooked to your liking. Wrap in foil and let rest for 10 minutes.

5 Add remaining stock, wine and thyme to the pan-juices and cook over a medium heat for 5 minutes or until the liquid has reduced by a third.

6 Serve the veal on a bed of mashed potatoes with pan-juices and sage leaves.

Serves 4

osso bucco

Method:

1 Melt butter in a frypan and cook carrot, onions, celery and garlic gently for 5 minutes, or until vegetables are softened. Remove vegetables from pan and place in an ovenproof dish.

2 Coat veal in flour. Heat oil in a frypan and cook veal until golden on each side. Remove from pan and arrange over vegetables.

3 Add tomatoes and cook, stirring constantly, for 5 minutes. Blend in wine, stock, bay leaf and black pepper to taste, bring to the boil and simmer for 5 minutes. Whisk in butter mixture and pour over meat and vegetables.

4 Cover dish and bake at 180°C/350°F/Gas 4 for 1½ hours or until meat is tender.

5 To make Gremolata, combine parsley, lemon rind, garlic and anchovy. Sprinkle over meat just prior to serving.

Note: Luxurious slow baking, intriguing stuffings and the use of unusual cuts characterise the cooking of most meats in Italy. Learn the secrets: the name of this recipe means 'hollow bones' and is a specialty from Milan.

Serves 4

ingredients

30g/1oz butter
1 carrot, chopped
2 onions, chopped
2 stalks celery, chopped
2 cloves garlic, crushed
4 thick slices shin veal on the bone
flour
2 tablespoons olive oil
8 tomatoes, peeled and chopped
125mL/4fl oz dry white wine
250mL/8fl oz beef stock
1 bay leaf
freshly ground black pepper
1 tablespoon butter mixed with
2 tablespoons flour
<u>Gremolata</u>
4 tablespoons fresh parsley, chopped
1 tablespoon lemon rind, finely grated
1 clove garlic, crushed
1 anchovy, finely chopped

Oven temperature 180°C, 350°F, Gas 4

chargrilled
lamb with mint pesto and creamy potatoes

Method:

1 *Preheat oven to 180°C/350°F/Gas 4. Season lamb with salt and freshly ground pepper to taste and set aside.*

2 *Lightly grease an ovenproof dish with butter and arrange the potato slices in overlapping rows in the dish, seasoning between each layer with salt and pepper, garlic and nutmeg.*

3 *Mix the flour and Parmesan cheese into the cream and pour over the potatoes. Sprinkle with extra Parmesan cheese then bake in the oven for 40-45 minutes or until potatoes are cooked.*

4 ***To make the pesto:*** *place the mint, parsley, garlic, pine nuts and cheeses in the bowl of a food processor, and process until finely chopped. Add the olive oil in a steady stream with the processor still running. Season with salt and pepper then set aside.*

5 *Preheat the chargrill plate (or pan), and grease lightly with a little oil. Chargrill the lamb on both sides for approximately 5-10 minutes or until done to your liking.*

6 *Serve the lamb sliced diagonally, on a bed of creamy potatoes with the mint pesto.*

Serves 4-6

ingredients

4 lamb backstraps (450g/1 lb in total)
salt and freshly ground black pepper
<u>Creamy potatoes</u>
500g/1 lb potatoes, thinly sliced
salt and freshly ground black pepper
1 garlic clove, crushed
1 teaspoon nutmeg
1 tablespoon plain flour
¹/₃ cup/40g/1¹/₃oz Parmesan cheese, grated
1 cup/250mL/8fl oz cream
2 tablespoons Parmesan cheese, grated (extra)
<u>Mint pesto</u>
1 cup/60g/2oz mint leaves
¹/₂ cup/30g/1oz parsley leaves
2 cloves garlic
¹/₂ cup/90g/3oz pine nuts, toasted
3 tablespoons Parmesan cheese, grated
3 tablespoons pecorino cheese, grated
¹/₃ cup/85mL/2¹/₂fl oz olive oil

meat

seared beef
with mushrooms and garlic

Method:

1 Soak the porcini mushrooms in boiling water for 20 minutes. Drain and chop. Set aside.

2 Heat the oil in a shallow pan, and cook the beef for a few minutes on each side. Remove from pan. Sauté the onion and the garlic (for a few minutes), then add all of the mushrooms and cook over high heat (until they are soft).

3 Add the wine and stock, bring to the boil, and then simmer for 10 minutes. Remove from the heat, add the parsley and season with salt and pepper.

4 Serve the beef with the mushrooms and sprinkle with extra chopped parsley.

ingredients

50g/1³/₄oz dried porcini mushrooms
60mL/2fl oz olive oil
1.2kg/2¹/₂ lb rump or fillet steak
(cut into 6 steaks)
1 brown onion, chopped
2 garlic cloves, crushed
350g/12oz shiitake/button mushrooms
60mL/2fl oz red wine
250mL/9fl oz brown stock
2 tablespoons parsley, chopped
salt and pepper
parsley, chopped (extra)

Serves 6

pork
braised in milk

Method:

1 Heat butter and oil in a large saucepan. When butter is foaming, add pork and brown on all sides.

2 Add milk, pepper to taste and bring to the boil. Reduce heat to low, cover and cook for 1¹/₂-2 hours or until pork is cooked. Brush pork occasionally with milk during cooking.

3 At end of cooking time, milk should have coagulated and browned in bottom of pan. If this has not occurred remove lid, and bring, liquid to the boil and boil until brown.

4 Remove meat from pan and set aside to cool slightly. Remove string from pork, cut into slices and arrange on a serving platter. Set aside to keep warm.

5 Remove any fat from pan, stir in water and bring to the boil, scraping residue from base of the pan. Strain and spoon pan juices over pork to serve.

Note: This dish originates from Bologna and is often preceded by dishes with a Bolognese sauce. Pork cooked this way also goes well with artichokes.

Serves 4

ingredients

30g/1oz butter
1 tablespoon vegetable oil
1kg/2 lb boneless loin pork,
rolled and tied
500mL/16fl oz milk
freshly ground black pepper
3 tablespoons warm water

lamb shanks
with root vegetables

Method:

1 Heat half the oil in a large heavy-based saucepan, add root vegetables and onions and cook quickly until brown. Set aside on a plate. Add remaining oil to pan and brown the garlic and shanks for a few minutes.

2 Add the stock, water, red wine, tomato paste, rosemary, bouquet garni, pepper and salt to the pan. Bring to the boil, reduce the heat, and leave to simmer with the lid on for 20 minutes.

3 Return the vegetables to the pan and continue to cook for another 30 minutes until vegetables and lamb are cooked.

4 Before serving, remove the bouquet garni and adjust the seasoning to taste.

Serves 4

ingredients

40mL/1¹/₂fl oz olive oil
2 parsnips, peeled, cut into large chunks
1 medium kumera, peeled,
cut into large chunks
1 swede, peeled, and cut into large chunks
1 bunch spring onions, trimmed
2 cloves garlic, crushed
4 lamb shanks
200mL/7fl oz beef stock
65mL/2¹/₄fl oz water
125mL/4¹/₂fl oz red wine
1 tablespoon tomato paste
2 sprigs rosemary, chopped bouquet garni
salt and freshly ground pepper

garlic
veal steaks

Method:

1 Heat half the oil in a nonstick frying pan over a low heat. Add garlic and cook, stirring, until golden and soft. Remove garlic from pan and set aside.

2 Increase heat to high, add veal, lemon rind and thyme and cook veal for 1-1½ minutes each side. Remove steaks from pan, top with garlic, set aside and keep warm.

3 Heat remaining oil in frying pan over a high heat, add eggplant (aubergine) and stir-fry for 3 minutes. Add wine, tomatoes and basil and stir-fry for 3 minutes longer or until eggplant (aubergine) is tender. Season to taste with black pepper.

4 To serve, arrange veal, garlic and eggplant (aubergine) mixture on serving plates and serve immediately.

Note: This dish is also delicious made with lamb steaks or chops instead of veal.

Serves 4

ingredients

1 tablespoon vegetable oil
6 cloves garlic
4 veal steaks or chops
2 teaspoons finely grated lemon rind
1 tablespoon chopped fresh thyme or
1 teaspoon dried thyme
1 eggplant (aubergine), cut into matchsticks
¼ cup/60mL/2fl oz red wine
2 tomatoes, chopped
1 tablespoon chopped fresh basil
freshly ground black pepper

sausage and roast capsicum
(pepper) salad

salads

In Italy, vegetables are often ordered

*as separate side dishes, and much importance
is attached to their taste and appearance.
Salads are also being treated with growing
reverence and innovation.*

marinated
mushroom salad

Method:

1 Whisk together basil, parsley, garlic, lemon juice, red and white wine vinegars and oil.

2 Place red capsicums (peppers) and mushrooms in a bowl. Pour over dressing. Toss. Cover. Marinate in the refrigerator for 3 hours.

ingredients

8 roasted red capsicums (peppers), skinned and cut into thick strips
125g/4oz mushrooms, sliced
<u>Herb and garlic dressing</u>
1 tablespoon chopped basil
1 tablespoon chopped parsley
2 cloves garlic, crushed
2 tablespoons lemon juice
2 tablespoons red wine vinegar
2 tablespoons white wine vinegar
2 tablespoons safflower oil

spiral
pasta salad

Method:

1 *Cook pasta in boiling water in a large saucepan following packet directions. Drain, rinse under cold running water and set aside to cool completely.*

2 *Place pasta, sun-dried tomatoes, artichokes, sun-dried or roasted peppers, olives, basil, Parmesan cheese, oil and vinegar in a bowl and toss to combine. Cover and refrigerate for 2 hours or until ready to serve.*

Note: *A wonderful salad that combines all the best flavours of Italy. It is delicious served with crusty bread and baked ricotta cheese. If you can, make it a day in advance so that the flavours have time to develop.*

Serves 4

ingredients

500g/1 lb spiral pasta
100g/3¹/₂oz sun-dried tomatoes, thinly sliced
100g/3¹/₂oz marinated artichoke hearts, chopped
75g/2¹/₂oz sun-dried or roasted peppers, chopped
125g/4oz marinated black olives
12 small fresh basil leaves
60g/2oz Parmesan cheese shavings
1 tablespoon olive oil
3 tablespoons balsamic or red wine vinegar

sausage
and roast capsicum (pepper) salad

Photograph opposite

sausage and roast capsicum (pepper) salad

ingredients

125g/4oz penne, cooked and cooled
2 red peppers, roasted and cut into strips
2 yellow or green peppers, roasted and cut into strips
125g/4oz button mushrooms, sliced
155g/5oz pitted black olives
5 English spinach leaves, stalks removed and leaves finely chopped
<u>**Herbed beef sausages**</u>
500g/1 lb lean ground beef
185g/6oz sausage meat
2 cloves garlic, crushed
1 teaspoon chopped fresh rosemary
1 tablespoon finely chopped fresh basil
2 slices proscuitto or lean ham, finely chopped
1 tablespoon olive oil
freshly ground black pepper
<u>**Herb dressing**</u>
1/2 cup/125mL/4fl oz olive oil
1/4 cup/60mL/2fl oz balsamic or red wine vinegar
2 teaspoons chopped fresh basil or 1 teaspoon dried basil
1 teaspoon chopped fresh oregano or 1/4 teaspoon dried oregano
freshly ground black pepper

Method:

1 *To make sausages, place beef, sausage meat, garlic, rosemary, basil, proscuitto or ham, olive oil and black pepper to taste in a bowl and mix to combine. Shape mixture into 10 cm/ 4in long sausages. Cook sausages under a preheated medium grill, turning occasionally, for 10-15 minutes or until brown and cooked through. Set aside to cool slightly, then cut each sausage into diagonal slices.*

2 *To make dressing, place olive oil, vinegar, basil, oregano and black pepper to taste in a screwtop jar and shake well to combine.*

3 *Place sausage slices, penne, red peppers, yellow or green peppers, mushrooms and olives in bowl, spoon over dressing and toss to combine. Line a serving platter with spinach leaves, then top with sausage and vegetable mixture.*

Note: *To prevent pasta that is for use in a salad from sticking together, rinse it under cold running water immediately after draining. All this mouth-watering salad needs to make a complete meal is some crusty bread or wholemeal rolls.*

Serves 4

145

spicy asparagus
with pine nuts

Method:

1 *Steam or microwave asparagus until just tender. Drain and rinse under cold running water to refresh, then drain again and set aside.*

2 *Heat butter in a frypan and cook pine nuts and salami until lightly browned. Add asparagus and basil and cook, stirring constantly, for 1 minute or until heated through. Sprinkle with Parmesan cheese and serve immediately.*

Note: *This recipe makes a delicious entrée. Use bacon instead of salami for a less spicy flavour.*

Serves 4

ingredients

**500g/1 lb fresh asparagus spears, trimmed
and cut into 5cm/2in pieces
15g/¹/₂oz butter
60g/2oz pine nuts
125g/4oz hot Italian salami,
cut into 5mm/¹/₄in cubes
2 tablespoons fresh basil, chopped
3 tablespoons fresh Parmesan cheese, grated**

radicchio anchovy salad

radicchio
anchovy salad

ingredients

**1 radicchio lettuce, washed
and leaves separated
¹/₂ bunch curly endive,
washed and leaves separated
1 witloof (chicory),
washed and leaves separated
8 radishes, washed and sliced
3 tablespoons chopped fresh
Italian flat-leaf parsley
Dressing
60mL/2fl oz olive oil
60mL/2fl oz lemon juice
60mL/2fl oz dry white wine
3 anchovy fillets, drained and chopped
¹/₂ teaspoon sugar**

Method:

1 *Arrange radicchio, endive and witloof (chicory) attractively on a large platter. Top with radishes and parsley.*

2 *To make dressing, place oil, lemon juice, wine, anchovies, garlic and sugar in a food processor or blender and process until smooth. Drizzle dressing over salad just before serving.*

Serves 6

fennel
and orange salad

Method:

1 Place endive on a large serving platter. Arrange fennel, oranges, onion and olives attractively over endive.

2 To make dressing, place oil, vinegar, fennel leaves, orange rind, sugar and black pepper to taste in a screw-top jar. Shake well to combine. Pour dressing over salad and serve immediately.

Serves 6

ingredients

**1 bunch curly endive,
leaves separated and washed
1 small fennel bulb, cut into thin strips
3 oranges, peeled and segmented
1 onion, sliced
20 black olives
<u>Orange dressing</u>
3 1/2 tablespoons olive oil
3 tablespoons white wine vinegar
1 tablespoon chopped fresh fennel leaves
1/2 teaspoon grated orange rind
1/2 teaspoon sugar
freshly ground black pepper**

cassata siciliana

desserts

When you see what treats are in

store for dessert, you might just decide to
serve nothing but these creamy, sugary, crunchy,
divinely indulgent delights. La dolce vita!

lemon
and basil granita

Method:

1 Combine basil, sugar and wine in a saucepan over medium heat. Bring to the boil. Cook, stirring, for 3 minutes.

2 Strain mixture. Discard solids. Cool to room temperature. Stir in lemon and lime juices and lemon rind.

3 Pour mixture into a shallow freezerproof container. Freeze until ice crystals start to form around the edges. Using a fork, stir to break up ice crystals. Repeat the process once more. Transfer mixture to ice cube trays. Freeze until firm.

ingredients

30g/1oz basil leaves, chopped
¼ cup/60g/2oz castor sugar
2 cups/500ml/16fl oz sweet white wine
1 cup/250ml/8fl oz lemon juice
¼ cup/60ml/2fl oz lime juice
1 tablespoon grated lemon rind

tiramisu

Method:

1 Place mascarpone, cream, brandy and sugar in a bowl, mix to combine and set aside. Dissolve coffee powder in boiling water and set aside.

2 Line the base of a 20 cm/8 in square dish with one-third of the sponge fingers. Sprinkle one-third of the coffee mixture over sponge fingers, then top with one-third of the mascarpone mixture. Repeat layers finishing with a layer of mascarpone mixture, sprinkle with grated chocolate and chill for 15 minutes before serving.

Note: Mascarpone is a fresh cheese made from cream. It is available from delicatessens and some supermarkets. If unavailable, mix one part sour cream with three parts lightly whipped cream (double) and use in its place.

Serves 4

ingredients

250g/8oz mascarpone
1/2 cup/125mL/8fl oz cream (double)
2 tablespoons brandy
1/4 cup/60g/2oz sugar
2 tablespoons instant coffee powder
1 1/2 cups/375mL/12fl oz boiling water
1 x 250g/8oz packet sponge fingers
250g/8oz grated chocolate

cassata
siciliana

Method:

1 Beat ricotta and sugar together until light and fluffy. Divide mixture in half. Fold pistachios and fruit through one half of mixture. Mix cinnamon, chocolate and Amaretto into other half. Cover and set aside.

2 Line base and sides of a 20cm/8in bowl or mould with plastic foodwrap, then with three-quarters of the cake slices. Fill with ricotta mixture and cover with remaining cake slices. Cover and freeze for 2 hours.

3 When mixture is set, pour chocolate mixture over it, return to freezer until set.

4 To make topping, whip cream and Amaretto together until soft peaks form. Just prior to serving, turn out cassata, spread completely with cream and decorate with glacé fruit.

Note: This is a simple do-ahead dinner party dessert that looks spectacular when decorated with extra glacé fruit. It is best prepared a day before serving.

ingredients

500g/1 lb ricotta cheese
250g/8oz sugar
2 tablespoons chopped pistachios
3 tablespoons chopped glacé fruit
¼ teaspoon ground cinnamon
60g/2oz dark chocolate, grated
2 tablespoons Amaretto liqueur
20cm/8in-round sponge cake,
cut into 1cm/½in slices
Topping
250mL/8fl oz pure (single) cream
1 tablespoon Amaretto liqueur
a selection of glacé fruit

Serves 8

fig
and mascarpone cake

Method:

1 To make custard, place custard powder, sugar, milk, cream and vanilla essence in a saucepan and whisk until mixture is smooth. Cook over a low heat, stirring constantly, until custard thickens. Remove pan from heat and set aside to cool. Fold mascarpone into cooled custard and set aside.

2 Line a 23cm/9in springform tin with nonstick baking paper and line the base with half the sponge fingers. Sprinkle with half the marsala, top with half the sliced figs and half the custard. Repeat layers to use all ingredients. Cover with plastic food wrap and refrigerate for 4 hours or until cake has set.

3 Remove cake from tin. Decorate the top with extra figs.

Note: When figs are not in season, fresh strawberries make a suitable substitute for this elegant charlotte.

Makes a 23cm/9in round cake

ingredients

32 sponge fingers
¹/₂ cup/125mL/4fl oz marsala
or sweet sherry
6 fresh figs, sliced
extra figs to decorate

Mascarpone custard
3 tablespoons custard powder
2 tablespoons caster sugar
1 cup/250mL/8fl oz milk
1 cup/250mL/8fl oz cream (double)
1 teaspoon vanilla essence
375g/12oz mascarpone

breads

Basic pizza dough

ingredients

**1³/₄ teaspoons active dry yeast,
or 15g/¹/₂oz fresh yeast, crumbled
pinch sugar
335mL/10¹/₂fl oz warm water
125mL/4fl oz olive oil
500g/1 lb plain flour, sifted
1¹/₄ teaspoons salt**

1 *Dissolve yeast and sugar in water in a large mixing bowl. Set aside in a draught-free place for 5 minutes or until foamy. Stir in oil, flour and salt and mix until a rough dough forms. Turn out onto a lightly floured surface and knead for 5 minutes or until soft and satiny. Add more flour if necessary.*

2 *Lightly oil a large bowl then roll dough around in it to cover surface with oil. Seal bowl with plastic foodwrap and place in a warm, draught-free spot for 1¹/₂-2 hours or until dough has doubled in volume.*

3 *Knock down and remove dough from bowl. Knead briefly before rolling out on a floured surface to desired shape. If dough feels too stiff, set aside to rest for a few minutes and start again.*

4 *Transfer to an oiled pizza pan and finish shaping by hand, forming a slightly raised rim. The dough should be approximately 5mm/¹/₄in thick. For a thicker crust, cover with a clean tea-towel and set aside for 30 minutes to rise again. The pizza is now ready for topping and baking.*

To make in a food processor:
Dissolve yeast and sugar in water in a small bowl. Set aside for 5 minutes or until foamy. Put flour and salt in food processor and pulse once or twice to sift. With machine running, slowly pour in yeast mixture and process for 10-15 seconds longer. Transfer to a lightly floured surface and knead by hand for 3-4 minutes. Continue as for basic recipe.

**Dough for a 38-40cm/
15-16in-round pizza**

Focaccia dough

ingredients

**1¹/₄ teaspoons active dry yeast
1 teaspoon sugar
315mL/9¹/₂fl oz lukewarm water
1 tablespoon olive oil
500g/1 lb plain flour, sifted**

1 *Place yeast and sugar in a large bowl and stir in all but 1 tablespoon water. Cover and set aside in a warm place for 8-10 minutes or until foaming.*

2 *Stir in remaining water and oil. Add one-third flour and stir until smooth. Stir in the next one-third flour, beat, then add remaining flour. Mix until a rough dough forms. Transfer to a floured board and knead for 8-10 minutes, or until dough is smooth and satiny.*

3 *Place dough in a lightly oiled bowl; roll around to coat dough with oil. Cover bowl tightly with plastic foodwrap. Set aside in a warm, draught-free spot for 1¹/₂ hours or until doubled in size.*

4 *Knock dough down, knead once or twice, then roll to desired shape. Place on an oiled oven tray, brush surface with a little oil, cover with a clean tea-towel and set aside to rise for 30 minutes longer.*

5 *Using your fingertips, dimple entire surface of dough, pushing in about halfway. Traditionally this serves to create little pools for the olive oil, but it also kneads the dough one last time. Re-cover with tea-towel and set aside again to rise for 1¹/₂-2 hours or until doubled. The focaccia is now ready for dressing and baking.*

To make in a food processor:
In a small bowl, stir yeast and sugar into warm water, cover and set aside in a warm place for 8-10 minutes or until foamy. Put flour and salt in processor bowl and pulse 2 or 3 times to mix. With machine running, pour in additional water, yeast and oil. Process until a rough dough forms, then continue to process to knead dough into a firm ball. Transfer to a floured board and knead by hand for 2-3 minutes.

**Dough for a 28x38cm/
11x15in focaccia**

Spinach, olive and onion bread

ingredients

1 recipe Focaccia Dough, (page 154)
1 tablespoon olive oil
1 egg white, lightly beaten
Filling
2 tablespoons olive oil
1 large red onion, sliced
1 clove garlic, crushed
1 tablespoon sultanas
750g/1 1/2 lb spinach, stalks removed and leaves shredded
125g/4oz stuffed green olives, sliced
3 tablespoons fresh mozzarella cheese, grated
freshly ground black pepper

1 *Prepare Focaccia Dough, as described in recipe through to end of Step 3.*
2 *To make filling, heat olive oil in a large frypan and cook onion until soft. Add garlic and sultanas and cook 1 minute longer.*

Add spinach and olives and cook over a medium heat until spinach just begins to wilt. Remove from heat and mix in mozzarella. Season to taste with black pepper. Set aside.
3 *Knock down dough and knead lightly. Divide dough into four portions, and roll each out into 5mm/1/4in-thick circles. Place two circles on lightly oiled baking trays, then spread with filling to within 2.5cm/1in of edge. Cover with remaining circles and pinch sides together to seal edges.*
4 *Brush top with olive oil. Cover with a clean tea-towel and set aside to rise in a warm place until doubled in size.*
5 *Brush top with egg white and bake at 200°C/ 400°F/Gas 6 for 25 minutes, or until golden brown and well risen.*
Note: *A filled bread, almost a pie, this flat loaf makes a delicious snack or supper dish.*
Serves 8

pizzas

Artichoke, mozzarella and salami pizza

ingredients

¹/₂ recipe Basic Pizza Dough (page 154)
olive oil
300g/9¹/₂oz fresh mozzarella,
thinly sliced
100g/3¹/₂oz Milano salami, thinly sliced
4 canned artichoke hearts, thinly
sliced lengthways
freshly ground black pepper

1 *Roll dough into rectangle 1cm/¹/₂in thick and press into a lightly oiled, shallow 28x18cm/ 11x7in tin and bring dough up at edges to form a slight rim. Brush with olive oil.*
2 *Place slices of mozzarella, slices of salami and slices of artichoke heart slightly overlapping in lines along width of dough. Continue forming rows of mozzarella, salami and artichoke heart until surface is covered. Sprinkle generously with olive oil, and season to taste with black pepper.*
3 *Bake at 220°C/425°F for 15 minutes, then reduce heat to 190°C/375°F and bake for 10 minutes longer or until cheese is bubbling and crust golden brown. Remove from oven and rest briefly before serving.*
Note: *Not all pizzas need a layer of tomato sauce to give them flavour and keep them moist. This tasty combination of toppings is a delicious and striking example.*
Makes 1 pizza

Pizza Supremo

ingredients

2 quantities Basic Pizza Dough (page 154)
³/₄ cup/185mL/6 fl oz tomato
paste (purée)
1 green pepper, chopped
155g/5oz sliced peperoni or salami
155g/5oz ham or prosciutto, sliced
125g/4oz mushrooms, sliced
440g/14oz canned pineapple
pieces, drained
60g/2oz pitted olives
125g/4oz mozzarella cheese, grated
125g/4oz tasty cheese (mature
Cheddar), grated

1 *Prepare pizza dough as described in recipe. Divide dough into two portions and shape each to form a 30cm/12in round. Place rounds on lightly greased baking trays and spread with tomato paste (purée).*
2 *Arrange half the green pepper, peperoni or salami, ham or prosciutto, mushrooms, pineapple and olives attractively on each pizza base.*
3 *Combine mozzarella cheese and tasty cheese (mature Cheddar) and sprinkle half the mixture over each pizza. Bake for 25-30 minutes or until cheese is golden and base is crisp.*
Note: *If you only want to make one pizza, halve the topping ingredients and use only one quantity of dough. But remember everyone loves pizza and they always eat more than you – or they – think they will.*
Serves 8

risotto

and other rice dishes

rice
king of kernels

Rice was the first grain cultivated by humans. In fact, it has been the staple diet of more than one third of the world's population for thousands of years.

There are over 60,000 varieties of rice grown on earth, wherever climate conditions are suitable, and it is still one of the world's most valued natural foods. The carbohydrate it contains provides a sustaining supply of energy to the body, and rice is a useful asset in any regimen to lose weight. All rice is cholesterol-free and the high fibre content of brown varieties promotes good digestion. Apart from its many healthy features, rice also looks good and is easy to prepare.

The chapter titled 'The Grain of Taste' contains all the basic rice cooking methods, each carefully explained. If in doubt, always follow these simple directions and you will have no problems with your rice cooking.

The recipes have all been carefully selected, tested, and adapted to appeal to the busy home cook, encourage the new cook, and inspire the amateur chef. There are no very lengthy recipes using complicated cooking terms; all recipes are written in a style that everyone can understand. The ingredients are listed in the order of use and the methods of preparation are clearly stated.

Rice makes an ideal starting point for all sorts of dishes. Don't forget that rice salads – using rice straight from the fridge – make a quick and easy meal when mixed with your choice of favourite ingredients.

Wide use is made of all the wonderful fresh foods available but canned may be substituted for fresh, and vice versa. All ingredients are readily obtainable. Most are not really expensive, and rice is certainly one of the cheapest basic foods. Also suggestions are made for ingredients which may be substituted if you wish.

Most of the recipes featured have been illustrated with enticing colour pictures which enable you to see at a glance how to present the meals to give instant appetite appeal.

Cooking can be fun, especially when you are creating something new. Using this book you will see that rice is an ideal ingredient as it's so wonderfully versatile and can be combined with many ingredients. Using the recipes in this book as your guide you will produce meals to delight your family and friends. Also you will be inspired to create your own special rice recipes.

The grain of nutrition

Rice contains a range of essential nutrients which our bodies need for good health. Like other cereal grains, rice supplies energy, complex carbohydrate, protein, B-group vitamins and minerals. Brown rice, containing the outer bran layers of the grain, supplies fibre or roughage, now recognised as an important factor in the prevention of many illnesses. Furthermore, rice is very low in fat and salt, which – in addition to its bland flavour – makes it light and easy to digest.

The protein supplied by rice is of high biological quality. Protein is essential for the growth and renewal of our bodies' tissues, organs and hormones. Rice protein, eaten together with a small supplement of protein from beans, fish or eggs, can provide all our daily requirements for protein. In fact, many people throughout the world rely on rice for almost all their protein needs, a fact often overlooked in Western society.

Nutrition authorities in many countries around the world have recently recommended changes to our eating habits in order to reduce the problem of 'overweight' or obesity, and to prevent nutrition-related illnesses, such as diabetes, coronary heart disease, gallstones, hypertension and some types of cancer. We are now urged to **reduce** our intake of fatty foods, sugar and salt and to increase the amount of complex carbohydrate and fibre we eat. Including rice on the menu is an excellent way to achieve this. Rice alone is low in fat, sugar and salt (and remember, you can control the amount of salt you add during cooking) and it provides carbohydrate and fibre.

White or brown

Brown rice contains the outer bran layers and the germ, both of which have a high concentration of vitamins, minerals and fibre. During rice milling, brushes remove most of the bran and germ to produce white rice, which consequently is lower in these nutrients. The most significant loss occurs with thiamin (vitamin B1), white rice having only about one-quarter the thiamin found in brown. Regarding fibre, white rice has approximately two-thirds that of brown. However the kilojoule (calorie) count of white and brown is very similar, brown being slightly higher due to the rich oils present in the germ.

Dieting with rice

Rice is part of a balanced weight-reducing diet plan. For many years, dieters have avoided starchy carbohydrate in the belief that they were somehow 'too fattening'. Today, however, nutritionists recognise that slow-burning carbohydrate is needed to balance a diet, and that fatty foods, alcohol and sugar should be restricted.

A sensible weight-reducing plan of 5000 kilojoules (1200 calories), which would be suitable for most women, includes 4 or 5 serves of complex carbohydrate foods a day. Half a cup of cooked rice, white or brown, has only 380 kilojoules (90 calories). It can substitute for other high carbohydrate foods, such as bread, potatoes, starchy vegetables or breakfast cereals. Rice complements foods with strong flavours, including meat, fish and low-kilojoule vegetables (celery, capsicum, shallots, mushrooms, onions), especially when cooked with herbs and spices. Oils and fats should be used sparingly when preparing rice as they are concentrated and quickly add kilojoules. Similarly, when making rice salads, mayonnaise must be counted as part of the daily fat allowance. Alternatively, low-fat salads can be made by substituting yoghurt or commercial low-kilojoule dressing.

Rice for special dishes

Rice is suitable for many therapeutic modified diets. It is free of gluten and forms the basis of gluten-free diets for coeliac disease and allergies. Being delicate and easy to digest, it is suitable for invalids and children. Cooked without salt, rice is ideal for low-sodium diets; a salt-free 'rice diet' was first developed in the 1940s and proved most effective in lowering high blood pressure. Diabetics can use rice as a substitute for bread or potatoes, following the quantities specified in their diet plan. As a carbohydrate exchange, one half cup of cooked rice (preferably brown for fibre) can be swapped for one slice of bread or 1 medium potato.

The goodness of rice

To summarise the nutritional value of rice, let's look at the nutrients supplied by a bowl (300g) of cooked brown rice. It supplies:

21% of your daily energy requirements,
14% of your daily protein requirements,
13% of your daily iron requirements,
49% of your daily thiamin requirements,
39% per cent of your daily niacin requirements,
<5% of your daily calcium/riboflavin requirements.*

*Based on Australian Average Dietary Allowances, Apparent Consumption of Foodstuffs and Nutrients, Australian Bureau of Statistics, Canberra.

starters

fragrant asian seafood soup

Many of the recipes in this chapter

will also stand on their own as light meals or snacks. Starting a meal with a dish based on rice is an economical way to fill hungry teenagers.

With a soothing texture and subtle, nutty flavour you never tire of, rice blends comfortably and graciously into almost any menu. A fragrant bed of perfectly cooked rice provides a pleasing background for kebabs, curries, and a myriad of sauces.

fragrant
asian seafood soup

Method:

1 Heat the vegetable stock and when simmering, add the Malaysian sweet soy, fish sauce, mirin and ginger. Stir well.

2 Meanwhile, wash the bok choy very well and cut off the leaves and set them aside. Slice the crunchy white stems and set asdie.

3 Chop the spring onions and add to the simmering broth then add the sliced oyster and shiitake mushrooms (if using). Add the shellfish and fish, trimmed and chopped to your liking and simmer for 5 minutes.

4 Add the white bok choy stems and simmer for 2 more minutes. If you wish, ginger can be removed at this stage.

5 Prepare each bowl by placing a scoop of rice in the centre and several bok choy leaves around. Ladle the simmering broth and other ingredients into each bowl and garnish with fresh coriander leaves. Serve immediately.

Serves 6-8

ingredients

1 1/2 litres fish or vegetable stock (or a mix)
2 tablespoons Malaysian sweet soy (Kecap Manis)
2 tablespoons fish sauce
2 tablespoonsn mirin
2 tablespoons finely sliced ginger
6 spring onions, both green and white parts,
100g. oyster mushrooms
100g fresh shiitake mushrooms (optional)
1kg fish or shellfish or your choice - prawns, calamari and salmon
4 baby bok choy
2 cups steamed white rice
1/2 bunch coriander

sizzling
rice cakes

Method:

1 In a heavy saucepan over high heat, bring rice and 2 cups/500mL/16oz water to a boil. Cover pan, reduce heat to low, and simmer 20 minutes, or until all water has been absorbed. Do not stir.

2 Drizzle oil over surface of rice. Loosen rice from pan and cut into cakes about 5 x 8 cms/ 2 x 3ins.

3 Pour oil into a skillet to a depth of 1 1/4cm/ 1/2 inch. Heat until a grain of rice dropped in oil sizzles. Fry rice cakes until light golden brown, then return cakes to hot oil for final crisping just before serving. Drain and serve hot.

Makes about 8 rice cakes

ingredients

1 cup/220g/7oz long-grain rice, washed and drained
1-2 tablespoons peanut oil, for deep-frying as needed

dolmades

Method:

1 Place vine leaves in a saucepan, cover with water and set aside for 5 minutes. Bring to the boil, then drain and cool.

2 To make filling, place rice, lentils, spring onions, tomato, pine nuts, lemon rind, lemon juice, basil, garlic and oil in a bowl and mix well to combine. Divide filling between twenty vine leaves and roll up leaves tightly to form neat parcels.

3 Place rolls close together in a large heavy-based frying pan and cover with remaining vine leaves. Place a plate over rolls to prevent them from unrolling during cooking. Add stock to cover rolls. Cover pan, bring to the boil, then reduce heat and simmer for 45 minutes.

Makes 20

ingredients

375g/12oz packaged vine leaves, rinsed
2 cups/500mL/16fl oz vegetable or
chicken stock
Rice and lentil filling
60g/2oz brown rice, cooked
60g/2oz red lentils, cooked
2 spring onions, chopped
1 small tomato, peeled and chopped
2 tablespoons chopped toasted pine nuts
1/2 teaspoon finely grated lemon rind
1 tablespoon lemon juice
2 teaspoons chopped fresh basil
1 clove garlic, minced
2 teaspoons olive oil

kappa-maki

Method:

1 *Place a layer of rice over seaweed on bamboo mat (or plastic sheet).*
2 *Place cucumber on rice spread with wasabi and sprinkled sesame seeds.*
3 *Roll up bamboo mat gently and firmly.*
4 *Using sharp knife cut along the cylinder at regular intervals to form rounds approximately 2¹/₂cm/1 in each.*

Serves 1

ingredients

1 sheet of dried seaweed (Nori)
¹/₂ cup/80g/2¹/₂ oz short-grain rice
cooked in the Sushi manner (page 219)
1 pinch wasabi (green mustard)
1 pinch sesame seeds
¹/₄ thinly sliced cucumber

brown
rice broth

Method:

1 *Combine stock with prepared vegetables in a large saucepan. Add bay leaf, tomato paste and rice. Season to taste. Cover and simmer for 1 1/2 hours. Serve sprinkled with chopped parsley.*

Serves 6

10 cups/2 1/2L/86fl oz beef stock
4 carrots, chopped
1 onion, chopped
1 stick celery, chopped
1 small turnip, chopped
3 whole parsley stalks
1 bay leaf
1 tablespoon tomato paste,
salt reduced
1/2 cup/65g/3oz brown rice
2 tablespoons chopped parsley

chilli rice
balls

Makes 16

ingredients

1 tablespoon olive oil
1 onion, finely chopped
1 1/2 cups/275g/9oz rice
1/2 teaspoon ground tumeric
3 cups/750mL/24fl oz chicken stock
1/2 teaspoon chilli powder
freshly ground black pepper
3 spring onions, finely chopped
15g/1/2oz butter
3 tablespoons grated tasty cheese
(mature cheddar)
2 eggs lightly beaten
125g/4oz mozzarella cheese,
cut into 16 cubes
3/4 cup/90g/3oz dried breadcrumbs
oil for deep frying

Method:

1 Heat olive oil in frying pan, add onion and cook for 2-3 minutes or until soft. Stir in rice and tumeric and cook, stirring, for 1-2 minutes longer or until rice is coated with oil.

2 Pour 3/4 cup/190mL/6fl oz of stock into frying pan and bring to boil. Cook, stirring frequently, until liquid has almost evaporated. Add chilli powder, black pepper to taste,then remaining stock, and simmer for 10-15 minutes or until liquid has been absorbed and rice is tender. Remove pan from heat and stir in spring onions, butter and tasty cheese(mature cheddar).

3 Fold eggs into rice mixture, taking care not to mash the grains. Divide rice mixture into sixteen equal portions. Take a cheese cube and, using wet hands, mould one portion of rice around a cheese cube, to form a ball. Repeat with remaining rice and cheese.

4 Roll balls in breadcrumbs, place on a plate lined with plastic food wrap and refridgerate for 30 minutes. Heat oil in a deep sauce pan until a cube of bread dropped in browns in 50 seconds. Cook 4-5 rice balls at a time for 5 minutes, or until golden brown. Using a slotted spoon, remove balls and drain on absorbent kitchen paper. Serve immediately.

Easy paella

main meals

Rice makes imaginative, economical,

healthy main-course fare. The recipes in this chapter have artfully combined rice with meats, poultry, fish, legumes, vegetables and fruits. You will find rice transforms itself into kedgeree, paella, pilaf, risotto, stirfry, and dozens of other rice dishes to fit every occasion.

salmon
rice loaf

10 spinach leaves, stalks removed
440g/14oz canned salmon, drained
and flaked
3 eggs, beaten
3 tablespoons sour cream or
natural yoghurt
2 tablespoons mayonnaise
1 tablespoon lemon juice
2 tablespoons rice, cooked
2 tablespoons grated Parmesan cheese
freshly ground black pepper

Serves 4

Oven temperature 200°C, 400°F, Gas 6

Method:

1 Boil, steam or microwave spinach leaves until tender.
2 Line the base and sides of a greased ovenproof 11x21cm/4^1/$_2$x8^1/$_2$in loaf tin with half the spinach leaves, allowing some of the leaves to hang over the sides of the pan.
3 Squeeze excess moisture from the remaining leaves and chop. Place chopped leaves, salmon, eggs, sour cream or yoghurt, mayonnaise, lemon juice, rice, Parmesan cheese and black pepper to taste in a bowl and mix to combine.
4 Spoon salmon mixture into prepared loaf tin and fold overhanging leaves over top of mixture. Cover with aluminium foil and bake for 45 minutes or until the filling is firm. Allow the loaf to stand for 10 minutes before turning out and serving.

Note: This loaf cooks quickly in the microwave. Remember to use a microwave-safe dish. Preparation of the loaf is the same, but cover the dish with microwave-safe plastic food wrap, then cook on HIGH (100%) for 13 minutes. Stand for 5 minutes before turning out and serving.

You will find that 2 tablespoons of uncooked rice as used in this recipe will cook up to about 6 tablespoons of cooked rice. So if you have leftover rice it could be used to make this delicious loaf.

easy
paella

main meals

Method:
1 Heat butter in a large frying pan, add onion and cook for 5 minutes or until soft.
2 Add rice and cook, stirring, for 2 minutes. Stir in stock and bring to the boil. Reduce heat, cover and simmer for 40 minutes or until rice is tender.
3 Stir in chicken, ham, prawns, lemon juice and black pepper to taste and cook for 4-5 minutes longer. Just prior to serving, sprinkle with parsley.

Serves 6

ingredients

30g/1oz butter
1 onion, chopped
$^2/_3$ cup/140g/4$^1/_2$oz brown rice
2 cups/500mL/16fl oz chicken stock
250g/8oz cooked chicken, chopped
250g/8oz ham, chopped
250g/8oz cooked prawns, shelled, deveined and chopped
2 tablespoons lemon juice
freshly ground black pepper
2 tablespoons chopped fresh parsley

rice-filled
eggplant

Method:
1 Cut eggplant (aubergines) in half lengthwise and scoop out the centre leaving a 2cm/$^3/_4$in-thick shell. Sprinkle with salt, place upside down on absorbent kitchen paper and set aside for 15 minutes.
2 Rinse eggplant (aubergines) and pat dry with absorbent kitchen paper.
3 To make filling, place oil, onion, garlic, bacon, tomatoes, thyme, egg, breadcrumbs, rice and Parmesan cheese in a bowl and mix to combine. Divide mixture between eggplant (aubergine) shells, place in a lightly greased baking dish and bake for 30 minutes.

Serves 4

ingredients

2 eggplants (aubergines) & salt

Rice and cheese filling
2 tablespoons olive oil
1 onion, chopped
1 clove garlic, minced
2 rashers bacon, chopped
3 canned tomatoes, drained and chopped
1 teaspoon chopped fresh thyme
or $^1/_2$ teaspoon dried thyme
1 egg
$^1/_2$ cup/60g/2oz dried breadcrumbs
$^1/_3$ cup/75g/2$^1/_2$oz rice, cooked
60g/2oz grated Parmesan cheese

Oven temperature 180°C, 350°F, Gas 4

rice terrine

Method:

1 Melt butter in a frying pan, add onion and cook for 4-5 minutes or until soft. Remove pan from heat and set aside.

2 Place rice, milk, eggs, chilli paste (sambal oelek), Parmesan cheese, parsley, black pepper to taste and cooked onions in a bowl and mix to combine.

3 Spoon one-third of the rice mixture into a greased 11 x 21cm/4¹/₂ x 8¹/₂in loaf tin and top with half the pimentos. Repeat layers, ending with a layer of rice, and bake for 35-40 minutes. Allow to stand for 10 minutes before turning out and serving.

Serves 8

main meals

ingredients

15g/¹/₂oz butter
1 onion, chopped
1¹/₄ cups/280g/9oz rice, cooked
1 cup/250mL/8fl oz milk
3 eggs
1 teaspoon chilli paste (sambal oelek)
3 tablespoons grated Parmesan cheese
2 tablespoons chopped fresh parsley
freshly ground black pepper
440g/14oz canned pimentos, drained

Oven temperature 180°C, 350°F, Gas 4

sausage-filled
capsicum

Method:

1 Cut tops from capsicums (peppers) and remove seeds and membranes. Set aside.

2 To make filling, heat oil in a large frying pan, add onion and garlic and cook for 4-5 minutes or until onion is soft.

3 Add sausages, coriander, tomatoes, tomato paste (purée), cumin, beans and cream to pan and cook over a high heat, stirring occasionally, for 20 minutes or until mixture reduces and thickens.

4 Stir rice into tomato mixture and spoon filling into capsicum (pepper) shells. Place filled red capsicums in a greased baking dish and bake for 25 minutes.

Serves 4

ingredients

4 red capsicums/peppers
Sausage filling
1 tablespoon vegetable oil
1 onion, chopped
3 cloves garlic, crushed
4 thin beef sausages, cooked and chopped
2 teaspoons ground coriander
315g/10oz canned tomatoes,
drained and mashed
2 teaspoons tomato paste (purée)
2 teaspoons ground cumin
440g/14oz canned red kidney beans, drained
1 cup/250mL/8fl oz cream (double)
1/3 cup/75g/2 1/2oz rice, cooked

rice with
cheese & herbs

Method:

1 *Place water in a large saucepan and bring to the boil. Stir in rice and cook, covered, for 15-20 minutes or until rice is tender. Stir occasionally during cooking to prevent sticking.*

2 *Drain, then return rice to same pan. Stir in butter and chopped herbs. Fold mozzarella and Parmesan cheeses into rice mixture and season to taste with black pepper. Transfer to a warm serving dish and serve immediately.*

Serves 4

ingredients

8 cups/2L/3¹/₂pt water
1¹/₂ cups/330g/10¹/₂oz arborio rice
90g/3oz butter, cut into small pieces
2 tablespoons chopped mixed fresh herbs
250g/8oz grated mozzarella cheese
60g/2oz grated Parmesan cheese
freshly ground black pepper

cheesy brown
rice pie

Method:

1 Place rice, tasty cheese (mature Cheddar), Parmesan cheese, spring onions, zucchini (courgettes), red capsicum (pepper), asparagus, pine nuts, eggs, yoghurt and black pepper to taste in a bowl and mix to combine.

2 Spoon rice mixture into a greased, deep-sided 23cm/9 in springform tin and bake for 40 minutes or until firm. Allow to stand for 5 minutes in tin before turning out and serving. Serve cut into wedges.

Serves 6

ingredients

³/₄ cup/170g/5¹/₂oz brown rice, cooked
250g/8oz grated tasty cheese
(mature Cheddar)
4 tablespoons grated Parmesan cheese
2 spring onions, chopped
2 zucchini (courgettes), grated
I red capsicum(pepper), diced
31g/10oz canned asparagus cuts, drained
3 tablespoons pine nuts, toasted
3 eggs, lightly beaten
I cup/20g/6¹/₂oz natural yoghurt
freshly ground black pepper

prawn
jambalaya

Method:

1 Cook bacon in a frying pan over a medium heat for 5 minutes or until crisp. Remove bacon from pan and drain on absorbent kitchen paper.

2 Add onion to pan and cook, stirring, for 5 minutes or until onion is soft, but not brown. Add green pepper, celery and garlic and cook for minutes. Add rice and cook, stirring frequently, for 5 minutes or until rice becomes translucent.

3 Stir in stock, tomatoes, spice mix and thyme and bring to the boil. Cover, reduce heat to low and cook for 15 minutes. Stir in prawns and ham, cover and cook for 10 minutes longer or until rice is tender and liquid absorbed. Sprinkle with spring onions and serve immediately.

Serves 4

ingredients

3 rashers bacon, cut into strips
1 large onion, finely chopped
1 green pepper, diced
1 stalk celery, chopped
3 cloves garlic, crushed
1 cup/220g/7oz long-grain rice
1¹/₂-2 cups/375-500mL/12-16fl oz boiling
chicken stock
440g/14oz canned tomatoes,
drained and mashed
2 teaspoons Cajun spice mix
1 teaspoon dried thyme
500g/1 lb uncooked medium prawns,
shelled and deveined
155g/5oz smoked ham in one piece,
cut into 1cm/¹/₂in cubes
3 spring onions, finely chopped

butterfly prawns
in lemon sauce

Method:

1 *Shell the prawns leaving on the tails. With a small sharp knife slit along the back of each prawn and remove vein. Rinse and pat dry.*

2 *Mix marinade ingredients in a bowl, add prawns, stir to coat well, cover and allow to marinate in refrigerator for at least half an hour.*

3 *Heat the oil in a wok or skillet and fry prawns a few at a time until just pink. Remove to a heated plate as they are cooked.*

4 *Add stir fry vegetables and stir fry two minutes. Add zest and lemon juice, sugar, salt, pepper and vegetable stock, stir a few times then add blended cornflour. Toss over heat until sauce thickens and coats the vegetables. Return prawns to wok and toss for one minute. Serve over hot steamed rice.*

Serves 2

500g/1lb green prawns
<u>Marinade</u>
2 teaspoons sherry
1 teaspoon soy sauce
1 egg white
¹/₂ teaspoon grated root ginger
1 teaspoon cornflour
<u>Stir-Fry</u>
3 tablespoons olive oil
250g/8oz packet stir-fry frozen vegetables
1 teaspoon grated lemon zest
juice of 1 lemon
1 teaspoon sugar
salt, pepper to taste
³/₄ cup/190ml/12fl oz vegetable stock
2 teaspoons cornflour, blended with
2 teaspoons water
steamed rice for serving

rice with chicken
livers, pine nuts and currants

Method:

1 *Wash chicken livers, and remove any sinew. Chop livers into bite-size pieces.*

2 *Heat butter in a large saucepan and sauté the shallots for five minutes (until tender). Add the chicken livers, and cook for a further few minutes (until they change colour).*

3 *Add the rice and chicken stock to the saucepan, bring to the boil, then simmer (with the lid on), stirring occassionally, for approximately 30 minutes (until the liquid has been absorbed and the rice is cooked). If the rice is not cooked (and the mixture is looking a little dry) add a further cup of water, and cook for a another five minutes.*

ingredients

1 kg/2lb chicken livers
75g/3oz butter
12 shallots (chopped)
1 1/2 cups/330g/10oz short-grain rice
600mL/20fl oz chicken stock
1/2 cup/30g/1oz parsley (chopped)
100g/3oz pine nuts
100g/3oz currants

4 *When rice is cooked, toss the chopped parsley, pinenuts and currants through the rice, and serve.*

Serves 8

luncheon
fish rolls

Method:

1. Heat and sauté onion until tender. Add rice and toss to blend. Season to taste.
2. Pat fish dry; season. Cut wide fillets in half lengthwise. Remove 6 tablespoons rice from pan and combine with egg, parsley, lemon rind and mayonnaise. Place 2 teaspoons of rice mixture at the end of each fillet, roll up, and secure with a toothpick.
3. Spoon remaining rice into a lightly greased oven-proof dish. Blend soup with milk. Add ¹/₂ cup/125mL/4oz of the soup to rice mixture; combine well. Place broccoli in centre of rice. Arrange fish rolls around broccoli.
4. Pour remaining soup over fish and broccoli, and sprinkle with cheese. Cover, cook in a moderate oven 180°C/350°F for 25-30 minutes or until fish flakes when tested with a fork.

Serves 4-6

ingredients

30mL/1fl oz olive oil
1 medium onion, finely chopped
4 cups/620g/20oz cooked brown rice
750g/240oz fresh or frozen fish fillets
1 hard-boiled egg, finely chopped
1 tablespoon chopped parsley
1 teaspoon grated lemon rind
2 tablespoons mayonnaise (light)
440g/140oz can cream of mushroom soup
(salt reduced)
¹/₂ cup/125mL/40fl oz skimmed milk
1 head broccoli, broken
into florets and cooked
¹/₂ cup/65g/20oz grated tasty
cheese(mature cheddar)

Risotto with baby spinach & gorgonzola

risottos

In this chapter we will temp you with

risotto delicacies with a wide variety of tastes. Correctly cooked, risotto is creamy, moist and flavoursome and the methods shown in this chapter will assist you to cook risotto like the professionals. Arborio rice (traditionally used for risottos), can absorb several times its own weight in stock, rendering it tender and creamy. Unlike pilaf a risotto is stirred continuously over low heat. Always ensure the stock is simmering on the stove and that you add it slowly, and by the ladle-full, to the risotto. All the time keep stirring and only add the next ladle when earlier addition has been absorbed. Risotto should be served as soon as it is cooked; for specific ingredients and cooking times, refer to the recipe you are using.

risotto with baby spinach & gorgonzola

Method:
1. Place stock in a saucepan. Bring to the boil. Leave simmering.
2. Heat oil in a large saucepan, add garlic and onion, and cook for 5 minutes (or until soft). Add rice, and stir(until well coated)
3. Pour in wine, and cook (until the liquid has been absorbed). Add the stock (ladle at a time), stirring continuously (until liquid has been absorbed), before adding the next ladle of stock. Keep adding stock this way, and stirring, until all stock is used, and until the rice is cooked (but still a little firm to bite).
4. Add the spinach, cheese and seasonings, stir, and cook (until spinach is just wilted and cheese has melted).
5. Serve immediately.
   Serves 6

ingredients

1 litre/35fl oz chicken stock
2 tablespoons olive oil
2 cloves garlic, minced
1 onion (finely chopped)
2 cups/440g/14oz arborio rice
125mL/4fl oz white wine
200g/6oz baby spinach
200g/6oz Gorgonzola cheese
(in small pieces)
salt & freshly ground pepper

chicken risotto

Method:
1. Heat the first teaspoon of olive oil and sauté garlic until golden. Increase heat and add chicken tenderloins, leek and parsley and sauté until the chicken changes colour. Remove from heat, set aside.
2. Heat remaining teaspoon olive oil. Add rice, stirring to coat. Add wine and allow liquid to be absorbed. Begin adding stock, half a cup at a time, stirring well after each addition.
3. When adding second quantity of stock, add all the chicken mixture and its juices, stirring well to combine. When half the stock has been absorbed, add diced green capsicums (peppers) and continue adding stock and stirring well after each addition.
4. When all the stock has been added, remove the saucepan from the heat and add the yoghurt, Parmesan cheese and extra tablespoon of stock. Season with salt and pepper to taste.
   Note: Garnish with finely diced green capsicum (pepper) and serve.
   Serves 4

ingredients

1 teaspoon olive oil
3 cloves garlic
600g/20oz chicken tenderloins
1 leek, white part only, washed and finely chopped
1/2 cup/30g/1oz parsley
1 teaspoon olive oil
400g/13oz arborio rice
200mL/7fl oz white wine
850mL/20oz vegetable stock, simmering
2 green capsicums (peppers), diced
1 tablespoon yoghurt
1 tablespoon Parmesan cheese
1 tablespoon stock, extra
salt & pepper to taste
1 green capsicum (pepper) finely diced, for garnish

creamy mushroom risotto

Method:

1 Place mushrooms in a bowl and cover with boiling water. Set aside to soak for 20 minutes or until mushrooms are tender. Drain, remove stalks if necessary and chop mushrooms.

2 Melt butter in a large saucepan, add onion and garlic and cook for 5 minutes or until onion is soft. Add rice, prepared dried mushrooms and button mushrooms and cook, stirring, for 1 minute.

3 Stir in ladle of hot stock and cook, stirring constantly, until liquid is absorbed. Continue adding stock, a ladle at a time, stirring constantly and allowing stock to be absorbed before adding
any more. Stir in parsley, Parmesan cheese and black pepper to taste and serve immediately.

Serves 4

30g/1oz dried mushrooms
boiling water
60g/2oz butter
1 onion, chopped
2 cloves garlic, minced
1 cup/220g/7oz arborio rice
250g/8oz button mushrooms, sliced
2 cups/500mL/16fl oz hot chicken
or vegetable stock
3 tablespoons chopped fresh parsley
3 tablespoons grated Parmesan cheese
freshly ground black pepper

seafood
risotto

ingredients

ı tablespoon olive oil
2 cloves garlic, minced
200g calamari, washed and cut into rings
200g raw green prawns, heads and shells removed
200g fillet of fresh Atlantic salmon, skin removed, cut into bite-sized pieces, or sliced thinly
¹/₂ cup minced parsley
ı tablespoon olive oil
10 spring onions, chopped
400g arborio rice
300ml dry white wine
800ml rich fish stock, simmering
4 roma tomatoes, finely chopped
ı tablespoon sour cream
2 tablespoons grated Parmesan cheese
¹/₂ cup finely chopped parsley

Method:

1 *Heat the olive oil and gently sauté the garlic. Add the prepared seafood and cook briefly until the fish and shellfish is opaque, adding the parsley at the last moment. Remove from heat and set aside.*

2 *Heat the remaining tablespoon of olive oil and sauté the spring onions. Add the rice, stirring to coat. Add the white wine and allow it to be absorbed, then add the first addition of fish stock together with the finely chopped tomatoes. Continue cooking, adding further additions of stock as the previous one is absorbed.*

3 *When there is only a small quantity of stock left, add the cooked fish mixture and all its juices with the last addition of stock and continue simmering for about 2 minutes, or until most of the liquid is absorbed. Add sour cream, cheese and parsley, stir well to incorporate and serve immediately.*

Note: *Risotto is a perfect vehicle for serving shellfish. The liquid stock helps to keep the seafood moist and tender, while allowing the seafood to impart its lovely briny flavours. I like to cook the seafood briefly before beginning the risotto to ensure even cooking of the fish, and also to avoid the risk of over-cooking. The seafood is then added with the last addition of stock. If the specified seafoods are not available, simply use other varieties of your choice that equal the same weight. Although not regarded as etiquette, I like to add a little Parmesan cheese with seafood; if you prefer to not to, simply leave it out.*

prawn
risotto

Method:

1 Melt half the butter in a large frying pan, add leeks and garlic and cook, stirring, for 5 minutes or until leeks are tender. Add prawns and cook for 3-4 minutes or until prawns just change colour. Remove pan from heat and set aside.

2 Melt remaining butter in a large saucepan, add rice and cook, stirring constantly, for 2 minutes. Stir in wine and cook until liquid is absorbed. Stir in a ladle of boiling stock and cook, stirring constantly, until liquid is absorbed. Continue adding stock a ladle at a time, stirring constantly and allowing stock to be absorbed before adding any more. Stir in prawn mixture, basil and black pepper to taste and cook for 3-4 minutes longer or until heated through. Serve immediately.

ingredients

125g/4oz butter
2 leeks, white part only, sliced
2 cloves garlic, minced
500g/1lb uncooked large prawns, shelled and deveined, tails left intact
1 1/2 cups/330g/10 1/2oz arborio rice
1/2 cup/125mL/4fl oz dry white wine
3 1/2 cups/875mL/1 1/2pt simmering fish or chicken stock
3 tablespoons chopped fresh basil
freshly ground black pepper

Serves 4

mixed mushroom risotto

Method:

1 In a pan, heat the butter, add the mushrooms, and cook (for a few minutes). Remove from heat and set aside.

2 Heat the oil in a large heavy-based saucepan, add the garlic and leek, and cook for 5-6 minutes (until cooked). Meanwhile, place stock in saucepan and simmer gently.

3 Add the rice to the garlic and leek mixture and stir for one minute (to coat the rice). Add the white wine and cook until liquid is absorbed. Start adding the stock, a ladle at a time, stirring continuously, until liquid has been absorbed. Continue adding stock (a ladle at a time), until all stock is used and rice is cooked.

4 Stir in mushrooms, lemon rind, cheese and parsley, serve immediately.

Serves 6-8

ingredients

2 tablespoons butter
500g/16oz mixed mushrooms (oyster, shiitake, flat, enoki, Swiss, sliced
40mL/1 ¹/₂fl oz olive oil
2 cloves garlic (minced)
1 leek (finely sliced)
1L/35fl oz chicken stock
2 cups/440g/14oz arborio rice
¹/₂ cup/125mL/4fl oz white wine
rind of 1 lemon (finely grated)
¹/₂ cup/60g/2oz pecorino cheese (grated)
¹/₂ cup/60g/2oz Parmesan cheese (grated)
2 tablespoons parsley (chopped)

risotto
with cheese

Method:

1 Place stock in a large saucepan and bring to the boil. Reduce heat and simmer.
2 Heat oil and 30g/1oz butter in a separate saucepan, add onion and cook over a low heat for 5-6 minutes or until lightly browned. Add rice and cook, stirring, for 1-2 minutes. This will coat the grains well with the butter mixture. Pour in $^3/_4$ cup/185mL/6fl oz boiling stock and stir over medium heat until liquid is absorbed.
3 Continue cooking in this way until all the stock is used and rice is just tender; this will take 18-20 minutes. Stir frequently during cooking to prevent sticking.
4 Stir in Parmesan cheese, remaining butter and black pepper to taste. Serve immediately.

ingredients

5 cups/1$^1/_4$L/2pt chicken
or beef stock
2 tablespoons vegetable oil
45g/1$^1/_2$oz butter
1 small onion, chopped
1$^1/_2$cups/330g/10$^1/_2$oz arborio rice
60g/2oz grated Parmesan cheese
freshly ground black pepper

risotto
variations

Risotto with Asparagus and Bacon:

For this variation you will require the ingredients for Risotto with Cheese, plus 2 rashers bacon, chopped and 500g/1lb fresh asparagus. Make up Risotto with Cheese, cooking the bacon with the onion. Cook the asparagus in the boiling stock. When tender, remove and set aside to cool, then cut into 5cm/2in pieces. Fold into risotto just prior to serving.

Risotto with Spinach and Herbs:

For this variation you will require the ingredients for Risotto with Cheese, plus 2 cloves garlic, crushed, 1 bunch/500g/1lb spinach, 1 tablespoon finely chopped fresh basil, and 1 tablespoon finely chopped fresh oregano or 1 teaspoon dried oregano. Make up Risotto with Cheese, cooking the garlic with the onion. Boil, steam or microwave spinach until tender and chop finely. Fold cooked spinach, basil and oregano into cooked risotto.

Oven temperature 200°C, 400°F, Gas 6

moulded
tomato risotto

Method:

1 Heat oil in a large frying pan, add onions and cook over a medium heat for 10 minutes or until golden. Stir in rice and cook for 2 minutes longer.

2 Add tomatoes, tomato paste (purée) and stock and cook, stirring frequently, until liquid is absorbed and rice is cooked.

3 Stir in butter, Parmesan cheese, basil and black pepper to taste. Spoon rice mixture into a well-greased ovenproof bowl, cover and bake for 10-15 minutes. Allow to stand 5-10 minutes before turning out and serving.

Serves 6

ingredients

3 tablespoons olive oil
2 onions, chopped
2 cups/440g/14oz arborio rice
440g/14oz canned tomatoes, undrained and mashed
3 tablespoons tomato paste (purée)
4 cups/1L/1¾pt boiling chicken stock
90g/3oz butter
125g/4oz grated Parmesan cheese
2 tablespoons chopped fresh basil
freshly ground black pepper

italian mushroom risotto

Method:

1 Place butter in frypan, add onions and garlic and cook until onions are golden. Add mushrooms and cook over low heat for 2 minutes. Add rice, toss and cook for a few minutes. Add wine, tomato paste and half the stock. Stir until it reaches boiling point. Allow to simmer over low heat, about 5 minutes, and add remaining stock. Continue simmering until rice is tender, about 20-25 minutes. Remove from heat, and add extra butter and cheese and toss with fork to blend.

Serves 6

ingredients

60g/2oz butter
1 onion, finely chopped
1 clove garlic, minced
250g/8oz mushrooms, sliced
1 tablespoon tomato paste
5 cups/1¼L/2pts hot beef
or chicken stock
30g/1oz butter, extra
2 tablespoons Parmesan cheese
2 cups/440g/14oz arborio rice
½ cup/125mL/4fl oz dry white wine
(or use extra stock)

risotto
mould

Method:

1 Heat oil in a frying pan and sauté onions until golden. Add mushrooms and cook for 2-3 minutes or until tender.

2 Stir in rice; toss to combine with mixture. Pour in boiling stock, a little at a time, stirring constantly until the rice is cooked and liquid is absorbed – about 15 minutes.

3 Fold through margarine and Parmesan. Season to taste. Risotto should be slightly creamy. Spoon mixture into a suitable lightly greased ovenproof mould or bowl and bake at for 10 minutes.

4 Turn out onto a platter or flat serving dish. Garnish with red capsicum(pepper) and pile cooked peas around risotto.

Serves 6-8

ingredients

¹/₄ cup/60mL/2oz olive oil
2 onions, finely chopped
440g/14oz mushrooms, sliced
2 cups/370g/12oz arborio rice
1L/35fl oz chicken stock
30g/1oz polyunsaturated margarine
¹/₂ cup/60g/2oz grated Parmesan cheese
<u>Garnish</u>
red capsicum(pepper) strips brushed with
a little olive oil, baked and skin removed
500g/16oz cooked fresh peas

artichoke
risotto

Method:
1 Melt butter in a large frying pan, add onion and cook for 5 minutes or until soft.
2 Add rice to pan and cook, stirring frequently, for 5 minutes. Combine stock, wine and reserved artichoke liquid. The total amount of liquid should equal 3 1/2 cups/875 mL/1 1/2 pt. Top up with additional stock, if necessary. Pour one-third of the liquid over the rice and cook over a low heat, stirring, until liquid is absorbed. Continue adding liquid a little at a time and cook, stirring frequently, until all liquid is absorbed.
3 Cut artichokes into quarters. Fold artichokes, parsley, ham, Parmesan cheese and tomatoes into rice. Season to taste with black pepper and serve immediately.

Serves 4

ingredients

60 g/2oz butter
1 onion, chopped
1 1/2 cups/330g/10oz arborio rice
2 cups/500mL/16fl oz chicken stock
1/2 cup/125mL/4fl oz dry white wine
440g/14oz canned artichoke hearts,
drained and liquid reserved
2 tablespoons chopped fresh parsley
4 thick slices ham, cut into strips
60g/2oz grated Parmesan cheese
4 cherry tomatoes, quartered
freshly ground black pepper

risotto
milanese

Method:
1 Heat the chicken stock in a saucepan, reduce the heat, and leave simmering.
2 Heat the oil in a heavy-based pan, add the onion and garlic, and cook (until soft).
3 Add rice, and stir (until coated with the mixture). Then add the wine and cook (until the liquid had been absorbed), stirring continuously.
4 Add the chicken stock (a ladle at a time), stirring continuously (until the liquid has been absorbed), before adding another ladle of stock. Continue adding the stock a ladle at a time until all the stock is used, and until the rice is cooked (but still firm to bite). It may be necessary to add a little more liquid.
5 Stir in the cheese and parsley, and serve immediately.

Serves 6

ingredients

1L/32fl oz chicken stock
2 tablespoons olive oil
1 onion (finely chopped)
1 clove garlic ground
2 cups/440g/14oz arborio rice
1 cup/250mL/8fl oz white wine
1/2 cup/60g/2oz pecorino cheese (grated)
2 tablespoons parsley (finely chopped)

Method:

1 Heat the olive oil and sauté the leek, shallots and garlic until softened, about 5 minutes.

2 Add the rice and stir to coat the rice, then add the wine and allow to be absorbed. Begin adding the stock, half a cup at a time, stirring well after each addition. When half the stock has been absorbed, add the sun-dried tomatoes, capsicums and artichokes and continue adding stock as required, stirring.

3 With the last addition of stock, add the basil and Fontina and cook for 2 minutes more. Remove the risotto from the heat and stir very well. Garnish with extra basil leaves and Parmesan cheese and serve immediately.

Variation – Risotto with Preserved Vegetables and Rabbit

One of the most popular meats in Tuscany is rabbit. It is inexpensive and has a good, rich flavour. Rabbit fillets pair well with the strong flavours of vegetables preserved in oil and make a nice change for those who enjoy meat. The addition of rabbit will also make this dish much more hearty, requiring only a green salad and some good bread for a well rounded meal.

Purchase 500g rabbit fillets, and dice. Add to the risotto with the leek/shallot mixture and cook until the meat changes colour. Continue with the risotto as above.

tuscan
risotto

ingredients

2 tablespoons olive oil
(from preserved vegetables if possible)
1 leek, cleaned and chopped
6 shallots, finely chopped
3 garlic cloves, minced
400g arborio rice
200ml white wine
800ml rich vegetable stock
10 sun-dried tomatoes (in oil, drained)
4 sun-dried capsicums (in oil, drained)
4 roasted artichokes,
drained and sliced or quartered
10 fresh basil leaves, finely shredded
1/2 cup grated Fontina cheese
2 tablespoons Parmesan cheese
extra basil leaves to garnish

warm rice salad

salads

Rice offers you the ultimate in easy

salad preparation, just cook and cool for the perfect base. Add your favourite flavours, be it meat, fruit, vegetables and nuts and you have a salad or even a meal to tempt any member of the family.

warm rice
salad

Method:

1 Heat oil in a large frying pan, add vinegar, orange juice and garlic and cook for 1 minute.
2 Add celery, sun-dried tomatoes, mushrooms, squash or zucchini (courgettes) and peas and cook for 3 minutes. Stir in artichokes, rice, carrots and olives and cook, stirring, for 4-5 minutes or until heated through. Season to taste with black pepper. Serve warm.

Note: This warm salad will add a Mediterranean feel to any meal. It is delicious served with grilled meat or poultry.

ingredients

1 tablespoon olive oil
3 tablespoons white wine vinegar
2 tablespoons orange juice
2 cloves garlic, crushed
2 stalks celery, chopped
3 tblspns chopped sun-dried tomatoes
60g/2oz button mushrooms, sliced
2 baby squash, quartered, or
2 zucchini (courgettes), sliced
60g/2oz fresh or frozen peas
440g/14oz canned artichokes, drained and halved
3/4 cup/170g/5 1/2oz rice, cooked
2 carrots, grated
8 black olives, pitted and sliced
freshly ground black pepper

Serves 6

summer
rice salad

ingredients

Method:

1 Combine cooked rice with ham, prawns and spring onions. Blend French dressing with paprika; stir into rice.
2 Pile rice in the centre of a salad platter, surround with orange and cucumber slices and sprinkle with chives.

Serves 6

3 cups/465g/15oz cooked long-grain rice
1/2 cup/90g/3oz chopped ham
1/2 cup/90g/3oz cooked prawns, shelled and deveined
4 spring onions, chopped
1/2 cup/125mL/4fl oz French dressing
1/2 teaspoon paprika
2 oranges, thinly sliced
1/2 cucumber, sliced
1 tablespoon chopped chives

saffron
rice

Method:

1 Slowly cook rice with stock and saffron for about $^1/_2$ hour. Drain, and when cool, add Spanish onion and fresh basil leaves. Garnish the salad with fresh or tinned artichokes, tomatoes, roasted capsicum (peppers) and black olives.

2 A great dressing can be made by placing $^1/_3$ balsamic vinegar, $^2/_3$ light olive oil and freshly ground pepper in a jar. Shake vigorously, use to dress salad

Serves 6

ingredients

2 cups/440g/14oz brown rice
1 L/35fl oz chicken stock
$^1/_2$ teaspoon saffron threads infused in
1 cup/250mL/8fl oz boiling water
salt, to taste
1 Spanish onion, finely diced
1 cup finely chopped
fresh basil leaves

seafood
paella salad

Serves 8

4 cups/1L/1³/₄pt chicken stock
500g/1lb uncooked large prawns
1 uncooked lobster tail (optional)
500g/1lb (mussels) clams in shells, cleaned
2 tablespoons olive oil
1 onion, chopped
2 ham steaks, cut into 1cm/¹/₂ in cubes
2 cups/440g/14oz rice
¹/₂ teaspoon ground turmeric
125g/4oz fresh or frozen peas
1 red capsicum(pepper), diced
<u>Garlic dressing</u>
¹/₂ cup/125mL/4fl oz olive oil
¹/₄ cup/60mL/2fl oz white wine vinegar
3 tablespoons mayonnaise
2 cloves garlic, minced
2 tablespoons chopped fresh parsley
freshly ground black pepper

Method:

1 Place stock in a large saucepan and bring to the boil. Add prawns and cook for 1-2 minutes or until prawns change colour. Remove and set aside. Add lobster tail and cook for 5 minutes or until lobster changes colour and is cooked. Remove and set aside. Add mussels and cook until shells open – discard any mussels that do not open after 5 minutes. Remove and set aside. Strain stock and reserve. Peel and devein prawns, leaving tails intact. Refrigerate seafood until just prior to serving.

2 Heat oil in a large saucepan, add onion and cook for 4-5 minutes or until soft. Add ham, rice and turmeric and cook, stirring, for 2 minutes. Add reserved stock and bring to the boil. Reduce heat, cover and simmer for 15 minutes or until liquid is absorbed and rice is cooked and dry. Stir in peas and red capsicum (pepper) and set aside to cool. Cover and refrigerate for at least 2 hours.

3 To make dressing, place oil, vinegar, mayonnaise, garlic, parsley and black pepper to taste in a food processor or blender and process to combine.

4 To serve, place seafood and rice in a large salad bowl, spoon over dressing and toss to combine.

thai chicken salad

Method:

1 *Cook the rice as per the instructions on the packet. Slice the chicken breasts into strips, removing any visible fat. Combine all marinade ingredients in a bowl and marinate the chicken for at least 1 hour.*

2 *In a large frying pan or wok over very high heat, fry the chicken pieces in canola oil for about 1 minute. Do not overcook. Remove to a warm place. Stir in the capsicum (peppers), nuts, garlic, onions and snow pea (mange tout) in the same pan for a couple of minutes.*

2 *Toss chicken with other ingredients in the pan. For the dressing, shake together the oil and lime juice with the coriander (cilantro). Place the lettuce on a platter and place the chicken on top. Sprinkle with the dressing. Serve with the rice.*

Serves 4-6

ingredients

2 cups/440g/14oz Jasmine fragrant rice
1kg/2lb chicken breasts, skin & bone removed
1 tablespoon canola oil
1 red capsicum(pepper), finely sliced
100g/3oz unsalted cashews or peanuts
1 clove garlic, finely chopped
4-5 spring onions, sliced into
bite-sized pieces
200g/7oz snow peas
assortment of lettuce leaves
<u>Marinade</u>
¹/₂ teaspoon sesame oil
¹/₂ teaspoon canola oil
1 teaspoon chilli sauce
1 tablespoon olive oil
1 tablespoon reduced salt soy sauce
<u>Dressing</u>
1 tablespoon olive oil
juice of 1 lime or ¹/₂ lemon
2 tablespoons fresh coriander (cilantro),
finely chopped (or ¹/₂ teaspoon dried)

st. clement's
rice salad

Method:
1 Bring orange juice, rind and chicken stock to boil, add rice, stir well, cover and simmer about 20-25 minutes till rice is tender. Remove from heat, uncover and allow to stand 10 minutes. Toss with fork and refrigerate till cold.

2 Blend all dressing ingredients thoroughly. Add spring onions to rice mixture, pour two-thirds dressing over rice. Place rice on salad platter, garnish centre with orange segments and chicken. Pour over remaining dressing. Decorate with mint sprigs.

Serves 6

1 cup/250mL/8fl oz orange juice
grated rind of 1 orange
2½ cups/600mL/20fl oz chicken stock
2 cups/440g/14oz long-grain rice
4 spring onions, chopped
2 cups/370g/12oz orange segments,
fresh or canned
3 cups/600g/20oz cooked chicken,
cut in bite-sized pieces
Citrus Dressing
6 tablespoons oil
2 tablespoons lemon juice
grated rind and juice of 1 orange
½ teaspoon paprika
salt and pepper to taste
2 teaspoons sherry, optional
sprigs of mint

nasi goreng

Makes 16

ingredients

4 tablespoons oil
2 eggs, beaten
2 cloves garlic, crushed
2 onions, thinly sliced
I red or yellow capsicum
(pepper), chopped
2 chillies, chopped, optional
250g/8oz pork fillet, diced
250g/8oz chicken breast, diced
250g/8oz peeled prawns
I cup/125g/4oz fresh bean sprouts
I tablespoon soy sauce
6 cups/1kg/2lb cooked short-grain rice
(allowed to stand in refrigerator overnight)

Meatballs
250g/8oz minced beef
I onion, finely chopped
pinch chilli powder or dash of
Tabasco sauce
salt to taste
I teaspoon curry powder
I beaten egg white

Method:

I *Heat I tablespoon oil, add pinch salt to beaten eggs. Add to pan and cook without stirring until set and golden. Remove egg, cut half into dice. Cut remainder into long thin strips, reserve. Add remainder of oil to pan, fry garlic, onions, capsicum (pepper) and chillies. Stir-fry, add pork fillet, chicken breast and prawns, cook for I0 minutes. Add bean sprouts. Add rice and toss continuously until heated. Season to taste with soy sauce. If not using chillies add pinch chilli powder or Tabasco. Add reserved chopped egg to rice. Spoon rice onto serving platter.*

Top with reserved egg strips in lattice pattern. Garnish with meat balls and thin cucumber slices.

Meatballs:
Blend all ingredients thoroughly then shape with wet hands into small meatballs. Brown in hot oil then thread onto short bamboo skewers. Top with a little chilli sauce.

Additional Garnishes:
Fried pineapple, bananas, cucumber and tomato slices, chutney, fried prawn crisps, dry fried onion rings.

Serves 6

mustard beef curry

quick meals

& side dishes

As a side dish, simple steamed rice

is an international winner on your table. While rice is one of the most versatile foods in your kitchen, it is also the most perfect partner for many other taste delights. Pure, steamed rice adds fluffy contrast to chicken, beef and lamb, pork and vegetables, its hungry grains eager to eat up the juices and flavours of those more substantial foods. In this way rice proves to be the most international of ingredients.

208

mustard
beef curry

Method:

1 Melt ghee or butter in large saucepan over a medium heat, add onion, garlic and ginger and cook, stirring, for 3 minutes or until onion is soft.

2 Add beef and cook, stirring, for 5 minutes or until beef is brown. Stir mustard, chilli powder, mustard seeds, stock and coconut milk into pan and bring to simmering. Simmer, stirring occasionally, for 50 minutes or until beef is tender. Sprinkle with coriander and serve. Serve with steamed long-grain rice.

Note: A typical Sri Lankan meal consists of one or two curries, rice, a soup, vegetables and several sambola. A sambola is the equivalent to the Indian sambal.

Serves 4

ingredients

60g/2oz ghee or butter
I large onion, chopped
3 cloves garlic, crushed
2 tablespoons finely grated fresh ginger
500g/I kg rump steak, cut into
2cm/³/₄in cubes
2 teaspoons French mustard
I teaspoon chilli powder
I tablespoon yellow mustard seeds
I cup/250 mL/8 fl oz beef stock
³/₄ cup/185 mL/6 fl oz coconut milk
2 tablespoons chopped fresh coriander

Serves 8

vegetable
& rice patties

Method:

1 Place rice, bran, flour, onion, garlic, ginger, sweet corn, carrot, zucchini (courgette) and pine nuts in a bowl and mix to combine. Place peanut butter, soy sauce, yoghurt and egg whites in a food processor or blender and process to combine. Add peanut-butter mixture to rice mixture and combine well.

2 Shape rice mixture into sixteen patties and coat with breadcrumbs. Heat oil in a nonstick frying pan and cook patties for 5 minutes each side or until golden and cooked through. Drain on absorbent kitchen paper.

ingredients

³/₄ cup/170g/5¹/₂oz brown rice, cooked
³/₄ cup/30g/1oz unprocessed bran
³/₄ cup/90g/3oz flour
I onion, grated
I clove garlic, minced
I teaspoon grated fresh ginger
250g/8oz canned sweet corn kernels, drained
I carrot, grated
I zucchini (courgette), grated
3 tablespoons toasted pine nuts
2 tablespoons peanut butter
2 teaspoons soy sauce
3 tablespoons natural yoghurt
2 egg whites
I¹/₂ cups/185g/6oz dried breadcrumbs
2 tablespoons olive oil

nutty
chicken curry

Method:

1 Place chicken, garlic, ginger and coriander in a bowl and mix to combine. Shape mixture into small balls.
2 Heat 1 tablespoon of oil in a wok over a medium heat and cook meatballs in batches for 5 minutes or until brown. Remove meatballs from pan and drain on absorbent kitchen paper.
3 Heat remaining oil in wok, add onion and stir-fry for 3 minutes or until golden. Stir in curry paste and cook for 3 minutes longer or until fragrant.
4 Stir peanut butter and coconut milk into curry paste mixture and bring to the boil. Reduce heat and simmer for 15 minutes. Return meatballs to pan, add basil and bring to simmering. Simmer, stirring occasionally, for 10 minutes. Serve with steamed long-grain rice.

Note: In Thailand curries are usually served over moulds of rice. The rice absorbs and is flavoured by the large proportion of liquid in the curry.

ingredients

500g/1 lb ground chicken
1 clove garlic, crushed
1 tablespoon finely grated fresh ginger
1 tablespoon chopped fresh coriander
2 tablespoons vegetable oil
1 onion, chopped
2 tablespoons Thai Red Curry Paste
2 tablespoons crunchy peanut butter
1 1/2 cups/375mL/12fl oz coconut milk
1 tablespoon chopped fresh basil
jasmine or basmati rice

The fragrant rices such as jasmine and basmati are perfect accompaniments for Thai curries.
Serves 4

cheddar
chicken rice

Method:

1 Melt butter, gently sauté onions, mushrooms and capsicum (pepper). Remove from pan. Add flour and cook 1 minute, gradually stir in milk and bring to boil, add three-quarters of the cheese and seasonings. Stir until cheese has melted. Add chicken, cooked vegetables, olives and almonds, simmer. Cook rice using the rapid boil method. Gently stir chopped parsley through rice. Place rice on a heated serving plate and mound the chicken in the centre. Sprinkle remaining cheese over top of chicken.

Serves 4-6

ingredients

30g/1oz butter
2 spring onions, sliced diagonally
1 cup/125g/4oz sliced fresh mushrooms
1/3 cup/60g/2oz green capsicum(pepper),
1 tablespoon plain flour
1 cup milk
250g/8oz Cheddar cheese, grated
salt and pepper
2 cups/380g/12oz diced cooked chicken
1/3 cup/60g/2oz sliced stuffed olives,
1/2 cup/60g/2oz slivered almonds, toasted
2 cups/440g/14oz short-grain rice
1/4 cup/30g1oz chopped parsley

stir-fried
chicken & rice

Method:

1 Remove fat, skin and bone from chicken. Cut breast in half lengthwise. Slice crosswise into thin strips.

2 Heat oil in a frying pan or wok, then stir-fry capsicum (peppers), shallots, garlic and ginger for 1-2 minutes. Remove. Set aside.

3 Add chicken to pan and stir-fry until just tender (about 3-4 minutes). Return vegetables to pan. Combine stock, soy sauce and tomato sauce. Blend cornflour with sherry and add to stock. Pour stock mixture over chicken and heat, stirring, until mixture boils and thickens.

4 Serve chicken spooned over hot rice and garnished with toasted slivered almonds.

Serves 4-6

ingredients

1 whole chicken breast
2 tablespoons olive oil
1 small red and 1 green capsicum(pepper), cut into thin strips
4 spring onions, cut on diagonal
1 clove garlic, minced
1/2 teaspoon grated fresh ginger
3/4 cup/185mL/6fl oz chicken stock
1 tablespoon soy sauce, salt reduced
1 tablespoon tomato sauce, salt reduced
2 teaspoons cornflour
1 tablespoon dry sherry
6 cups/1kg/2lb hot cooked long-grain rice
1/4 cup/30g/1oz slivered almonds, toasted

broccoli
& rice soufflé

Serves 4

ingredients

125g/4oz broccoli, cut into small florets
1g/¹/₂oz butter
¹/₂ onion, chopped
2 tablespoons flour
1 cup/250mL/8fl oz hot milk
¹/₄ teaspoon ground nutmeg
freshly ground black pepper
3 eggs, separated
60g/2oz grated tasty cheese
(mature Cheddar)
¹/₃ cup/75g/2¹/₂oz rice, cooked

Method:

1 Boil, steam or microwave broccoli until tender. Drain and refresh under cold, running water. Drain again and set aside.

2 Melt butter in a small saucepan, add onion and cook for 2 minutes. Stir in flour and cook, stirring constantly, for 2 minutes longer. Remove pan from heat and gradually whisk in hot milk. Return pan to heat and cook, stirring constantly, for 5 minutes or until sauce boils and thickens. Stir in nutmeg and black pepper to taste.

3 Beat egg yolks into sauce, then add broccoli, cheese and rice to sauce and mix well to combine.

4 Place egg whites in a large bowl and beat until stiff peaks form. Stir one-quarter egg whites into sauce mixture, then carefully fold in remaining egg whites. Spoon soufflé mixture into four lightly greased ³/₄ cup/185mL/6fl oz capacity soufflé dishes and bake for 25 minutes or until soufflés are puffed and golden. Serve immediately.

Serves 4

apple
rice

Method:

1 *Delicious with roast pork or pork chops. Just cook 1 cup/220g/7oz short-grain rice in 1 cup/250mL/8oz apple juice, 1 cup/250mL/ 8oz stock, salt to taste. Garnish with chopped apple.*

lemon
rice

Method:

1 *Perfect with fish. Cook 1 cup/220g/7oz short-grain rice using 1 3/4 cups/420mL/14fl oz water, 1/4 cup/60mL/2fl oz lemon juice, 1 teaspoon grated lemon peel and 1/4 teaspoon turmeric. Salt to taste.*

onion
rice

Method:

1 *Great with steaks or any kinds of chops. Cook 1 cup/220g/7oz short-grain rice, 1/2 package dehydrated onion soup mix and 2 cups water, salt to taste. Garnish with fried onion rings.*

orange
rice

Method:

1 *Great served with chicken. Cook 1 cup/ 220g/7oz short-grain rice with 1 cup/250mL/ 8fl oz orange juice, 1 cup/250mL/8fl oz stock, salt to taste. If you like, add nuts and sultanas.*

tomato
rice

Method:

1 *Great with steak and burgers. Cook 1 cup/ 220g/7oz short-grain rice in 1 cup/250mL/8 fl oz tomato juice, 1 cup/250mL/8 fl oz beef stock, salt to taste. Garnish with sliced green onions.*

yellow
rice

Method:

1 *Cook 2 cups/440g/14oz short-grain rice to directions for rapid boil method (page 76), adding 1 teaspoon turmeric to the water. When cooked, drain well and toss with 1 teaspoon grated lemon rind.*

fried rice

Method:

1 Soak mushrooms in hot water 20 minutes or until tender. Cut into small dice. Heat half the oil with garlic and ginger ,then fry eggs without stirring until set and golden. Remove, cut in small dice and reserve. Heat remaining oil and fry mushrooms, chicken and prawns and spring onions. Add rice and toss continuously with egg slice or fork till heated. Season with salt. Add reserved egg. Combine soy sauce and wine. Sprinkle over rice, toss again. Serve garnished with shallot curls.

Serves 6 *(with other dishes)*

ingredients

6 dried mushrooms, optional
4 tablespoons peanut oil
1 small clove garlic, crushed
1/2 teaspoon root ginger, chopped
2 eggs, beaten with little soy sauce
1/2 cup/90g/3oz cooked diced chicken
or barbecued pork
1/2 cup/90g/3oz shelled prawns
6 spring onions, chopped
6 cups/1kg/2lb cooked short-grain rice
(place in refrigerator overnight)
salt
1 tablespoon soy sauce or to taste
1 tablespoon Chinese rice wine

steamed
rice

Method:

1 Place rice in sieve or colander and run cold water over rice till water runs quite clear. Allow rice to drain and dry. Place rice in heavy-bottomed saucepan, and add enough cold water to cover 2.5cm/1in above rice. (This measurement applies to any quantity of rice.) Add salt. Bring to boil, boil rapidly till steam holes appear in rice. Turn heat down as low as possible. Cover with lid, seal with foil if not a good fit.

Allow rice to simmer gently till tender 15-20 minutes. Remove from heat, uncover and allow to stand 5 minutes before serving.

Serves 8

ingredients

2 cups/440g/14oz short-grain rice
water
1/2 teaspoon salt

Serves 6

sushi
rice

ingredients

3 1/3 cups/730g/24oz short-grain rice
4 cups/1L/35fl oz water
<u>Vinegar mixture</u>
6 tablespoons rice vinegar
5 tablespoons sugar
1 teaspoon salt

Method:

1 Wash rice until water runs clear and drain in strainer for 1 hour. Put the drained rice in a rice cooker or a pot with a tight-fitting lid and add water. Cover tightly and bring to boil over medium heat. Continue boiling over high heat for 2 minutes, reduce heat and boil for a further 5 minutes. Cook gently over a low heat for 15 minutes, or until all the water has been absorbed. Remove from heat. Take off lid, spread a clean kitchen towel over the top of the pot, replace lid and let stand for 15 minutes.

2 While rice is cooking, combine the vinegar mixture ingredients in a bowl and heat gently till the sugar has dissolved, stirring constantly. Remove from heat. To cool quickly, place in a bowl of ice cubes.

3 Empty rice into a hangiri (or other non-metallic tub) and spread evenly over the base with a large wooden spoon. Run the spatula through the rice in right-and-left slicing motion to separate the grains. As you do this, slowly add the vinegar mixture. You may not need it all. The rice must not be mushy. Continue the slicing motion with the spatula as you add the vinegar. Do not refrigerate the rice, but keep it in the tub covered with a clean cloth until ready for use. Sushi rice lasts only one day and does not lend itself to the usual ways of dealing with leftovers.

dishes

sweet
rice
dishes

tropical touch parfait

sweet
rice
dishes

Combine rice with fruits, sweetners

and spices and you will reap sweet success. Try a fragrant, Creamy Rice with Warm Berries, or a Tropical Touch Parfait, the results will delight you. Rice is remarkable in its ability to complement, contrast, or provide a vehicle to enhance the flavours and textures of many foods.

tropical
touch parfait

Method:

1 Combine rice with pineapple liquid, rind and juice of oranges, honey and butter. Place over moderate heat and stir occasionally till liquid is almost absorbed. Allow to cool. Fold into rice half the cream and half the passionfruit. Add pineapple and blend thoroughly. Spoon into parfait glasses. Decorate with remaining cream, top with banana slices and remaining passionfruit.

Serves 4

ingredients

2 cups/310g/10oz cooked short-grain rice
450g/14oz can pineapple pieces
or fruit salad (keep liquid)
grated rind and juice 2 oranges
1 tablespoon of honey or sugar to taste
1 tablespoon butter
1 cup/250mL/8oz whipping cream
3 passionfruit
1 banana, sliced, soaked in lemon juice

creamy rice
with warm berries

Method:

1 In a medium saucepan bring milk to the boil with vanilla beans. Add rice and reduce heat. Simmer over medium heat, stirring from time to time until rice is tender – about 25 minutes. When rice is cooked, remove from heat and take out vanilla beans. Scrape tiny vanilla seeds from pods into rice. Allow to cool.

2 To prepare berries:
In a non-reactive saucepan, combine the berries, sugar and water. Bring to a gentle simmer, remove from stove. Serve warm berries over creamy rice.

Serves 6

ingredients

325g/10oz sugar
3 1/2 cups/875mL/28fl oz milk
2 vanilla beans, split lengthwise
1 cup/220g/7oz short-grain rice
For Berries:
1 cup/125g/4oz blueberries
1 cup/125g/4oz raspberries
1 cup/125g/4oz blackberries
1 cup/125g/4oz strawberries,
hulled and halved
60g/2oz sugar
1/4 cup/60mL/2fl oz water

cherry jubilee
parfait

Method:

1   *Place rice in saucepan with butter, milk and sugar, simmer, stirring occasionally, till creamy, about 15 minutes. Cool. Make 1 port wine and cherry jelly, with liquid from canned cherries plus water to make 1 1/2 cups/375ml/8oz liquid. When almost set add cherries, chill till firm. Place alternate layers creamy rice and jelly in parfait glasses. Top with cream.*

Serves 4

ingredients

1 1/2 **cups/250g/8oz cooked**
shortgrain rice
1 **tablespoon butter**
1 1/2 **cups/375ml/12oz milk**
1/2 **cup/250g/8oz sugar**
1 **medium can cherries**
1 **packet port wine flavoured gelatine**

chocolate
ricotta rice

Method:

1 *Beat ricotta cheese in a basin until smooth. Add caster sugar, Tia Maria and cream, and beat until combined. Add rice and grated chocolate. Divide between 4 dessert glasses.*

2 *Place water and chopped extra chocolate in a saucepan and stir over medium heat until chocolate has melted. Remove from heat. Set aside.*

3 *Combine extra caster sugar and extra water in a saucepan and stir over low heat until sugar has dissolved. Bring to the boil. Boil rapidly for 5 minutes or until mixture forms a soft ball when a small amount is dropped into cold water. Beat egg yolks until pale-coloured. Pour boiling sugar syrup, in a thin stream, into egg yolks, beating until cool (about 2 minutes). Beat in melted chocolate. Pour over ricotta mixture and refrigerate until firm. Decorate with whipped cream and grated chocolate, if desired.*

Serves 4

ingredients

250g/8oz ricotta cheese
2 tablespoons caster sugar
1 tablespoon Tia Maria
1 tablespoon cream
³/₄ cup/125g/4oz cooked brown rice
60g/2oz dark chocolate, grated
3 tablespoons water
185g/6oz dark chocolate, extra
¹/₂ cup/80g/2¹/₂ oz caster sugar, extra
¹/₄ cup/60mL/2fl oz water, extra

fruit salad
rice

Method:

I Heat orange juice, add rice, bring to the boil, then lower heat to simmer. Stir occasionally until almost all juice is absorbed. Remove from heat, add honey and allow to cool. Fold whipped cream through rice. Combine kiwifruit, honeydew, pawpaw and strawberries, then spoon fruits into a ring over rice. Spoon over passionfruit pulp. Serve with extra whipped cream.

Serves 4

ingredients

2¹/₂ cups/625mL/20oz orange juice
3 cups/500g/16oz cooked short-grain rice
2 tablespoons honey or to taste
I cup/250mL/8oz whipped cream
2 kiwifruit, sliced
I cup/190g/6oz diced honeydew melon
I cup/190g/6oz diced pawpaw
250g/8oz punnet strawberries, sliced
3 passionfruit

orange rice
pudding

Method:

1 Boil rice in water till liquid has been absorbed (about 15 minutes). Add orange juice and water with butter. Bring to boil then simmer till rice is quite tender (about 25 minutes). Add honey, extra orange juice and rind. Spoon into serving dish. Top with ring of sliced oranges. Heat marmalade with sherry then spoon over orange slices. Serve with cream or ice cream.

Note: Canned mandarin segments may be used to replace fresh oranges.

Serves 4

ingredients

1 cup/220g/7oz short-grain rice
2 cups/500mL/16fl oz water
1/2 cup/125mL/4oz orange juice
1 1/2 cups/375mL/12oz water
1 tablespoon butter
1/2 cup/125mL/4oz honey or
sugar to taste
2 extra tablespoons orange juice
grated rind 1 orange
2 peeled oranges, thinly sliced
1/2 cup/125mL/4oz orange marmalade
or use apricot jam
2 teaspoons sherry, optional

pineapple
chocolate
trifle

Serves 6-8

ingredients

1¼ **cups/185g/6oz cooked long-grain rice**
3¾ **cups/920mL/30fl oz milk**
¾ **cup/60g/2oz sugar**
1 **teaspoon vanilla**
440g/14oz **can crushed pineapple, drained**
1 **cup/250mL/8oz cream, whipped**
2 **tablespoons custard powder**
2 **eggs, separated**
60g/2oz **dark chocolate, grated**
1 **chocolate sponge layer**
⅓ **cup/85mL/2½oz Tia Maria**
4 **kiwifruit, peeled and sliced**
250g/8oz **punnet strawberries, hulled and sliced**

Method:

1 Place rice and one-third of milk in a saucepan. Simmer over low heat until all of the milk has been absorbed. Remove from heat and stir in one-third of the sugar and the vanilla. Fold pineapple and cream into cooled rice. Set aside.

2 Blend custard powder with the remaining milk. Add the remaining sugar. Stir over low heat until the mixture boils and thickens. Remove from heat, and whisk in egg yolks and chocolate. Stir until chocolate has melted and is well blended. Cool. Fold in gently beaten egg whites.

3 Cut sponge cake into cubes and arrange in the bottom of a large glass serving dish (alternatively serve on individual plates). Sprinkle with Tia Maria and then add layers of kiwifruit, strawberries, chocolate custard and pineapple rice cream. Decorate top with whipped cream and chocolate curls, if desired.

the grain
of taste

How to Rapid Boil Rice

Pour 8 cups/2litres/3^1/2 pts of water into a large saucepan. Use a large saucepan, because when you bring the water to boil, you're setting up the maximum saucepan area for the rice grains to expand. Add 2 teaspoons of salt to the boiling water, then slowly add 1 cup of rice. Stir the rice several times with a fork and boil rapidly in the uncovered saucepan for 12 to 15 minutes. Remember, 1 cup/220g/7oz of uncooked rice becomes 3 cups/660g/21oz cooked rice. Tip the expanded cooked rice into a colander, drain well, then fluff up the rice with a fork.

How to Cook Rice by the Absorption Method

Bring 2 cups/500mL/16oz of water or stock to the boil, then slowly add 1 cup/220g/7oz of rice and some salt to taste. Reheat to boil and stir once. Cover tightly with a saucepan lid, then turn heat as low as possible. Simmer gently for 25 minutes or until all the rice is tender and all the liquid is absorbed.

How to Fry Rice

You can use refrigerated or even frozen rice to make Chinese Fried Rice. Finely chop ^{1}/2 cup/60g/2oz of shallots,^{1}/2 cup/60g/2oz of mushrooms, ^{1}/2 cup/60g/2oz of green capsicum (pepper) and add a chopped fried egg. Heat ^{1}/4 cup/60ml/2fl oz of oil in a wok or electric frying pan and stir in vegetables. Toss for three to four minutes. Add the refrigerated boiled rice and keep tossing. Add salt and soy sauce to taste, and for the final touch, if it takes your fancy, one tablespoon of sherry.

How to Store Rice

Just store the rice in an airtight container – pop the pack into the fridge. Rice can be kept as long as fresh milk in the fridge. If you want to keep it longer, just pop it into the freezer.

How to Reheat Rice

Place rice in colander over simmering water and allow to heat through. Or a microwave oven does it perfectly.

Cooking Brown Rice

Absorption Method: Bring 2 cups/500mL/16fl oz of water to the boil. Add 1 cup/220g/7oz brown rice slowly. Salt to taste. Return to the boil, stir once, cover and turn heat as low as possible. Simmer gently for 1 hour or till all the liquid is absorbed.

Rapid Boil Method: Bring 8 cups/2L/3^1/2 pts of water or stock to boil in a large saucepan. Add 2 teaspoons of salt or to taste. Slowly add 1 cup/220g/7oz of brown rice. Stir several times with a fork. Boil rapidly uncovered for 35-40 minutes. Tip into colander. Drain well. Fluff up with fork.

Variations: Stock made from soup cubes is ideal for this method, or use a combination of tomato and vegetable juices. For chicken or seafood dishes, use half chicken broth and half oyster liquid. When preparing rice for desserts, fruit juices using the above method will give an ideal result. A further interesting variation for savoury dishes to fry lightly in butter any of the following: onion, crushed garlic, shallots, celery, green capsicum (pepper), mushrooms, etc. Add the raw rice, toss a few minutes over moderate heat then add 2 cups/500ml/16fl oz boiling liquid and continue cooking as above.

At least one-third of the human race eats rice as a staple food. There are many varieties and no preparation is required. Cooking varies according to the type of rice and the recipe.

Short-grain rice: The most popular all-purpose rice, particularly suited to dishes where grains need to cling together.

Long-grain rice: Known for its fluffy texture, long-grain rice is good for pilaus, salads and stuffings.

Brown rice: Natural unpolished rice that has a distinctive nutty taste.

Basmati rice: Grown in Bangladesh and Pakistan, this rice is a delicious aromatic rice ideal for highly spiced Indian dishes.

Arborio or risotto rice: An Italian rice that is ideal for absorbing a great deal of liquid. Generally used for risotto and jambalaya.

Wild rice: Although related to the rice family, wild rice is actually a seed from an aquatic grass that grows in North America. It has an appealing distinctive nutty flavour. It is quite expensive, and is used more commonly in gourmet cooking.

Rice cooking chart

Method	White Rice	Brown Rice
Rapid boil	Place 8 cups/2L/3¹/₂pts water in a large saucepan and bring to the boil. Stir in 1 cup/220g/7oz rice and return to the boil. Boil rapidly for 12-15 minutes or until rice is tender. Drain through a sieve or colander and serve.	Place 8 cups/2L/3¹/₂pts water in a large saucepan and bring to the boil. Stir in 1 cup/220g/7oz rice and return to the boil. Boil rapidly for 30-40 minutes or until rice is tender. Drain and serve.
Absorption An easy way to cook rice, and the grains stay separate and fluffy.	Place 1¹/₂ cups/375mL/12fl oz water in a large saucepan, stir in 1 cup/220g/7oz rice. Cover and simmer for 20-25 minutes. Uncover, toss with a fork and stand for a few minutes before serving.	Place 2 cups/500mL/16fl oz water in a large saucepan and bring to the boil. Stir in 1 cup/220g/7oz rice, cover and simmer for 55 minutes or until all the liquid is absorbed. Toss with a fork and serve.
Steaming This is a popular Chinese method of cooking rice.	Wash 1 cup/220g/7oz rice, then drain and set aside to dry. Place rice in a heavy-based saucepan and add enough water to cover the rice by 2.5cm/1in. Bring to the boil and boil rapidly until steam holes appear on the surface of the rice. Reduce heat to as low as possible, cover with a tight-fitting lid, or foil, and steam for 10 minutes. Remove lid, or foil, toss with a fork and stand 5 minutes before serving.	Wash 1 cup/220g/7oz rice, then drain and set aside to dry. Place rice in a heavy-based saucepan and add enough water to cover the rice by 2.5cm/1in. Bring to the boil and boil rapidly until steam holes appear on the surface of the rice. Reduce heat to as low as possible, cover with a tight-fitting lid, or foil, and steam for 25-30 minutes. Remove lid or foil, toss with a fork and stand 5 minutes before serving.
Microwave Cooking rice in the microwave does not save time but it does guarantee a perfect result and there is no messy saucepan at the end of the cooking time.	Place 1 cup/220g/7oz rice and 2 cups/500mLl/16fl oz water in a large microwave-safe container. Cook, uncovered, on HIGH (100%) for 12-15 minutes or until liquid is absorbed. Cover and stand for 5 minutes. Toss with a fork and serve.	Place 1 cup/220g/7oz rice and 3 cups/750mL/1¹/₂ pts water in a large microwave-safe container. Cook, uncovered, on HIGH (100%) for 30-35 minutes or until liquid is absorbed. Stir occasionally during cooking. Cover and stand for 5 minutes. Toss with a fork and serve.

pasta
perfect

Pasta in all its forms has graced tables in Italy and indeed all over the globe for thousands of years. Recognised as one of the world's most beloved foods, pasta possesses qualities that quite possibly will make it the 21st century's food of choice. Pasta's superior nutritional benefits have earned it superfood status. It is also the ideal staple; economical, convenient to store and prepare, it is versatile and highly pleasurable to eat. In fact one could quite easily call pasta "the perfect food".

Pasta Fresh **and Dried:**

Pasta is made from grain combined with liquid (and sometimes with other ingredients for flavouring and colouring). Kneading produces a smooth dough or paste (hence the word pasta), that can be rolled out or cut and formed into any of hundreds of varieties. Making sense out of the multitude of pasta varieties is simplified by dividing pasta into two categories: fresh and dried.

Basic **ingredients:**

The basic ingredients of fresh pasta are flour and eggs, with perhaps a little oil or water added to make the dough easier to work, with some salt for flavour.

Most commercially produced dried pasta is made from water and semolina, a special variety of flour ground from high quality durum wheat.

Semolina creates a firm, elastic dough that is sturdy enough to be shaped by a machine. It can also be used in homemade pasta, either alone or mixed with all-purpose flour, to strengthen the dough and enhance the texture of the finished product.

Nutritional **value**

Pasta is valued as a high-energy, low-fat food, and a high source of dietary fibre. It supplies moderate amounts of protein and some of the B group vitamins, especially thiamine.

The sauces and their ingredients served with pasta will increase the nutritive content. With an informed choice, fat content can remain low, making pasta meals ideal for healthy eating.

How to cook **value**

You need to follow only a few well-trodden rules to achieve perfect pasta every time. If you adhere to the following steps you will never produce pasta that is soggy or sticky.

Use a big pan and lots of water. As the Italian's love to say, "pasta loves to swim".

Let the water come to full boiling point before adding salt.

With the water boiling freely add the pasta a few handfuls at a time and stir gently to stop it sticking together.

Cover the pan to allow the water to return to the boil quickly, but watch to ensure that the pot does not boil over. When foam rises to the top of the pan lower the heat to maintain a soft boil.

Test pasta by biting into a selected strand. The pasta is done when it tastes good, with just that little bit of firmness. It should be deliciously chewy without a floury taste, what the Italian's call "al dente", which means "just right to the tooth".

Different thicknesses of dried pasta require different cooking times. It should also be noted that fresh pasta, with its higher moisture content, will usually cook much more quickly than even the thinnest dried pasta. When cooked immediately drain the pasta. Do not rinse it, unless the directions specifically say so as washing will reduce the nutrients in the meal.

Always sauce the pasta at once, to keep it from sticking, tossing well to distribute the sauce evenly.

Pasta that is to be sauced and baked, should be undercooked slightly: otherwise it will be too soft after baking.

With spaghetti, apply a light sauce to a fine stick, such as angel-hair, and a more robust sauce to a thicker strand. A rule of thumb, therefore, would be to ensure that the sauce grades increase with the thickness of the spaghetti, linguine or fettuccine used.

When using tubular pasta try a clinging sauce that will stick to them both inside and out, whilst shell shaped pasta is shaped just right for holding puddles of sauce and pieces of meat, fish or poultry.

Twists are more versatile as they will allow a robust sauce to wrap around them for a full-flavour dish, or they can accept a light vinaigrette when served in a cold salad.

Sauce ingredients are only limited by the cook's imagination and desire to experiment. We have included a number of very tasty sauces throughout this book, however we would encourage you to experiment and experience the delight of creating your own marvellous dish, using your favourite pasta as a base.

The best oils for **pasta**

The subtle flavour of pasta is enhanced by good-quality olive oil. The flavour and quality of olive oil varies according to the type of olives it was pressed from, where the olives were grown and the method of pressing. Olive oils are graded according to how much oleic acid they contain and the procedure used to make them. The oil must be pressed from olives that were not chemically treated in order to qualify for one of the following top four categories:

- Virgin (no more than 4 percent oleic acid)
- Fine virgin (no more than 3 percent oleic acid)
- Superfine virgin (no more than 2 percent oleic acid)
- Extra virgin (no more than 1 percent oleic acid)

Storing and using **olive oil**

- Choose olive oil with a clean, fruity aroma, full body, and fruity or peppery flavour
- Store olive oil where it will not be exposed to heat or light, which can cause it to become rancid. Use within a years time.
- Use a good-tasting affordable olive oil for sautéed and baked disks; save the finest grades for pesto and other uncooked dishes or for drizzling over cooked foods just before serving.

Campellini with tomatoes

Healthy soups are made hearty by

the addition of pasta; add it to vegetables, meat and vegetable or chicken soups.

Vermicelli is a fine-strand pasta, suitable for inclusion in broths or puréed soups (first break the strands into 5cm/2in pieces). Elbows, spirals, trivelle and rigatoni are more suitable for big "chunky" soups.

What better choice for an entrée than pasta with a delicious sauce to stimulate the appetite. Fettuccine is perhaps the most popular choice and will go well when matched with a variety of sauces. You will find a very tasty of sauces to make within this chapter.

Like many other dishes based on pasta, soups and salads offer creative, delicious opportunities for using up leftover shellfish, poultry, meats or vegetables.

capellini
with tomatoes

Photograph Page 237

Photograph Page 237

Method:
1 *Heat 60mL/2oz of the oil in a pan, add the garlic, and cook over a medium heat (until the garlic is slightly browned and golden).*
2 *Reduce the heat, and add the tomatoes, basil, salt and pepper, and cook for 5 minutes (or until tomatoes are just heated through).*
3 *Cook cappellini pasta in boiling salted water (until al dente). Add remaining oil.*
4 *Serve with tomato mixture over cappellini pasta.*
Serves 4-6

ingredients

**120mL/4 fl oz olive oil
6 cloves garlic, thinly sliced
550g/17oz Roma tomatoes, seeded and diced
1/3 cup fresh basil, shredded
salt
freshly ground black pepper
400g/13oz cappellini**

spaghetti
basil soup

Photograph opposite

Photograph opposite

ingredients

Method:
1 *Cook spaghetti in boiling water in a large saucepan following packet directions. Drain and set aside.*
2 *Heat oil in a large saucepan and cook onion, garlic and almonds, stirring over a medium heat for 6-7 minutes or until onions are transparent.*
3 *Add stock and basil to pan and bring to the boil, reduce heat, cover and simmer for 10 minutes. Stir in spaghetti and season to taste with black pepper. Spoon soup into bowls and serve immediately.*
Serves 4

**155g/5oz spaghetti, broken into pieces
2 tablespoons vegetable oil
1 onion, chopped
2 cloves garlic, crushed
60g/2oz slivered almonds
4 cups/1L/1 3/4pt chicken stock
30g/1oz fresh basil leaves, shredded
freshly ground black pepper**

caviar
fettuccine

Method:

1 Cook fettuccine in boiling water in a large saucepan, following packet directions. Drain, set aside and keep warm.

2 Heat oil in a large frying pan and cook garlic over low heat for 3-4 minutes. Add fettuccine, chives, red and black caviar, and eggs to pan. Toss to combine. Serve immediately, topped with sour cream.

Serves 4

ingredients

300g/9¹/₂oz fettuccine
2 tablespoons olive oil
2 cloves garlic, crushed
2 tablespoons finely snipped fresh chives
3 tablespoons red caviar
3 tablespoons black caviar
2 hard-boiled eggs, chopped
4 tablespoons sour cream

fettuccine
with coriander (cilantro) sauce

Method:

1 Cook fettuccine in boiling water in a large saucepan following packet directions. Drain, set aside and keep warm.

2 To make sauce, place garlic, walnuts, coriander (cilantro) and parsley in a food processor or blender and process to finely chop. With machine running, add oil in a steady stream. Add Parmesan cheese and black pepper to taste, and process to combine.

3 Spoon sauce over pasta and toss to combine. Serve immediately.

Serves 6

ingredients

500g/1 lb fettuccine
Coriander (cilantro) sauce
2 cloves garlic, chopped
60g/2oz walnut pieces
60g/2oz coriander (cilantro) leaves
15g/¹/₂oz fresh parsley leaves
4 tablespoons vegetable oil
60g/2oz grated Parmesan cheese
freshly ground black pepper

tomato
pasta rolls

ingredients

Method:

1 Place flour, eggs, water, tomato paste (purée) and oil in a food processor and process to combine. Turn dough onto a lightly floured surface and knead for 5 minutes or until it is smooth and elastic. Wrap dough in plastic food wrap and set aside to stand for 15 minutes.

2 To make filling, place spinach, ricotta or cottage cheese, eggs, Parmesan cheese, nutmeg and black pepper (to taste) in a bowl, and mix to combine.

3 Divide dough in two halves and roll out one half to form a rectangle 30x45cm/12x18in. Spread with half the filling mixture, leaving a 2.5cm/1in border, then top with half the prosciutto or ham and half the mozzarella cheese. Fold in borders on long sides, then roll up from the short side. Wrap roll in a piece of washed calico cloth and secure ends with string. Repeat with remaining ingredients to make a second roll.

4 Half fill a baking dish with water and place on the stove top. Bring to the boil, add rolls, reduce heat, cover dish with aluminium foil or lid and simmer for 30 minutes. Turn rolls once or twice during cooking. Remove rolls from water and allow to cool for 5 minutes. Remove calico from rolls and refrigerate until firm. To serve, cut rolls into slices.

Serves 12

2 cups/250g/8oz flour
2 eggs
2 tablespoons water
2 tablespoons concentrated
tomato paste (purée)
I tablespoon olive oil
<u>Spinach filling</u>
500g/I lb frozen spinach, thawed
and well drained
375g/12oz ricotta or
cottage cheese
2 eggs
90g/3oz grated Parmesan cheese
I teaspoon ground nutmeg
freshly ground black pepper
12 slices prosciutto or thinly sliced ham
500g/I lb sliced mozzarella cheese

spaghetti
and pesto

Method:

1 Cook spaghetti in boiling water in a large saucepan following packet directions. Drain, set aside and keep warm.

2 To make Pesto, place basil, pine nuts and garlic in a food processor or blender and process to finely chop all ingredients. With machine running, add oil in a steady steam. Season to taste with black pepper.

3 Add Pesto to spaghetti and toss to combine. Serve immediately.

Serves 6

500g/1 lb spaghetti
Pesto
125g/4oz fresh basil leaves
3 tablespoons pine nuts
4 cloves garlic, crushed
4 tablespoons olive oil
freshly ground black pepper

chicken
& leek rolls

Method:

1. *Cook lasagne sheets in boiling water in a large saucepan until tender. Drain, set aside and keep warm.*
2. *To make filling, heat oil in a large frying pan and cook leeks and chicken, stirring, for 4-5 minutes or until chicken is brown. Stir in stock, cornflour mixture, mustard and basil and cook, stirring, for 2 minutes longer. Season to taste with black pepper.*
3. *Place spoonfuls of filling on lasagne sheets, roll up, top with Parmesan cheese and serve immediately.*

Serves 6

ingredients

12 spinach lasagne sheets
<u>Chicken and leek filling</u>
2 teaspoons vegetable oil
3 leeks, finely sliced
3 chicken breast fillets, cut into thin strips
¹/₂ cup/125mL/4 fl oz chicken stock
3 teaspoons cornflour blended with
2 tablespoons water
1 teaspoon French mustard
2 teaspoons chopped fresh basil
freshly ground black pepper
2 tablespoons grated fresh
Parmesan cheese, for garnish

minestrone

Method:

1 Place dried beans and 4 cups/1L/1³/₄ pt water in a large bowl, cover and set aside to soak for 8 hours or overnight.

2 Drain beans and rinse in cold water. Place beans and stock in a large saucepan, bring to the boil and boil for 10 minutes, then reduce heat, cover and simmer for 1 hour or until beans are tender.

3 Add mushrooms, green beans, carrots, zucchini (courgettes), leek and remaining water to pan. Bring to the boil, then reduce heat, cover and simmer for 30 minutes. Stir pasta and tomatoes into soup and cook for 10 minutes longer or until pasta is tender. Season to taste with black pepper. Sprinkle with Parmesan cheese and serve immediately.

Serves 6

ingredients

315g/10oz dried white beans
6 cups/1.5L/2¹/₂pt water
6 cups/1.5L/2¹/₂pt chicken stock
125g/4oz mushrooms, sliced
155g/5oz green beans, chopped
2 carrots, chopped
2 zucchini (courgettes), sliced
1 leek, sliced
155g/5oz small shell pasta
440g/14oz canned tomatoes,
undrained and mashed
freshly ground black pepper
grated Parmesan cheese

noodles
with bok choy sauce

Method:

1 Cook noodles in boiling water in a large saucepan, following packet directions. Drain, set aside and keep warm.
2 To make sauce, heat oil in a wok or frying pan over a high heat, add bok choy and stir-fry for 2-3 minutes. Add soy sauce, sesame oil, kechap manis, chilli sauce and ginger. Bring to a simmer and cook for 1 minute.
3 Add tofu and bean sprouts and stir-fry for 2-3 minutes or until heated through. Add noodles to pan and toss to combine. Serve immediately.

Serves 4

250g/8oz quick-cooking noodles
Bok choy sauce
1 tablespoon vegetable oil
2 bunches/500g/1 lb baby bok choy, leaves separated and trimmed
1/3 cup/90mL/3 fl oz soy sauce
2 tablespoons sesame oil
2 tablespoons kechap manis
2 tablespoons sweet chilli sauce
2 tablespoons pickled ginger
315g/10oz tofu, cut into 1 cm/1/2in cubes
15g/5oz bean sprouts

crispy noodles
and vegetables

Method:

1 Cook noodles in boiling water in a large saucepan for 2-3 minutes, drain and dry on absorbent kitchen paper. Heat oil in a large saucepan over a medium heat until a cube of bread dropped in browns in 50 seconds. Deep-fry noodles, in batches, for 2-3 minutes or until puffed and crispy. Drain on absorbent kitchen paper, set aside and keep warm.
2 Cook mixed vegetables following packet directions. Drain, set aside and keep warm.
3 To make sauce, place peanut butter, sugar, garlic, coconut milk, soy sauce and chilli sauce in a saucepan and cook over a low heat, stirring, for 3-5 minutes or until hot. To serve, divide noodles between serving plates, top with vegetables and sauce.

Serves 4

315g/10oz fresh thin egg noodles
vegetable oil for deep-frying
500g/1 lb packaged frozen Chinese stir-fry mixed vegetables
Peanut sauce
3/4 cup/200g/6 1/2oz crunchy peanut butter
1 tablespoon brown sugar
1 clove garlic, crushed
1 1/2 cups/375mL/12 fl oz coconut milk
2 tablespoons light soy sauce
2 teaspoons hot chilli sauce

Ravioli and vegetable medley

meat & poultry

For nutritious and filling main

meals, pasta served with a substantial sauce of meat or poultry is the answer.

For one-pot pasta dinners, braise cubes of meat or chicken pieces with onion and garlic for 30 minutes, then add 220g/7oz shell pasta or pasta spirals, 2 tablespoons tomato paste and enough hot water to cover. Continue to simmer for a further 25 minutes and the meal is ready.

Serve with a sprinkling of grated Romano or Parmesan cheese.

penne
bacon & basil

Method:

1 Cook penne in boiling water in a large saucepan, following packet directions. Drain, set aside and keep warm.

2 Heat oil in a large frying pan and cook garlic over a medium heat for 1 minute. Add bacon and cook for 2-3 minutes longer or until bacon is crispy. Add basil, walnuts and penne to pan, season to taste with black pepper and toss to combine. Sprinkle with Parmesan cheese and serve immediately.

Serves 4

ingredients

500g/1 lb penne
1 tablespoon olive oil
2 cloves garlic, minced
6 rashers bacon, chopped
2 tablespoons chopped fresh basil
60g/2oz chopped walnuts
freshly ground black pepper
30g/1oz grated Parmesan cheese

ravioli
with vegetable medley

Photograph Page 249

Method:

1 Cook ravioli in boiling water in a large saucepan, following packet directions. Drain, set aside and keep warm.

2 Melt butter in a large frying pan and cook garlic and mushrooms for 2-3 minutes. Add beans and tomatoes, season to taste with black pepper and cook for 2 minutes longer.

3 Add ravioli and Parmesan cheese to pan and toss to combine. Serve immediately.

Serves 4

ingredients

500g/1 lb ravioli of your choice
30g/1oz butter
2 cloves garlic, minced
125g/4oz button mushrooms, halved
125g/4oz green beans, cut into 1cm/¹/₂in lengths
125g/4oz cherry tomatoes, quartered
freshly ground black pepper
30g/1oz grated Parmesan cheese

fettuccine
with leeks

Method:

1 Cook fettuccine in boiling water in a large saucepan following packet directions. Drain, set aside and keep warm.

2 Heat butter in a large frying pan and cook leeks for 8-10 minutes or until tender. Add ham and red capsicum (pepper) and cook for 2-3 minutes longer. Stir in cream, bring to the boil, then reduce heat and simmer for 4-5 minutes.

3 Add fettuccine to pan and toss to combine. Season with black pepper (to taste), and serve immediately.

Serves 4

500g/1 lb fettuccine
60g/2oz butter
2 large leeks, halved and thinly sliced
185g/6oz ham, cut into strips
1 red capsicum (pepper), cut into strips
1 cup/250mL/8 fl oz thickened (double) cream
freshly ground black pepper

cheesy meatballs
& spaghetti

Method:

1 *To make meatballs, place beef, parsley, Parmesan cheese, tomato paste (purée) and egg in a bowl, and mix to combine. Form mixture into small balls and cook in a non-stick frying pan for 4-5 minutes or until brown. Remove meatballs from pan and drain on absorbent kitchen paper.*

2 *To make sauce, melt butter in a large frying pan and cook onion, basil and oregano for 2-3 minutes or until onion is soft. Stir in tomatoes, tomato paste (purée), beef stock, wine and sugar. Bring to the boil, then reduce heat and simmer, stirring occasionally, for 30 minutes or until sauce reduces and thickens. Season to taste with black pepper. Add meatballs to sauce and cook for 5 minutes longer.*

3 *Cook spaghetti in boiling water in a large saucepan following packet directions. Drain, place in a warm serving bowl and top with meatballs and sauce. Serve immediately.*

What's the easiest way to eat ribbon pasta?

Firstly, serve it in a shallow bowl or on a plate with a slight rim. To ensure that the pasta stays hot while you are eating it, heat the plates before serving. To eat the pasta, slip a few strands on to your fork, then twirl them against the plate, or a spoon, into a ball — the trick is to take only small forkfuls and to wind the pasta tightly so that there are no dangling strands.

Serves 4

ingredients

250g/8oz spaghetti
<u>Cheesy meatballs</u>
500g/1 lb lean ground beef
**2 tablespoons finely chopped
fresh parsley**
¹/₂ cup/60g/2oz grated Parmesan cheese
2 teaspoons tomato paste (purée)
1 egg, beaten
<u>Tomato sauce</u>
15g/¹/₂oz butter
1 onion, finely chopped
2 teaspoons dried basil
1 teaspoon dried oregano
**440g/14oz canned tomatoes,
undrained and mashed**
2 tablespoons tomato paste (purée)
¹/₂ cup/125mL/4 fl oz beef stock
¹/₂ cup/125mL/4 fl oz white wine
1 teaspoon caster sugar
freshly ground black pepper

fettuccine
carbonara

Method:

1 Cook pasta in boiling water in a large saucepan following packet directions. Drain, set aside and keep warm.

2 To make sauce, cook ham, prosciutto or bacon in a frying pan over a medium heat for 3 minutes or until crisp.

3 Stir in stock and cream, bring to simmering and simmer until sauce is reduced by half.

4 Remove pan from heat, whisk in eggs, parsley and black pepper to taste. Return pan to heat and cook, stirring, for 1 minute. Remove pan from heat, add hot pasta to sauce and toss to combine. Serve immediately.

Serves 6

ingredients

500g/1 lb fettuccine
<u>**Carbonara sauce**</u>
250g/8oz ham, prosciutto or bacon, chopped
½ cup/125mL/4fl oz chicken stock
1 cup/250mL/8fl oz cream (double)
7 eggs, lightly beaten
2 tablespoons chopped flat-leaf parsley
freshly ground black pepper

hot shallot
& semi-dried tomato pasta

Hot shallot & semi-dried tomato pasta

Serves 4

meat &
poultry

ingredients

¹/₂ bunch spring onions
250g/1 lb bow pasta
1 teaspoon butter
1 tablespoon olive oil
1 small chilli, seeded and sliced
2 tablespoons brandy
300mL/10 fl oz cream
¹/₃ cup sun-dried tomatoes
freshly ground black pepper to taste

Method:

1 *Wash and trim spring onions. Slice into 2cm/³/₄in lengths. Place pasta in boiling water and cook until al dente. Drain, and place in warm serving bowl.*

2 *Heat butter and oil in frying-pan, sauté shallots and chilli for 1 minute. Add brandy, cream and sliced sun-dried tomatoes. Simmer until sauce thickens. Season with pepper.*

3 *Pour over pasta. Serve with Parmesan cheese and sprinkle with freshly ground black pepper.*

traditional
lasagne

Method:

1 To make cheese sauce, melt butter in a saucepan over a medium heat. Stir in flour and cook, stirring, for 1 minute. Remove pan from heat and whisk in milk. Return pan to heat and cook, stirring, for 4-5 minutes or until sauce boils and thickens. Stir in cheese and black pepper to taste and set aside.

2 To make meat sauce, heat oil in a frying pan over a medium heat. Add onions and garlic and cook, stirring, for 3 minutes or until onions are soft. Add beef and cook, stirring, for 5 minutes or until beef is brown. Stir in tomatoes, wine and herbs, bring to simmering point and simmer, stirring occasionally, for 15 minutes or until sauce reduces and thickens. Season to taste with black pepper.

3 Line the base of a large greased baking dish with 6 lasagne sheets. Top with one-quarter of the meat sauce and one-quarter of the cheese sauce. Repeat layers to use all ingredients, ending with a layer of cheese sauce.

4 Sprinkle top of lasagne with mozzarella cheese and bake for 30-40 minutes or until it is hot and bubbling and top is golden.

Serves 6

ingredients

24 sheets instant* lasagne
60g/2oz mozzarella cheese, grated
Cheese sauce
75g/2¹/₂oz butter
¹/₃ cup/45g/1¹/₂oz flour
2 cups/500mL/16 fl oz milk
90g/3oz tasty cheese
(mature Cheddar), grated
freshly ground black pepper
Meat sauce
2 teaspoons vegetable oil
2 onions, chopped
2 cloves garlic, crushed
1.25kg/2¹/₂ lb ground beef
2 x 440g/14oz canned tomatoes,
undrained and mashed
³/₄ cup/185mL/6 fl oz red wine
2 tablespoons chopped mixed herbs

*No precooking required

Oven temperature 180°C, 350°F, Gas 4

smoked chicken
pappardelle

Method:

1 Cook pasta in boiling water in a large saucepan following packet directions. Drain, set aside and keep warm.

2 Heat a non-stick frying pan over a medium heat, add chicken and cook, stirring, for 1 minute. Add wine, cream, chives and black pepper to taste, bring to a simmer and cook for 2 minutes. To serve, top pasta with chicken mixture and nasturtium butter.

Nasturtium butter: Mix all ingredients well together.

Serves 6

ingredients

750g/1½ lb pappardelle
1.5kg/3 lb smoked chicken, skin removed and flesh sliced
½ cup/125mL/4 fl oz white wine
1 cup/250mL/8 fl oz cream
2 tablespoons snipped fresh chives
freshly ground black pepper
<u>Nasturtium butter</u>
125g/4oz butter, softened
1 clove garlic, crushed
1 tablespoon lime juice
6 nasturtium flowers, finely chopped

pasta shapes
with avocado sauce

Method:

1 Cook pasta in boiling water in a large saucepan, following packet directions. Drain, set aside and keep warm.

2 To make sauce, place avocado, ricotta cheese, lime juice, lime rind, milk, coriander (cilantro) and black pepper (to taste) in a food processor or blender and process until smooth. Set aside.

3 Boil, steam or microwave snow peas (mangetout) and squash or zucchini (courgettes) separately until just tender. Drain well. Add vegetables to hot pasta and toss to combine. To serve, top pasta with sauce and shavings of Parmesan cheese, if using.

Serves 6

ingredients

500g/1 lb pasta shapes of your choice
125g/4oz snow peas
(mangetout), trimmed
125g/4oz yellow squash or
zucchini (courgettes), sliced
fresh Parmesan cheese (optional)
<u>Avocado sauce</u>
1 avocado, stoned and peeled
1 cup/250g/8oz ricotta cheese, drained
1 tablespoon lime juice
2 teaspoons finely grated lime rind
2 tablespoons milk
2 tablespoons chopped fresh coriander (cilantro)
freshly ground black pepper

chicken
and mango pasta salad

Method:

1 Cook pasta in boiling water in a large saucepan, following packet directions. Drain, rinse under cold running water, then drain again.
2 Place pasta, chicken, water chestnuts and mangoes in a bowl and toss to combine.
3 To make dressing, place mayonnaise, chutney, spring onions, coriander (cilantro) and black pepper (to taste) in a bowl and mix to combine. Spoon dressing over salad and toss to combine. Cover and chill until required.

Serves 6

ingredients

500g/1 lb large shell pasta
Flesh of 1 cooked chicken,
cut into bite-sized pieces
220g/7oz canned water chestnuts,
drained and sliced
440g/14oz canned mangoes,
drained and sliced
<u>Mango chutney dressing</u>
1 cup/250g/8oz low-fat mayonnaise
1/2 cup/155g/5oz sweet mango chutney
2 spring onions, finely chopped
2 tablespoons chopped fresh coriander (cilantro)
freshly ground black pepper

gnocchi
with gorgonzola sauce

Method:

1 Cook gnocchi in boiling water in a large saucepan, following packet directions. Drain, set aside and keep warm.

2 To make sauce, place Gorgonzola or blue cheese, milk and butter in a saucepan and cook over low heat, stirring, for 4-5 minutes or until cheese melts. Stir in walnuts, cream and black pepper to taste. Bring to a simmer and cook for 5 minutes or until sauce reduces and thickens. Spoon sauce over hot gnocchi and toss to combine.

Serves 6

ingredients

500g/1 lb potato gnocchi
Gorgonzola sauce
200g/6¹/₂oz Gorgonzola or blue cheese, crumbled
³/₄ cup/185mL/6fl oz milk
60g/2oz butter
60g/2oz walnuts, toasted and chopped
200mL/6¹/₂fl oz thickened cream (double)
freshly ground black pepper

spaghetti
bolognaise

Method:

1 To make sauce, heat oil in a frying pan over a medium heat. Add garlic and onion and cook, stirring, for 3 minutes or until onion is soft.

2 Add beef and cook, stirring, for 5 minutes or until meat is well browned. Stir in tomato purée (passata), wine or water, oregano and thyme. Bring to a simmer and cook, stirring occasionally, for 15 minutes or until sauce reduces and thickens. Season to taste with black pepper.

3 Cook pasta in boiling water in a large saucepan following packet directions. Drain well. To serve, spoon sauce over hot pasta and top with Parmesan cheese.

Serves 4

ingredients

500g/1 lb spaghetti
grated Parmesan cheese (optional)
Bolognaise sauce
2 teaspoons vegetable oil
1 clove garlic, minced
1 onion, chopped
500g/1 lb ground beef
440g/14oz canned tomato purée (passata)
¹/₄ cup/60mL/2fl oz red wine or water
1 tablespoon chopped fresh oregano or ¹/₂ teaspoon dried oregano
1 tablespoon chopped fresh thyme or ¹/₂ teaspoon dried thyme
freshly ground black pepper

chicken
pasta toss

Method:

1 Cook pasta in boiling water in a large saucepan, following packet directions. Drain, set aside and keep warm.
2 Melt butter in a large frying pan and cook onion and garlic, stirring, over a medium heat for 3-4 minutes. Add chicken and stock, and cook for 4-5 minutes longer.
3 Add spinach and pasta to pan, season to taste with black pepper and toss to combine. Sprinkle with pine nuts and serve immediately.

Serves 4

ingredients

500g/1 lb shell pasta
30g/1oz butter
1 onion, finely chopped
1 clove garlic, crushed
250g/8oz cooked chicken, shredded
1/2 cup/125mL/4fl oz chicken stock
6 spinach leaves, shredded
freshly ground black pepper
60g/2oz pine nuts, toasted

pepperoni
toss

Method:

1 Cook spaghetti in boiling water in a large saucepan, following packet directions. Drain, set aside and keep warm.
2 Heat oil in a large frying pan and cook onion over a medium heat for 5-6 minutes or until onion is transparent. Add olives and salami and cook for 2 minutes longer.
3 Add spaghetti to pan and toss to combine. Serve immediately.

Serves 6

375g/12oz spaghetti
1 tablespoon olive oil
1 onion, finely chopped
90g/3oz black olives, chopped
125g/4oz pepperoni salami, chopped

spirelli
with ham

Method:

1 Cook spirelli in boiling water in a large saucepan, following packet directions. Drain, set aside and keep warm.
2 Heat oil in a frying pan and cook ham and artichokes for 1-2 minutes.
3 Add spirelli to pan and toss to combine. Remove from heat and quickly stir in egg mixture. Season to taste with black pepper. Serve as soon as the eggs start to stick to spirelli – this will take only a few seconds.

Serves 4

ingredients

500g/1 lb fresh or 410g/13oz
dried spirelli or spiral pasta
2 teaspoons olive oil
315g/10oz ham, cut into strips
6 canned artichoke hearts,
sliced lengthwise
3 eggs, beaten with 1 tablespoon
grated fresh Parmesan cheese
freshly ground black pepper

spaghetti
carbonara

Method:

1 Cook ham in a non-stick frying pan for 2-3 minutes. Place eggs, cream and Parmesan cheese in a bowl and beat lightly to combine.

2 Cook spaghetti in boiling water in a large saucepan following packet directions. Drain spaghetti, add egg mixture and ham and toss so that the heat of the spaghetti cooks the sauce. Season to taste with black pepper and serve immediately.

Serves 4

ingredients

185g/6oz slices ham, cut into strips
4 eggs
1/3 cup/90mL/3fl oz pure cream (single)
90g/3oz grated fresh Parmesan cheese
500g/1 lb spaghetti
freshly ground black pepper

warm pasta
and salami salad

Method:

1 Cook pasta in boiling water in a large saucepan, following packet directions. Drain, set aside and keep warm.

2 Heat oil in a large frying pan and cook garlic and pine nuts, stirring constantly, over a medium heat for 1-2 minutes. Remove pan from heat and stir in salami and parsley. Add salami mixture to pasta and toss to combine. Serve while still warm.

Serves 4 as a light meal

ingredients

250g/8oz large shell pasta
1 tablespoon olive oil
2 cloves garlic, minced
60g/2oz pine nuts
125g/4oz salami, thinly sliced
1 tablespoon chopped fresh parsley

pork-and-sage
filled ravioli

Method:

I To make filling, place ricotta cheese, bacon, pork, parsley, sage and Parmesan cheese in a bowl. Mix to combine and season to taste with nutmeg and black pepper. Cover and set aside while making pasta.

Assemble, following directions for making ravioli.

ingredients

ingredients

1 quantity Homemade Pasta dough (see recipe page 307)
grated fresh Parmesan cheese
<u>Pork and sage filling</u>
315g/10oz ricotta cheese, drained
60g/2oz lean bacon, finely chopped
155g/5oz lean cooked pork, finely diced
1 teaspoon finely chopped fresh parsley
¹/₂ teaspoon finely chopped fresh sage
1 teaspoon grated fresh Parmesan cheese
grated nutmeg
freshly ground black pepper

chicken
pasta salad

Method:

1 Cook plain, spinach and tomato tagliatelle together in boiling water in a large saucepan, following packet directions. Drain, rinse under cold running water, then drain again and set aside to cool completely.

2 Heat oil in a large frying pan and cook onions and garlic, stirring, over a medium heat for 2-3 minutes. Add chicken, oregano and basil and cook, stirring, for 10 minutes longer or until chicken is cooked. Remove pan from heat and set aside to cool completely. Place cooked chicken mixture, artichokes, red capsicum (pepper), olives and tagliatelle in a large salad bowl. Season to taste with black pepper and toss to combine.

Serves 6

ingredients

155g/5oz plain tagliatelle
155g/5oz spinach tagliatelle
155g/5oz tomato tagliatelle
2 tablespoons olive oil
2 red onions, cut into eighths
2 cloves garlic, minced
500g/1 lb chicken breast fillets, chopped
1 tablespoon finely chopped fresh oregano
or 1 teaspoon dried oregano
1 tablespoon finely chopped fresh basil
or 1 teaspoon dried basil
440g/14oz canned artichoke hearts, drained and halved
1 red capsicum (pepper), cut into strips
90g/3oz green olives, drained
freshly ground black pepper

vegetable
pasta salad

Photograph opposite

Method:

1 Cook pasta in boiling water in a large saucepan, following packet directions. Drain, rinse under cold running water, then drain again and set aside to cool completely.

2 Boil, steam or microwave broccoli for 2-3 minutes or until it just changes colour. Refresh under cold running water. Drain, then dry on absorbent kitchen paper.

3 To make dressing, place vinegar, oil, Parmesan cheese, garlic and black pepper to taste in a screw-top jar and shake to combine.

4 Place pasta, broccoli, tomatoes, spring onions and olives in a salad bowl. Pour dressing over and toss to combine.

Serves 8

ingredients

500g/1 lb small pasta shapes of your choice
250g/8oz broccoli, broken into florets
250g/8oz cherry tomatoes, halved
6 spring onions, cut into 2¹/₂cm/1in lengths
12 black olives
Red wine dressing
2 tablespoons red wine vinegar
¹/₄ cup/125mL/4fl oz olive oil
2 tablespoons grated fresh Parmesan cheese
1 clove garlic, crushed
freshly ground black pepper

seafood

Spaghetti with tuna and cress

Seafood and pasta team well

together as do their nutritional values. The high-protein low-fat seafood combined with the complex-carbohydrate pasta make a nutritionally well-balanced meal. Add a tossed salad to complete your nutritional requirements.

Shellfish is a wonderful ingredient for pasta dishes. Quick to cook, attractive to serve, and a delight to eat, what could be better than seafood pasta and a glass of good wine?

Fresh fish or canned varieties are equally suitable to use. Simmer your favourite seafood in any of the wide range of sauces provided in this book and serve with your favourite pasta.

scallop
and capsicum pasta

ingredients

Method:
1 To make Gremolata, place garlic, parsley and lemon rind in a bowl and mix well to combine.
2 Cook pasta in boiling water in a large saucepan , following packet directions. Drain, set aside and keep warm.
3 Heat oil in a frying pan over a medium heat. Add scallops and prosciutto or ham and cook, stirring, for 3 minutes or until scallops just turn opaque and prosciutto or ham is crisp. Remove pan from heat, stir in lemon juice, basil and black pepper to taste and set aside.
4 Place stock in a saucepan, bring to a simmer and cook until reduced by half. Add red capsicum (pepper) and leeks and simmer for 3 minutes. Add pasta and scallop mixture to stock mixture. Toss to combine and top with Gremolata.

Serves 4

ingredients

500g/1 lb tagliarini
1 tablespoon olive oil
500g/1 lb scallops
100g/3¹/₂oz prosciutto or lean ham, cut into thin strips
2 tablespoons lemon juice
2 tablespoons chopped fresh basil or 1 teaspoon dried basil
freshly ground black pepper
1 cup/250mL/8fl oz chicken stock
1 red capsicum(pepper), cut into strips
2 leeks, cut into strips
Gremolata
3 cloves garlic, minced
¹/₂ bunch flat-leaf parsley, leaves finely chopped
1 tablespoon finely grated lemon rind

spaghetti
with tuna & cress

Photograph Page 271

ingredients

Method:
1 Cook pasta in boiling water in a large saucepan of boiling water, following packet directions. Drain well and place in a large serving bowl.
2 Add tuna, watercress, olives, lime rind, ginger, vinegar, oil and lime juice to hot pasta and toss to combine. Serve immediately.

Serves 4

500g/1 lb spaghetti
500g/1 lb tuna steaks, thinly sliced
1 bunch/250g/8oz watercress, leaves removed and stems discarded
125g/4oz black olives
1 tablespoon finely grated lime rind
2 teaspoons finely grated fresh ginger
¹/₄ cup/60mL/2fl oz balsamic or red wine vinegar
1 tablespoon olive oil
2 tablespoons lime juice

raspberry
salmon pasta

Method:

1 To make mayonnaise, place raspberries in a food processor or blender and process until smooth. Push purée through a fine sieve and discard seeds. Add mayonnaise, mustard and lemon juice to purée, mix to combine and set aside.

2 Cook pasta in boiling water in a large saucepan, following packet directions. Drain, set aside and keep warm.

3 Heat oil in a frying or grill pan over a medium heat. Brush salmon with lemon juice and sprinkle with dill. Place salmon in pan and cook for 2-3 minutes each side or until flesh flakes when tested with a fork. Remove salmon from pan and cut into thick slices.

4 To serve, divide pasta between six serving plates. Top with salmon slices and drizzle with raspberry mayonnaise. Serve immediately.

Serves 6

ingredients

**500g/1 lb pepper or plain fettuccine
1 tablespoon vegetable oil
500g/1 lb salmon fillet, bones and skin removed
2 tablespoons lemon juice
2 tablespoons chopped fresh dill
<u>Raspberry mayonnaise</u>
200g/6¹/₂oz raspberries
1 cup/250g/8oz low-fat mayonnaise
2 teaspoons wholegrain mustard
1 tablespoon lemon juice**

lobster
in pasta nets

Method:

1 Cook pasta in boiling water in a large saucepan until almost cooked. Drain, rinse under cold running water, drain again and pat dry on absorbent kitchen paper. Set aside.

2 To make lime cream, place mayonnaise, sour cream, lime rind, lime juice, mustard and tarragon in a bowl and mix to combine. Set aside.

3 Dust lobster pieces with flour. Wrap a few stands of pasta around each lobster piece. Continue wrapping with pasta to form a net effect around lobster.

4 Heat oil in a large saucepan until a cube of bread dropped in browns in 50 seconds. Cook pasta-wrapped lobster in batches for 2-3 minutes or until golden. Drain on absorbent kitchen paper and serve immediately with lime cream.

ingredients

375g/12oz angel-hair pasta
3 uncooked lobster tails, shelled and flesh cut into 4 cm/1 ¹/₂in pieces,
flour
vegetable oil for deep frying
<u>Lime cream</u>
¹/₂ cup/125g/4oz mayonnaise
¹/₄ cup/60g/2oz sour cream
1 tablespoon finely grated lime rind
1 tablespoon lime juice
1 tablespoon wholegrain mustard
2 tablespoons chopped fresh tarragon
or 1 teaspoon dried tarragon

Lobster in pasta nets

Serves 4

avocado
salmon salad

ingredients

375g/12oz bow pasta
1 large avocado, stoned, peeled and roughly chopped
1 teaspoon finely grated orange rind
2 tablespoons fresh orange juice
freshly ground black pepper
4 slices smoked salmon
4 sprigs fresh dill
1 orange, segmented

Method:

1 Cook pasta in boiling water in a large saucepan, following packet directions. Drain, rinse under cold running water, then drain again and set aside to cool completely.

2 Place avocado, orange rind, orange juice and black pepper (to taste) in a food processor or blender and process until smooth.

3 Place pasta in a bowl, top with avocado mixture and toss to combine. Roll salmon slices into cornets and fill with a dill sprig. Divide salad between four serving plates and top with salmon cornets and orange segments.

Serves 4 as a light meal

pasta
with broccoli and anchovy sauce

Method:

1 Cook broccoli florets in boiling water for 1-2 minutes, ensuring they are still crisp.

2 In a frying-pan heat the oil. Cook anchovy fillets and garlic slivers, stirring until anchovies disintegrate. Stir in the chilli and add cooked broccoli and pepper to taste.

3 Meanwhile, cook the pasta in boiling, salted water until al dente. Drain and add sauce. Mix carefully and serve

Serves 4-6

ingredients

500g/1lb broccoli, cut into florets
125mL/4fl oz olive oil
6 anchovy fillets, drained
3 garlic cloves, peeled and thinly sliced
1/2 teaspoon freshly chopped chilli
freshly ground black pepper
410g/13oz pasta of choice

quick fettuccine
with scallops

Method:

1 Cook fettuccine in boiling water in a large saucepan, following packet directions. Drain, set aside and keep warm.

2 To make sauce, melt butter in a large frying pan and cook red capsicum (pepper) and spring onions for 1-2 minutes. Add cream and bring to the boil, then reduce heat and simmer for 5 minutes or until sauce reduces slightly and thickens.

3 Stir scallops into sauce and cook for 2-3 minutes or until scallops are opaque. Season to taste with black pepper. Place fettuccine in a warm serving bowl, top with sauce and sprinkle with parsley.

Serves 4

ingredients

500g/1 lb fettuccine
Scallop sauce
30g/1oz butter
1 red capsicum (pepper), cut into strips
2 spring onions, finely chopped
1 cup/250mL/8 fl oz
thickened cream (double)
500g/1 lb scallops
freshly ground black pepper
1 tablespoon finely chopped
fresh parsley

tagliatelle
with chilli octopus

Method:

1 To make marinade, place sesame oil, ginger, lime juice and chilli sauce in a large bowl and mix to combine. Add octopus, tossing to coat, then cover and marinate in the refrigerator for 3-4 hours.

2 Cook pasta in boiling water in a large saucepan, following packet directions. Drain, set aside and keep warm.

3 To make sauce, heat oil in a saucepan over a medium heat. Add spring onions and cook, stirring, for 1 minute. Stir in tomato purée (passata), bring to a simmer and cook for 4 minutes.

4 Cook octopus under a preheated hot grill for 5-7 minutes or until tender. Add octopus to sauce and toss to combine. Spoon octopus mixture over hot pasta and toss to combine.

Serves 4

ingredients

1kg/2 lb baby octopus, cleaned
500g/1 lb spinach tagliatelle
Chilli ginger marinade
1 tablespoon sesame oil
1 tablespoon grated fresh ginger
2 tablespoons lime juice
2 tablespoon sweet chilli sauce
Tomato sauce
2 teaspoons vegetable oil
3 spring onions, sliced diagonally
440g/14oz canned tomato
purée (passata)

pasta
shells with anchovy sauce

Method:

1 Cook pasta shells in boiling water in a large saucepan, following packet directions. Drain, set aside and keep warm.

2 To make sauce, heat oil in a large frying pan and cook onions and garlic over a medium heat for 10 minutes or until onions are soft. Stir in wine and anchovies and bring to the boil. Cook for 2-3 minutes or until wine reduces by half.

3 Stir in rosemary and stock and bring back to the boil. Cook until sauces reduces and thickens slightly. Add chilli and pasta to sauce, toss to combine, sprinkle with Parmesan cheese and serve immediately.

Serves 4

ingredients

500g/1 lb small shell pasta
60g/2oz grated fresh Parmesan cheese
<u>**Anchovy sauce**</u>
2 tablespoons olive oil
3 onions, chopped
1 clove garlic, minced
1/2 cup/125mL/4fl oz dry white wine
8 canned anchovies
1 tablespoon chopped fresh rosemary leaves or 1 teaspoon dried rosemary
1 cup/250mL/8fl oz beef or chicken stock
1 fresh red chilli, seeded and cut into rings

macaroni
with tomato sauce

Photograph opposite

Method:

1 Cook macaroni in boiling water in a large saucepan, following packet directions. Drain, set aside and keep warm.

2 To make sauce, heat oil in a frying pan and cook onion for 3-4 minutes or until soft. Stir in garlic, tomatoes and wine and cook, stirring constantly, over a medium heat for 5 minutes. Bring to the boil, then reduce heat and simmer, uncovered, for 10-15 minutes or until sauce reduces and thickens. Add basil and season to taste with black pepper.

3 Add sauce to hot macaroni and toss to combine. Serve immediately.

Serves 4

ingredients

500g/1 lb wholemeal macaroni
<u>**Chunky tomato sauce**</u>
2 tablespoons olive oil
1 onion, chopped
1 clove garlic, minced
2 x 440g/14oz canned Italian-style tomatoes, undrained and mashed
1/4 cup/60mL/2fl oz dry white wine
1 tablespoon chopped fresh basil
freshly ground black pepper

oriental
vegetable noodles

Method:

1 Cook noodles in boiling water in a large saucepan following packet directions. Drain and set aside to keep warm.
2 Heat oil in a wok or large frying pan over a high heat, add garlic, ginger, fish and prawns and stir-fry for 2 minutes or until prawns just change colour.
3 Add spring onions, red capsicum (pepper) and bok choy (Chinese cabbage) to pan and stir-fry for 3 minutes longer. Add sweet corn, snow peas (mangetout), and mushrooms and stir-fry for 3 minutes.
4 Add mint, chilli sauce, soy sauce, plum sauce, lime juice and noodles and stir-fry for 3 minutes or until heated through. Serve immediately.

ingredients

315g/10oz fresh egg noodles
1 tablespoon sesame oil
1 clove garlic, crushed
1 tablespoon grated fresh ginger
185g/6oz firm white fish fillets,
cut into 2cm/³/₄in pieces
155g/5oz green prawns, shelled and deveined
4 spring onions, sliced
1 red capsicum (pepper), sliced
250g/8oz bok choy (Chinese cabbage), chopped
375g/12oz canned whole baby sweet corn,
125g/4oz snow peas (mangetout)
125g/4oz fresh shiitake mushrooms, sliced
2 tablespoons chopped fresh mint
2 tablespoons sweet chilli sauce
2 tablespoons sweet soy sauce
1 tablespoon plum sauce
1 tablespoon lime juice

pasta
with anchovies & basil sauce

Method:

1 Heat the oil and sauté garlic and anchovies until garlic is only just yellow in colour. Turn heat to very low, and then toss halved tomatoes, basil leaves, sun-dried tomatoes and capers in with the anchovies and oil.

2 Cook pasta in boiling, salted water until al dente and drain thoroughly. Pour sauce over fresh pasta and garnish with fresh chopped basil and sprinkle black pepper to taste.

Serves 4

ingredients

250mL/8fl oz olive oil
2 cloves garlic, minced
8 anchovy fillets, reserve oil
2 punnets cherry tomatoes, halved
20 fresh basil leaves, roughly chopped
12 sun-dried tomatoes, sliced
2 teaspoons capers
500g/1 lb egg fettuccine
$^1/_2$ cup fresh basil, chopped
freshly ground black pepper

penne with tuna
olives & artichokes

Method:

1 Cook the pasta in boiling salted water until al dente. Drain, and rinse in cold water.
2 Heat 2 tablespoons of the oil in a pan, add the garlic and chilli, and cook for 2-3 minutes. Return the cooked pasta to the pan, add the remaining ingredients and heat through.
3 Serve immediately with Parmesan cheese.

Serves 4-6

ingredients

500g/1 lb penne pasta
6 tablespoons olive oil
2 cloves garlic, minced
3 chillies, seeded and finely chopped
1 cup black olives, seeded
400g/13oz can artichokes
2 tablespoons capers, finely chopped
425g/14oz can tuna, drained

tuna-filled
shells

Method:

1 Cook 8 pasta shells in a large saucepan of boiling water until al dente. Drain, rinse under cold running water and drain again. Set aside, then repeat with remaining shells, ensure cooked shells do not overlap.

2 To make filling, place ricotta cheese and tuna in a bowl and mix to combine. Mix in red capsicum (pepper), capers, chives and 2 tablespoons grated Swiss cheese, nutmeg and black pepper to taste.

3 Fill each shell with ricotta mixture, and place in a lightly greased, shallow ovenproof dish. Sprinkle with Parmesan cheese and remaining Swiss cheese. Place under a preheated grill and cook until cheese melts.

Makes 16

ingredients

16 giant pasta shells
Tuna filling
250g/8oz ricotta cheese, drained
440g/14oz canned tuna in brine, drained and flaked
1/2 red capsicum (pepper), diced
1 tablespoon chopped capers
1 teaspoon snipped fresh chives
4 tablespoons grated Swiss cheese
pinch ground nutmeg
freshly ground black pepper
2 tablespoons grated fresh Parmesan cheese

vegetabl

llnguine with chilli and lemon

A healthy way to enjoy pasta is

with vegetable sauces. Any vegetable combination enriched with fresh herbs, spiced up with garlic, chilli or curry, may be tossed through your favourite pasta. Vegetarian eating has become increasingly popular. Whether it's the committed vegetarian or simply the cook looking for new and interesting ways to make the most of fresh vegetables and delicious pasta, there are recipes that will appeal in this chapter.

You will also discover that Italy is not the only country with a cuisine that includes pasta — many European countries also have wonderful pasta dishes. Of course, there is also Oriental pasta which includes such delicacies as Chinese egg and rice noodles and Japanese soba noodles.

fettuccine
with spinach sauce

Method:

1 Cook pasta in boiling water in a large saucepan, following packet directions. Drain, set aside and keep warm.

2 To make sauce, melt butter in a saucepan over a medium heat, add garlic and leek and cook, stirring, for 3 minutes. Add spinach and cook for 3 minutes longer or until spinach wilts.

3 Place spinach mixture, cream cheese, grated Parmesan cheese and stock in a food processor or blender and process until smooth. Return sauce to a clean saucepan, bring to a simmer and cook, stirring constantly, for 5-6 minutes or until sauce thickens and is heated through.

4 Spoon sauce over hot pasta and toss to combine. Serve topped with shavings of Parmesan cheese.

Serves 4

ingredients

500g/1 lb fettuccine
fresh Parmesan cheese
<u>**Spinach sauce**</u>
15g/¹⁄₂oz butter
1 clove garlic, minced
1 leek, sliced
500g/1 lb English spinach, chopped
250g/8oz low-fat cream cheese
2 tablespoons grated Parmesan cheese
¹⁄₂ cup/125mL/4fl oz chicken stock

linguine
with chilli & lemon

Photograph Page 285

ingredients

Method:

1 Cook pasta in boiling water in a large saucepan, following packet directions. Drain, set aside and keep warm.

2 Heat oil in a frying pan over a low heat, add garlic and chillies and cook, stirring, for 6 minutes or until garlic is golden. Add garlic mixture, rocket (arugola), lemon rind, lemon juice, black pepper (to taste) and Parmesan cheese to hot pasta and toss to combine.

Serves 4

500g/1 lb fresh linguine or spaghetti
2 tablespoons olive oil
6 cloves garlic, peeled
2 fresh red chillies, seeded and sliced
125g/4oz rocket (arugola), shredded
3 teaspoons finely grated lemon rind
2 tablespoons lemon juice
freshly ground black pepper
90g/3oz grated Parmesan cheese

penne
napolitana

Method:
1 Cook pasta in boiling water in a large saucepan, following packet directions. Drain, set aside and keep warm.
2 To make sauce, heat oil in a saucepan over a medium heat. Add onions and garlic and cook, stirring, for 3 minutes or until onions are soft.
3 Stir in tomatoes, wine, parsley, oregano and black pepper to taste. Bring to a simmer and cook for 15 minutes or until sauce reduces and thickens.
4 To serve, spoon sauce over hot pasta and top with shavings of Parmesan cheese.
Serves 4

ingredients

500g/1 lb penne
fresh Parmesan cheese
<u>Napolitana sauce</u>
2 teaspoons olive oil
2 onions, chopped
2 cloves garlic, minced
2 x 440g/14oz canned tomatoes,
undrained and mashed
³/₄ cup/185mL/6fl oz red wine
1 tablespoon chopped flat-leaf parsley
1 tablespoon chopped fresh oregano
or ¹/₂ teaspoon dried oregano
freshly ground black pepper

fettuccine
pesto

Method:

1 Cook pasta in boiling water in a large saucepan, following packet directions. Drain, set aside and keep warm.

2 To make pesto, place Parmesan cheese, garlic, pine nuts and basil in a food processor or blender and process to finely chop. With machine running, gradually add oil and continue processing to form a smooth paste. To serve, spoon pesto over hot pasta and toss to combine.

Serves 4

ingredients

500g/1 lb fettuccine
Basil pesto
100g/3¹/₂oz fresh Parmesan cheese, chopped
2 cloves garlic, minced
60g/2oz pine nuts
1 large bunch basil, leaves removed and stems discarded
¹/₄ cup/60mL/2fl oz olive oil

vegetable
& chilli pasta

Method:

1 Cut eggplant (aubergines) into 2cm/³/₄in cubes. Place in a colander, sprinkle with salt and set aside to drain for 10 minutes. Rinse eggplant under cold running water and pat dry.

2 Cook pasta in boiling water in a large saucepan, following packet directions. Drain, set aside and keep warm.

3 Heat oil in a large frying pan over a medium heat and cook eggplant in batches, for 5 minutes or until golden. Remove eggplant from pan, drain on absorbent kitchen paper and set aside.

4 Add onions, chillies and garlic to pan and cook, stirring, for 3 minutes or until onions are golden. Stir in tomatoes, wine and basil, bring to a simmer and cook for 5 minutes. To serve, spoon sauce over hot pasta.

Serves 4

ingredients

2 eggplant, (aubergines)
salt
500g/1 lb pasta shells
¹/₄ cup/60mL/2fl oz olive oil
2 onions, chopped
2 fresh red chillies, seeded and chopped
2 cloves garlic, minced
2 x 440g/14oz canned tomatoes, undrained and mashed
¹/₂ cup/125mL/4fl oz dry white wine
2 tablespoons chopped fresh basil or
1 teaspoon dried basil

289

tortellini
& avocado cream

Method:
1 Cook tortellini in boiling water in a large saucepan following packet directions. Drain, set aside and keep warm.
2 To make Avocado Cream, place avocado, cream, Parmesan cheese and lemon juice in a food processor or blender and process until smooth. Season to taste with black pepper.
3 Place tortellini in a warm serving bowl, add Avocado Cream and toss to combine. Serve immediately.

Serves 4

ingredients

500g/1 lb tortellini
<u>Avocado cream</u>
1/2 ripe avocado, stoned and peeled
1/4 cup/60mL/2fl oz cream (double)
30g/1oz grated fresh Parmesan cheese
1 teaspoon lemon juice
freshly ground black pepper

rigatoni
with pumpkin

Method:

1 Cook rigatoni in boiling water in a large saucepan, following packet directions. Drain, set aside and keep warm.

2 Melt 60g/2oz butter in a large saucepan and cook pumpkin over a medium heat for 5-10 minutes or until tender.

3 Stir chives, nutmeg, Parmesan cheese, black pepper (to taste), rigatoni and remaining butter into pumpkin mixture and toss to combine. Serve immediately.

Serves 4

500g/1 lb rigatoni
90g/3oz butter
250g/8oz pumpkin,
cut into small cubes
1 tablespoon snipped fresh chives
pinch ground nutmeg
30g/1oz grated fresh Parmesan cheese
freshly ground black pepper

macaroni
with basil

Method:

1 Cook macaroni in boiling water in a large saucepan, following packet directions. Drain, set aside and keep warm.

2 Heat oil in a large frying pan and cook garlic, mushrooms and tomatoes over a medium heat for 4-5 minutes. Stir in basil and season to taste with black pepper.

3 Add macaroni to mushroom mixture and toss to combine. Serve immediately.

Serves 4

ingredients

375g/12oz wholemeal macaroni
1 tablespoon olive oil
2 cloves garlic, minced
250g/8oz button mushrooms, sliced
6 sun-dried tomatoes, drained and
cut into strips
2 tablespoons chopped fresh basil
freshly ground black pepper

chilli
broad bean salad

Method:

1 Cook pasta in boiling water in a large saucepan, following packet directions. Drain, rinse under cold running water, then drain again and set aside to cool completely.

2 Heat oil in a large frying pan and cook broad beans and chilli paste over a medium heat for 3 minutes. Stir in stock, bring to a simmer, cover and cook for 10 minutes. Drain off any remaining liquid and set aside to cool.

3 To make dressing, place oil, vinegar, garlic and black pepper to taste in a screw-top jar. Shake well to combine.

4 Place pasta, broad bean mixture, radishes, parsley and Parmesan cheese in a salad bowl. Pour dressing over and toss to combine.

Serves 4

ingredients

375g/12oz small shell pasta
1 tablespoon vegetable oil
250g/8oz shelled or frozen broad beans
1 teaspoon chilli paste (sambal selek)
1 1/2 cups/375mL/12fl oz chicken stock
6 radishes, thinly sliced
2 tablespoons chopped fresh parsley
30g/1oz grated fresh Parmesan cheese
<u>Garlic dressing</u>
1/4 cup/60mL/2fl oz olive oil
1 tablespoon cider vinegar
1 clove garlic, minced
freshly ground black pepper

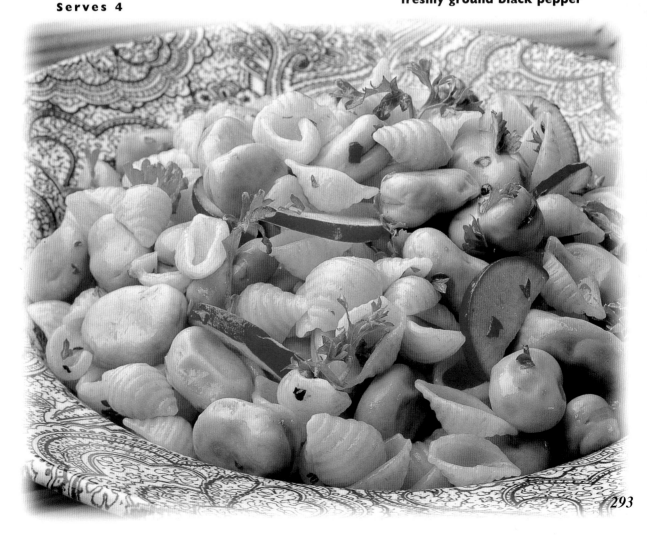

ravioli
with lemon sauce

Method:

1 Cook pasta in boiling water in a large saucepan, following packet directions. Drain, set aside and keep warm.

2 To make sauce, melt butter in a frying pan over a low heat, add garlic and cook, stirring, for 1 minute. Stir in cream, lemon juice, Parmesan cheese, chives and lemon rind, bring to a simmer and cook for 2 minutes. Add parsley and black pepper to taste and cook for 1 minute longer. Spoon sauce over pasta and toss to combine. Scatter with almonds and serve.

Serves 4

ingredients

500g/1 lb cheese and spinach ravioli
30g/1oz slivered almonds, toasted
<u>**Lemon cream sauce**</u>
30g/1oz butter
1 clove garlic, minced
1 1/4 cups/315mL/10fl oz thickened (double)cream
1/4 cup/60mL/2fl oz lemon juice
30g/1oz grated fresh Parmesan cheese
3 tablespoons snipped fresh chives
1 teaspoon finely grated lemon rind
2 tablespoons chopped fresh parsley
freshly ground black pepper

fettuccine
with corn sauce

Method:

1 Cook pasta in boiling water in a large saucepan, following packet directions. Drain, set aside and keep warm.

2 To make sauce, heat oil in a saucepan over a medium heat, add red capsicum (pepper) and cook, stirring, for 2 minutes or until capsicum (pepper) is soft. Stir in sweet corn, water, chilli sauce, coriander (cilantro) and black pepper to taste and cook for 2 minutes longer or until sauce is hot. Spoon sauce over pasta and toss to combine.

Serves 4

ingredients

500g/1 lb fresh fettuccine
<u>Corn and coriander sauce</u>
1 tablespoon olive oil
1 red capsicum (pepper), chopped
440g/14oz canned creamed sweet corn
¹/₄ cup/60mL/2fl oz water
2 teaspoons hot chilli sauce
2 tablespoons chopped fresh coriander (cilantro)
freshly ground black pepper

crests
with mushrooms

Method:

1 Cook pasta in boiling water in a large saucepan , following packet directions. Drain, set aside and keep warm.

2 To make sauce, melt butter in a saucepan over a medium heat, add mushrooms, onion and garlic and cook, stirring occasionally, for 5 minutes or until onions and mushrooms are soft.

3 Stir in paprika, wine and tomato paste (purée), bring to a simmer and cook for 5 minutes. Remove pan from heat, stir in sour cream and parsley and cook over a low heat for 3-4 minutes or until heated through. Season to taste with black pepper. Spoon sauce over pasta and serve immediately.

Serves 4

ingredients

375g/12oz cresti di gallo pasta
Mushroom and paprika sauce
30g/1oz butter
125g/4oz mushrooms, sliced
1 onion, thinly sliced
1 clove garlic, minced
1 tablespoon ground paprika
1/2 cup/125mL/4fl oz white wine
2 tablespoons tomato paste (purée)
1 1/4 cups/315g/10oz sour cream
1 tablespoon chopped fresh parsley or
1 teaspoon dried parsley flakes
freshly ground black pepper

tomato
& cheese lasagne

Method:

1. Place ricotta cheese, parsley, basil and black pepper (to taste) in a bowl and mix to combine. Set aside.

2. Place pecorino or Parmesan and mozzarella cheeses in a bowl and mix to combine. Set aside.

3. To make sauce, heat oil in a saucepan over a medium heat, add garlic and onion and cook, stirring, for 3 minutes or until onion is soft. Add tomatoes and cook, stirring for 4 minutes longer.

4. Add tomato paste (purée), bay leaf, thyme, ham or bacon bone, water and sugar and bring to the boil. Reduce heat and simmer, stirring occasionally, for 45 minutes or until sauce reduces and thickens. Remove ham or bacon bone from sauce and discard.

5. Place three lasagne sheets in the base of a greased 18x28cm/7x11in ovenproof dish. Top with one-third of the tomato sauce, then one-third of the ricotta mixture and one-third of the cheese mixture. Repeat layers twice more to use all ingredients, finishing with a layer of cheese. Bake for 30 minutes or until hot and bubbling and top is golden.

Serves 6

1 cup/250g/8oz ricotta cheese, drained
1 tablespoon chopped fresh parsley
1 tablespoon chopped fresh basil
freshly ground black pepper
60g/2oz grated pecorino or Parmesan cheese
125g/4oz grated mozzarella cheese
9 sheets instant* lasagne
Fresh tomato sauce
2 teaspoons olive oil
2 cloves garlic, minced
1 onion, chopped
7 tomatoes, peeled, seeded and chopped
2 tablespoons tomato paste (purée)
1 bay leaf
3 sprigs fresh thyme or
1/2 teaspoon dried thyme
1 small ham or bacon bone
1/2 cup/125mL/4fl oz water
1 teaspoon sugar

*No pre-cooking required

grilled
vegetable salad

grilled vegetable salad

Serves 6

vegetables

ingredients

250g/8oz fresh angel-hair pasta
1 large eggplant (aubergine)
salt
1 large red capsicum(pepper),
seeded and quartered
1 large green capsicum(pepper),
seeded and quartered
4 spring onions, sliced diagonally
Sesame and chilli dressing
2 fresh red chillies, seeded and diced
1 clove garlic, crushed
¹/₂ cup/125mL/4fl oz olive oil
¹/₃ cup/90mL/3fl oz soy sauce
2 tablespoons sesame oil
2 tablespoons honey
2 tablespoons red wine vinegar

Method:

1 Cook pasta in boiling water in a large saucepan , following packet directions. Drain and rinse under cold running water. Drain again and set aside.

2 Cut eggplant (aubergine) into 1cm/¹/₂in-thick slices and place in a colander. Sprinkle with salt and set aside for 1 hour. Rinse eggplant under cold running water, then pat dry with absorbent kitchen paper.

3 To make dressing, place chillies, garlic, olive oil, soy sauce, sesame oil, honey and vinegar in a bowl and whisk to combine.

4 Brush eggplant slices with some of the dressing and cook under a preheated hot grill for 5 minutes each side or until golden. Set aside to cool, then cut into strips.

5 Place red and green capsicum (pepper) quarters, skin side up, under a hot grill and cook for 5-10 minutes or until skins are blistered and charred. Place capsicums in a plastic or paper bag and set aside until cool enough to handle. Remove skins and cut flesh into chunks.

6 Place pasta, eggplant, red and green capsicums, and spring onions in a large bowl and toss gently. Pour over remaining dressing and toss to coat pasta and vegetables. Cover and chill until required.

tortellini
with onion confit

Method:

1 To make confit, melt butter in a saucepan over a medium heat, add onions and cook, stirring, for 3 minutes or until onions are soft. Stir in sugar and cook for 2 minutes longer. Add thyme, wine and vinegar, bring to a simmer and cookr, stirring frequently, for 40 minutes or until mixture reduces and thickens.

2 Place stock in a saucepan, bring to the boil and cook until reduced by half. Keep warm.

3 Cook pasta in boiling water in a large saucepan, following packet directions. Drain well. Add pasta, confit, peas and tarragon to stock, bring to a simmer and cook for 2-3 minutes or until peas are just cooked.

Serves 4

ingredients

1¹/₂ cups/375mL/12fl oz beef stock
750g/1¹/₂ lb beef or veal tortellini
250g/8oz small peas
2 tablespoons chopped fresh tarragon
or 1 teaspoon dried tarragon
Onion confit
30g/1oz butter
2 onions, thinly sliced
2 teaspoons sugar
1 tablespoon chopped fresh thyme or
¹/₂ teaspoon dried thyme
1 cup/250mL/8fl oz red wine
2 tablespoons red wine vinegar

penne
with gorgonzola sauce

Method:

1. Cook pasta in boiling water in a large saucepan, following packet directions. Drain, set aside and keep warm.
2. To make sauce, place cream, stock, wine and Gorgonzola or blue cheese in a saucepan and cook, over a medium heat, stirring constantly, until smooth. Bring to a simmer and cook for 8 minutes or until sauce thickens.
3. Add parsley, nutmeg and black pepper (to taste) to sauce, bring to a simmer and cook for 2 minutes. Spoon sauce over hot pasta.

Serves 4

ingredients

500g/1 lb penne
<u>**Gorgonzola sauce**</u>
1 cup/250mL/8fl oz thickened double cream
1/2 cup/125mL/4fl oz vegetable stock
1/2 cup/125mL/4fl oz white wine
125g/4oz Gorgonzola or blue cheese, crumbled
2 tablespoons chopped flat-leaf parsley,
1/2 teaspoon ground nutmeg
freshly ground black pepper

pasta
with six-herb sauce

pasta with six-herb sauce

Serves 4

ingredients

500g/1 lb pasta shapes of your choice
Six-herb sauce
30g/1oz butter
2 tablespoons fresh rosemary, chopped
12 small fresh sage leaves
12 small fresh basil leaves
2 tablespoons fresh marjoram leaves
2 tablespoons fresh oregano leaves
2 tablespoons chopped fresh parsley
2 cloves garlic, chopped
1/4 cup/60mL/2fl oz white wine
1/4 cup/60mL/2fl oz vegetable stock

Method:

1 *Cook pasta in boiling water in a large saucepan, following packet directions. Drain, set aside and keep warm.*

2 *To make sauce, melt butter in a saucepan over a medium heat. Add rosemary, sage, basil, marjoram, oregano, parsley and garlic and cook, stirring, for 1 minute.*

3 *Stir in wine and stock, bring to a simmer and cook for 4 minutes. To serve, spoon sauce over hot pasta and toss to combine.*

Know your pasta

Angel-hair *pasta:* *Also labelled as capelli di angelo, this is an extremely long thin pasta that is dried in coils to prevent it from breaking. Because of its delicate nature angel-hair pasta is best served with a light sauce.*

Cannelloni: This large hollow pasta is most often stuffed, topped with a sauce and cheese, then baked. Cannelloni can also be stuffed and deep-fried until crisp.

If deep-frying, the tubes will need to be boiled before stuffing and frying. Lasagne sheets can also be used for baked cannelloni – spread the filling down the centre of the pasta then roll up.

Farfalle: Meaning 'butterflies', this bow-shaped pasta is ideal for serving with meat and vegetable sauces, as the sauce becomes trapped in the folds.

Fettuccine: A flat ribbon pasta that is used in a similar way to spaghetti. Often sold coiled in nests, fettuccine is particularly good with creamy sauces, which cling better than heavier sauces.

Lasagne: These flat sheets of pasta are most often layered with a meat, fish or vegetable sauce, topped with cheese, then baked to make a delicious and satisfying dish. Instant lasagne that you do not have to cook before using is also available.

Linguine: This long thin pasta looks somewhat like spaghetti but has square-cut ends. It can be used in the same way as spaghetti, fettuccine and tagliatelle.

Macaroni: Short-cut or 'elbow' macaroni, very common outside of Italy, is most often used in baked dishes and in the ever-popular macaroni cheese.

Orecchiette: Its name means 'little ears' and this is exactly what this pasta looks like. It is made without eggs and tends to have a chewier and firmer texture than some other pastas. Traditionally a homemade pasta, it can now be purchased dried from Italian food stores and some supermarkets.

Pappardelle: This very wide ribbon pasta was traditionally served with a sauce made of hare, herbs and wine, but today it is teamed with any rich sauce.

Penne: A short tubular pasta, similar to macaroni, but with ends cut at an angle rather than straight. It is particularly suited to being served with meat and heavier sauces, that catch in the hollows.

*Shell *pasta:* Also called conchiglie, if large, or conchigliette, if smaller. The large shells are ideal for stuffing and a fish filling is often favoured because of the shape of the pasta. Small shells are popular in casseroles, soups and salads.*

Spaghetti: Deriving its name from the Italian word spago meaning 'string', spaghetti is the most popular and best known of all pastas outside of Italy. It can be simply served with butter or oil and is good with almost any sauce.

*Spiral *pasta:* Also called fusilli, this pasta is great served with substantial meat sauces, as the sauce becomes trapped in the coils or twists.*

Tagliarini: Similar to fettuccine, this is the name often given to homemade fettuccine.

Tagliatelli: Another of the flat ribbon pastas, tagliatelle is eaten more in northern Italy than in the south and is used in the same ways as fettuccine.

Cooking pasta

Cook pasta in a large, deep saucepan of water: the general rule is 4 cups/1 litre/1^3/$_4$pt water to 100g/3^1/$_2$oz pasta. Bring the water to a rolling boil, toss in salt to taste (in Italy, 1 tablespoon per every 100g/3^1/$_2$oz is usual), then stir in pasta. If you wish, add some oil. When the water comes back to the boil, begin timing. The pasta is done when it is 'al dente', that is tender but with resistance to the bite. Remove the pasta from the water by straining through a colander or lifting out of the saucepan with tongs or a fork.

You will find that the pasta quantities used in this book are fairly generous. In many cases, all you will need to make a complete meal is a tossed green or vegetable salad and some crusty bread or rolls.

Basic egg dough

1^1/$_2$ cups/185g/6oz plain flour
1 egg
1 teaspoon salt
1 tablespoon safflower oil

Method:

1 Mix flour and salt in a bowl until blended.

2 If using a food processor, process all ingredients for about 30 seconds. If the mixture forms a ball immediately and is wet to the touch, mix in flour by the tablespoon until the dough feels soft but not sticky.

Note: If the mixture is too dry to work with, blend in water by the teaspoon until the dough just forms a ball.

3 If you have a pasta machine, the dough may be immediately kneaded and rolled out. If not using a pasta machine it may be better to wrap dough in plastic film and allow it to rest for about 15-30 minutes before rolling out.

Adjusting flour & liquid in dough

The moisture content of pasta dough is affected by a number of variables, including the type of wheat used, the age of the flour, its moisture content, and the degree of humidity in the air. For this reason, even when you measure the ingredients very carefully, you may need to adjust the proportions of flour and liquid if the dough seems too sticky or too dry to handle. Also, keep in mind that dough for filled pasta varieties will need to be more moist than dough for flat or tubular pasta. Add flour and water (no more than ^{1}/$_2$ teaspoon water or 1 tablespoon flour at a time as necessary, until the dough is the proper consistency for rolling, cutting or shaping.

Designer doughs

Using basic egg dough as a foundation, you can add different ingredients to create your own "designer" pastas with exciting colours and flavours. Experiment to your heart's content. Just remember that the colour and flavour of the pasta you make should compliment whatever sauce you plan to serve with it. Depending on which of the following ingredients you add, you may need to adjust the proportions of liquid and flour to form a dough of proper consistency.

- Puréed vegetables: cooked beetroot, roasted red, green or yellow capsicum (peppers), cooked pumpkin.
- Fresh puréed garlic
- Spices and seasonings: black pepper, cayenne, cinnamon, chilli powder, curry, nutmeg, saffron
- Fresh or dried black olives, finely chopped
- Fresh or canned hot chillies, finely chopped.

Making pasta by hand

Machines can be convenient for making pasta, but they are not essential. With only a bowl, a fork, and a rolling pin, you can turn out professional-quality fresh pasta in 10 minutes.

1 *Make a ring of flour blended with salt on a clean work surface. Place beaten egg in centre of well. Use a fork or your fingertips to incorporate the flour into beaten egg so as to form a firm dough. On a flour-dusted work surface, knead dough until it is smooth and cohesive (5-8 minutes). Cover with a damp cloth for 15 minutes.*

2 *Lightly flour work surface. Begin with one third of the dough at a time. Starting from the centre and moving to the edge, roll the pasta using as few strokes as possible. If dough becomes too elastic, cover it for a few minutes with a damp cloth to prevent it from drying out. Roll out about .2 -.3cm ($^1/_8$–$^1/_{16}$) in-thick.*

3 *Lightly flour dough and roll into a sponge-roll shape. Cut by hand to desired thickness for flat shapes (such as linguine, fettuccine, or lasagne). Dry 10-15 minutes on a pasta rack before cooking.*

Making tortellini

Tortellini can be made with a variety of fillings, including the pumpkin filling shown here. Tortellini can be formed a few hours ahead and spread on lightly floured baking sheets. Make sure they do not touch. Cover and refrigerate or freeze before cooking. Follow directions for freezing as for ravioli.

1 *The dough should be quite thin. Cut 5cm/2in) circles from dough. Put a scant teaspoon of filling in centre of each. Brush edges lightly with cold water.*

2 *Fold circle in half to enclose filling. Press edges firmly to seal.*

3 *With sealed edge out, plac folded circle over index finge Bring ends toward each othe under the finger, turnin sealed outer edge up to forr a cuff. Pinch ends togethe firmly. Let dry for a fe minutes on a lightly floure surface before cooking.*

Preparing ravioli

Ravioli can be made with a variety of doughs and fillings.

Use the basic egg dough shown above, or your favourite flavoured dough recipe. The dough and filling should be compatible in flavour and colour.

The dough should be rolled quite thin. Using a mold to form the ravioli simplifies the process, but it is not essential. Ravioli can be prepared a few hours ahead of serving time and spread on lightly floured baking sheets. Make sure they do not touch.

Cover and refrigerate or freeze. Place in a lock-top plastic bag and use within 3 months. After cooking, ravioli can be added to broth or your favourite sauce.

Method for making ravioli:

1 *Roll pasta dough into thin sheets. Place mounds of filling, about $^3/_4$ teaspoon each, at regular intervals the length of the pasta. Brush lightly with cold water between the mounds.*

2 *Place another sheet of pasta over the first and use your fingers to press the sheets together between the mounds of filling.*

3 *Cut ravoli with a pizza cutter or pastry wheel. Use a fork to crimp and seal the edges.*

1

2

3

How much pasta to serve		
Pasta type	**First course**	**Main Meal**
Dried pasta	60-75g 2-2 $^1/_{20}$z	75-100g 2 $^1/_2$-3 $^1/_2$ oz
Fresh pasta	75-100g 2 $^1/_2$-3 $^1/_{20}$z	125-155g 4-5 oz
Filled pasta	155-185g 5-6oz	185-200g 6-6 $^1/_2$ oz

beans

pulses and legumes

introduction

All pulses are members of the legume family, one of the world's most important food groups. Their genus is Phaseolus. Technically, legumes are plants that carry their seeds in a pod. Beans of every shape and colour, peas and peanuts are all legumes. An exceptionally nutritious component in the human diet, they have on average twice the protein of grains and a good dose of iron and vitamin B. With some legumes, such as peanuts and mature English peas, we eat only the seeds and discard the pods. Other legumes such as sugar snap peas and snow peas (mange tout), are edible in their entirety. Most beans consist of a pod with a single section that holds one row of seeds. Some varieties are cultivated more for their edible pod than their seeds; others have tough, stringy pods and are cultivated primarily for their seeds, which may be used either fresh or dried. There are hundreds of varieties of fresh and dried beans.

Beans with edible pods are enjoyed as a salad and as a side dish. French cooks serve tiny haricots verds both cold and hot; the cold beans are normally served with vinaigrette or mayonnaise, and hot with melted butter or olive oil.

Chinese cooks often stir-fry beans with titbits of seasoned ground pork or with oyster sauce. Italians add edible-podded beans to vegetable soups or saute them with pancetta (unsmoked bacon). Indian cooks braise green beans with coconut and spices. Shell beans may also be eaten as a cold salad or a hot side dish. They add body and flavour to soups and stews.

It is best to store fresh beans in the refrigerator in a perforated plastic bag; they may be kept for four to five days. Store fresh shell beans with inedible pods similarly and use within two or three days; shell just before using. Store dried beans in an air-tight container in a cool place; they will keep for about a year.

Preparation varies depending upon bean; check specific recipes for preparation information. Most dried beans (except lentils) require soaking before cooking. Cover with plenty of cold water and soak at least 8 hours or, better still, overnight.

You may use the "quick soak" method: boil beans and water

2 minutes; cover and let stand 1 hour. remember to discard water before proceeding with recipe.

A full description of beans and cooking times can be seen on pages 78 and 79 of this book. In our health-conscious world, grains, pulses and beans have been elevated from humble peasant food. Which, until recently, was thought of as fattening and stodgy but is now regarded as fashionable and very good for you. This new status has inspired recipes and ideas that turn these foods into gourmet dishes. It has also created an awareness of different cuisines as we look at new ways in which to use them.

In this book you will find a host of wonderful dishes, including traditional recipes, as well as new and innovative delights.

winter vegetable soup

starters

Many of the recipes in this chapter

will also stand on their own as light meals or snacks.
Starting a meal with a dish based on legumes, beans or
grains is an economical way to fill hungry teenagers.

curried
lentil soup
Photograph on right

Method:

1 *Heat oil in a large saucepan, add onion, curry powder and cumin and cook, stirring occasionally, for 4-5 minutes or until onion is soft. Stir in tomato paste (purée) and stock and bring to the boil. Reduce heat, add lentils, cover and simmer for 30 minutes.*

2 *Add broccoli, carrots, parsnip and celery and cook, covered, for 30 minutes longer or until vegetables are tender. Season to taste with black pepper. Just prior to serving, stir in parsley.*

Serves 6

ingredients

**2 tablespoons vegetable oil
I onion, chopped
2 teaspoons curry powder
¹/₂ teaspoon ground cumin
I tablespoon tomato paste (purée)
6 cups/I¹/₂ litres/2¹/₂pt vegetable stock
125g/4oz red or green lentils
I small head broccoli, broken into florets
2 carrots, chopped
I parsnip, chopped
I stalk celery, chopped
freshly ground black pepper
I tablespoon chopped fresh parsley**

winter
vegetable soup
Photograph on right

Method:

1 *Heat oil in a large saucepan, add onion, garlic, celery, carrots and turnip and cook, stirring occasionally, for 4-5 minutes or until vegetables are just tender.*

2 *Stir in tomatoes, tomato paste (purée), basil, oregano, sugar and stock and bring to the boil. Reduce heat and simmer for 30-45 minutes.*

3 *Stir in pasta and beans. Season to taste with black pepper and simmer, uncovered, for 30 minutes.*

Serves 6

ingredients

**2 tablespoons vegetable oil
I large onion, sliced
I clove garlic, minced
2 stalks celery, chopped
2 carrots, chopped
I turnip, chopped
440g/14oz canned tomatoes,
undrained and mashed
2 tablespoons tomato paste (purée)
I tablespoon finely chopped fresh basil
I teaspoon dried oregano
I teaspoon sugar
6 cups/I¹/₂ litres/2¹/₂pt vegetable stock
125g/4oz small pasta shells
315g/10oz canned red kidney beans,
drained and rinsed
freshly ground black pepper**

hearty
bean soup

Method:

1 Place beans in a large bowl, cover with water and set aside to soak overnight.

2 Drain beans, place in a large saucepan with enough water to cover and bring to the boil. Boil for 10 minutes, reduce heat and simmer for 1 hour or until beans are soft. Drain and reserve 2 cups/500mL/16fl oz of cooking water. Place reserved cooking water and half the beans in a food processor or blender and process until smooth.

3 Heat oil in a large saucepan, add onions and garlic and cook, stirring, for 4-5 minutes or until onions are soft. Add carrots, celery, potatoes, tomatoes, water, beans and bean purée and bring to the boil. Reduce heat and simmer for 20 minutes or until vegetables are tender. Stir in parsley and season to taste with black pepper.

Serves 4

ingredients

185g/6oz dried haricot beans
1 tablespoon oil
2 onions, chopped
2 cloves garlic, minced
2 carrots, sliced
2 stalks celery, sliced
2 potatoes, chopped
440g/14oz canned tomatoes,
undrained and mashed
6 cups/1 1/2 litres/2 1/2pt water
2 tablespoons chopped fresh parsley
freshly ground black pepper

mushroom
& barley soup

Method:

1 *Place mushrooms, tomato, carrots, onion, celery, parsley, barley and water in a large saucepan and bring to the boil. Reduce heat, cover and simmer for 1 hour or until barley is tender. Season to taste with black pepper.*

Serves 4

ingredients

500g/16oz button mushrooms, sliced
1 tomato, chopped
2 carrots, chopped
1 onion, chopped
2 stalks celery, chopped
2 tablespoons chopped fresh parsley
1/2 cup/100g/3 1/2oz barley
6 cups/1 1/2 litres/2 1/2pt water
freshly ground black pepper

cream
of lentil soup

Photograph on right

Method:

1 Heat oil in a large saucepan. Add onion, leeks and garlic and cook over a medium heat, stirring constantly, for 5 minutes or until onions are golden.

2 Stir in lentils and stock or water and bring to the boil. Reduce heat and simmer for 30 minutes or until lentils are tender. Add rocket and lemon juice and simmer for 5 minutes longer. Remove pan from heat and set aside to cool slightly.

3 Place lentil mixture, in batches, in a food processor or blender and process until smooth.

4 Return soup to a clean saucepan, bring to the boil and simmer over a medium heat for 2-3 minutes or until soup is hot. Stir in cream or yoghurt.

Serves 6

ingredients

2 teaspoons vegetable oil
I onion, chopped
2 leeks, chopped
2 cloves garlic, minced
315g/10oz green lentils
6 cups/1.5 litres/2¹/₂pt vegetable stock or water
12 rocket leaves, roughly chopped
I tablespoon lemon juice
¹/₂ cup/125mL/4fl oz cream (single) or
¹/₂ cup/100g/3¹/₂oz natural yoghurt

snow pea
soup

Photograph on right

Method:

1 Melt butter in a large saucepan. Add leeks and garlic and cook over a medium heat, stirring, for 4 minutes or until leeks are soft.

2 Stir in stock or water and snow peas (mange-tout), bring to simmering and simmer for 20 minutes. Remove pan from heat and set aside to cool slightly. Place soup mixture, in batches, in a food processor or blender and process until smooth. Push mixture through a sieve.

3 Return purée to a clean saucepan, stir in cream or milk, mint and black pepper to taste. Bring to simmering and simmer for 2 minutes or until soup is hot.

4 To make Cheese toasts, toast bread slices under a preheated medium grill until golden on one side. Place cream cheese, Parmesan cheese, Swiss cheese and black peppercorns in a bowl and mix to combine. Spread cheese mixture over untoasted side of bread and cook under grill until cheese melts. Serve with hot soup.

Serves 6

ingredients

15g/¹/₂oz butter
2 leeks, chopped
I clove garlic, minced
6 cups/1.5 litres/2¹/₂pt vegetable stock or water
375g/12oz snow peas (mange-tout), trimmed and halved
³/₄ cup/185mL/6fl oz cream (single) or milk
I tablespoon chopped fresh mint
freshly ground black pepper
<u>Cheese toasts</u>
I small French bread stick, cut into slices
100g/3¹/₂oz cream cheese
45g/1¹/₂oz grated Parmesan cheese
45g/1¹/₂oz grated Swiss cheese
I teaspoon crushed black peppercorn

chickpea
and eggplant dip

Method:

1 Place eggplant (aubergines) on a baking tray and bake for 30 minutes or until very soft. Set aside to cool, then remove skins.

2 Place eggplant (aubergine) flesh, chickpeas, yoghurt, lemon juice, garlic, mint and black pepper in a food processor or blender and process until smooth. Place dip in a serving dish and serve with warm flatbread.

Serves 4

ingredients

2 eggplant (aubergines)
200g/6¹/₂oz canned chickpeas, drained and rinsed
1 cup/200g/6¹/₂oz low-fat natural yoghurt
¹/₄ cup/60mL/2fl oz lemon juice
1 clove garlic, minced
1 tablespoon chopped fresh mint
freshly ground black pepper

chilli bean
potatoes

Method:

1 Bake potatoes for 45-60 minutes or until soft. Remove from oven and allow to cool slightly.

2 Cut tops from potatoes and scoop out flesh, leaving a thin shell. Place potato flesh, tomato paste (purée) and chilli sauce in a bowl and mash. Stir in beans and season to taste with black pepper.

3 Spoon potato mixture into potato shells, dust with paprika and bake for 10-15 minutes or until heated through and lightly browned.

Serves 4

ingredients

4 potatoes, scrubbed
1 tablespoon tomato paste (purée)
1-2 teaspoons chilli sauce, or
according to taste
315g/10oz canned red kidney beans,
drained and rinsed
freshly ground black pepper
paprika

Oven temperature 220°C, 425°F, Gas 7

chunky
lamb soup

Method:

1 Melt the butter in a large saucepan over moderate heat. Add lamb cubes, onion, parsley, paprika, saffron and pepper. Cook for 5 minutes, stirring frequently. Add the stock.

2 Drain chickpeas and add them to pan with tomatoes and lemon juice. Bring to the boil, boil for 10 minutes, then cover pan and simmer mixture for 1-1¼ hours.

3 Stir in rice. Cook for 15-20 minutes or until tender. Serve at once, in heated bowls.

Serves 6

ingredients

30g/1oz butter
500g/1lb lamb fillet,
cut into 2cm/³⁄₄in cubes
1 large onion, chopped
1 tablespoon chopped fresh parsley
2 teaspoons paprika
1 teaspoon saffron powder
1 teaspoon ground black pepper
1.5 litres/2¹⁄₂pt lamb or chicken stock
60g/2oz chickpeas, soaked overnight in
water to cover
500g/1lb tomatoes, peeled,
seeded and chopped
4 tablespoons lemon juice
60g/2oz long-grain rice

hummus

Method:

1 Drain chickpeas and place into a large saucepan. Cover with fresh water, bring to the boil, and simmer for 1-1¼ hours or until tender. Drain, reserving 250mL/8fl oz of cooking water.

2 Purée chickpeas with the reserved cooking water, tahini, salt, pepper, lemon juice, garlic and ricotta until smooth.

3 Spoon hummus onto a shallow plate, sprinkle with paprika and drizzle with olive oil. Serve with pitta bread.

Serves 6

ingredients

220g/7oz chickpeas, soaked for
4 hours in enough water to cover
125mL/4fl oz tahini
(sesame seed paste)
½ teaspoon salt
½ teaspoon freshly ground pepper
60mL/2fl oz lemon juice
3 gloves garlic, minced
90g/3oz ricotta cheese
paprika
3 tablespoons olive oil

chilli bean tortillas

quick meals

Some of the following recipes

require the beans to be presoaked, but once this is done they are quick to prepare.

When cooking beans and grains be sure to cook extra so that you have them on hand to make quick meals such as the ones in this chapter. Cooked legumes, beans and grains freeze well or will keep in the refrigerator for 3-4 days.

chilli bean
tortillas

Photograph page 325

ingredients

12 tortillas
**¹/₂ cup/60g/2oz grated reduced-fat
Cheddar cheese**
<u>Chilli bean filling</u>
I onion, chopped
I clove garlic, minced
**440g/14oz canned tomatoes,
undrained and mashed**
**I tablespoon chopped fresh coriander
(cilantro)**
I teaspoon ground cumin
**2 fresh red chillies,
seeded and chopped**
**440g/14oz canned red kidney beans,
rinsed and drained**
¹/₃ cup/90mL/3fl oz red wine
2 tablespoons tomato paste (purée)

Method:

1 *To make filling, place onion, garlic and I tablespoon juice from tomatoes in a nonstick frying pan and cook over a medium heat, stirring, for 3 minutes or until onions are soft.*

2 *Add coriander (cilantro), cumin and chillies and cook for I minute longer. Stir in tomatoes, beans, wine and tomato paste (purée) and bring to the boil. Reduce heat to simmering and simmer, stirring occasionally, for 8-10 minutes or until mixture reduces and thickens.*

3 *Divide filling between tortillas and roll up. Place tortillas in a baking dish, sprinkle with cheese and bake for 10 minutes or until tortillas are heated and cheese melts.*

Serves 6

Oven temperature 180°C, 350°F, Gas 4

spicy
chickpeas

ingredients

30g/1oz ghee or butter
I tablespoon curry paste
2 tablespoons finely grated fresh ginger
3 spring onions, chopped
750g/1¹/₂lb canned chickpeas, drained
3 large tomatoes, chopped
I tablespoon chopped fresh mint

Method:

1 *Melt ghee or butter in a saucepan over a medium heat, add curry paste and cook, stirring, for 3 minutes or until fragrant.*

2 *Add ginger and spring onions and cook for 3 minutes or until spring onions are soft.*

3 *Stir in chickpeas, tomatoes and mint, and cook, stirring frequently, for 15 minutes.*

Serves 4

bean
cottage pie

Method:

1 *Heat oil in a large frying pan, add garlic, leeks and carrots and cook, stirring, for 5 minutes or until leeks are tender. Add tomatoes, bring to the boil, then reduce heat and simmer for 10 minutes or until mixture reduces and thickens. Stir in beans and cook for 3-4 minutes longer. Season to taste with black pepper.*

2 *Transfer bean mixture to a greased ovenproof dish, top with mashed potato and sprinkle with cheese. Bake for 20 minutes or until top is golden.*

Serves 4

ingredients

1 tablespoon vegetable oil
2 cloves garlic, minced
2 leeks, white parts only, sliced
2 large carrots, sliced
440g/14oz canned tomatoes, undrained and mashed
440g/14oz canned lima or butter beans, drained
freshly ground black pepper
750g/1¹/₂lb potatoes, cooked and mashed
60g/2oz grated tasty mature Cheddar cheese

Oven temperature 180°C, 350°F, Gas 4

lentil burger

Photograph on right

Method:

1 To make sauce, place yoghurt and mint in a small bowl and mix to combine.

2 Place lentils, mashed potato, milk, egg, spring onions, garlic, cumin, coriander, curry powder and black pepper to taste in a bowl and mix to combine.

3 Shape lentil mixture into eight patties and cook under a preheated grill for 5 minutes each side or until golden and heated through.

4 Place two patties on the bottom half of each bread roll, then top with sauce and top of roll.

Serves 4

ingredients

90g/3oz red lentils, cooked, drained and mashed
125g/4oz instant mashed potato
³/4 cup/185mL/6fl oz milk
I egg, lightly beaten
4 spring onions, chopped
I clove garlic, minced
I teaspoon ground cumin
I tablespoon chopped fresh coriander (cilantro)
I teaspoon curry powder
freshly ground black pepper
4 bread rolls, split and toasted
<u>**Yoghurt mint sauce**</u>
I cup/200g/6¹/₂oz natural yoghurt
I tablespoon chopped fresh mint

tuscan
bean soup

Method:

1 Drain beans, put in a saucepan and add vegetable stock or water. Bring to the boil and boil vigorously for 10 minutes. Lower heat and simmer for 1 hour; drain.

2 Heat oil in a saucepan, add carrots, celery and zucchini (courgettes) and fry for four minutes.. Stir in tomatoes and garlic and cook for 10 minutes, stirring constantly.

3 Add chicken stock and beans. Bring to the boil, then simmer for 30 minutes. Add cabbage and cook for 2 minutes more.

Serves 6-8

ingredients

185g/6oz dried red kidney beans, soaked overnight in water to cover
I litre/I³/4pt unsalted vegetable stock or water
125ml/4fl oz olive oil
2 carrots, chopped
2 sticks celery, sliced
4 zucchinis (courgettes), chopped
I x 410g/13oz can chopped tomatoes with basil
3 cloves garlic, minced
1.2 litres/2pt chicken stock
250g/8oz cabbage, chopped

bean-filled
tacos

Method:

1 To make filling, heat oil in a large frying pan, add onion and cook for 5 minutes. Stir in taco seasoning and chilli powder and cook for 1 minute longer.

2 Add red capsicum (pepper) and zucchini (courgette) and cook, stirring, for 3-4 minutes. Stir in beans, mashed tomatoes and tomato paste (purée), bring to simmering and simmer for 10 minutes or until mixture reduces and thickens.

3 Place taco shells on a baking tray and heat in the oven for 5 minutes. Half-fill each taco shell with filling, then top with avocado slices and serve immediately with cottage cheese, lettuce, chopped tomato and chilli sauce, if desired.

Serves 4

ingredients

12 taco shells
1 avocado, sliced and brushed with
2 tablespoons lemon juice
125g/4oz cottage cheese
¼ lettuce, shredded
1 tomato, chopped
1 tablespoon chilli sauce (optional)
<u>Spicy bean filling</u>
1 tablespoon vegetable oil
1 onion, chopped
45g/1½oz packet taco seasoning
¼ teaspoon chilli powder
1 red capsicum (pepper), chopped
1 zucchini (courgette), chopped
315g/10oz canned red kidney beans, drained
440g/14oz canned tomatoes, undrained and mashed
3 tablespoons tomato paste (purée)

Oven temperature 180°C, 350°F, Gas 4

lentil
pockets

Method:

1 Place lentils in a large saucepan, cover with water and bring to the boil. Reduce heat and simmer for 30 minutes or until lentils are tender. Drain and set aside.

2 Melt butter in a large saucepan, add onion and garlic and cook over a medium heat, stirring, for 5 minutes or until onion is soft. Add carrots, tomato, oregano and water and bring to the boil. Reduce heat and simmer for 10 minutes or until carrots are tender.

3 Add spinach, lemon juice and lentils to pan, bring to simmering and simmer for 15 minutes or until mixture reduces and thickens.

4 Spoon lentil mixture into pitta bread pockets and serve immediately.

Serves 6

ingredients

200g/6¹/₂oz red lentils
15g/¹/₂oz butter
1 onion, chopped
2 cloves garlic, minced
3 carrots, chopped
1 tomato, chopped
1 tablespoon chopped fresh oregano
or 1 teaspoon dried oregano
¹/₂ cup/125mL/fl oz water
1 bunch/500g/1lb spinach, stalks
removed and leaves chopped
1 tablespoon lemon juice
6 large pitta bread rounds,
warmed and cut in half

barley
vegetable curry

ingredients

Method:

1 Melt butter in large saucepan, add leeks, stir over heat until tender. Add garlic, curry powder and garam masala, stir over heat for 1 minute.

2 Add pearl barley, potatoes, pumpkin and water, cover and bring to the boil, then simmer for 10 minutes. Add broccoli and simmer for a further 10 minutes or until vegetables and barley are tender

Serves 4

60g/2oz butter
4 leeks, sliced (white part only)
2 cloves garlic, minced
2 teaspoon curry powder
1/2 teaspoon garam masala
375g/12 1/2oz pearl barley,
rinsed and drained
2 large potatoes, peeled and cut into
2cm/3/4in cubes
375g/12 1/2oz pumpkin, cut into
2cm/3/4in cubes
4 cups/1 litre/35fl oz water
250g/8oz broccoli, broken into florets

okra
& chickpea salad

Method:

1 *Place chickpeas in a bowl, cover with cold water and set aside to soak overnight. Drain and place chickpeas in a large saucepan with enough cold water to cover chickpeas by 5cm/2in. Bring to the boil and boil rapidly for 5 minutes then reduce heat and simmer for 1-1½ hours or until chickpeas are tender. Drain, and reserve 2 tablespoons of cooking liquid.*

2 *Heat oil in a large frying pan and cook onions over a low heat for 10 minutes or until golden. Add garlic, okra, chickpeas and reserved cooking liquid and cook for 4-5 minutes or until okra is tender.*

3 *Add tomatoes, coriander (cilantro), lemon juice and black pepper to taste and toss to combine. Serve hot or cold.*

ingredients

200g/6½ oz dried chickpeas
2 tablespoons olive oil
12 small onions, peeled
1 clove garlic, minced
500g/1lb okra, trimmed
4 tomatoes, skinned and quartered
4 tablespoons, chopped fresh coriander
(cilantro)
2 tablespoons lemon juice
freshly ground black pepper

mung-bean
frittata

Photograph on right

mung bean frittata

Serves 6

ingredients

100g/3¹/₂oz dried mung beans
2 eggs
2 tablespoons vegetable oil
I onion, sliced
2 potatoes, grated
2 carrots, grated
2 zucchinis (courgettes), grated
125g/4oz canned sweetcorn kernels,
drained
3 tablespoons chopped fresh basil
freshly ground black pepper
125g/4oz grated tasty
mature Cheddar cheese
Coconut cream
¹/₂ cup/125mL/4fl oz coconut milk
I tablespoon lemon juice
2 tablespoons chopped fresh mint

Method:

I Place mung beans in a bowl, pour over boiling water to cover and set aside to soak for 30 minutes. Drain beans and place in a food processor or blender with eggs and process until smooth. Transfer to a large bowl.

2 Heat I tablespoon oil in a frying pan, add onion and cook over a low heat for 3-4 minutes. Add potatoes, carrots and zucchini (courgettes) and cook, stirring, for 5 minutes or until vegetables are tender. Remove vegetables from pan and drain on absorbent kitchen paper.

3 Add cooked vegetables, sweetcorn, basil and black pepper to taste to bean mixture and mix well to combine.

4 Heat remaining oil in a large nonstick frying pan, add vegetable mixture, sprinkle with cheese and cook over a low heat for 5-8 minutes or until just firm. Place pan under a preheated grill and cook for 3 minutes or until top of frittata is browned.

5 To make Coconut cream, place coconut milk, lemon juice and mint in a screwtop jar and shake well to combine. Invert frittata onto a serving plate, cut into wedges and serve with Coconut cream.

barley casserole

main meals

Legumes, beans and grains can

form the basis of many satifying main course dishes. Combine them with fish or meat to extend these foods or with vegetables for a tasty vegetarian meal – add some herbs and spices and you have a wonderful balance of flavours, textures and nutrients.

barley
casserole

Photograph page 337

Method:

1 Place barley in a large bowl, cover with water and set aside to soak for 2 hours. Drain well and set aside.

2 Heat oil in a large frying pan, add barley and cook over a medium heat, stirring constantly, for 10 minutes.

3 Add tomatoes, wine and tomato paste (purée) to pan, bring to simmering and simmer for 20 minutes. Add onion and cook for 5 minutes longer. Stir in olives and serve immediately.

Serves 8

ingredients

1 cup/200g/6¹/₂oz barley
2 tablespoons vegetable oil
440g/14oz canned tomatoes, undrained and mashed
¹/₄ cup/60mL/2fl oz dry white wine
3 tablespoons tomato paste (purée)
1 large onion, chopped
12 stuffed green olives, halved

black bean
hot pot

Photograph on right

Method:

1 Place beans in a large bowl, cover with water and set aside to soak overnight. Drain beans. Place beans, celery, onion and bay leaf in a saucepan with enough water to cover and bring to the boil. Boil for 10 minutes then reduce heat and simmer for 1 hour or until beans are tender. Drain beans, reserving ³/₄ cup/185mL/6fl oz of cooking liquid, and discard remaining liquid and vegetables.

2 Cook sausages under a preheated grill for 5-6 minutes each side or until cooked. Slice sausages diagonally.

3 Heat reserved cooking liquid in a large frying pan, add red wine vinegar, tomato purée, red onion, capsicum (red pepper), beans and black pepper to taste, simmer for 20-25 minutes or until liquid is reduced by half. Add sausages and cook for 5 minutes longer.

Serves 6

ingredients

250g/8oz dried black-eyed beans
1 stalk celery, chopped
1 onion, chopped
1 bay leaf
8 spicy sausages
3 tablespoons red wine vinegar
3 tablespoons tomato purée
1 red onion, chopped
1 capsicum (red pepper), chopped
freshly ground black pepper

vegetable
chilli

Method:

1 Place eggplant (aubergine) in a colander, sprinkle with salt and set aside to stand for 15-20 minutes. Rinse under cold, running water and pat dry with absorbent kitchen paper.

2 Heat oil in a large frying pan, add eggplant (aubergine) and cook, stirring, for 5 minutes or until soft. Transfer eggplant (aubergine) to a large casserole dish.

3 Add onion, garlic and capsicum (green pepper) to frying pan and cook for 5 minutes or until onion is soft. Stir in tomatoes, zucchini (courgettes), chilli powder, cumin, parsley, beans and black pepper to taste and bring to the boil. Transfer bean mixture to casserole dish with eggplant (aubergine) and bake for 1½ hours or until the skin of the eggplant (aubergine) is tender.

Serves 6

ingredients

1 large eggplant (aubergine),
cut into 1cm/½in cubes
salt
4 tablespoons olive oil
1 large onion, chopped
1 clove garlic, minced
1 green capsicum (green pepper), sliced
440g/14oz canned tomatoes,
undrained and mashed
2 zucchinis (courgettes), sliced
1 teaspoon hot chilli powder
½ teaspoon ground cumin
2 tablespoons chopped fresh parsley
500g/1lb canned three bean mix
freshly ground black pepper

Oven temperature 180°C, 350°F, Gas 4

lima bean
hot pot

Method:

1 Place beans in a large bowl, cover with water and set aside to soak overnight. Drain beans, place in a saucepan with enough water to cover and bring to the boil. Boil for 10 minutes, then reduce heat and simmer for 1 hour or until beans are tender. Drain and set aside.

2 Heat oil in a saucepan, add onions and green capsicum (green pepper) and cook, stirring occasionally, for 4-5 minutes or until vegetables are soft. Add tomatoes, stock or water, oregano and chilli sauce and bring to the boil. Reduce heat and simmer, uncovered, for 15 minutes or until sauce reduces and thickens. Stir in beans and black pepper to taste.

3 Transfer bean mixture to an ovenproof dish, sprinkle with cheese and bake for 20 minutes.

Serves 4

ingredients

**250g/8oz dried lima or butter beans
2 tablespoons oil
2 onions, chopped
1 green capsicum (green pepper), chopped
4 tomatoes, chopped
1/2 cup/125mL/4fl oz vegetable stock
or water
1 tablespoon chopped fresh oregano
or 1 teaspoon dried oregano
2 teaspoons chilli sauce
freshly ground black pepper
125g/4oz grated tasty,
mature Cheddar cheese**

pumpkin
with bean filling

Method:

1 Cut tops from pumpkins and scoop out seeds. Bake or microwave pumpkins until just tender. Drain off any liquid that accumulates during cooking and place pumpkins in a lightly greased baking dish.

2 To make filling, soak burghul (cracked wheat) in water for 30 minutes. Drain and set aside. Heat oil in a large frying pan, add garlic, leek and mushrooms and cook, stirring, over a medium heat for 4-5 minutes.

3 Stir in beans, tomato sauce, Worcestershire sauce, chilli sauce and burghul and cook for 3-4 minutes longer or until heated through. Season to taste with black pepper.

4 Divide filling evenly between pumpkins, sprinkle with cheese and bake for 10 minutes or until cheese melts.

ingredients
4 golden nugget pumpkins
Bean filling
15g/¹/₂oz burghul (cracked wheat)
1 tablespoon olive oil
2 cloves garlic, minced
1 small leek, sliced
60g/2oz mushrooms, sliced
315g/10oz canned red kidney beans, drained and rinsed
1 tablespoon tomato sauce
2 teaspoons Worcestershire sauce
¹/₂ teaspoon chilli sauce
freshly ground black pepper
90g/3oz grated mozzarella cheese

Oven temperature 180°C, 350°F, Gas 4

vegetable
& bean risotto

Method:

1 Heat oil in a large frying pan, add poppy and mustard seeds and cook until they begin to pop. Add rice and cook, stirring, for 5 minutes.

2 Place chilli powder, turmeric, cumin, ground coriander and a little water in a small bowl and mix to form a paste. Stir spice mixture, eggplant (aubergine), red capsicum (red pepper), and beans into rice mixture and cook, stirring, for 5 minutes.

3 Place remaining water, tomato purée, stock and coconut milk in a bowl and whisk to combine. Add to rice mixture, bring to simmering and simmer for 30-40 minutes or until most of the liquid is absorbed and rice is cooked. Stir in fresh coriander (cilantro) and black pepper to taste. Serve immediately.

Serves 6

ingredients

1 tablespoon olive oil
1 teaspoon poppy seeds
1 teaspoon mustard seeds
1 cup/220g/7oz long-grain rice
1/4 teaspoon chilli powder
1 teaspoon ground turmeric
1 teaspoon ground cumin
1 teaspoon ground coriander
1 cup/250mL/8fl oz water
1 eggplant (aubergine), cut
into 5mm/1/4in cubes
1/2 red capsicum (red pepper) chopped
315g/10oz canned lima or butter
beans, drained and rinsed
1 1/2 cups/375mL/12fl oz tomato purée
1 1/2 cups/375mL/12fl oz chicken stock
1/2 cup/125mL/4fl oz coconut milk
1 tablespoon chopped fresh coriander
(cilantro)
freshly ground black pepper

broad beans
and ham

Method:

1 Boil, steam or microwave broad beans until tender. Drain and set aside.

2 Heat oil in a large frying pan, add ham and cook over a medium heat for 1 minute. Stir in flour and cook for 1 minute longer.

3 Stir wine, stock, cream and black pepper to taste into pan and bring to the boil, stirring constantly. Reduce heat and simmer for 5 minutes or until sauce thickens. Add broad beans and herbs and cook for 1 minute longer.

Serves 4

ingredients

500g/1lb shelled or frozen broad beans
1 tablespoon vegetable oil
185g/6oz ham, cut into thin strips
1 tablespoon flour
1/4 cup/60mL/2fl oz dry white wine
3/4 cup/185mL/6fl oz chicken or vegetable stock
1 tablespoon cream (double)
freshly ground black pepper
1 tablespoon chopped mixed fresh herbs

broad beans
with yoghurt

Method:

1 *Heat oil in a large saucepan, add broad beans and chives and cook, stirring constantly, for 3 minutes.*

2 *Stir in lemon juice, dill and water and bring to the boil. Reduce heat and simmer for 10 minutes. Drain beans, transfer to a serving dish and set aside to cool.*

3 *Place yoghurt and garlic in a small bowl and mix to combine. Spoon yogurt mixture over beans and serve immediately or chill.*

Serves 6

ingredients
2 tablespoons olive oil
1kg/2lb shelled or frozen broad beans
2 tablespoons snipped fresh chives
1/4 cup/60mL/2fl oz lemon juice
2 tablespoons chopped fresh dill
2 cups/500mL/16fl oz water
3/4 cup/185g/6oz natural yoghurt
2 cloves garlic, minced

chilli con carne

ingredients

Method:

1 Heat oil in a saucepan over a medium heat, add onion, chillies and garlic and cook, stirring, for 3 minutes or until onions are golden. Add mushrooms and red capsicum (red pepper) and cook for 3 minutes or until vegetables are just tender.

2 Add beef and cumin and cook, stirring frequently, for 5 minutes or until beef is brown. Add tomatoes, wine, tomato paste (purée) and Tabasco sauce, if using, and bring to the boil. Reduce heat and simmer for 30 minutes or until mixture reduces and thickens. Stir in coriander (cilantro).

3 To make salsa, place avocado, green capsicum (green pepper), onion, tomato, garlic, lemon juice in a bowl, mix to combine.

4 To make chips, brush bread lightly with oil, place on a baking tray and bake for 10 minutes or until bread is crisp. Break into bite-sized pieces.

To serve, top beef with yoghurt and accompany with salsa and chips.

Serves 4

1 tablespoon polyunsaturated vegetable oil
1 onion, finely chopped
4 small fresh red chillies, finely chopped
2 cloves garlic, crushed
125g/4oz button mushrooms, sliced
1 red capsicum (pepper), finely chopped
500g/1lb lean ground beef
1 teaspoon ground cumin
440g/14oz canned tomatoes, undrained and mashed
¼ cup/60mL/2fl oz red wine
1 tablespoon tomato paste (purée)
Tabasco sauce (optional)
2 tablespoons chopped fresh coriander (cilantro)
3 tablespoons low-fat natural yoghurt
Avocado and pepper salsa
1 avocado, halved, stoned, peeled and chopped
1 green capsicum (pepper), chopped
1 red onion, finely chopped
1 tomato, chopped
1 clove garlic, chopped
1 tablespoon lemon juice
Crispy chips
2 sheets lavash bread or
2 large pitta bread rounds
1 tablespoon vegetable oil

Oven temperature 190°C, 375°F, Gas 5

spicy lime
couscous

Method:

1 Place couscous in a bowl, cover with water and toss with a fork until couscous absorbs all the liquid.

2 Heat oil in a nonstick frying pan over a medium heat, add leek and chillies and cook, stirring, for 3 minutes or until leeks are golden.

3 Stir in sweet potato, garam masala, stock and lime juice, bring to simmering and simmer for 15 minutes or until sweet potato is tender.

4 Add beans and tomatoes and cook for 5-10 minutes or until beans are just cooked. Remove pan from heat, stir in raisins, pine nuts and coriander (cilantro). To serve, line a large platter with couscous and top with vegetable mixture.

Serves 4-6

ingredients

2 cups/375g/12oz couscous
3 cups/750mL/1 1/4 pt boiling water
1 tablespoon olive oil
1 leek, sliced
2 small fresh red chillies,
finely chopped
250g/8oz sweet potato, diced
1 teaspoon garam masala
1/2 cup/125mL/4fl oz chicken stock
2 tablespoons lime juice
125g/4oz green beans, halved
2 large tomatoes, peeled,
seeded and chopped
90g/3oz raisins
60g/2oz pine nuts, toasted
3 tablespoons chopped fresh coriander (cilantro)

monks butter
bean salad

Method:

1 Heat sesame and vegetable oils together in a wok over a medium heat, add garlic and onion and stir-fry for 5 minutes or until onion is soft.
2 Add turmeric, chilli powder and cardamom and stir-fry for 2 minutes longer or until fragrant.
3 Stir in beans and water, bring to simmering and simmer for 15 minutes or until mixture thickens slightly. Sprinkle with coriander (cilantro) and serve immediately.

Serves 4

ingredients

1 tablespoon sesame oil
1 tablespoon vegetable oil
2 cloves garlic, crushed
1 large onion, finely chopped
1 teaspoon ground turmeric
$^1/_2$ teaspoon chilli powder
$^1/_2$ teaspoon ground cardamom
2 x 315g/10oz canned butter beans, drained
1 cup/250mL/8fl oz water
1 tablespoon chopped fresh coriander (cilantro)

spicy lamb
tagine

Method:

1 Heat a non-stick frying pan over a medium heat. Add lamb and cook, stirring, for 5 minutes or until lamb is brown. Remove lamb from pan and place in casserole.

2 Add onions, cinnamon, cloves and garam masala to pan and cook, stirring, for 3 minutes or until onions are soft.

3 Add onion mixture, tomatoes, stock, chickpeas, potatoes, carrots, sultanas and orange rind to casserole dish and bake for 75-90 minutes or until lamb is tender.

4 Stir cornflour mixture into lamb mixture, return to oven and cook for 5-10 minutes longer or until tangine thickens slightly. Serve with couscous.

Serves 4

ingredients

500g/1lb lean diced lamb
2 onions, chopped
1 teaspoon ground cinnamon
1/2 teaspoon ground cloves
1 teaspoon garam masala
440g/14oz canned tomatoes, undrained and mashed
2 cups/500mL/16fl oz beef stock
250g/8oz canned chickpeas, drained and rinsed
3 potatoes, chopped
2 carrots, chopped
45g/1 1/2oz sultanas
2 teaspoons finely grated orange rind
3 teaspoons cornflour, blended with one tablespoon water
couscous for serving

marinated bean salad

vegetari

Legumes, beans and grains should

form the basis of a balanced vegetarian diet. These foods supply much of the protein, vitamins and minerals that non-vegetarians obtain from meat. While there are many meatless dishes in this book, the recipes in this chapter have been specially chosen for those following a vegetarian diet.

marinated
bean salad

Photograph page 351

Method:

1 Boil, steam or microwave green beans, zucchini (courgettes) and carrot, separately, until just tender. Drain and refresh under cold, running water.

2 To make dressing, place oil, vinegar, garlic and black pepper to taste in a screwtop jar and shake well to combine.

3 Place cooked vegetables, red kidney beans, chickpeas, pinto beans, water chestnuts, capsicum (pepper), parsley and basil in a large salad bowl. Spoon over dressing and toss to combine. Cover and refrigerate for 4-6 hours or overnight. Just prior to serving, toss again.

Serves 6

ingredients

125g/4 oz green beans, cut in half
2 zucchini (courgettes), cut into matchsticks
1 carrot, cut into matchsticks
250g/8oz canned red kidney beans, drained and rinsed
250g/8oz canned chickpeas, drained and rinsed
250g/8oz canned pinto beans, drained and rinsed
125g/4oz water chestnuts, drained
1 red capsicum(red pepper), cut into strips
2 tablespoons chopped fresh parsley
1 tablespoon chopped fresh basil
<u>Italian dressing</u>
¹/₄ cup/60mL/2fl oz olive oil
2 tablespoons red wine vinegar
1 clove garlic, minced
freshly ground black pepper

warm broad bean
salad with prosciutto

Method:

1 Line a platter with radicchio leaves. Pod broad beans, if necessary. Bring a saucepan of lightly salted water to the boil, add fresh or frozen broad beans and cook until tender. Drain thoroughly and pat dry with paper towels.

2 Tip broad beans into a bowl, add the onion, prosciutto, parsley and dressing. Season with salt and pepper, if required. Toss lightly. Spoon mixture onto lettuce-lined platter. Serve immediately.

Serves 4

ingredients

radicchio leaves to line platter
1kg/2lb broad beans in the pod or 375g/12oz frozen broad beans
3 tablespoons finely chopped spanish onion
60g/2oz prosciutto, cut into fine strips
2 tablespoons finely chopped parsley
4-5 tablespoons your favourite dressing
salt
freshly ground black pepper

broad beans
with grilled haloumi & lemon

Method:

1 *Slice the haloumi cheese very thinly, then brush with olive oil, and grill under a griller (until just starting to brown).*

2 *Place the broad beans and haloumi in a bowl, and add the lemon juice, olive oil, salt and ground black pepper, and serve. Serve with toasted pita bread.*

Note: *If broad beans are large, blanch and peel off outer skins.*

Serves 4

ingredients

**100g/3¹/₂oz haloumi cheese (halved)
oil for brushing
250g/8oz broad beans
(fresh or frozen)
65ml/2fl oz lemon juice
80ml/3fl oz olive oil
salt and ground black pepper
4 rounds pita bread**

vegetable
& lentil curry

Photograph on right

Method:

1 *Heat oil in a large saucepan, add onion, garlic, cumin, coriander, turmeric and carrots and cook for 5 minutes or until onion is soft.*

2 *Stir in lentils, tomatoes and stock or water and bring to the boil. Reduce heat, cover and simmer for 15 minutes.*

3 *Add chilli sauce, pumpkin and cauliflower and cook for 15-20 minutes longer or until pumpkin is tender. Stir in almonds and black pepper to taste. To serve, ladle curry into bowls and top with a spoonful of yoghurt.*

Serves 4

ingredients

1 tablespoon olive oil
1 onion, sliced
1 clove garlic, minced
1 teaspoon ground cumin
1 teaspoon ground coriander
1 teaspoon ground turmeric
2 carrots, sliced
100g/3¹/₂oz red lentils
440g/14oz canned tomatoes, undrained and mashed
1¹/₂ cups/375mL/12fl oz vegetable stock or water
1 teaspoon chilli sauce, or according to taste
500g/1lb pumpkin or potatoes, cut into 2cm/³/₄in cubes
¹/₂ cauliflower, cut into florets
2 tablespoons blanched almonds
freshly ground black pepper
4 tablespoons natural yoghurt

spicy vegetable
loaf

Photograph on right

Method:

1 *Heat oil in a large frying pan, add garlic, onion, chilli powder, cumin, coriander and turmeric and cook for 4-5 minutes or until onion is soft.*

2 *Add lentils, carrot, potato, tomatoes and stock and bring to the boil. Reduce heat, cover and simmer for 30 minutes or until lentils are tender. Remove pan from heat and set aside to cool slightly.*

3 *Place egg whites in a bowl and beat until stiff peaks form. Fold egg whites into lentil mixture.*

4 *Stir rolled oats into lentil mixture and season to taste with black pepper. Spoon into a lightly greased 11 x 21cm/4¹/₂ x 8¹/₂in loaf tin and bake for 1 hour.*

Serves 6

ingredients

1 tablespoon olive oil
1 clove garlic, minced
1 onion, chopped
¹/₂ teaspoon chilli powder
¹/₂ teaspoon ground cumin
¹/₂ teaspoon ground coriander
¹/₂ teaspoon ground turmeric
500g/1lb red lentils
1 carrot, grated
1 large potato, grated
440g/14oz canned tomatoes, undrained and mashed
2 cups/500mL/16fl oz vegetable stock
3 egg whites
1¹/₂ cups/140g/4¹/₂oz rolled oats
freshly ground black pepper

Oven temperature 180°C, 350°F, Gas 4

beans in rich
tomato sauce

Method:

1 Place beans in a large bowl, cover with water and set aside to soak overnight.

2 Drain beans, place in a saucepan with enough water to cover and bring to the boil. Boil for 10 minutes, then reduce heat and simmer for 1 hour or until tender. Drain and set aside.

3 Heat oil in a large saucepan, add garlic and onion and cook, stirring, for 3 minutes or until onion is golden. Add parsley, rosemary and tomatoes and bring to the boil. Reduce heat and simmer, stirring occasionally, for 20 minutes or until mixture reduces and thickens. Stir in beans and black pepper to taste and cook for 15 minutes longer.

Serves 6

ingredients

**500g/1lb dried lima beans
1 tablespoon olive oil
1 clove garlic, minced
1 onion, finely chopped
3 tablespoons chopped fresh parsley
1 tablespoon chopped fresh rosemary
or 1 teaspoon dried rosemary
440g/14oz canned tomatoes,
undrained and mashed
freshly ground black pepper**

bean patties
with avocado sauce

Method:

1 *To make patties, place half the beans in a bowl and mash. Add carrot, breadcrumbs, eggs, tomato sauce, chives, black pepper to taste and remaining beans and mix well to combine. Shape bean mixture into twelve patties, using wet hands. Roll patties in dried breadcrumbs to coat, place on a tray or plate lined with plastic food wrap, cover and refrigerate for 30 minutes.*

2 *Heat oil in a nonstick frying pan and cook patties for 4-5 minutes each side or until golden and heated through.*

3 *To make sauce, place sour cream, avocado, lemon juice and chilli powder in a small saucepan and heat until just warm.*

Serve sauce with patties.

Makes 12 patties

ingredients

2 x 315g/10oz canned lima or butter
beans, drained and rinsed
1 large carrot, grated
3 cups/185g/6oz breadcrumbs, made
from stale bread
2 eggs, lightly beaten
4 tablespoons tomato sauce
2 tablespoons snipped fresh chives
freshly ground black pepper
1 cup/125g/4oz dried breadcrumbs
2 tablespoons vegetable oil
<u>Avocado Sauce</u>
1/2 cup/125g/4oz sour cream
1/2 avocado, mashed
2 teaspoons lemon juice
pinch chilli powder

okra & bean stew

Method:

1 Heat oil in a large saucepan. Add garlic, chillies and onions and cook over a medium heat, stirring constantly, for 5 minutes or until onions are soft and golden.

2 Add okra, eggplant (aubergines), tomatoes, beans, tofu, wine and sugar. Bring to the boil, then reduce heat and simmer for 30 minutes. Stir in basil and black pepper to taste.

Serves 4

ingredients

2 teaspoons vegetable oil
2 cloves garlic, crushed
2 fresh red chillies, chopped
2 onions, sliced
250g/8oz okra
2 eggplant (aubergines), chopped
2 x 440g/14oz canned peeled tomatoes, undrained and mashed
440g/14oz canned red kidney beans, rinsed
250g/8oz firm tofu, cut into chunks
1/2 cup/125mL/4fl oz red wine
1 tablespoon brown sugar
3 tablespoons chopped fresh basil
freshly ground black pepper

chickpea
and tomato curry

Method:

1 *Heat oil in a large saucepan over a medium heat, add garlic, ginger and onion and cook, stirring, for 3 minutes or until onion is golden. Add cumin, coriander and curry paste and cook for 2 minutes longer.*

2 *Add tomatoes and chickpeas and bring to the boil. Reduce heat and simmer for 10 minutes.*

3 *Stir in mushrooms, eggs and mint and cook for 3 minutes or until curry is heated through. Season to taste with black pepper, sprinkle with coconut and serve immediately.*
Note: *Made from fresh red chillies, red curry paste lends distinctive colour to Malaysian-style curries. If you prefer, substitute green curry paste (prepared from green chillies) or any of the many varieties of curry pastes available from gourmet or international sections of supermarkets and in Oriental food stores.*

Serves 4

ingredients

1 tablespoon vegetable oil
1 clove garlic, crushed
2 tablespoons finely grated fresh ginger
1 onion, chopped
1 tablespoon ground cumin
1 tablespoon ground coriander
1 tablespoon red curry paste
440g/14oz canned tomatoes, undrained and mashed
440g/14oz canned chickpeas, rinsed and drained
125g/4oz button mushrooms, halved
3 hard-boiled eggs, quartered
3 tablespoons chopped fresh mint
freshly ground black pepper
60g/2oz shredded coconut, toasted

beans con carne

Photograph on right

Method:
1 Heat water in a saucepan, add onion and garlic and cook, stirring, for 3-4 minutes or until onion is soft.
2 Add red capsicum (red pepper), red kidney beans, carrots, green beans, tomatoes, tomato juice and chilli powder and bring to the boil. Reduce heat and simmer, stirring occasionally, for 15-20 minutes or until mixture reduces and thickens. Stir in parsley and serve.

Serves 6

ingredients

3 tablespoons water
2 onions, chopped
2 cloves garlic, minced
1 red capsicum (pepper), chopped
2 x 440g/14 oz canned red kidney beans, drained
2 carrots, diced
250g/8oz green beans, cut into 2.5cm/1in pieces
2 x 440g/14oz canned tomatoes, undrained and mashed
1 cup/250mL/8fl oz tomato juice
1/4 teaspoon chilli powder, or according to taste
4 tablespoons chopped fresh parsley

capsicum
(peppers) filled with beans

Photograph on right

Method:
1 Cut capsicums (peppers), in half lengthwise and remove seeds and pith. Place capsicums (peppers), shells on a lightly greased baking tray and set aside.
2 Heat oil in a large saucepan, add onion and cook, stirring, for 2-3 minutes or until onion is soft.
3 Add cumin, garlic, tomato paste (purée), stock, tomatoes and red kidney beans to pan and bring to the boil. Reduce heat and simmer, uncovered, for 10 minutes or until mixture reduces and thickens. Season to taste with black pepper.
4 Spoon filling into prepared capsicum (pepper) shells and bake for 20 minutes or until capsicums (peppers), are tender.

Serves 4

ingredients

4 red or green capsicums (peppers)
Bean filling
2 tablespoons olive oil
1 onion, chopped
2 tablespoons ground cumin
1 clove garlic, minced
3 tablespoons tomato paste (purée)
1/4 cup/60mL/2fl oz chicken or vegetable stock
440g/14oz canned tomatoes, undrained and mashed
440g/14oz canned red kidney beans, drained
freshly ground black pepper

Oven temperature 180°C, 350°F, Gas 4

salad nicoise

salads

Salads made with legumes, beans

and grains make satisfying and substantial side dishes. When these ingredients are teamed with fish or meat you have a wonderful main course. So next time you are looking for a warm weather main dish why not try black-eyed bean or tuna bean salad?

salad niçoise

Photograph Page 59

Method:

1 Arrange lettuce leaves, beans, red capsicum (red pepper) artichokes, tomatoes, cucumber, spring onions, anchovy fillets, tuna, olives and eggs on a large serving platter or in a large salad bowl. Drizzle with oil and season to taste with black pepper.

Serves 4-6

ingredients

1 lettuce of your choice,
leaves separated
500g/1lb fresh young broad
beans, shelled
1 large red capsicum (pepper), cut
into thin strips
8 marinated artichoke hearts, halved
250g/8oz cherry tomatoes
1 large cucumber, cut into strips
3 spring onions, chopped
12 canned anchovy fillets, drained
250g/8oz canned tuna
in water, drained
185g/6oz marinated black olives
6 hard-boiled eggs, quartered
1/4 cup/60mL/2fl oz olive oil
freshly ground black pepper

warm
chickpea salad

Photograph on right

ingredients

Method:

1 Place chickpeas in a large bowl, cover with cold water and set aside to soak overnight. Drain. Place chickpeas, stock, garlic, thyme sprig, bay leaves and quartered onion in a large saucepan and bring to the boil. Boil for 10 minutes, then reduce heat and simmer for 45-60 minutes or until chickpeas are tender. Drain.

2 To make dressing, place vinegar, oil, thyme and garlic in a small bowl and whisk to combine. Add onion, spring onions and black pepper to taste and mix to combine.

3 Spoon dressing over warm chickpeas, toss to combine and sprinkle with parsley. Serve warm or at room temperature.

Serves 6

185g/6oz dried chickpeas
6 cups/1.5 litre/2 1/2pt vegetable or
chicken stock
1 clove garlic, minced
1 sprig fresh thyme
2 bay leaves
1 onion, quartered
3 tablespoons chopped fresh parsley
Fresh thyme dressing
1/2 cup/60mL/2fl oz red wine vinegar
1/4 cup/60mL/2fl oz olive oil
2 teaspoons finely chopped fresh
thyme or 1/2 teaspoon dried thyme
1 clove garlic, crushed
1 small onion, thinly sliced
2 spring onions, finely chopped
freshly ground black pepper

tuna bean
salad

Method:

1 Place beans in a large bowl, cover with water and set aside to soak overnight, then drain. Place beans and onion in a saucepan with enough water to cover and bring to the boil. Boil for 10 minutes, then reduce heat and simmer for 1 hour or until beans are tender. Remove onion and discard, drain beans and set aside to cool.

2 Place beans, tuna, spring onions, red capsicum (pepper) and parsley in a salad bowl.

3 Place oil, vinegar and black pepper to taste in a screwtop jar and shake well to combine. Pour dressing over bean mixture and toss to combine. Serve immediately.

Serves 6

ingredients

375g/12oz dried haricot beans
1 onion, halved
440g/14oz canned tuna,
drained and flaked
4 spring onions, chopped
1 red capsicum (pepper), diced
4 tablespoons chopped fresh parsley
4 tablespoons olive oil
2 tablespoons cider vinegar
freshly ground black pepper

prawn & bean
salad

Method:

1 Heat oil in a large frying pan and cook garlic, bay leaf, oregano, thyme, onions and green capsicum (pepper), over a medium heat, stirring for 5 minutes or until onions are soft.

2 Stir in beans, tomato paste (puree) and bring to simmering. Cook, uncovered, for 15-20 minutes or until most of the liquid evaporates.

3 Remove pan from heat and set aside to cool completely. Add prawns and season to taste with black pepper. Serve at room temperature.

Serves 6

ingredients

2 tablespoons olive oil
2 cloves garlic, minced
1 bay leaf
3 teaspoons chopped fresh oregano or
1 teaspoon dried oregano
3 teaspoons chopped fresh thyme or
1 teaspoon dried thyme
3 onions, sliced
1 green capsicum (pepper), cut into strips
440g/14oz canned haricot or lima beans, drained
440g/14oz canned tomatoes, undrained and mashed
1 tablespoon tomato paste (purée)
24 large cooked prawns, shelled and deveined
freshly ground black pepper

red hot beans

Photograph on right

Method:

1 *Place beans in a large bowl, cover with water and set aside to soak overnight, then drain.*
2 *Place beans, eggplant (aubergine), red capsicum (pepper), onion, garlic, tomatoes, tomato purée, chilli sauce and water in a large saucepan and bring to the boil. Boil for 15 minutes then reduce heat and simmer, stirring occasionally, for 1 hour or until beans are tender. Season to taste with black pepper and sprinkle with coriander (cilanto).*

Serves 4

ingredients

250g/8oz dried red kidney beans
1 eggplant (aubergine), diced
1 red capsicum (pepper), cut into strips
1 onion, sliced
1 clove garlic, crushed
4 large tomatoes, skinned and chopped
2 tablespoons tomato purée
2 teaspoons chilli sauce
1 cup/250mL/8fl oz water
freshly ground black pepper
2 tablespoons chopped fresh coriander (cilantro)

lentil
salad

Photograph on right

ingredients

200g/6¹/₂ oz red lentils
200g/6 oz yellow lentils
6 cups/1.5 litres/2¹/₂pt vegetable stock
1 teaspoon cumin seeds
2 tomatoes, diced
2 stalks celery, sliced
¹/₂ green capsicum (pepper), diced
¹/₂ red capsicum (pepper), diced
1 small onion, chopped
1 small avocado, stoned, peeled and chopped
2 tablespoons snipped fresh chives
<u>Spicy dressing</u>
¹/₄ teaspoon ground coriander
¹/₄ teaspoon ground turmeric
pinch chilli powder
1 clove garlic, minced
4 tablespoons cider vinegar
1 tablespoon olive oil
freshly ground black pepper

Method:

1 *Place red and yellow lentils, stock and cumin seeds in a saucepan and bring to the boil. Reduce heat and simmer for 20 minutes or until lentils are tender. Drain and set aside to cool.*
2 *Place cold lentils, tomatoes, celery, green and red capsicums (peppers), onion and avocado in a large salad bowl.*
3 *To make dressing, place coriander, turmeric, chilli powder, garlic, vinegar, oil and black pepper to taste in a screwtop jar and shake well to combine. Spoon dressing over salad and toss to combine. Sprinkle with chives and serve immediately.*

Serves 6

bean & bacon salad

Method:

1 Boil, steam or microwave broccoli and snow peas (mangetout), separately, until just tender. Drain and place in a large salad bowl.

2 Cook bacon in a frying pan, stirring constantly, for 4-5 minutes or until lightly browned. Remove and drain on absorbent kitchen paper.

3 To make dressing, place oil, vinegar, mustard and black pepper to taste in a screwtop jar and shake well to combine.

4 Add bacon, beans and parsley to salad bowl. Pour over dressing and toss to combine. Serve immediately.

Note: This warm salad makes an interesting starter to a winter meal.

Serves 4

ingredients

**1 small head broccoli,
broken into small florets**
185g/6oz snow peas (mangetout)
6 rashers bacon, cut into strips
**440g/14oz canned lima or butter
beans, drained and rinsed**
1 tablespoon chopped fresh parsley
<u>French dressing</u>
¹/₄ cup/60mL/2fl oz olive oil
1 tablespoon cider vinegar
1 teaspoon Dijon mustard
freshly ground black pepper

lentil
& mushroom salad

Method:

1 Bring a large saucepan of water to the boil. Add lentils, reduce heat and simmer for 30 minutes or until lentils are soft. Drain, rinse under cold running water and drain again.

2 Place lentils, mushrooms, spring onions, pumpkin seeds, grapes, capsicum (pepper) and spinach leaves in a large bowl. Toss to combine.

3 To make dressing, place garlic, honey, soy sauce, vinegar, oil and grape juice in a screwtop jar and shake well to combine.

4 Spoon dressing over salad, cover and marinate at room temperature for 3 hours.

Serves 4-6

ingredients

375g/12oz red lentils
250g/8oz button mushrooms, halved
4 spring onions, sliced diagonally
4 tablespoons pumpkin seeds
250g/8oz grapes
1 yellow or red capsicum (pepper), chopped
4 spinach leaves, shredded
<u>Honey dressing</u>
2 cloves garlic, minced
1 tablespoon honey
2 tablespoons soy sauce
3 tablespoons tarragon vinegar
2 tablespoons vegetable oil
1/3 cup/90 mL/3floz grape juice

black-eyed
bean salad

Method:

1 *Place beans in a large bowl, cover with water and set aside to soak overnight, then drain. Bring a large saucepan of water to the boil, add beans and boil for 10 minutes. Reduce heat and cook for 20-30 minutes or until beans are soft. Drain and set aside to cool.*

2 *Place beans, vinegar, onion, tomatoes, basil and mint in a bowl, toss to combine and set aside for 20 minutes.*

3 *Brush eggplant (aubergine) slices lightly with oil. Place under a preheated hot grill and cook for 2 minutes each side or until golden.*

4 *Arrange lettuce leaves, bean mixture and eggplant (aubergine) on a serving platter. Serve at room temperature.*

ingredients

250g/8oz black-eyed beans
2 tablespoons balsamic or red wine vinegar
I red onion, finely chopped
3 ripe tomatoes, chopped
2 tablespoons chopped fresh basil
I tablespoon chopped fresh mint
I eggplant (aubergine), sliced
2 tablespoons olive oil
200g/6¹/₂oz assorted lettuce leaves

Serves 4

bean
& artichoke

Method:

1 *Boil, steam or microwave green beans until just tender. Drain and refresh under cold running water. Set aside.*

2 *Place red capsicum (pepper), strips in a bowl of iced water for 20 minutes or until curled.*

3 *Place green beans, red capsicum(pepper), lima or butter beans, artichoke hearts, oil, vinegar and black pepper to taste in a bowl and toss to combine.*

Serves 4

ingredients

250g/8oz green beans, cut into 2cm/³/₄in pieces
1 red capsicum (pepper), cut into thin strips
250g/8oz canned lima or butter beans, drained and rinsed
440g/14oz canned artichoke hearts, drained and halved
2 tablespoons olive oil
4 tablespoons vinegar
freshly ground black pepper

indian
dhal

Photograph on right

ingredients

250g/8oz brown or red lentils
4 cups/1litre/1³/₄pt water
1 teaspoon ground turmeric
1 clove garlic, crushed
30g/1oz ghee or clarified butter
1 large onion, chopped
1 teaspoon garam masala
¹/₂ teaspoon ground ginger
1 teaspoon ground coriander
¹/₂ teaspoon cayenne pepper

1

2

3

Method:

1 *Wash lentils in cold water.*

2 *Place lentils, water, turmeric and garlic in a large saucepan and bring to simmering. Cover and simmer, stirring occasionally, for 30 minutes or until lentils are cooked. Remove cover from pan, bring to the boil and boil to reduce excess liquid.*

3 *Melt ghee or butter in a large frying pan, add onion and cook for 5 minutes or until onion is soft. Stir in garam masala, ginger, coriander and cayenne pepper and cook for 1 minute. Stir spice mixture into lentils and serve immediately.*

Note: *Dhal is an Indian vegetarian dish made from lentils. In Hindustani the word for pulses (lentils, split peas and beans) is dhal. Yellow lentils are called toor dhal, pink lentils masoor dhal and yellow split peas channa dhal.*

Serves 6

1

2

falafel
in pitta bread

4 large pitta bread rounds, warmed
shredded lettuce
onion slices
tomato slices
<u>Falafels</u>
440g/14oz canned chickpeas, drained
1 onion, quartered
2 cloves garlic, crushed
2 slices white bread
1/2 teaspoon cumin seeds
4 small dried chillies, seeded and minced
1 tablespoon chopped fresh parsley
1 egg, lightly beaten
freshly ground black pepper
1/3 cup/45g/1 1/2oz dried breadcrumbs
vegetable oil for deep-frying

Method:

1 To make falafels, place chickpeas, onion, garlic, bread, cumin seeds and chillies in a food processor or blender and process until smooth. Transfer mixture to a bowl and stir in parsley, egg and black pepper to taste.

2 Divide mixture into eight equal portions and roll into balls. Roll balls in dried breadcrumbs, then flatten slightly to make an oval shape.

3 Heat oil in a deep saucepan until a cube of bread dropped in browns in 50 seconds. Cook falafels a few at a time for 3 minutes or until golden. Remove and drain on absorbent kitchen paper.

4 Cut each pitta bread round in half and fill each half with a falafel, some lettuce and a few slices of onion and tomato. Serve immediately.

Makes 8

vegetable couscous

1

2

2 cups/250g/8oz couscous
2 cups/500mL/16fl oz water
4 tablespoons olive oil
2 onions, chopped
1 eggplant (aubergine), diced
500g/1lb pumpkin, acorn squash
or marrow, diced
2 carrots, sliced
1 teaspoon chilli paste (sambal oelek)
2 tomatoes, peeled and chopped
2 tablespoons tomato purée
2 cups/500mL/16fl oz vegetable or
chicken stock
440g/14oz canned chickpeas, drained
2 zucchini (courgettes), sliced
60g/2oz sultanas
2 tablespoons chopped fresh parsley

Method:

1 Place couscous and water in a large bowl and set aside to soak for 15 minutes or until water is absorbed. Heat oil in a large saucepan, add onions, eggplant (aubergine), pumpkin or squash and carrots and cook, stirring, for 5 minutes. Stir in chilli paste (sambal oelek), tomatoes, tomato purée and stock and bring to the boil.

2 Line a large metal sieve or colander with muslin or all-purpose kitchen cloth and place over saucepan. Place couscous in sieve or colander, then cover with aluminium foil and steam for 20 minutes. Remove sieve or colander and stir chickpeas, zucchini (courgettes) and sultanas into vegetable mixture. Replace sieve or colander, fluff up couscous with a fork, cover and steam for 20 minutes longer.

3 Spread couscous around the edge of a large serving dish. Stir parsley into vegetable mixture and spoon into the centre of the serving dish.

Serves 6

crunchy
split peas

Photograph on right

ingredients

**185g/6oz yellow split peas or
(90g/3oz yellow split peas and
90g/3oz green split peas)
2 teaspoons bicarbonate of soda
oil for deep-frying
¹/₂ teaspoon chilli powder
¹/₂ teaspoon ground coriander
pinch ground cinnamon
pinch ground cloves
I teaspoon salt**

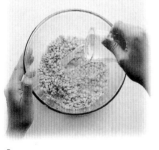

1

2

3

Method:

1 *Place split peas in a large bowl, cover with water, stir in bicarbonate of soda and set aside to soak overnight.*

2 *Rinse split peas under cold running water and drain thoroughly. Set aside for at least 30 minutes, then spread out on absorbent kitchen paper to dry. Heat about 5cm/2in oil in a frying pan and cook split peas in batches until golden. Using a slotted spoon, remove peas and drain on absorbent kitchen paper.*

3 *Transfer cooked peas to a dish, sprinkle with chilli powder, coriander, cinnamon, cloves and salt and toss to coat. Allow peas to cool and store in an airtight container.*

Note: *Take care when frying the peas as even when completely dry they tend to cause the oil to bubble to the top of the pan.*

Serves 8

Legumes

Adzuki beans: Small reddish brown beans with a cream-coloured seam. Their creamy texture is particularly popular in Japan and China where they are used in soups, patés and savoury dishes.

Black beans: Small, almost round, black beans with a white seam, black beans are popular in the West Indies and Chinese cuisine. They are a sweet-tasting

bean that can be used in soups, salads and savoury dishes.

Broad beans: Flat beans native to North Africaranging in colour from olive greem to brown cream. Initially cultivated by the ancient Egyptians and Greeks, they are known in Europe as Fava beans and are mostly eaten dried. Broad beans are also eaten fresh.

Butter beans: Native to South America, these large plump, white beans are similar in shape to broad beans. They are available fresh, dried, canned and frozen.

Cannellini: White kidney beans with square ends. Popular in Italian cuisine, they are delicious in soups and salads or in place of haricot beans to make baked beans.

Chickpeas: Available as white garbanzo or small, brown desi chickpeas. Both are round and rough textured with a pointed beard at one end. They are crunchy with a nutty flavour and are popular in Middle Eastern cooking where they are combined with tahini, lemon and garlic to make a version of falafel. In Greece. roasted chickpeas are served with drinks.

Haricot/Navy beans: Small white oval beans. The term haricot derives from medieval times when dried beans were used chiefly in a pot containing a haricot of meat. Probably best known for their use in commercial baked beans, they were commonly served to the US Navy, hence the alternative name. These beans are also delicious in casseroles.

Lentils: Popular in European and Indian cuisine, lentils are available in brown, green, orange, yellow, and black. They are lens-shaped and may be bought whole or split. Used in soups and casseroles, they are also the main ingredient of the well-known Indian stew, dhal.

Lima beans: Native to South America, lima beans are flat kidney-shaped beans which can be either small and green or large and white. They have a soft floury texture and are popular in both salads and hot dishes.

Mung beans: Widely cultivated in India and China, these small olive green beans are available whole, split and skinless. They are commonly used in stews and salads but are best known in their sprouted form as bean sprouts.

Red kidney beans: Sweet-tasting, red, kidney-shaped beans. They are mostly used in soups, stews and salads, and traditionally found in Creole cooking and in the Mexican dish Chilli Con Carne.

Soya beans: These small, hard, oval, beige beans are extremely versatile. Originally cultivated in China, soya beans are possibly the most nutritious of all beans and are best known for their by-products, which include soy sauce, tofu (bean curd) and miso (fermented bean paste). Soya beans are also used to make textured vegetable protein (TVP) and soy bean milk.

Split peas: Green and yellow peas are available. The green pea is traditionally used in English pease pudding. The yellow variety is puréed for soup. In Sweden, this soup is traditionally served on a Thursday evening to commemorate the day of the last supper of the unpopular King Eric XIV, who was poisoned by a dash of arsenic in his split pea soup!

Cooking legumes

You win two ways when you cook with beans: firstly in your wallet, as these dietary staples are remarkably economical; secondly in your health, as there are few foods more nutritious.

Tips for cooking legumes

All legumes except lentils and split peas require soaking before cooking. Soaking helps to clean and soften them.

- Soaking lentils and split peas will speed up the cooking time. Depending on how much time is available, legumes can either have a long or a short soak.
- Do not add salt to the cooking water as this causes the skins to split and the insides to toughen.
- The cooking time depends on the type, age and quality of the beans. The fresher the beans, the shorter the cooking time.
- All legumes should be brought to the boil and boiled rapidly for at least 5 minutes.
- Red kidney beans should be boiled for 10-15 minutes to kill the toxins in them.
- Always cook legumes in a large saucepan with enough cold water to cover them by 5cm/2in.

Long soak

This method of preparation requires a little forethought. To prepare legumes, rinse, then place them in a large bowl. Cover with cold water, then cover the bowl and set aside to soak overnight at room temperature. If soaking lentils or split peas, only 10 minutes is required. Drain and replace the water before cooking.

Short soak

For this method simply place the legumes in a large saucepan, cover them with water and bring to the boil. Reduce the heat and simmer for 5 minutes. Remove the pan from the heat and set aside to soak for 1-2 hours (see Legume Cooking Chart for the time required). Drain and rinse before using.

Legume Cooking Chart

Legume	Short soak time	Cooking time
Adzuki beans	1 hour	30-45 minutes
Black-eyed beans	1 hour	45-60 minutes
Borlotti beans	1 hour	1¼-1½ hours
Butter or Lima beans	1 hour	1-1½ hours
Cannellini beans	1 hour	1-1½ hours
Chickpeas	2 hours	1-1½ hours
Haricot beans	1 hour	1 hour
Lentils	—	30 minutes
Pinto beans	1 hour	1¼ hours
Red kidney beans	1 hour	1¼-1½ hours
Soya beans	2 hour	2-4 hours
Split peas	—	30 minutes

red hot

gourmet

introduction

introduction

introduction

The passionate pursuit of foods that make us gasp for breath and perspire is nothing new. Early attempts at food preservation often involved liberal applications of pepper and other strong-tasting seasonings—the same ingredients used to help mask the taste of decay when victuals had passed there prime. Many of the hottest cuisines originated in very warm climates, where particular foods have long been revered for the ability to induce sweating, thereby triggering a kind of natural air-conditioning when the sweat evaporates. Throughout history pepper, garlic, chiles, and other hot foods have been acclaimed as digestives, antiseptics, antidepressants, and even aphrodisiacs.

Practical benefits aside, certain edibles possess an irresistible quality that keeps human palates begging for more. The fascination with hot stuff—foods capable of producing a mix of pleasure and pain—has developed into a hot love affair, and it's getting hotter every day.

Cuisines the world over rely on certain ingredients with a reputation for feistiness to add heat, not to mention exciting flavour. Just as the name of these foods vary from culture to culture, so do individual tolerances for heat and spiciness: What's exquisitely hot to you may not seem hot at all to someone else. In preparing the recipes in this book, let your own taste and tolerance level be your guide. Adapt the recipes to suit yourself, adding more or less of the following heat sources:

Onions and Garlic: Eaten raw, both onions and garlic release a strong-tasting acid. Cooked at low heat, the acid breaks down and the harshness dissipates. Most varieties of onions and garlic have powerful personalities but are easy to get along with when handled properly. Fresh, firm onions and young, ivory-coloured heads of garlic provide the best flavour.

Mustard: The seeds of the mustard plant are virtually flavourless and odourless. But when crushed and steeped 15 minutes in water or other liquid, mustard can be blistering in its effects—literally. The volatile oils in mustard were traditionally considered powerful medicine for a number of ailments, with mustard poultices and foot baths among the most common remedies.

Prepared mustards made from yellow, brown, or black mustard seed run the gamut from mild table varieties to fiery Asian blends. Wasabi, a fire-breathing cousin to mustard, is often served with sushi and other Japanese dishes.

Ginger: Ginger imparts a refreshingly clean, hot taste that adds sparkle to sweet and spicy foods alike. It is available fresh, pickled, candied, and powdered.

Note: For the recipes in this book, powdered ginger is not an acceptable substitute for fresh ginger.

Pepper: A member of the Piper nigrum family, pepper is available in three forms: black peppercorns (the result of drying ripe pepper berries); white (produced by hulling the ripe berries); and green peppercorns (made by pickling the immature berries). Pepper's hot bite and flavour can't be duplicated; like mustard, it releases its heat and flavour only when cracked or ground.

Chile: Chiles are the hot-blooded relatives of sweet, mild bell peppers, both members of the genus Capsicum. Hot chiles, fresh or dried, are among the most potent of all heat sources. The amount of heat in chiles varies (depending upon the variety, growing conditions, and method of processing). Chiles have 60 percent of the substance that makes them hot— capsaicin— in the ribs and veins, 30 percent in the seeds, and 10 percent in the skin. Because small chiles have a proportionately larger volume of ribs and seeds (the hottest areas) than larger chiles, they usually pack more firepower. One of the hottest is the tiny tabasco, the main ingredient in the famous bottled condiment from Louisiana. Chiles also vary in size (from short to long), shape (from blocky to slim), and colour (from pale green to yellow, orange, or red.)

There are a multitude of different names for the same chiles, the similarity of varieties can be confusing. For example, the habanero, a H-bomb of a chile native to the Yucatán peninsula, differs slightly in colour and flavour from the equally potent Jamaican Scotch Bonnet. Both chiles have their zealous fans, but the two are generally regarding as different varieties of the same species and can be substituted for one another.

Note: A chile by any other name is just as hot; always exercise caution in handling and tasting any chile, especially if it is unfamiliar.

Any cook can become a red hot gourmet. It's a matter of selecting authentic ingredients, mastering basic techniques, and applying them to well-crafted recipes like the ones developed for this book and the adaptations you'll create yourself. You'll find red hot recipes to tingle your mouth, clear your head, and warm your soul.

stir-fried tamarind prawns

stir-fries

Stir-frying is a very quick cooking

process, it is therefore very important that all preparation such as cutting and chopping have been completed before the cooking starts. In this chapter you will find succulent stir-fries ranging from Beef with Peppercorns to Coconut Prawns and Scallops.

chicken
with chilli jam

Method:

1 *To make jam, heat oil in a wok over a medium heat, add chillies, ginger and shrimp paste and stir-fry for 1 minute or until golden. Stir in sugar, water and lime juice and cook, stirring, for 3 minutes or until mixture is thick. Remove jam from wok and set aside.*

2 *Heat oil in a clean wok over a high heat for 1 minute, add chicken and shallots and stir-fry for 3 minutes or until chicken is lightly browned.*

3 *Add broccoli, snow peas (mangetout), cashews and soy sauce and stir-fry for 3 minutes longer or until vegetables change colour and are cooked.*

4 *To serve, place chicken on serving plate and top with Chilli Jam.*

   Note: *Serve this tasty chicken dish with steamed jasmine rice. If you prefer, the Chilli Jam can be served separately so that each diner can season their serving according to individual taste.*

Serves 4

ingredients

2 teaspoons vegetable oil
3 chicken breast fillets or 4 boneless thigh fillets, cut into thin strips
4 red or golden shallots, chopped
185g/6oz broccoli, chopped
125g/4oz snow peas (mangetout), halved
60g/2oz unsalted, roasted cashews
2 tablespoons light soy sauce
<u>Chilli jam</u>
2 teaspoons vegetable oil
4 fresh red chillies, sliced
1 tablespoon shredded fresh ginger
1 teaspoon shrimp paste
1/3 cup/90g/3oz sugar
1/3 cup/90ml/3fl oz water
2 tablespoons lime juice

beef
with peppercorns

Method:

1 Heat oil in a wok over a high heat. Add garlic and chilli and cook for 1 minute. Add beef and peppercorns and stir-fry for 3 minutes or until beef is browned.

2 Stir in green pepper, coriander (cilantro), coconut milk and fish sauce and cook for 2 minutes longer.

Serves 4.

ingredients

2 teaspoons vegetable oil
2 cloves garlic, minced
1 fresh green chilli, chopped
500g/1 lb topside or round steak, sliced
1 tablespoon green peppercorns in brine, drained and lightly crushed
1 green pepper, chopped
3 tablespoons fresh coriander (cilantro) leaves
1/3 cup/90mL/3fl oz coconut milk
2 teaspoons Thai fish sauce (nam pla)

coconut
prawns and scallops

Method:

1 Dip prawns in egg whites, then roll in coconut to coat. Heat vegetable oil in a large saucepan until a cube of bread dropped in browns in 50 seconds and cook prawns, a few at a time, for 2-3 minutes or until golden and crisp. Drain on absorbent kitchen paper and keep warm.

2 Heat peanut oil in a wok over a high heat, add red and green chillies, garlic, ginger and lime leaves and stir-fry for 2-3 minutes or until fragrant.

3 Add scallops to wok and stir-fry for 3 minutes or until opaque. Add cooked prawns, snow pea (mangetout) leaves or sprouts, sugar, lime juice and fish sauce and stir-fry for 2 minutes or until heated.

Note: If snow pea (mangetout) leaves or sprouts are unavailable watercress is a good alternative for this dish.

Serves 6

ingredients

1 kg/2 lb large uncooked prawns, shelled and deveined, tails left intact
3 egg whites, lightly beaten
90g/3oz shredded coconut
vegetable oil for deep-frying
1 tablespoon peanut oil
4 fresh red chillies, seeded and sliced
2 small fresh green chillies, seeded and sliced
2 cloves garlic, minced
1 tablespoon shredded fresh ginger
3 kaffir lime leaves, finely shredded
375g/12oz scallops
125g/4oz snow pea (mangetout) leaves or sprouts
2 tablespoons palm or brown sugar
1/4 cup/60ml/2fl oz lime juice
2 tablespoons Thai fish sauce (nam pla)

stir-fried
duck with greens

Method:

1 Slice meat from duck, leaving the skin on, and cut into bite-sized pieces. Reserve as many of the cavity juices as possible.

2 Heat oil in a wok over a medium heat, add curry paste, shrimp paste, lemon grass and chillies and stir-fry for 3 minutes or until fragrant.

3 Add duck and reserved juices and stir-fry for 2 minutes or until coated in spice mixture and heated. Add broccoli or chard, sugar, tamarind and fish sauce and stir-fry for 3-4 minutes or until broccoli is wilted.

Note: Chinese broccoli (gai lum) is a popular Asian vegetable. It has dark green leaves on firm stalks often with small white flowers. The leaves, stalks and flowers are all used in cooking, however the stalks are considered to be the choicest part of the plant. To prepare, remove leaves from stalks and peel, then chop both leaves and stalks and use as directed in the recipe.

Serves 4

ingredients

1 ¹/₄ kg/2¹/₂ lb Chinese barbecued or roasted duck
2 teaspoons vegetable oil
1 tablespoon Thai red curry paste
1 teaspoon shrimp paste
1 stalk fresh lemon grass, finely sliced, or ¹/₂ teaspoon dried lemon grass, soaked in hot water until soft
4 fresh red chillies
1 bunch Chinese broccoli (gai lum) or Swiss chard, chopped
1 tablespoon palm or brown sugar
2 tablespoons tamarind concentrate
1 tablespoon Thai fish sauce (nam pla)

pork
and pumpkin stir-fry

Method:

1 Place curry paste in wok and cook, stirring, over a high heat for 2 minutes or until fragrant. Add onions and cook for 2 minutes longer or until onions are soft. Remove from pan and set aside.

2 Heat oil in wok, add pork and stir-fry for 3 minutes or until brown. Remove pork from pan and set aside.

3 Add pumpkin, lime leaves, sugar, coconut milk and fish sauce to pan, bring to simmering and simmer for 2 minutes. Stir in curry paste mixture and simmer for 5 minutes longer. Return pork to pan and cook for 2 minutes or until heated.

Note: Spoons and forks are used in Thailand for eating, not chopsticks. Like us, Thais would only use chopsticks when eating Chinese food.

Serves 4

ingredients

2 tablespoons Thai red curry paste
2 onions, cut into thin wedges, layers separated
2 teaspoons vegetable oil
500g/1 lb lean pork strips
500g/1 lb peeled butternut pumpkin (squash), cut into 2cm/³⁄₄in cubes
4 kaffir lime leaves, shredded
1 tablespoon palm or brown sugar
2 cups/500ml/16fl oz coconut milk
1 tablespoon Thai fish sauce (nam pla)

pork
with garlic and pepper

Method:

1 Heat oil in a wok or frying pan over a medium heat, add garlic and black peppercorns and stir-fry for 1 minute. Add pork and stir-fry for 3 minutes or until brown.

2 Add bok choy (Chinese greens), coriander, sugar, soy sauce and lime juice and stir-fry for 3-4 minutes or until pork and bok choy are tender.

Note: Bok choy is also known as Chinese chard, buck choy and pak choi. It varies in length from 10-30cm/4-12in. For this recipe the smaller variety is used. It has a mild, cabbage-like flavour. Ordinary cabbage could be used for this recipe.

Serves 4

ingredients

2 teaspoons vegetable oil
4 cloves garlic, sliced
1 tablespoon crushed black peppercorns
500g/1 lb lean pork strips
1 bunch/500g/1 lb baby bok choy (Chinese greens), chopped
4 tablespoons fresh coriander (cilantro) leaves
2 tablespoons palm or brown sugar
2 tablespoons light soy sauce
2 tablespoons lime juice

stir-fried
bitter melon

Method:

1 Rub each slice of bitter melon (gourd) with salt, place in a colander and set aside for 30 minutes. Rinse under cold water and drain thoroughly.

2 Heat oil in a wok over a medium heat, add dried prawns, shallots, garlic and lemon grass or rind and stir-fry for 4 minutes or until shallots are golden.

3 Add chillies and bitter melon (gourd) and stir-fry for 4 minutes or until melon is tender. Add pawpaw, snow peas (mangetout) and tamarind and stir-fry for 2 minutes or until snow peas (mangetout) are tender.

Note: This dish is delicious served on a bed of cellophane noodles and topped with fried onions. Bitter melon (gourd) looks somewhat like a cucumber with a lumpy skin and as the name suggests has a bitter taste. It should always be degorged with salt before using.

Serves 4

ingredients

1 medium bitter melon (gourd), peeled, seeds removed, cut into 1cm/¹/₂ in thick slices
2 tablespoons salt
1 tablespoon vegetable oil
3 tablespoons small dried prawns
6 red or golden shallots, sliced
2 cloves garlic, sliced
2 stalks fresh lemon grass, finely sliced, or 1 teaspoon finely grated lemon rind
3 fresh green chillies, finely sliced
1 small red pawpaw, cut into 3cm/1¹/₄in cubes
125g/4oz snow peas (mangetout), halved
1 tablespoon tamarind concentrate

eggplant
and basil stir-fry

Method:

1 Place eggplant (aubergines) in a colander, sprinkle with salt and set aside for 20 minutes. Rinse under cold running water and pat dry on absorbent kitchen paper.

2 Heat oil in a wok or frying pan over a high heat, add onions, chillies, garlic and lemon grass and stir-fry for 3 minutes. Add eggplant (aubergines), beans and coconut cream and stir-fry for 5 minutes or until eggplant (aubergines) are tender. Stir in basil.

Note: Stir-frying is a very quick cooking process – this dish takes less than 10 minutes – it is therefore very important that all preparation such as cutting and chopping have been completed before the cooking starts.

Serves 6

ingredients

3 eggplant (aubergines), halved lengthways and cut into 1 cm/¹/₂in thick slices
salt
1 tablespoon vegetable oil
2 onions, cut into thin wedges, layers separated
3 fresh red chillies, chopped
2 cloves garlic, sliced
1 stalk fresh lemon grass, chopped, or ¹/₂ teaspoon dried lemon grass, soaked in hot water until soft
250g/8oz green beans, trimmed
1 cup/250mL/8fl oz coconut cream
45g/1¹/₂oz basil leaves

stir-fried
tamarind prawns

Photograph also on page 387

Method:

1 Place tamarind pulp and water in a bowl and stand for 20 minutes. Strain, reserve liquid and set aside. Discard solids.

2 Heat oil in a wok or frying pan over a high heat, add lemon grass or rind and chillies and stir-fry for 1 minute. Add prawns and stir-fry for 2 minutes or until they change colour.

3 Add mangoes, coriander, sugar, lime juice and tamarind liquid · and stir-fry for 5 minutes or until prawns are cooked.

Note: Tamarind is the large pod of the tamarind or Indian date tree. After picking, it is seeded and peeled, then pressed into a dark brown pulp. It is also available as a concentrate. Tamarind pulp or concentrate can be purchased from Indian food stores. In Oriental cooking it is used as a souring agent, if unavailable a mixture of lime or lemon juice and treacle can be used instead.

Serves 4

ingredients

2 tablespoons tamarind pulp
¹/₂ cup/125ml/4fl oz water
2 teaspoons vegetable oil
3 stalks fresh lemon grass, chopped, or
2 teaspoons finely grated lemon rind
2 fresh red chillies, chopped
500g/1 lb medium uncooked prawns,
shelled and deveined, tails intact
2 green (unripe) mangoes, peeled
and thinly sliced
3 tablespoons chopped fresh coriander
(cilantro) leaves
2 tablespoons brown sugar
2 tablespoons lime juice

mussels
with coconut vinegar

Method:

1 Place mussels, coriander (cilantro), lemon grass, ginger and water in a wok over a high heat. Cover and cook for 5 minutes or until mussels open. Discard any mussels that do not open after 5 minutes cooking. Remove mussels from wok, discard coriander (cilantro), lemon grass and ginger. Strain cooking liquid and reserve.

2 Heat oil in a wok over a medium heat, add onion and chillies and stir-fry for 3 minutes or until onion is soft. Add mussels, reserved cooking liquid and coconut vinegar and stir-fry for 2 minutes or until mussels are heated. Scatter with coriander leaves and serve.

Note: This dish is delicious served with boiled egg noodles and topped with coriander leaves and wok juices. Coconut vinegar is made from the sap of the coconut palm. It is available from Oriental food shops. If unavailable any mild vinegar can be used instead.

Serves 4

ingredients

1¹/₂kg/3 lb mussels (clams) in their shells
6 whole coriander (cilantro) plants, washed and roughly chopped
3 stalks fresh lemon grass, bruised, or 1¹/₂ teaspoons dried lemon grass, soaked in hot water until soft
5cm/2in piece fresh ginger, shredded
¹/₂ cup/125ml/4fl oz water
1 tablespoon vegetable oil
1 red onion, halved and sliced
2 fresh red chillies, sliced
2 tablespoons coconut vinegar
fresh coriander (cilantro) leaves

red beef curry

curries

This chapter offers a range of

curry dishes from some of the more popular Asian cuisines. From a Red Beef Curry to a Minted Bean Curry theres a dish sure to tantalise the taste buds.

cardamom
and orange duck

Method:

1 Remove meat from duck and cut into bite-sized pieces – reserve bones, skin and as many of the juices as possible. Place reserved bones, skin and juices, stock, chillies, galangal or ginger, lemon grass, coriander (cilantro) stems and roots, cardamom pods, lime leaves and orange rind in a saucepan and bring to the boil. Reduce heat and simmer, uncovered, for 15 minutes. Strain liquid and set aside. Discard solids.

2 Heat oil in a wok or large saucepan over a medium heat, add shrimp and curry pastes and garlic and cook, stirring, for 1-2 minutes or until fragrant.

3 Add duck pieces and stir to coat with spice paste. Add reserved liquid and simmer for 3-4 minutes or until liquid reduces slightly. Stir in orange segments, coriander (cilantro) leaves and sugar. Serve scattered with spring onions.

Serves 4

ingredients

1 1/2 kg/3 lb Chinese barbecued or roasted duck
3 cups/750ml/1 1/4pt chicken stock
2 small fresh red chillies, halved
3cm/1 1/4in piece fresh galangal or ginger, sliced, or 5 slices bottled galangal
2 stalks fresh lemon grass, cut into 3cm/1 1/4in pieces, bruised, or
1 teaspoon dried lemon grass, soaked in hot water until soft
6 whole coriander (cilantro) plants, washed, stems and roots removed, leaves reserved
6 cardamom pods, crushed
4 kaffir lime leaves, torn into pieces
1 large orange, peeled, all white pith removed from rind, flesh segmented and reserved
1 tablespoon vegetable oil
2 teaspoons shrimp paste
2 teaspoons Thai red curry paste
1 clove garlic, finely chopped
1 tablespoon palm or brown sugar
2 spring onions, cut into thin strips

thai green
chicken curry

Method:

1 Heat oil in a saucepan over a high heat, add onions and cook for 3 minutes or until golden. Stir in curry paste and cook for 2 minutes or until fragrant.

2 Add chicken, basil, lime leaves, coconut milk and fish sauce and bring to the boil. Reduce heat and simmer for 12-15 minutes or until chicken is tender and sauce is thick. Serve garnished with extra basil.

Note: The curry pastes of Thailand are mixtures of freshly ground herbs and spices and if you are able to make your own it is well worth the small effort required.

Serves 6

ingredients

1 tablespoon vegetable oil
2 onions, chopped
3 tablespoons Thai green curry paste
1 kg/2 lb boneless chicken thigh
or breast fillets, chopped
4 tablespoons fresh basil leaves
6 kaffir lime leaves, shredded
2¹/₂ cups/600ml/1pt coconut milk
2 tablespoons Thai fish sauce (nam pla)
extra fresh basil leaves

minted
bean curry

ingredients

6 whole coriander (cilantro) plants, roots
removedand washed, reserve
leaves for another use
2 stalks fresh lemon grass, finely sliced, or
1 teaspoon dried lemon grass, soaked in
hot water until soft
6 kaffir lime leaves, shredded
2 teaspoons palm or brown sugar
3 cups/750mL/1¼pt water
3 tablespoons Thai fish sauce (nam pla)
2 teaspoons peanut oil
3 small fresh green chillies,
shredded (optional)
5cm/2in piece fresh ginger, shredded
2 teaspoons Thai green curry paste
220g/7oz pea eggplant (aubergines)
220g/7oz snake (yard-long) or green beans,
cut into 2½cm/1in pieces
440g/14oz canned tomatoes,
drained and chopped
2 tablespoons tamarind concentrate
60g/2oz fresh mint leaves

Method:

1 Place coriander (cilantro) roots, lemon grass, lime leaves, sugar, water and fish sauce in a saucepan and bring to the boil. Reduce heat and simmer for 10 minutes. Strain, discard solids and set stock aside.

2 Heat oil in a wok or large saucepan over a medium heat, add chillies (if using), ginger and curry paste and stir-fry for 2-3 minutes or until fragrant. Add eggplant (aubergines) and beans and stir to coat with spice mixture. Stir in reserved stock and simmer for 10 minutes or until vegetables are tender. Add tomatoes and tamarind and simmer for 3 minutes or until hot. Stir in mint.

Note: Pea eggplant (aubergines) are tiny green eggplant (aubergines) about the size of green peas and are usually purchased still attached to the vine. They are used whole, eaten raw or cooked and have a bitter taste. If unavailable green peas can be used instead.

Serves 4

green
chilli and prawn curry

Method:

1 Heat 2 teaspoons oil in a saucepan over a medium heat, add reserved prawn shells and heads and cook, stirring, for 3-4 minutes or until shells change colour. Add lemon grass, the halved green chillies, galangal or ginger and water and bring to the boil. Using a wooden spoon break up galangal or ginger, reduce heat and simmer for 10 minutes. Strain, discard solids and set stock aside.

2 Heat remaining oil in a wok or saucepan over a medium heat and stir-fry curry paste for 2-3 minutes or until fragrant.

3 Add prawns, cucumber, 5 whole green chillies (if using), sugar, reserved stock, fish sauce, vinegar and tamarind and cook, stirring, for 4-5 minutes or until prawns change colour and are cooked through.

Serves 4

ingredients

1 tablespoon vegetable oil
1¹/₂kg/3 lb medium uncooked prawns, shelled and deveined, shells and heads reserved
2 stalks fresh lemon grass, bruised, or 1 teaspoon dried lemon grass, soaked in hot water until soft
2 long fresh green chillies, halved
4cm/1¹/₂in piece fresh galangal or ginger, or 6 slices bottled galangal
3 cups/750mL/1¹/₄pt water
2 teaspoons Thai green curry paste
1 cucumber, seeded and cut into thin strips
5 whole fresh green chillies (optional)
1 tablespoon palm or brown sugar
2 tablespoons Thai fish sauce (nam pla)
1 tablespoon coconut vinegar
2 teaspoons tamarind concentrate

red
beef curry

Photograph also on page 399

Method:

1 Place coconut cream in a saucepan and bring to the boil over a high heat, then boil until oil separates from coconut cream and it reduces and thickens slightly. Stir in curry paste and boil for 2 minutes or until fragrant.

2 Add beef, eggplant (aubergines), bamboo shoots, lime leaves, sugar, coconut milk and fish sauce, cover and simmer for 35-40 minutes or until beef is tender. Stir in coriander (cilantro) and chillies.

Note: In Thailand curries are usually served over moulds of rice. The rice absorbs and is flavoured by the large proportion of liquid in the curry. The fragrant rices such as jasmine and basmati are perfect accompaniments for Thai curries.

Serves 4

ingredients

1 cup/250ml/8fl oz coconut cream
3 tablespoons Thai red curry paste
500g/1 lb round or blade steak, cubed
155g/5oz pea eggplant (aubergines) or
1 eggplant (aubergine), diced
220g/7oz canned sliced bamboo shoots
6 kaffir lime leaves, crushed
1 tablespoon brown sugar
2 cups/500ml/16fl oz coconut milk
2 tablespoons Thai fish sauce (nam pla)
3 tablespoons fresh coriander
(cilantro) leaves
2 fresh red chillies, chopped

cashew
and chilli beef curry

Method:

1 Place galangal or ginger, lemon grass, lime leaves, chopped chillies, shrimp paste, fish sauce and lime juice in a food processor and process to make a thick paste, adding a little water if necessary.

2 Heat 1 tablespoon oil in a wok or large saucepan over a medium heat, add shallots, garlic, sliced red chillies and spice paste and cook, stirring, for 2-3 minutes or until fragrant. Remove and set aside.

3 Heat remaining oil in wok over a high heat and stir-fry beef, in batches, until brown. Return spice paste to pan, stir in stock and okra and bring to the boil. Reduce heat and simmer, stirring occasionally, for 15 minutes.

4 Stir in cashews, sugar and soy sauce and simmer for 10 minutes longer or until beef is tender.

Note: Fish sauce 'nam pla' is characteristic of Thai cooking and appears as a seasoning in many dishes. Thai cooks take pride in making their own fish sauce and the ability to make a good sauce is the hallmark of an accomplished cook.

Serves 4

ingredients

3cm/1¼in piece fresh galangal or ginger, chopped or 5 slices bottled galangal, chopped
1 stalk fresh lemon grass, finely sliced, or ½ teaspoon dried lemon grass, soaked in hot water until soft
3 kaffir lime leaves, finely shredded
2 small fresh red chillies, seeded and chopped
2 teaspoons shrimp paste
2 tablespoons Thai fish sauce (nam pla)
1 tablespoon lime juice
2 tablespoons peanut oil
4 red or golden shallots, sliced
2 cloves garlic, chopped
3 small fresh red chillies, sliced
500g/1 lb round or blade steak, cut into 2cm/³⁄₄in cubes
2 cups/500ml/16fl oz beef stock
250g/8oz okra, trimmed
60g/2oz cashews, roughly chopped
1 tablespoon palm or brown sugar
2 tablespoons light soy sauce

chicken
phanaeng curry

Method:

1 Place coconut milk in a saucepan and bring to the boil over a high heat, then boil until oil separates from coconut milk and it reduces and thickens slightly. Stir in curry paste and boil for 2 minutes or until fragrant.
2 Add chicken, beans, peanuts, sugar and fish sauce and simmer for 5-7 minutes or until chicken is tender. Stir in coconut cream, basil and coriander(cilantro). Serve garnished with slices of chilli.

Serves 4

ingredients

2 cups/500ml/16fl oz coconut milk
3 tablespoons Thai red curry paste
500g/1 lb chicken breast fillets, sliced
250g/8oz snake (yard-long)
or green beans
3 tablespoons unsalted peanuts, roasted
and finely chopped
2 teaspoons brown or palm sugar
1 tablespoon Thai fish sauce (nam pla)
1/2 cup/125ml/4fl oz coconut cream
2 tablespoons fresh basil leaves
2 tablespoons fresh coriander (cilantro) leaves
sliced fresh red chilli

chicken
with lime and coconut

Method:

1 Place chicken and curry paste in a bowl and toss to coat. Heat oil in a wok or large saucepan over a high heat, add chicken and stir-fry for 4-5 minutes or until lightly browned and fragrant.
2 Add sugar, lime leaves, lime rind, coconut cream and fish sauce and cook, stirring, over a medium heat for 3-4 minutes or until the sugar dissolves and caramelises.
3 Stir in vinegar and coconut and simmer until chicken is tender. Serve with chillies in a dish on the side.

Note: For something a little different serve this dish with egg noodles.

Serves 4

ingredients

1 kg/2 lb chicken thigh or breast
fillets, cut into thick strips
1 tablespoon Thai red curry paste
1 tablespoon vegetable oil
3 tablespoons palm or brown sugar
4 kaffir lime leaves
2 teaspoons finely grated lime rind
1 cup/250ml/8fl oz coconut cream
1 tablespoon Thai fish sauce (nam pla)
2 tablespoons coconut vinegar
3 tablespoons shredded coconut
4 fresh red chillies, sliced

salads

hot and cold

introduction

introduction

introduction

In this book you will find many delightful surprises, especially for those who thought that salads could only be served on a hot summer's day, and for those, too, who imagine a salad to be the usual greenery served time and time again.

Salads need not have a special season; simple, easy-to-prepare green salads with a special dressing or mixed vegetable salads make wonderful accompaniments to meats, chicken, fish, omelettes and quiches at any time of the year.

Whole or torn, leaves add colour and flavour to salads. Shredded, or shaped into cups for individual portions, they also play an important supporting role in the presentation of cold dishes made with other vegetables, meat, poultry or fish.

The secret to a successful salad is simple: always choose fresh, unblemished salad ingredients, then prepare them in an imaginative way. Combine flavours and textures of salad ingredients carefully and always complement your salads with a compatible dressing or mayonnaise.

We know you will enjoy the salads presented in this book. You will find that the recipes contain a variety of ingredients but are simple to prepare.

Fine food comes in many guises, but seldom is it as convenient, flavoursome or healthful as when it is gathered from the garden or garnered from a greengrocer with garden-fresh produce.

Fresh fruits and vegetables are relatively inexpensive, easy to prepare and full of fibre and nutrients. They come in a glorious array of colours, offer a wide range of tastes and textures and provide raw energy on a sustained level, unlike the quick gratification offered by sugary snacks.

Small wonder that salads — whether simple or carefully composed — are becoming more and more a staple of our daily diet. It is so easy to introduce raw foods in the form of a salad, either at the start of meal, as an accompaniment or, in the French fashion, as a separate course served after the main and before the dessert (to cleanse the palate and, equally importantly, to avoid any conflict between the dressing and the wine).

A hearty main-course salad can be a meal in itself, at any season. If you've never sampled a warm salad, now's the time to experience the contrast in textures and temperatures offered by Warm Steak Salad with Pawpaw and Spanish Onion. And, while Fruit salads are conventionally served as desserts, recipes like Melon and Onion Salad also make excellent savouries.

This comprehensive collection includes over a hundred recipes for salads of every description, plus dozens of dressings.

knowing
your greens

In recent years the availability of various types of salad vegetables has increased so much that a trip to the greengrocer or fruit and vegetable section of any supermarket can be mind-boggling. Use the following as a guide to help you identify, and know how best to use, some of those exotic-looking salad greens.

Witloof or Chicory

Sometimes called Brussels chicory or Belgian endive, this vegetable can be eaten raw or cooked. It has tightly clustered, smooth, white leaves with greenish yellow tips and looks somewhat like an oblong tight-headed lettuce. Witloof means 'white leaf' and when buying this vegetable always look for the whitest witloof. Slightly bitter in taste, it is a versatile vegetable that combines well with a range of flavours.

Curly Endive

Another member of the chicory family, curly endive has large, curly, frilly-edged leaves with a slightly bitter flavour. The leaves graduate from a pale, green yellow to dark green. Use the paler heart leaves and stalks. Sold in large bunches, curly endive makes an attractive bed for a meat or chicken salad and is an interesting addition to a mixed green salad.

Butter or Round Lettuce

There are a several varieties of butter lettuce which include Bibb, Boston and Butterhead. The one thing they have in common is that they are a soft, smallish lettuce with a mild flavour. Often grown hydroponically, the butter lettuce lacks the crunch of iceberg or cos, but is popular in mixed lettuce salads.

Cos or Romaine Lettuce

Popular with the Romans, this lettuce was named by them because they claim to have discovered it on the Greek island of Cos. Later the English and Europeans renamed it Romaine lettuce after the Romans. Today it is known by both names depending on where in the world you reside. This lettuce has an elongated head of dark green oval leaves and a crisp pale green heart. It has a pungent flavour and stays crisp. Its main claim to fame is its use in the traditional Caesar Salad.

Iceberg or Crisp Head Lettuce

Probably the most popular and well known of lettuces, the iceberg lettuce is a large lettuce with crisp outer leaves and a firm, sweet heart. It is the basis of many salads as it combines well with other lettuces and salad greens.

Red Leaf Lettuces

These are among the prettiest of lettuces and include mignonette, lollo rosso and red oakleaf. They are characterised by their soft, smallish leaves with pink- to red-tinged edges. These lettuces have a delicate sweet flavour. The red leaf lettuces are usually interchangeable in a recipe and more often than not are used to give a salad colour and interest.

Radicchio

Yet another member of the chicory family, the radicchio is beetroot-coloured with white veins and has a tightly packed head. It has a tangy, slightly bitter flavour and is a much loved salad vegetable in Italy where it is called red chicory. In Italy, radicchio is the name generally used for chicory.

Rocket

Also known as arugula, roquette and rugula, this plant has small, peppery, dark green leaves and should be used while still young. Rocket first grew wild in the Mediterranean area and was a popular salad green with the ancient Romans. Still rare in many areas, it is in fact easy to grow and for something different in your salads, it is well worth the effort.

English Spinach or Spinach

The young, fresh, dark green leaves of this vegetable are delicious eaten raw. One of the most popular spinach salads consists of roughly torn spinach leaves, crisp bacon pieces and croutons, with a dressing made from the cooking juices of the bacon, lemon juice and freshly ground black pepper.

Watercress

Watercress has smooth round leaves, crunchy stems and a pungent, slightly peppery flavour. Use young outer leaves and tender stems for salads. The remainder can be used in soups. Watercress has long been used as both a food and a medicine and can be traced back to the ancient Greeks. It combines well with other milder salad greens and is popular as a garnish for salads and open sandwiches. Watercress does not keep well and should be stored upright in the refrigerator in a container of water, and covered with a plastic food bag. Change the water daily for to ensure lasting freshness.

salad
vegetables

While lettuce, chicory and a variety of other greens form the basis of many salads, there are also a number of other salad vegetables which are popular and should not be forgotten when creating wonderful salads.

Cabbage

One of the oldest cultivated vegetable species, the cabbage family includes white cabbage, red cabbage and yellow and green savoy cabbage. Used raw and finely shredded, it is the basis of the ever popular coleslaw. Red cabbage, usually cooked, is also delicious raw, and when shredded and combined with green cabbage makes an attractive slaw. Store cabbage in a plastic food bag in the crisper section of the refrigerator.

Red, green or yellow capsicum

Also called peppers and bell peppers, when sliced or chopped these add colour and crunch to salads. Always choose well-shaped, firm capsicums with a glossy, smooth skin. Dull-looking capsicums, those with soft spots and wrinkled skins should be avoided. Remove the stalk, seeds and white membrane before use. Roasted capsicum also make an interesting salad garnish. Capsicums should keep in the crisper section of the refrigerator for 5-7 days.

Celery

Use either sliced, cut into sticks or as celery curls (see Techniques section). The leaves also make a tasty and attractive salad garnish.

Cucumber

The variety of cucumbers available include apple, green or ridge, Lebanese and telegraph cucumber. The green or ridge and telegraph cucumbers are the most widely available. To prepare cucumbers you need only peel them if the skin is tough or bitter as leaving the skin on is said to help with digestion. Cucumbers (except the apple variety) should have bright green skins with a firm, fresh appearance. Apple cucumbers should have a pale yellow-white skin.

Onions

All types of onions can be used raw in salads. White and brown onions have a strong, hot, pungent taste and should be used sparingly. The red onion is a mild sweet onion that adds a pretty colour to any salad. Spring onions, also known as scallions or green onions, give a mild fresh onion flavour. Use onions either sliced or chopped in salads or as a garnish.

Radishes

These small, crisp red bulbs can be used whole, sliced, chopped or grated in salads. Select radishes with fresh-looking leaves and bright-coloured bulbs.

Sprouts

There are a number of sprout varieties available, the most popular being alfalfa and bean sprouts. To save wastage, you might like to grow your own sprouts – see Sprouting Know-how. Sprouts should be kept in a plastic food bag or the container in which you purchased them.

Tomatoes

Tomatoes should have a good red colour and firm flesh. Used whole or halved, cherry and the small, yellow teardrop tomatoes are also popular salad ingredients. For best flavour, tomatoes should always be used at room temperature.

Hydroponically grown lettuces last longer as they are still growing when you buy them and will continue to grow if kept in a plastic food bag in the crisper section of the refrigerator. Many varieties are now grown hydroponically making them available all year round.

Lettuce should be stored in the vegetable crisper section of your refrigerator. Place the whole lettuce in a plastic food bag or covered container. Separate leaves and wash just prior to using. Always remember to wash salad vegetables before using. To prepare lettuce, cut out the core using a stainless steel knife, then separate leaves and wash briefly in cold water. Dry the leaves by shaking off the excess water, then pat dry with a teatowel. The leaves can also be drained in a colander or salad basket, or use a salad spinner or centrifugal dryer (a piece of equipment especially designed for drying lettuce leaves). Always dress a lettuce salad as close to serving time as possible. The longer the dressing sits on the leaves the less crisp they will be.

veggie salads

chilli noodle salad

A sensational salad can add colour,

flavour and variety to an otherwise simple meal. Many of these easy salads can also double as light meals. What more delicious meal could there be than a Roasted Vegetable Salad served with crusty bread and a glass wine?

chargrilled
vegetable salad

Method:

1 Brush sweet corn cobs, eggplant (aubergines), red capsicum (peppers), zucchini (courgettes) and leeks with olive oil. Place vegetables on a preheated hot barbecue and cook, turning occasionally, for 15 minutes or until vegetables are golden and tender.

2 To make dressing, place basil, rosemary, chilli oil and vinegar in a screwtop jar and shake well to combine. Drizzle dressing over warm vegetables.

Note: Smoky flavoured, crisp on the outside and tender within, char-grilled vegetables taste quite unlike any other. You may substitute the proportions of vegetables listed here if any of them are in short supply.

Serves 6

ingredients

2 cobs fresh sweet corn, cut into
3 cm/1 1/4 in pieces
6 baby eggplant (aubergines),
halved lengthwise
3 red capsicums (peppers),
cut into quarters
6 zucchini (courgettes), halved lengthwise
6 small leeks, halved lengthwise olive oil
<u>Herb dressing</u>
2 tablespoons chopped fresh basil
1 tablespoon chopped fresh rosemary or
1 teaspoon dried rosemary
2 tablespoons chilli oil
2 tablespoons balsamic vinegar

marinated
eggplant salad

Method:

1 Place eggplant (aubergines) in a colander, sprinkle with salt and drain for 20 minutes. Rinse eggplant (aubergines) under cold water and pat dry with absorbent kitchen paper.

2 Preheat barbecue to a high heat. Brush eggplant (aubergine) slices with oil, place on barbecue grill and cook for 2 minutes each side or until tender and golden. Place in a shallow dish.

3 To make dressing, place onion, parsley, basil, chilli, vinegar and black pepper to taste in a screwtop jar and shake to combine. Pour dressing over eggplant (aubergines) and toss. Cover and marinate in the refrigerator for at least 1 hour before serving.

Note: This salad can be marinated for up to 24 hours. Salting eggplant (aubergine) degorges it of any bitter juices. For this recipe, it also ensures that you do not end up with excess juices coming out during marinating.

Serves 8

ingredients

3 large eggplant (aubergines), sliced
sea salt
2-3 tablespoons olive oil
<u>Herb and balsamic dressing</u>
1 red onion, sliced
2 tablespoons chopped fresh
flat-leaf parsley
2 tablespoons chopped fresh basil
1 fresh green chilli, seeded and
finely chopped
2/3 cup/170ml/5 1/2fl oz balsamic vinegar
freshly ground black pepper

Oven temperature 220°C, 425°F, Gas 7

moroccan
vegetable salad

Method:

1. To make marinade, place turmeric, cumin, cinnamon, harissa, garlic, oil, lime juice and honey in a glass or ceramic bowl and whisk to combine.
2. Add onions, garlic, carrots, fennel, parsnips and sweet potatoes to marinade and toss to coat. Cover and marinate in the refrigerator for 2-3 hours.
3. To make Herbed Yoghurt, place yoghurt, dill, mint and black pepper to taste in a bowl and mix to combine. Cover and refrigerate until required.
4. Transfer vegetables and marinade to a baking dish and bake for 1 hour or until vegetables are tender. Serve hot or warm with Herbed Yoghurt.

   Note: Harissa is a hot chilli paste used in North African cooking. It is available from specialty food shops or you can make a simple version yourself by combining 2 tablespoons each of chilli powder, ground cumin, tomato paste (purée) and olive oil with 1 teaspoon salt.

Serves 4

ingredients

10 baby onions, peeled
10 cloves garlic, peeled
3 carrots, cut into 5cm/2in lengths
1 bulb fennel, cut into wedges
4 parsnips, cut into quarters, lengthwise
500g/1 lb sweet potatoes, cut into
2cm/³/₄in thick rounds
Spicy lime marinade
1 teaspoon ground turmeric
1 teaspoon ground cumin
1 teaspoon ground cinnamon
¹/₂ teaspoon harissa
2 cloves garlic, crushed
¹/₂ cup/125ml/4fl oz olive oil
3 tablespoons lime juice
1 tablespoon honey
Herbed yoghurt
1 cup/200g/6¹/₂oz natural yogurt
2 tablespoons chopped fresh dill
2 tablespoons chopped fresh mint
freshly ground black pepper

gado gado

Method:

1 To make sauce, heat oil in a frying pan over a medium heat, add onion and chilli and cook, stirring, for 3 minutes or until onion is soft. Stir in peanut butter, coriander, coconut cream, kechap manis and chilli sauce and stirring, bring to the boil. Reduce heat and simmer for 5 minutes, then stir in sugar and lemon juice. Cool slightly. The sauce should be slightly runny, if it is too thick add a little water.

2 Boil, steam or microwave beans and carrots, separately, until they are bright green and bright orange, then rinse under cold running water and drain well.

3 Heat oil in a frying pan or wok over a high heat, add tofu and stir-fry until golden. Drain on absorbent kitchen paper and cool slightly.

4 To serve, arrange piles of beans, carrots, tofu, red capsicum (pepper), cucumbers, mushrooms and eggs on a large serving platter. Serve with sauce.

Note: Kechap manis is a thick sweet seasoning sauce used in Indonesian cooking. It is sometimes called Indonesian soy sauce. If unavailable, a mixture of soy sauce and dark corn syrup or golden syrup can be used in its place.

Serves 6

ingredients

125g/4oz green beans, sliced lengthwise
2 carrots, cut into thick strips
2 tablespoons vegetable oil
185g/6oz firm tofu,
cut into thick strips
1 large red capsicum (pepper), cut into thick strips
2 cucumbers, cut into thick strips
12 small button mushrooms
6 hard-boiled eggs, cut into wedges
<u>Peanut Sauce</u>
1 tablespoon peanut (groundnut) oil
1 onion, finely chopped
1 fresh red chilli, finely chopped
2/3 cup/170g/5 1/2oz peanut butter
1 tablespoon ground coriander
3/4 cup/185ml/6fl oz coconut cream
3 tablespoons kechap manis
2 teaspoons chilli sauce
1 teaspoon palm or brown sugar
1 tablespoon lemon juice

roasted
vegetable salad

Method:

1 *Place fennel, sweet potatoes and shallots in a nonstick baking dish and spray with olive oil. Sprinkle with cumin seeds and bake for 30-35 minutes or until vegetables are soft and golden. Set aside to cool for 10-15 minutes or until vegetables are warm.*

2 *Place vegetables in a serving bowl, add beans, rocket, cheese, vinegar and black pepper to taste and toss.*

Note: *The shallots used in this recipe are the French échalote. If unavailable red or yellow shallots used in Asian cooking or pickling onions can be used instead.*

Serves 4

ingredients

3 bulbs fennel, cut into wedges
2 sweet potatoes, peeled and chopped
12 shallots, peeled
olive oil spray
1 teaspoon cumin seeds
315g/10oz green beans, blanched
185g/6oz rocket leaves
155g/5oz reduced-fat feta cheese, chopped
2-3 tablespoons balsamic vinegar
freshly ground black pepper

golden
grain salad

Method:

1 Place rice, barley, couscous, corn, green pepper, carrot, celery and zucchini in a large serving bowl.

2 To make dressing, place orange juice, mustard, ginger, and black pepper to taste in a screwtop jar. Shake well to combine. Pour over salad and toss to combine.

Do ahead: Keep a selection of cooked rice, pasta and legumes in the refrigerator then you will always have a carbohydrate-rich food that can be made into a salad in minutes. Always cook extra of these foods to have on hand.

Serves 4

ingredients

1 cup/210g brown rice, cooked
1 cup/210g pearl barley, cooked
¹/₂ cup/60g couscous, cooked
**440g canned corn kernels,
no-added-salt, drained**
1 green pepper, cut into strips
1 carrot, peeled and cut into strips
2 stalks celery, cut into strips
1 zucchini, cut into strips

Orange dressing
¹/₂ cup/125mL orange juice
2 teaspoons wholegrain mustard
1 teaspoon finely grated fresh ginger
freshly ground black pepper

blue cheese
witloof and lettuce

Method:

1 To make dressing, puree basil leaves and 2 tablespoons oil in food processor or blender. Add egg yolk and blue cheese and process until smooth. Combine remaining olive oil and vinegar and with the machine running add to the basil mixture. Season to taste with pepper.

2 Toss avocado slices in the dressing. Arrange radicchio, butter lettuce and witloof leaves attractively in six individual salad bowls.

3 Sprinkle dressing over salad and top with avocado slices.

   Note: Arrange lettuce on plates, cover and refrigerate until ready to serve. Leave avocado slices in dressing until final preparation of salad. This strongly flavoured, colourful salad can be prepared in advance. Serve leftover dressing separately.

Serves 6

ingredients

1 avocado, peeled and cut into thin slices
1 radicchio, washed, leaves separated
1 butter lettuce, washed, leaves separated
2 witloof, washed, leaves separated

Blue cheese dressing
6 fresh basil leaves
1/2 cup/125mL olive oil
1 egg yolk
100g blue cheese
4 tablespoons white wine vinegar
freshly ground black pepper

roasted
capsicums with herbs

Photograph opposite

ingredients

3 red capsicums (peppers)
2 green capsicums(peppers)
4 medium fresh green chillies
2 onions, quartered
2 tablespoons fresh marjoram leaves
2 tablespoons fresh thyme leaves
¹/₄ cup/60ml/2fl oz lime juice
¹/₄ cup/60ml/2fl oz olive oil
freshly ground black pepper

roasted peppers with herbs

Method:

1 *Place red and green capsicums (peppers) and chillies in a hot frying pan or comal and cook until skins are blistered and charred. Place capsicums (peppers) and chillies in a plastic food bag and stand for 10 minutes or until cool enough to handle.*

2 *Carefully remove skins from capsicums (peppers) and chillies, then cut off tops and remove seeds and membranes. Cut into thick slices.*

3 *Place onions in frying pan or comal and cook for 5 minutes or until soft and charred.*

4 *Place capsicum (peppers), chillies, onions, marjoram, thyme, lime juice, oil and black pepper to taste in a bowl and toss to combine. Stand for 30 minutes before serving.*

Note: *A comal is a steel, cast iron or unglazed earthenware cooking disk, which is used for cooking and heating tortillas and for toasting other ingredients such as chillies and pumpkin seeds.*

Serves 6

warm
potato salad

Method:

1 Cook potatoes in boiling water until just tender. Drain well and place in a heatproof bowl.

2 To make dressing, place mustard, parsley, capers, garlic, lemon juice and black pepper to taste in a bowl and mix to combine. Spoon dressing over hot potatoes and toss to combine. Serve immediately.

Note: Iced water or mineral water makes a refreshing and light drink to serve with meals. For added appeal serve with a slice of lemon, lime or orange.

Serves 4

ingredients

500g/1 lb baby new potatoes
Mustard dressing
2 tablespoons wholegrain mustard
2 tablespoons chopped fresh parsley
2 teaspoons chopped capers
1 clove garlic, crushed
1 tablespoon lemon juice
freshly ground black pepper

chilli
noodle salad

Photograph also on page 419

Method:

1 *To make dressing, place sugar, garlic, chillies, lime juice and fish sauce in a bowl and whisk to combine.*

2 *Place vermicelli in a bowl, pour over boiling water to cover and soak for 10 minutes. Drain well and place in a serving bowl.*

3 *Add carrots, cucumbers, red capsicum (pepper), spring onions, mushrooms, bean sprouts and coriander leaves. Pour over dressing and toss to combine. Cover and refrigerate for 2 hours before serving.*

Note: *When trying to cool your mouth down after eating chilli-flavoured foods, do not drink water or beer. While this cools the tongue it spreads the burning chilli oil around the rest of your mouth and so makes the whole experience even more fiery. A glass of milk, a cool yoghurt sambal or dip, or neutral foods such as plain bread, rice, noodles or mashed potatoes are the most effective mouth coolers and neutralisers.*

Serves 4

ingredients

100g/3¹/₂oz rice vermicelli
2 carrots, cut into matchsticks
2 cucumbers, cut into matchsticks
1 red capsicum (pepper),
cut into matchsticks
3 spring onions, cut into thin strips
125g/4oz button mushrooms, quartered
30g/1oz bean sprouts
1 bunch fresh coriander
<u>Chilli and lime dressing</u>
¹/₄ cup/45g/1¹/₂oz brown sugar
1 clove garlic, crushed
2 fresh red chillies, finely chopped
¹/₂ cup/125ml/4fl oz lime juice
¹/₄ cup/60ml/2fl oz fish sauce

tomato
salad

Method:

1 Place egg (plum or Italian) tomatoes, cherry tomatoes, tomatoes, onion, vinegar, basil and black pepper to taste in a bowl and toss to combine. Set aside to stand for 30 minutes.

2 Line a large serving platter with lettuce leaves and top with tomato mixture.

   Note: This salad can be made using any combination of tomatoes - so check the market and use what is in season and available.

Serves 6

ingredients

6 egg (plum or Italian) tomatoes,
cut into wedges
250g/8oz cherry tomatoes, halved
3 tomatoes, sliced
1 red onion, chopped
2 tablespoons red wine vinegar
2 tablespoons chopped fresh basil
freshly ground black pepper
assorted lettuce leaves

warm
vegetable salad

Method:

1 To make vinaigrette, place olive oil, vinegar, thyme, sugar and black pepper to taste in a screwtop jar and shake well to combine. Set aside.

2 Heat 2 teaspoons vegetable oil in a wok over a high heat, add hazelnuts and stir-fry for 3 minutes. Set aside. Heat remaining oil in wok, add onions and stir-fry for 3 minutes or until golden.

3 Add carrots, zucchini (courgettes), snow peas (mangetout), mushrooms, green and red capsicums (peppers), spring onions and asparagus and stir-fry for 5 minutes. Return hazelnuts to wok, add vinaigrette and toss to combine.

Note:A heavy wok made of carbon steel will give better cooking results than a stainless steel or aluminium one.

Serves 4

ingredients

1 tablespoon vegetable oil
125g/4oz blanched hazelnuts
2 onions, chopped
2 carrots, sliced
2 zucchini (courgettes), chopped
155g/5oz snow peas (mangetout)
4 field mushrooms, sliced
1 green capsicum (pepper), sliced
1 red capsicum (pepper), sliced
6 spring onions, chopped
250g/8oz asparagus, halved
<u>**Red Wine and Thyme Vinaigrette**</u>
1/3 cup/90ml/3fl oz olive oil
1/4 cup/60ml/2fl oz red wine vinegar
1 tablespoons chopped fresh thyme
1 teaspoon sugar
freshly ground black pepper

greek
potato salad

Method:

1 Boil, steam or microwave potatoes until tender. Drain, place in a bowl and set aside to cool.

2 Heat vegetable oil in a frying pan, add onions and garlic and cook over a medium heat, stirring, for 3 minutes or until onions are soft. Add vinegar, olives, capers, parsley and olive oil to pan and mix to combine.

3 Remove pan from heat and set aside to cool. Spoon onion mixture over potatoes and toss gently to combine. Cover and refrigerate until required.

Note: The most popular black olive is the Kalamata olive from Greece. It is a large purplish black olive, which lends itself to marinating.

Serves 4

ingredients

1 kg/2 lb potatoes, roughly chopped
2 teaspoons vegetable oil
2 onions, sliced
1 clove garlic, crushed
3 tablespoons white wine vinegar
185g/6oz black olives
1 tablespoon capers, drained
2 tablespoons chopped
flat-leaved parsley
2 tablespoons olive oil

marinated
tomato salad

Method:

1 *Place tomatoes, cheese, onion and basil in a bowl and toss to combine.*

2 *To make dressing, place sugar, vinegar and black pepper to taste in a screwtop jar and shake well to combine. Pour dressing over tomato mixture and toss to combine. Cover and marinate, at room temperature, for 20 minutes before serving.*

Serves 4

4 tomatoes, thickly sliced
125g/4oz reduced-fat feta
cheese, chopped
¹/₂ red onion, sliced
3 tablespoons fresh basil leaves
<u>Balsamic dressing</u>
I tablespoon brown sugar
¹/₄ cup/60ml/2fl oz balsamic vinegar
freshly ground black pepper

salad
of roast tomatoes

Method:

1 Place tomatoes and garlic on a baking tray, sprinkle with black pepper to taste and oil and bake for 30 minutes or until tomatoes are soft and golden. Set aside to cool completely.

2 Arrange lettuce leaves, feta cheese, yellow or red capsicum (pepper), tomatoes and garlic attractively on serving plates.

3 To make dressing, place vinegar, tomato purée, Tabasco and black pepper to taste in a screwtop jar and shake well to combine. Drizzle dressing over salad and serve immediately.

Note: The sweet, rich flavour of roast tomatoes is a perfect partner for the creamy piquant feta cheese in this salad.

Serves 4

ingredients

6 plum (egg or Italian) tomatoes, halved
8 cloves garlic, peeled
freshly ground black pepper
2 tablespoons olive oil
315g/10oz assorted lettuce leaves
185g/6oz feta cheese, crumbled
1 yellow or red capsicum (pepper), sliced
<u>**Tangy dressing**</u>
3 tablespoons balsamic or red wine vinegar
3 tablespoons tomato purée
3 drops Tabasco sauce

Oven temperature 180°C, 350°F, Gas 4

oriental
coleslaw in curry

Method:

1 Place Chinese and red cabbages in a bowl and toss to combine, then arrange.

2 Place carrot, celery, spring onions, red capsicum (pepper), bean sprouts and mint and coriander leaves in a bowl and toss to combine. Arrange vegetable mixture on top of cabbage mixture.

3 To make dressing, place curry powder, sugar, yogurt, sour cream and lemon juice in a bowl and whisk to combine. Drizzle dressing over salad, then scatter with sesame seeds and serve with fried noodles.

Note: The thickness of the dressing will depend on the type of yogurt used, if it is too thick, whisk in a little water.

Serves 4

ingredients

¹/₄ **Chinese cabbage, finely shredded**
¹/₄ **red cabbage, finely shredded**
I carrot, cut into thin strips
2 stalks celery, cut into thin strips
4 spring onions, thinly sliced
¹/₂ **red capsicum (pepper),**
cut into thin strips
60g/2oz bean sprouts
¹/₂ **bunch fresh mint**
¹/₂ **bunch fresh coriander**
I tablespoon black sesame seeds, toasted
60g/2oz fried egg noodles
<u>Curry dressing</u>
I teaspoon curry powder
I teaspoon brown sugar
I cup/200g/6¹/₂ oz natural yogurt
2 tablespoons sour cream
I teaspoon lemon juice

grilled prawn salad

seafood
salads

As a main meal or as a starter,

a seafood salad is always welcome. In this chapter you will find exciting recipes for salads, such as Warm Seafood Salad or Grilled Prawn Salad. Whichever one you choose, you can be sure that it will not only taste great but will be good for you as well.

marinated
citrus fish

Method:

1 Place fish in a glass bowl with peppercorns and orange rind.
2 To make marinade, combine oil, orange, grapefruit and lime juices, vinegar and ginger. Pour marinade over fish, cover and refrigerate overnight.
3 To serve, use a slotted spoon to remove fish to a bowl. Add lychees, orange and grapefruit segments to fish mixture. Toss lightly to combine. Arrange watercress on a plate and top with fish salad. Spoon over a little of the marinade.

Serves 4

ingredients

500g/1 lb white fish fillets, cut into strips
2 teaspoons pink peppercorns
2 teaspoons orange rind
440g/14oz canned lychees, drained
1 orange, peeled and segmented
1 grapefruit, peeled and segmented
1/2 bunch fresh watercress
Marinade
1 tablespoon grape seed oil
125mL/4fl oz orange juice
1 tablespoon grapefruit juice
1 tablespoon lime juice
1 tablespoon tarragon vinegar
1 teaspoon grated fresh ginger

grilled
prawn salad

Method:

1 Place prawns, chilli, soy sauce and honey in a bowl, toss to combine and marinate for 5 minutes.
2 Arrange witlof (chicory), radicchio, mangoes, mint and coriander (cilantro) on serving plates. Combine sugar and lime juice and drizzle over salad.
3 Heat a nonstick frying pan over a high heat, add prawns and stir-fry for 2 minutes or until cooked. Place prawns on top of salad, spoon over pan juices and serve immediately.

Serves 4

ingredients

16 uncooked prawns, shelled and deveined, tails left intact
1 fresh green chilli, seeded and shredded
1/4 cup/60ml/2fl oz reduced-salt soy sauce
1 tablespoon honey
1 witlof (chicory), leaves separated
1 radicchio, leaves separated
2 green (unripe) mangoes, thinly sliced
4 tablespoons fresh mint leaves
3 tablespoons fresh coriander (cilantro) leaves
1 tablespoon brown sugar
2 tablespoons lime juice

chickpea
and trout salad

Method:

1 Arrange endive and rocket on a serving platter. Top with chickpeas, goat's cheese, onion and trout. Sprinkle salad with basil and top with red capsicum (pepper).

2 To make dressing, place yoghurt, mint, cumin, honey and lime juice in a bowl and mix to combine. Drizzle dressing over salad and serve immediately.

Note: Chickpeas are slightly crunchy and lend a nutty flavour to salads like this as well as casseroles, soups and other savoury dishes. Dried chickpeas can be used rather than canned if you wish. To cook chickpeas, soak overnight in cold water. Drain. Place in a large saucepan, cover with cold water and bring to the boil over a medium heat. Reduce heat and simmer for 45-60 minutes or until chickpeas are tender. Drain and cool.

Serves 4

ingredients

1 bunch curly endive, leaves separated
1 bunch rocket
440g/14oz canned chickpeas, rinsed and drained
125g/4oz herbed goat's cheese, crumbled
1 red onion, sliced
250g/8oz smoked trout, skin and bones removed, flesh flaked
2 tablespoons chopped fresh basil
1 red capsicum (pepper), halved, roasted, skin removed and sliced
<u>Honey lime dressing</u>
1/2 cup/100g/3 1/2oz natural yoghurt
1 tablespoon chopped fresh mint
1 tablespoon ground cumin
1 tablespoon honey
1 tablespoon lime juice

Method:

1 *Arrange salad leaves, teardrop tomatoes (if using) and cherry tomatoes, avocados, snow peas (mangetout) and asparagus on a large serving platter.*

2 *To make dressing, place vinegar, fish sauce, chilli sauce, basil, lemon juice and water in a small bowl and whisk to combine. Set aside.*

3 *Cut calamari (squid) tubes, lengthwise, and open out flat. Using a sharp knife, cut parallel lines down the length of the calamari (squid), taking care not to cut right through the flesh. Make more cuts in the opposite direction to form a diamond pattern. Cut each piece into 5 cm/2 in squares.*

4 *Melt butter in a large frying pan, add scallops and prawns and stir-fry for 3 minutes. Add calamari (squid) pieces and stir-fry for 1 minute longer. Arrange cooked seafood and smoked ocean trout or smoked salmon on salad and drizzle with dressing.*

Note: *This salad is great served warm, but also may be made ahead of time and served chilled. If serving chilled, prepare the salad, seafood and dressing and store separately in the refrigerator. Just prior to serving, assemble the salad as described in the recipe.*

Serves 8

warm
seafood salad

ingredients

500g/1 lb assorted salad leaves
250g/8oz yellow teardrop tomatoes (optional)
250g/8oz cherry tomatoes, halved
2 avocados, stoned, peeled and sliced
155g/5oz snow peas (mangetout), trimmed, blanched
250g/8oz asparagus spears, cut into 5cm/2in pieces, blanched
3 calamari (squid) tubes
30g/1oz butter
250g/8oz scallops
16 uncooked medium prawns, shelled and deveined, tails left intact
200g/6¹/₂oz thickly sliced smoked ocean trout or smoked salmon
Oriental dressing
1 tablespoon rice vinegar
1 tablespoon fish sauce
2 tablespoons sweet chilli sauce
1 tablespoon shredded fresh basil
1 tablespoon lemon juice
¹/₄ cup/60ml/2fl oz water

asparagus
and salmon salad

Method:

1 Boil, steam or microwave asparagus until tender. Drain, refresh under cold running water, drain again and chill. Arrange lettuce leaves, asparagus and salmon on serving plates.

2 To make sauce, place yogurt, lemon rind, lemon juice, dill and cumin in a small bowl and mix to combine.

3 Spoon sauce over salad. Sprinkle with black pepper, cover and chill until required.

Note: If fresh asparagus is unavailable, green beans or snow peas (mangetout) are good alternatives for this recipe.

ingredients

750g/1¹/₂ lb asparagus spears, trimmed
lettuce leaves of your choice
500g/1 lb smoked salmon slices
freshly ground black pepper
<u>Lemon yoghurt sauce</u>
1 cup/200g/6¹/₂oz natural
low-fat yoghurt
1 tablespoon finely grated lemon rind
1 tablespoon lemon juice
1 tablespoon chopped fresh dill
1 teaspoon ground cumin

scallops
and wilted spinach

Method:

1 Preheat barbecue to a medium heat.

2 To make salad, blanch spinach leaves in boiling water for 10 seconds. Drain spinach, refresh under cold running water, drain again and place in a bowl.

3 Place sesame seeds, soy sauce, lemon juice and sesame oil in a bowl and mix to combine. Spoon dressing over spinach and toss to combine. Divide salad between serving plates.

4 Place scallops in bowl, drizzle with a little vegetable oil and season to taste with black pepper. Sear scallops on barbecue plate (griddle) for 45-60 seconds or until golden and flesh is opaque. Place scallops on top of each salad and serve immediately.

Note: Alternatively the scallops can be seared in a hot frying pan.

Serves 6

ingredients

18 scallops
vegetable oil
crushed black peppercorns
Wilted spinach salad
185g/6oz baby English spinach leaves
2 teaspoons sesame seeds
2 tablespoons soy sauce
1 tablespoon lemon juice
2 teaspoons sesame oil

salad
of lobster with raspberries

Method:

1 Cut lobster tails into 1cm medallions and set aside.

2 Arrange radicchio, mignonette, sprouts or watercress, lobster, orange segments and strawberries attractively on a serving platter and refrigerate until required.

3 To make dressing, place raspberries in a food processor or blender and process until pureed. Push through a sieve to remove seeds. Combine raspberry puree with vinegar, oil, mint and sugar. Mix well to combine, pour over salad and serve immediately.

Note: Lobster would have to be the undisputed king of shellfish. In this recipe, it is taken to new heights with the addition of a raspberry dressing.

Serves 4

ingredients

2 lobster tails, cooked and shells removed
1 small radicchio, leaves separated
1 small mignonette lettuce,
leaves separated
100g/3oz snow pea sprouts or watercress
1 orange, segmented
250g/8oz strawberries, halved
<u>Dressing</u>
125g/4oz fresh or frozen raspberries
2 tablespoons raspberry vinegar
2 tablespoons vegetable oil
1 teaspoon finely chopped fresh mint
1 tablespoon sugar

thai
squid salad

Method:

1 Using a sharp knife, make a single cut down the length of each squid (calamari) tube and open out. Cut parallel lines down the length of the squid (calamari), taking care not to cut right the way through the flesh. Make more cuts in the opposite direction to form a diamond pattern.

2 Heat a nonstick char-grill or frying pan over a high heat, add squid (calamari) and cook for 1-2 minutes each side or until tender. Remove from pan and cut into thin strips.

3 Place squid (calamari), beans, tomatoes, pawpaw, spring onions, mint, coriander and chilli in a serving bowl.

4 To make dressing, place sugar, lime juice and fish sauce in a screwtop jar and shake well. Drizzle over salad and toss to combine. Cover and stand for 20 minutes before serving.

Serving suggestion: Soy Rice Noodles - boil 375g/12oz fresh rice noodles, drain and sprinkle with a little reduced-salt soy sauce. Scatter with a few toasted sesame seeds and toss to combine.

ingredients

3 squid (calamari) tubes, cleaned
185g/6oz green beans, sliced lengthwise
2 tomatoes, cut into wedges
1 small green pawpaw, peeled, seeded and shredded
4 spring onions, sliced
30g/1oz fresh mint leaves
30g/1oz fresh coriander (cilantro) leaves
1 fresh red chilli, chopped
<u>Lime dressing</u>
2 teaspoons brown sugar
3 tablespoons lime juice
1 tablespoon fish sauce

Serves 4

tuna
and lemon pasta

Method:

1 Cook fettuccine in boiling water in a large saucepan following packet directions. Drain and return pasta to saucepan.
2 Place pan over a low heat, add tuna, rocket, cheese, dill, lemon juice and black pepper to taste and toss to combine. Serve immediately.

Serves 4

ingredients

500g/1 lb fettuccine
440g/14oz canned tuna in spring water, drained and flaked
185g/6oz rocket leaves, roughly chopped
155g/5oz reduced-fat feta cheese, chopped
1 tablespoon chopped fresh dill
¹/₄ cup/60ml/2fl oz lemon juice
freshly ground black pepper

mediterranean
salad

Method:

1 Place couscous in a bowl, pour over boiling water and toss with a fork until couscous absorbs all the liquid. Add oil, vinegar and black pepper to taste and toss to combine. Set aside.

2 Place cucumber, green capsicum (pepper), fresh and dried tomatoes, artichokes, olives, prawns (if using), feta cheese, basil and lime or lemon rind in a salad bowl and toss to combine. Add couscous mixture and toss.

Note: Couscous is a cracked wheat product made from the endosperm of durum wheat and, like burghul wheat, is very versatile and quick to prepare. After soaking in water, mix couscous with salad ingredients and serve cold; toss with dried fruits, seeds and nuts and serve as a pilau or simply serve hot with milk and fresh fruit as a breakfast 'porridge'.

Serves 4

ingredients

185g/6oz couscous
2 cups/500ml/16fl oz boiling water
1 tablespoon olive oil
1 tablespoon balsamic vinegar
freshly ground black pepper
1 cucumber, sliced
1 green capsicum (pepper), chopped
3 plum (egg or Italian)
tomatoes, chopped
12 sun-dried tomatoes, sliced
60g/2oz marinated artichokes,
drained and sliced
60g/2oz pitted black olives, sliced
185g/6oz cooked prawns, shelled and
deveined (optional)
125g/4oz feta cheese, cut into
2cm/3/4in cubes
2 tablespoons chopped fresh basil or
2 teaspoons dried basil
2 teaspoons finely grated lime
or lemon rind

salmon
and lentil salad

Method:

1 To make dressing, place mayonnaise, stock, mustard and vinegar in a bowl and mix to combine. Set aside.

2 Arrange lettuce, cooked lentils, tomatoes and croûtons attractively on a serving platter. Set aside.

3 Heat oil in a frying pan over a medium heat, add salmon and cook, turning several times, for 4 minutes or until salmon is cooked. Remove from pan and arrange on top of salad. Drizzle dressing over salad and top with shavings of Parmesan cheese and black pepper to taste.

Note: The iron content of legumes such as lentils is fairly high, but as it occurs in an inorganic form, the human body needs help to absorb it. You can increase the body's ability to absorb the iron if you serve a Vitamin C-rich food (such as the salad and tomatoes here) as part of the same meal.

Use a vegetable peeler or a coarse grater to make shavings from a piece of fresh Parmesan cheese.

Serves 4

ingredients

Fish
1 cos lettuce, leaves separated and torn into large pieces
200g/6¹/₂oz green lentils, cooked and drained
200g/6¹/₂oz red lentils, cooked and drained
250g/8oz cherry tomatoes, halved
155g/5oz prepared wholemeal croûtons
1 tablespoon chilli oil or vegetable oil
375g/12oz salmon fillets, skin and bones removed, cut into 3cm/1¹/₄in wide strips
fresh Parmesan cheese
freshly ground black pepper
<u>**Creamy dressing**</u>
¹/₂ cup/125ml/4fl oz mayonnaise
2 tablespoons vegetable stock
1 tablespoon wholegrain mustard
1 tablespoon white wine vinegar

niçoise
salad

Method:

1 To make salad, place tuna, artichokes, if using, cheese, eggs, potatoes, tomatoes, onion, beans and olives in a large bowl and toss to combine.

2 To make dressing, place oil, vinegar, garlic, mustard and black pepper to taste in a screwtop jar and shake well to combine. Spoon dressing over salad and toss lightly.

3 Line a large serving platter with lettuce leaves and top with salad.

Note: For a complete meal, serve with crusty fresh or toasted French bread. A few anchovies and shavings of Parmesan cheese are delicious additions to this dish. Always buy the form of the product that best fits your menu. Less expensive shredded or flaked tuna is the perfect choice for a salad such as this - it's lower priced because of appearance, not quality. Feta cheese makes a delicious and more gourmet alternative to tasty cheese (mature Cheddar).

Serves 6

ingredients

lettuce leaves of choice
Tuna salad
440g/14oz canned tuna, drained and flaked
125g/4oz canned artichoke hearts, drained and sliced (optional)
125g/4oz tasty cheese (mature Cheddar), cubed
4 hard-boiled eggs, sliced
2 potatoes, cooked and sliced
2 tomatoes, sliced
1 onion, sliced
250g/8oz green beans, cooked
45g/1 1/2oz stuffed olives, sliced
Niçoise dressing
1/4 cup/60ml/2fl oz olive oil
2 tablespoons vinegar
1 clove garlic, crushed
1/2 teaspoon Dijon mustard
freshly ground black pepper

honeyed
squid salad

Method:

1 To make dressing, place oil, orange juice, vinegar, honey, garlic, mustard and black pepper to taste in a screwtop jar and shake well to combine.

2 Dry squid (calamari) rings on absorbent kitchen paper. Toss in flour and shake off excess. Heat oil in a frying pan over a medium heat, add squid (calamari) and stir-fry for 1-2 minutes or until golden. Drain on absorbent kitchen paper.

3 Place lettuce leaves, tomatoes and onion in a bowl and toss. Divide lettuce mixture between serving plates, top with hot squid (calamari) and drizzle with dressing. Serve immediately.

Note: To clean fresh squid (calamari), pull off tentacles, carefully taking with them the head, stomach and ink bag. Rub off the skin under cold running water. Slice tube (body) crosswise into rings. If fresh squid (calamari) is unavailable, use 375g/12oz frozen squid (calamari) rings instead.

Serves 4

ingredients

6 small squid (calamari), cleaned and
sliced into rings
¹/₄ cup/30g/1oz flour
olive oil for shallow-frying
lettuce leaves of your choice
250g/8oz cherry tomatoes, halved
1 onion, thinly sliced
<u>Honey orange dressing</u>
¹/₄ cup/60ml/2fl oz olive oil
1 tablespoon orange juice
1 tablespoon vinegar
1 teaspoon honey
1 clove garlic, crushed
¹/₄ teaspoon mild mustard
freshly ground black pepper

seafood
salads

tarragon
seafood salad

Method:

1 Place tarragon, lime juice, lime rind, chilli, oil and black pepper to taste in a bowl and mix to combine. Add lobster, toss to coat and set aside to marinate for 15 minutes.

2 Arrange snow pea sprouts or watercress, cucumber, carrot and red capsicum (pepper) on a large serving platter and set aside.

3 Heat a char-grill or frying pan over a high heat, add lobster mixture and cook, turning frequently, for 2 minutes or until lobster is tender. Arrange lobster over salad, spoon over pan juices and serve immediately.

Note: To make cucumber and carrot ribbons, use a vegetable peeler to remove strips lengthwise from the cucumber or carrot. This salad is also delicious made using prawns instead of lobster. If using prawns, shell and devein them before marinating.

Serves 4

ingredients

4 tablespoons chopped fresh tarragon
2 tablespoons lime juice
3 teaspoons grated lime rind
1 fresh red chilli, chopped
2 teaspoons olive oil
freshly ground black pepper
500g/1 lb uncooked lobster tail, flesh removed from shell and cut into large pieces or 500g/1 lb firm white fish fillets, cut into large pieces
250g/8oz snow pea sprouts or watercress
1 cucumber, sliced into ribbons
2 carrots, sliced into ribbons
1 red capsicum (pepper), cut into thin strips

Method:

1 To make dressing, place mayonnaise, olive oil, vinegar and mustard in a bowl, mix to combine and set aside.

2 Heat sesame oil in a frying pan over a high heat, add garlic and scallops and cook, stirring, for 1 minute or until scallops just turn opaque. Remove scallop mixture from pan and set aside. Add bacon to pan and cook, stirring, for 4 minutes or until crisp. Remove bacon from pan and drain on absorbent kitchen paper.

3 Place lettuce leaves in a large salad bowl, add dressing and toss to coat. Add bacon, croûtons and shavings of Parmesan cheese and toss to combine. Spoon scallop mixture over salad and serve.

seared
scallop salad

ingredients

2 teaspoons sesame oil
2 cloves garlic, crushed
375g/12oz scallops, cleaned
4 rashers bacon, chopped
1 cos lettuce, leaves separated
60g/2oz croûtons
fresh Parmesan cheese
Mustard dressing
3 tablespoons mayonnaise
1 tablespoon olive oil
1 tablespoon vinegar
2 teaspoons Dijon mustard

chicken and orange salad

meat
salads

Succulent strips or slices of meat

tossed or drizzled with a tangy dressing are the basis of these meat salads. Perfect as light meals, these salads are substantial enough to satisfy the hungriest diners.

green
mango salad

ingredients

125g/4oz mixed lettuce leaves
1 cucumber, thinly sliced
2 green (unripe) mangoes, peeled and
thinly sliced
250g/8oz cooked chicken, shredded
4 tablespoons fresh mint leaves
4 tablespoons fresh coriander leaves
<u>Chilli and lime dressing</u>
2 fresh red chillies, chopped
2 tablespoons palm or brown sugar
3 tablespoons lime juice
2 teaspoons Thai fish sauce (nam pla)

Method:

1 *Arrange lettuce, cucumber, mangoes, chicken, mint and coriander attractively on a serving platter.*

2 *To make dressing, place chillies, sugar, lime juice and fish sauce in a bowl and mix to combine. Drizzle dressing over salad and serve.*

Note: *Palm sugar is a rich, aromatic sugar extracted from the sap of various palms. The palm sugar used in Thailand is lighter and more refined than that used in other parts of Asia. Palm sugar is available from Oriental food shops. If green (unripe) mangoes are unavailable you might like to make this salad using tart green apples instead.*

Serves 4

chicken
caesar salad

Photograph page 453

ingredients

2 boneless chicken breast fillets
4 rashers bacon
1 cos lettuce, leaves separated
250g/8oz cherry tomatoes, halved
125g/4oz parmesan cheese shavings
<u>Crispy croutons</u>
250g/8oz bread cubes
2 tablespoons olive oil
<u>Creamy mustard dressing</u>
1/2 cup/125g/4oz sour cream
1/2 cup/125ml/4fl oz mayonnaise
2 tablespoons wholegrain mustard
3 anchovy fillets, chopped
1/4 cup/60ml/2fl oz water

Method:

1 *Preheat barbecue to a medium heat.*

2 *To make croûtons, place bread cubes in a baking dish, drizzle with oil and toss to coat. Bake for 15 minutes or until bread is crisp and golden. Cool.*

3 *Place chicken and bacon on oiled barbecue and cook for 2-3 minutes each side or until chicken is tender and bacon is crisp. Cool, then cut chicken into slices and chop bacon.*

4 *Arrange lettuce leaves, tomatoes, chicken and bacon in a bowl.*

5 *To make dressing, place sour cream, mayonnaise, mustard, anchovies and water in a food processor or blender and process until smooth. Just prior to serving, drizzle dressing over salad, then scatter with croûtons and parmesan cheese shavings.*

Note: *To make the bread cubes for the croûtons, take an unsliced loaf of stale bread and cut off all the crusts to make an evenly shaped rectangular loaf. Cut bread loaf into 5mm/¹/₄ in thick slices. Cut each bread slice into 5mm/¹/₄ in thick strips, then cut in the opposite direction at 5mm/¹/₄ in intervals to make 5 mm/¹/₄ in square bread cubes. Using a whole loaf of bread will make more croûtons than you require for this recipe, however, leftover croûtons will keep in an airtight container for several weeks.*

Serves 8

warm
beef and potato salad

Method:

1 Roll beef in black peppercorns. Heat 1 tablespoon oil in a frying pan over a medium heat, add beef and cook for 10-15 minutes, turning frequently, until well browned on all sides, continue cooking until beef is cooked to your liking. Remove beef from pan, cover, set aside and keep warm.

2 Wipe pan clean with absorbent kitchen paper. Add 5cm/2in of oil and heat until a cube of bread dropped in browns in 50 seconds. Cook potato slices and sweet potato slices in batches for 3-5 minutes or until golden and crisp. Remove from pan, drain on absorbent kitchen paper and sprinkle with salt.

3 To serve, slice beef thinly. Divide potato crisps and lettuce leaves between serving plates. Place beef slices on top of lettuce, sprinkle with vinegar and serve immediately.
Note: When the beef is browned it will be rare to medium. If this is how you like your meat, remove it from the pan at this stage. To test the degree of doneness of the meat,

500g/1 lb fillet of beef in one piece
2 tablespoons crushed black peppercorns
vegetable oil
4 potatoes, very thinly sliced
1 large orange sweet potato,
very thinly sliced
salt
assorted lettuce leaves
balsamic or red wine vinegar

press it with a pair of blunt tongs. Rare meat will feel springy to the touch, medium meat slightly springy and well-done meat will feel firm.

Serves 4

chicken
and nectarine salad

Method:

1 Arrange lettuce leaves, watercress, chicken, red pepper, nectarines and celery in a salad bowl or on a large serving platter.

2 To make dressing, place black peppercorns, oil and vinegar in a screwtop jar and shake well to combine. Spoon dressing over salad and serve immediately.

Note: This spectacular salad is ideal for a simple summer luncheon.

Serves 4

1 lettuce of your choice, leaves separated
1 bunch/250g/8oz watercress, broken into sprigs
500g/1 lb cooked chicken, chopped
1 red capsicum (pepper), sliced
4 nectarines, sliced
2 stalks celery, sliced
<u>Black pepper dressing</u>
3 teaspoons crushed black peppercorns
1 tablespoon olive oil
2 tablespoons red wine vinegar

cellophane
noodle salad

Method:

1 *Place noodles in a bowl and pour over boiling water to cover. Stand for 10 minutes, then drain well.*

2 *Heat oil in a frying pan over a high heat, add garlic and ginger and stir-fry for 1 minute. Add pork and stir-fry for 5 minutes or until pork is browned and cooked through.*

3 *Arrange mint, coriander, lettuce, shallots, chilli and noodles on a serving platter. Top with pork mixture, then drizzle with lemon juice and soy sauce.*

Note: *Cellophane noodles, also known as glass noodles, bean thread noodles or vermicelli, are made from mung bean flour and are either very thin vermicelli-style noodles or flatter fettuccine-style noodles. In the dried state they are very tough and difficult to break. For ease of use it is best to buy a brand which packages them as bundles.*

Serves 4

ingredients

155g/5oz cellophane noodles
2 teaspoons sesame oil
2 cloves garlic, crushed
1 tablespoon finely grated fresh ginger
500g/1 lb ground pork
15g/¹/₂oz mint leaves
15g/¹/₂oz coriander (cilantro) leaves
8 lettuce leaves
5 red or golden shallots, chopped
1 fresh red chilli, sliced
2 tablespoons lemon juice
1 tablespoon light soy sauce

Oven temperature 180°C

marsala
quail salad

Method:

1 *Place quails on a rack in a baking pan and bake for 20 minutes. Cool slightly, then break into serving-size portions.*

2 *Melt butter in a saucepan. Add cream and Marsala, bring to the boil, then reduce heat and simmer for 5 minutes. Add quail and cook for 5 minutes longer. Set aside to cool.*

3 *To make sauce, combine cream, mayonnaise and Marsala and beat well to combine.*

4 *Arrange endive, witloof, radicchio, watercress and pear in a serving bowl. Top with quail, sprinkle with pecans and drizzle sauce over. Serve immediately.*

Note: *In this salad the quail and marsala, with their distinctive flavours, mingle deliciously with the salad leaves. An elegant dish that can be served as a luncheon dish or starter.*

Serves 6

ingredients

6 quails
30g/1 oz butter
¹/₂ cup/125ml/4fl oz cream
³/₄ cup/185ml/6fl oz dry Marsala
1 curly endive, leaves separated
1 witloof, leaves separated
1 radicchio, leaves separated
1 bunch/200g/7oz watercress
1 pear, peeled, cored and sliced
45g/1¹/₂oz pecans
Marsala sauce
2 tablespoons mayonnaise
2 teaspoons dry Marsala

smoked
chicken in ginger dressing

ingredients

Method:

1 Place chicken, shallots, red capsicum (pepper), chilli, coriander (cilantro) and mint in a serving bowl. Season to taste with black pepper.

2 To make dressing, place oil, vinegar, orange juice, mustard, sugar and ginger in a screwtop jar and shake well to combine. Pour over chicken mixture and toss to combine. Cover and refrigerate.

Note: A pretty salad with a fresh taste that is easy to make and travels well. Put the salad in the serving bowl to marinate on the way to your picnic.

Serves 6

1 smoked chicken, 1-1½kg, meat removed and broken into bite-size pieces
4 green shallots, finely chopped
1 small red capsicum (pepper), finely sliced
1 small red chilli, seeded and finely sliced
1 tablespoon chopped fresh coriander (cilantro)
1 tablespoon chopped fresh mint
freshly ground black pepper
<u>Orange and ginger dressing</u>
3 tablespoons olive oil
2 tablespoons white wine vinegar
2 tablespoons freshly squeezed orange juice
1 teaspoon wholegrain mustard
1 teaspoon brown sugar
1 teaspoon finely grated fresh ginger

italian
chicken salad

Method:

1 *Heat a nonstick char-grill or frying pan over a high heat. Lightly spray chicken with olive oil, add to pan and cook for 2-3 minutes each side or until tender. Remove from pan and set aside to cool.*

2 *To make dressing, place prunes, oregano, lemon rind, sugar and vinegar in a saucepan over a low heat, bring to simmering and simmer for 5 minutes.*

3 *To assemble salad, cut chicken breasts into thin slices. Arrange spinach, beans, onion, chicken and capers attractively on serving plates. Drizzle a little warm dressing over the salad and serve immediately. Serve any remaining dressing separately.*

Serves 4

ingredients

**13 boneless chicken breast fillets,
all visible fat and skin removed
olive oil spray
125g/4oz baby English spinach leaves
125g/4oz green beans, blanched
1 red onion, thinly sliced
2 tablespoons small capers, drained
<u>Vinegar and Prune Dressing</u>
8 pitted prunes
1 tablespoon fresh oregano leaves
shredded rind of 1 lemon
1 teaspoon sugar
1/2 cup/125ml/4fl oz red wine vinegar**

warm
pork and mint salad

Method:

1 Heat a nonstick frying pan or wok over a medium heat, add shallots, ginger and chilli and cook, stirring, for 3 minutes.

2 Add pork and stir-fry for 3-4 minutes or until brown. Stir in mint, sugar, soy sauce, lime juice and fish sauce and stir-fry for 4 minutes or until pork is cooked.

3 Arrange lettuce leaves, cucumber and snow pea (mangetout) sprouts or watercress on a serving platter, top with pork mixture and serve immediately.

Note: For an easy dessert, serve Chilled Nashis with Lime - cut chilled nashis into thin slices, sprinkle with fresh lime juice and toss. Nashis are at their best during the winter months and this easy dessert is a refreshing and healthy way to end any meal. If Vietnamese mint is unavailable use ordinary mint instead.

Serves 4

ingredients

6 shallots, chopped
2 tablespoons shredded fresh ginger
1 fresh red chilli, chopped
500g/1 lb lean ground pork
3 tablespoons shredded Vietnamese mint
1 tablespoon brown sugar
1/4 cup/60ml/2fl oz reduced-salt soy sauce
2 tablespoons lime juice
2 teaspoons Thai fish sauce
250g/8oz assorted lettuce leaves
1 cucumber, sliced
60g/2oz snow pea (mangetout)
sprouts or watercress

chicken
and couscous salad

Method:

1 *Place couscous in a bowl, pour over boiling water and stock, cover and stand for 5 minutes or until water is absorbed. Toss with a fork to separate grains.*
2 *Arrange lettuce, couscous, chicken, tomatoes, cucumber, coriander and snow pea (mangetout) sprouts or watercress on a serving platter.*
3 *To make dressing, place mint, cumin, chilli powder and yoghurt in a bowl and whisk to combine. Drizzle a little dressing over salad and serve remaining dressing separately.*

Serves 4

ingredients

1 cup/185g/6oz couscous
¹/₂ cup/125ml/4fl oz boiling water
¹/₂ cup/125ml/4fl oz boiling chicken stock
1 cos lettuce, leaves separated
250g/8oz cooked chicken breast fillets,
cut into thick slices
2 tomatoes, chopped
1 cucumber, chopped
3 tablespoons fresh coriander
(cilantro) leaves
60g/2oz snow pea (mangetout) sprouts
or watercress
Yoghurt dressing
2 tablespoons chopped fresh mint
1 teaspoon ground cumin
¹/₂ teaspoon chilli powder
1 cup/200g/6¹/₂oz low-fat yoghurt

thai
beef salad

Method:

1 Heat a frying or char-grill pan over a high heat until hot, add beef and cook for 1-2 minutes each side or until cooked to your liking. Set aside to cool.

2 Arrange lettuce, tomatoes, cucumbers, onions and mint attractively on a serving platter.

3 To make dressing, place lemon grass or rind, coriander (cilanto), sugar, lime juice and soy, chilli and fish sauces in a bowl and mix to combine.

4 Slice beef thinly and arrange on salad, then drizzle with dressing and serve.

Note: When making a Thai salad, presentation is all important and a salad can be a spectacular centrepiece for any table. Traditionally Thai salads are served on flat plates - not in bowls - which means the full effect of the arrangement of ingredients can be appreciated.

Serves 4

ingredients

500g/1 lb rump or topside steak
185g/6 oz mixed lettuce leaves
185g/6oz cherry tomatoes, halved
2 cucumbers, peeled and chopped
2 red onions, sliced
3 tablespoons fresh mint leaves
<u>Lime and Coriander dressing</u>
1 stalk fresh lemon grass, chopped or
1 teaspoon finely grated lemon rind
3 tablespoons fresh coriander
(cilanto) leaves
1 tablespoon brown sugar
2 tablespoons lime juice
3 tablespoons light soy sauce
2 tablespoons sweet chilli sauce
2 teaspoons Thai fish sauce (nam pla)

nutty
pork ravioli salad

Method:

1 *To make filling, heat oil in a nonstick frying pan over a medium heat, add garlic and cook, stirring, for 2 minutes. Add pork and cook, stirring, for 5 minutes. Remove pan from heat, stir in peanut butter, chilli sauce, mint and soy sauce. Place a tablespoon of filling in the centre of each wrapper, brush edges with a little water, then top with a second wrapper and press edges to seal.*

2 *Place in a steamer set over a saucepan of boiling water, cover and steam in batches for 5 minutes or until ravioli is tender. Set aside and keep warm.*

3 *To make dressing, combine water, lime juice, chilli sauce, fish sauce and coriander (cilantro) in a bowl. Arrange lettuce leaves on a serving platter, top with warm ravioli and spoon over dressing.*

ingredients

32 spring roll or wonton wrappers, each 7¹/₂cm/3in square
assorted lettuce leaves
<u>Chilli pork filling</u>
1 tablespoon sesame oil
1 clove garlic, finely chopped
250g/8oz lean ground pork
1 tablespoon crunchy peanut butter
1 tablespoon sweet chilli sauce
1 tablespoon chopped fresh mint
2 teaspoons reduced-salt soy sauce
<u>Chilli dressing</u>
¹/₄ cup/60ml/2fl oz warm water
2 tablespoons lime juice
1 tablespoon sweet chilli sauce
1 tablespoon fish sauce
3 tablespoons chopped fresh coriander (cilantro)

thai
lamb salad

Method:

1 *To make dressing, place coriander (cilantro), sugar, soy and chilli sauces, lime juice and fish sauce in a bowl and mix to combine. Set aside.*

2 *Arrange lettuce leaves and cucumber on a serving platter and set aside.*

3 *Heat oil in a wok over a high heat, add lamb and stir-fry for 2 minutes or until brown. Place lamb on top of lettuce leaves, drizzle with dressing and serve immediately.*

Note: *This salad is also delicious made with pork fillet. Use a vegetable peeler to make long thin slices of cucumber - simply peel off lengthwise strips.*

Serves 4

ingredients

250g/8oz assorted lettuce leaves
1 cucumber, sliced lengthwise into thin strips
2 teaspoons vegetable oil
500g/1 lb lamb fillets, trimmed of all visible fat, thinly sliced
<u>Coriander and Chilli Dressing</u>
2 tablespoons chopped coriander (cilantro)
1 tablespoon brown sugar
¹/₄ cup/60ml/2fl oz soy sauce
2 tablespoons sweet chilli sauce
2 tablespoons lime juice
2 teaspoons fish sauce

new
mexico chicken salad

Method:

1 Arrange rocket, flowers and radicchio attractively on serving plates. Top with grapefruit and chicken.

2 To make dressing, place pine nuts, bay leaves, chillies, sugar, vinegar and oil in a bowl and whisk to combine. Just prior to serving, drizzle dressing over salad.

Note: Edible flowers you might like to choose from include nasturtiums, scented geraniums, roses, marigolds, violets, zucchini (courgette) flowers and the flowers of most herbs such as chives, rocket, borage, dill, rosemary, lavender and basil. Look out for mixed packs of edible flowers in greengrocers and specialty food shops.

Serves 4

ingredients

1 bunch young rocket
edible flowers of your choice
6 radicchio leaves, shredded
1 grapefruit, peeled, all white pith removed, segmented
2 smoked chicken breasts, sliced
Pine nut and chilli dressing
4 tablespoons pine nuts, toasted
6 bay leaves
2 fresh red chillies, finely chopped
2 tablespoons sugar
¹/₃ cup/90ml/3fl oz red wine vinegar
¹/₄ cup/60ml/2fl oz olive oil

chicken
and curry salad

Method:
1 Heat oil in a wok over a medium heat, add garlic, ginger, chillies and onion and stir-fry for 3 minutes or until onion is golden. Add curry paste and stir-fry for 3 minutes longer or until fragrant.
2 Stir chicken, fish sauce and sugar into pan and cook, stirring frequently, for 10 minutes or until chicken is tender. Remove pan from heat and set aside to cool slightly. Add mint and coriander and toss to combine.
3 To serve, line a large platter with cabbage, then top with spring onions, cucumbers, bean sprouts, red capsicum (pepper) and chicken mixture.
Serves 4

ingredients

1 tablespoon sesame oil
1 clove garlic, crushed
1 tablespoon finely grated fresh ginger
2 small fresh red chillies, finely chopped
1 onion, cut in wedges
1 tablespoon Thai green curry paste
500g/1 lb boneless chicken breast fillets, thinly sliced
1 tablespoon Thai fish sauce (nam pla)
1 tablespoon sugar
2 tablespoons chopped fresh mint
1 tablespoon chopped fresh coriander (cilantro)
1 Chinese cabbage, sliced
3 spring onions, sliced
2 cucumbers, sliced
125g/4oz bean sprouts
1 red capsicum (pepper), thinly sliced

spiced
grilled beef

Method:

1 *Place onion, garlic, coriander roots, peppercorns, soy sauce, lime juice and fish sauce in a food processor and process to make a paste. Coat beef with spice mixture and cook over a medium charcoal or gas barbecue, turning occasionally, for 15 minutes or until beef is cooked to medium doneness. Alternatively, bake beef in oven for 30-45 minutes or until cooked to medium .*

2 *Arrange lettuce, tomatoes and cucumber on a serving plate. Slice beef thinly and arrange over lettuce. Serve with lime wedges.*

Serves 4

ingredients

1 red onion, chopped
4 cloves garlic, crushed
2 fresh coriander (cilantro) roots
1 teaspoon crushed black peppercorns
2 tablespoons light soy sauce
2 teaspoons lime juice
2 teaspoons Thai fish sauce (nam pla)
500g/1 lb rib-eye (scotch fillet) of beef, in one piece
6 lettuce leaves
185g/6oz cherry tomatoes, halved
1 cucumber, cut into strips
lime wedges

bean, pasta & rice salads

mexican corn and bean salad

Salads made with beans, pasta

and rice make satisfying and substantial meals. Next time you are looking for a warm-weather main dish, why not try a Warm Rice or Marinated Bean Salad.

pasta
shell salad

Method:

1 Place pasta, avocado, sweet corn and tomato in a bowl and toss to combine. Mix together mayonnaise and yoghurt, drizzle over salad and toss to combine.

Serves 2

ingredients

75g/2¹/₂oz pasta shells, cooked
¹/₂ avocado, peeled and chopped
3 tablespoons drained, canned
sweet corn kernels
¹/₂ tomato, chopped
2 tablespoons mayonnaise
2 tablespoons natural yoghurt

mexican
corn bean salad

Photograph page 469

Method:

1 Place sweet corn, red kidney and green beans, red and green capsicum(peppers), tomatoes and avocados in a salad bowl and toss to combine.

2 To make dressing, place onion, chillies, garlic, coriander, cumin, vinegar and oil in a bowl and whisk to combine.

3 Drizzle dressing over salad and toss to combine. Cover and refrigerate for 1 hour before serving.

Note: To blanch green beans, bring a large saucepan of water to the boil, add beans and cook until they are bright green. Remove immediately and refresh under cold running water. For a delicious light meal serve this salad on fried tortillas or wrapped in pitta bread.

Serves 6

ingredients

375g/1 oz canned sweet corn kernels, drained
375g/12oz canned red kidney beans,
rinsed and drained
90g/3oz green beans, blanched
and cut into 5cm/2in pieces
1 large red capsicum (pepper), diced
1 large green capsicum (pepper), diced
3 tomatoes, chopped
2 avocados, chopped
<u>Chilli and herb dressing</u>
1 red onion, chopped
3 small fresh green chillies,
finely chopped
2 cloves garlic, crushed
3 tablespoons chopped fresh coriander
(cilantro)
2 teaspoons ground cumin
¹/₃ cup/90ml/3fl oz balsamic vinegar
¹/₄ cup/60ml/2fl oz olive oil

minestrone

Method:

1 Cook pasta in boiling water in a large saucepan following packet directions. Drain, rinse under cold running water and set aside to cool completely.

2 Place chickpeas, carrots, zucchini (courgettes), celery, red capsicum (pepper), beans, tomatoes and pasta in a bowl and toss to combine.

3 Arrange lettuce on a serving platter and top with pasta mixture.

4 To make dressing, place pesto, yoghurt and mayonnaise in a bowl and mix to combine. Drizzle over salad and serve.

Note: This dish makes the most of all the flavours ordinarily found in minestrone soup and serves them up as a salad! If plum (egg or Italian) tomatoes are not available, substitute ordinary tomatoes.

Serves 4

ingredients

250g/8oz pasta shells
440g/14oz canned chickpeas, rinsed and drained
2 carrots, diced
2 zucchini (courgettes), diced
2 stalks celery, diced
1 red capsicum (pepper), diced
155g/5oz green beans, blanched
3 plum (egg or Italian) tomatoes, cut into wedges
250g/8oz mixed lettuce leaves
__Pesto dressing__
125g/4oz ready-made pesto
1/2 cup/100g/3 1/2oz natural yoghurt
2 tablespoons mayonnaise

spicy
wild rice salad

Method:

1 Cook rice in boiling water following packet directions or until tender. Drain well and set aside to cool.

2 Heat oil in a nonstick frying pan over a medium heat, add onions, cumin, cinnamon, cloves and ginger and cook, stirring, for 10 minutes or until onions are soft and slightly caramelised. Add carrots and cook until tender. Stir in honey, then remove from heat and cool slightly.

3 Place rice, carrot mixture, oranges, pistachios, raisins, almonds, spring onions and dill in a bowl and toss to combine.

4 To make dressing, place mustard, oil, orange juice and vinegar in a bowl and whisk to combine. Pour dressing over salad and toss.

Note: If wild rice blend is unavailable use ³/₄ cup/170g/5¹/₂oz brown rice and ¹/₄ cup/60g/2oz wild rice. The two varieties of rice can be cooked together.

Serves 4

ingredients

2 cups/440g/14oz wild rice blend
(brown and wild rice mix)
2 tablespoons vegetable oil
2 onions, cut into thin wedges
1 teaspoon ground cumin
¹/₂ teaspoon ground cinnamon
¹/₄ teaspoon ground cloves
¹/₄ teaspoon ground ginger
2 carrots, thinly sliced
1 teaspoon honey
2 oranges, segmented
90g/3oz pistachios, toasted and
roughly chopped
90g/3oz raisins
60g/2oz flaked almonds, toasted
3 spring onions, sliced
3 tablespoons chopped fresh dill
<u>Orange mustard dressing</u>
1 teaspoon Dijon mustard
¹/₂ cup/125ml/4fl oz olive oil
¹/₄ cup/60ml/2fl oz orange juice
1 tablespoon red wine vinegar

pasta
and asparagus salad

Method:

1 Cook pasta in boiling water in a large saucepan following packet directions. Drain, rinse under cold running water, drain again and set aside.

2 Boil, steam or microwave asparagus until tender. Add asparagus and watercress to pasta and toss to combine.

3 Place butter and rosemary in a small saucepan and cook over a low heat until butter is golden. Divide pasta between serving bowls, then drizzle with rosemary-flavoured butter and top with black pepper and Parmesan cheese to taste. Serve with lime wedges.

Note: Chilli pasta is available from delicatessens and specialty food stores. If unavailable use ordinary pasta and add some chopped fresh chilli to the butter and rosemary mixture.

Serves 4

ingredients

**500g/1 lb chilli linguine
250g/8oz asparagus, cut in half
155g/5oz watercress, broken into sprigs
60g/2oz butter
2 tablespoons chopped fresh rosemary
freshly ground black pepper
fresh Parmesan cheese shavings
lime wedges**

bean
and broccoli salad

Method:

1 Boil, steam or microwave broccoli and beans, separately, until they just change colour. Drain and refresh under cold running water. Place in a bowl.

2 To make dressing, place pine nuts, basil, mint, lemon juice, oil and black pepper to taste in a bowl and mix to combine. Spoon dressing over vegetables and toss to combine.

Note: For a more colourful salad, use a combination of green and butter beans instead of just green.

Serves 8

ingredients

1kg/2 lb broccoli, broken into florets
155g/5oz green beans
Fresh herb dressing
60g/2oz pine nuts,
toasted and roughly chopped
2 tablespoons chopped fresh basil
1 tablespoon choppped fresh mint
1/3 cup/90ml/3fl oz lemon juice
1 tablespoon olive oil
freshly ground black pepper

beetroot
pasta salad

Method:

1 Cook beetroot in boiling water for 10-15 minutes or until tender. Drain and set aside to cool. Discard cooking water.

2 Cook pasta in clean boiling water in pan following packet directions. Drain, rinse under cold running water and set aside to cool completely.

3 Arrange lettuce leaves in a salad bowl, top with pasta, beetroot, carrots, zucchini (courgettes) and red capsicum (pepper).

4 To make dressing, place sesame seeds, oil, soy sauce and chilli sauce in a screwtop jar and shake well to combine. Spoon dressing over salad, cover and refrigerate until ready to serve.

Note: For an even quicker version of this dish canned baby beetroot could be used.

Serves 4

ingredients

Beetroot pasta salad
8 small beetroot, peeled and halved
375g/12oz fettuccine
250g/8oz assorted lettuce leaves
2 carrots, cut into thin strips
2 zucchini (courgettes), chopped
1 red capsicum (pepper), sliced
Sesame dressing
1 tablespoon sesame seeds
2 teaspoons sesame oil
2 tablespoons sweet soy sauce
2 tablespoons sweet chilli sauce

Oven temperature 180°C, 350°F, Gas 4

pasta
salad with roasted garlic

Method:

1 Place unpeeled garlic cloves on a lightly greased baking tray and bake for 10-12 minutes or until soft and golden. Peel garlic and set aside.

2 Cook bacon in a frying pan over a medium heat for 4-5 minutes or until crisp. Drain on absorbent kitchen paper.

3 Melt butter in a clean frying pan, add breadcrumbs, herbs and black pepper to taste and cook, stirring for 4-5 minutes or until breadcrumbs are golden.

4 Cook pasta in boiling water in a large saucepan following packet directions. Drain well and place in a warm serving bowl. Add garlic, bacon and breadcrumb mixture, toss and serve immediately.

Note: The garlic can be roasted and the bacon and breadcrumb mixture cooked several hours in advance, leaving just the cooking of the pasta and the final assembly of the salad to do at the last minute.

Serves 8

ingredients

**20 cloves unpeeled garlic
8 rashers bacon, chopped
30g/1oz butter
2 cups/125g/4oz breadcrumbs,
made from stale bread
4 tablespoons chopped fresh mixed
herb leaves
freshly ground black pepper
750g/1½ lb spinach, tomato
or plain linguine**

drunken summer fruits

fruit salads

A fruit salad makes a healthy,

refreshing and light dessert that few people can resist. The ways in which you can present your fruit are almost endless. This chapter presents a selection of fruit salads that you will be proud to serve with any meal.

orange
salad

Method:

1 Thinly peel the rind from 1 orange. Ensure all the white pith is removed, cut rind into thin strips and set aside. Peel remaining oranges, remove all the white pith, and slice all oranges crossways into 1 cm/½ in thick slices. Place in a heatproof bowl and set aside.

2 Place reserved orange rind, sugar, cinnamon stick, water and lemon juice in saucepan over a medium heat, bring to simmering and simmer for 3 minutes. Remove from heat, cool slightly and pour over oranges. Cover and chill for at least 2 hours or until ready to serve. Serve with yoghurt.

Note: When blood oranges are in season they make a spectacular alternative to ordinary oranges in this simple dessert salad. Blood oranges are in season during winter months, however their season is short and they are not always easy to find.

Serves 4

ingredients

4 oranges
¼ cup/60g/2oz sugar
1 cinnamon stick
¾ cup/185ml/6fl oz water
1 teaspoon lemon juice
4 tablespoons reduced-fat honey-flavoured yoghurt

drunken
summer fruits

Photograph page 477

Method:

1 Place berries, peaches and nectarines in a bowl. Pour wine and lime juice over fruit and toss gently to combine. Cover and chill for 20-30 minutes. Serve in deep bowls with some of the marinade and a spoonful of thick cream.

Note: When available, fresh apricots are a tasty addition to this summer dessert.

Serves 4-6

ingredients

375g/12oz mixed berries, such as raspberries, blueberries and strawberries
2 white peaches, quartered
2 nectarines, quartered
¾ cup/185ml/6fl oz dessert wine
2 tablespoons lime juice
thick cream

apple
strawberry and pecan salad

Method:

1 Combine apples, celery, strawberries, sultanas and pecans in a bowl.
2 To make dressing, blend together mint, yoghurt and lemon juice. Toss with apple mixture and refrigerate until required.
Note: A variation on the traditional Waldorf salad, with half the fat and no cholesterol.

Serves 4

ingredients

2 red apples, chopped
2 stalks celery, sliced
185g/6oz strawberries, halved
3 tablespoons sultanas
60g/2oz chopped pecans
Dressing
2 teaspoons finely chopped
fresh mint leaves
3 tablespoons low-fat natural yoghurt
2 tablespoons lemon juice

berries
and passion fruit salad

Method:

1 *To make vinaigrette, place passion fruit pulp, vinegar, sugar, mustard and black pepper to taste in a screwtop jar and shake well to combine.*

2 *Arrange watercress, lettuce leaves, blueberries, tomatoes and cucumber on a serving platter. Spoon vinaigrette over salad and serve immediately.*

Note: *Blackberries or any other fresh berries can be used in place of the blueberries in this salad. Delicious served with wholegrain or rye bread.*

Serves 4

ingredients

**250g/8oz watercress, broken into sprigs
I lettuce of your choice,
leaves separated
250g/8oz blueberries
250g/8oz yellow teardrop or red cherry
tomatoes, halved
I cucumber, seeded and chopped
<u>Passion Fruit Vinaigrette</u>
4 tablespoons passion fruit pulp
2 tablespoons white vinegar
I teaspoon sugar
2 teaspoons Dijon mustard
freshly ground black pepper**

melon
in ginger syrup

Method:

1 *Arrange watermelon, honeydew melon and rock melon (cantaloupe) on a serving platter. Cover and chill until required.*

2 *To make Ginger Syrup, place ginger, wine, sugar and lemon strips in a saucepan, bring to simmering over a medium heat and simmer, stirring occasionally, for 3 minutes. Transfer syrup to a bowl, cover and chill.*

3 *Just prior to serving, spoon syrup over melon.*

Note: *Use any combination of melons that are available for this recipe.*

Serves 6-8

ingredients

**400g/12¹/₂oz watermelon,
cut into thick strips
300g/9¹/₂oz honeydew melon,
cut into thick strips
300g/9¹/₂oz rock melon (cantaloupe),
cut into thick strips
<u>Ginger syrup</u>
45g/1¹/₂oz preserved ginger in syrup,
thinly sliced
1 cup/250ml/8fl oz sweet ginger wine
2 tablespoons sugar
1 tablespoon thin lemon rind strips**

dressings

Salads and Dressings

Salads take only minutes to prepare and are delicious eaten as an accompaniment or as a light meal on their own. Dressings add interest to any salad or vegetable and the ones in this chapter are quick to make and can be kept in the refrigerator for a week or more.

Oriental Mayonnaise

2 tablespoons soft brown sugar
2 teaspoons grated fresh ginger
I teaspoon fennel seeds
I clove garlic, crushed
¹/₃ cup/90ml/3fl oz soy sauce
2 tablespoons cider vinegar
2 egg yolks
¹/₂ teaspoon dry mustard
³/₄ cup/185ml/6 fl oz vegetable oil
2 teaspoons sesame oil
¹/₂ teaspoon hot chilli sauce

1 *Place sugar, ginger, fennel seeds, garlic, soy sauce and vinegar in a saucepan and bring to the boil. Reduce heat and simmer, uncovered, for 5 minutes or until mixture reduces by half. Remove from heat, strain and discard fennel seeds. Set aside to cool.*
2 *Place egg yolks and mustard in a food processor or blender and process until just combined. With machine running, gradually pour in vegetable and sesame oils and process until mayonnaise thickens.*
3 *Add soy mixture and process to combine. Mix in chilli sauce to taste.*
   Note: *Store mayonnaise in a jar or bottle in the refrigerator for up to I week.*
   Makes I ¹/₂ cups/37ml/12fl oz

Mayonnaise

¹/₄ teaspoon dry mustard
2 egg yolks
I cup/250ml/8fl oz olive oil
2 tablespoons lemon juice or white wine vinegar
freshly ground black pepper

Place mustard and egg yolks in a food processor or blender and process until just combined. With machine running, gradually pour in oil and process until mixture thickens. Blend in lemon juice or vinegar and black pepper to taste.

Green Herbed Mayonnaise: Purée

30g/1oz fresh basil leaves,
12 fresh chives,
2 tablespoons chopped fresh parsley and I clove garlic.

Prepare mayonnaise as above using vinegar rather than lemon juice. Stir basil purée into prepared mayonnaise.

Blue Cheese Mayonnaise: Crumble

90g/3oz blue cheese, add to prepared mayonnaise and process to combine.
Makes I ¹/₂ cups/375ml/12fl oz

oils and vinegars

Ginger and Soy Dressing

1 tablespoon grated fresh ginger
1 clove garlic, crushed (optional)
¹/₂ cup/125ml/4fl oz soy sauce
¹/₂ cup/125ml/4fl oz water
1 tablespoon cider vinegar
1 tablespoon sesame oil

Place ginger, garlic (if using), soy sauce, water, vinegar and oil in a screwtop jar and shake well to combine. Stand for at least 15 minutes before using.
Note: *Store dressing in the jar in which you made it, in the refrigerator for 2-3 weeks. Shake well and bring to room temperature before using.*

Makes 1 cup/250ml/8fl oz

Basic Vinaigrette

³/₄ cup/185ml/6fl oz olive oil
¹/₄ cup/60ml/2fl oz cider vinegar
1 tablespoon Dijon mustard
freshly ground black pepper

Place oil, vinegar, mustard and black pepper to taste in a screwtop jar and shake well to combine.

Walnut or Hazelnut Vinaigrette:

Replace olive oil with 3 tablespoons walnut or hazelnut oil and ¹/₂ cup/125ml/4fl oz vegetable oil.

Lemon Herb Vinaigrette:

Replace vinegar with lemon juice and add 60g/2oz mixed chopped fresh herbs such as basil, parsley, chives, rosemary, thyme or tarragon.
Note: *Store dressing in the jar in which you made it, in the refrigerator for 2-3 weeks. Shake well and bring to room temperature before using.*

Makes 1 cup/250ml/8fl oz

Yoghurt Dressing

2 tablespoons snipped fresh chives
1 clove garlic, crushed (optional)
³/₄ cup/155g/5oz natural yoghurt
2 tablespoons white wine vinegar

1 *Place chives, garlic (if using), yoghurt and vinegar in a bowl and whisk to combine.*

Mint Yoghurt Dressing:

Prepare Yoghurt Dressing as described. Mix in 2 tablespoons finely chopped fresh mint.

Curried Yoghurt Dressing:

Prepare Yoghurt Dressing as described. Mix in 1 teaspoon curry powder and a dash of chilli sauce.

Thousand Island Yoghurt Dressing:

1 *Prepare Yoghurt Dressing as described, omitting garlic. Mix in 2 tablespoons chopped green olives, 2 finely chopped spring onions, 1 chopped hard-boiled egg, 1 tablespoon finely chopped green capsicum (pepper), 1 tablespoon tomato paste (purée) and ¹/₂ teaspoon chilli sauce.*
Note: *Store dressing in a screwtop jar in the refrigerator for up to 1 week.*

Makes 1 cup/250ml/8fl oz

Low-oil Vinaigrette

¹/₂ teaspoon dry mustard
²/₃ cup/170ml/5¹/₂fl oz cider vinegar
¹/₃ cup/90ml/3fl oz olive oil
cayenne pepper
freshly ground black pepper

Place mustard, vinegar, oil and cayenne and black pepper to taste in a screwtop jar and shake well to combine.
Note: *Store dressing in the jar in which you made it, in the refrigerator for 2-3 weeks. Shake well and bring to room temperature before using.*
Makes 1 cup/250ml/8fl oz

Pesto Pasta Salad

45g/1¹/₂oz spiral pasta
4 cherry tomatoes, halved
1 slice leg ham, cut into thin strips
30g/1oz watercress or snow pea (mangetout) sprouts
Pesto sauce
15g/¹/₂oz fresh basil leaves
1 tablespoon pine nuts
1 clove garlic
2 tablespoons olive oil
1¹/₂tablespoons grated Parmesan cheese
freshly ground black pepper

1 *Cook pasta in boiling water in a saucepan following packet directions. Rinse under cold water, drain and set aside to cool.*
2 *To make sauce, place basil, pine nuts, garlic and 1 tablespoon oil in a food processor or blender and process until smooth. With machine running, gradually pour in remaining oil. Mix in Parmesan cheese and black pepper to taste.*
3 *Spoon sauce over pasta and toss to combine. Add tomatoes, ham and watercress or snow pea (mangetout) sprouts to salad and toss.*
Note: *This quantity is for a salad which is being served as a side dish, however it is also wonderful as a main course. To serve as a main course simply increase the pasta*

quantity to 60-90g/2-3oz. It is also delicious served warm - keep the pasta warm after cooking and complete recipe as directed.
Makes 1 serving

Julienne Vegetable Salad

1 small carrot, cut into thin strips
1 small zucchini (courgette), cut into thin strips
¹/₂ stalk celery, cut into thin strips
Ginger and Soy Dressing
1 teaspoon sesame seeds, toasted

1 *Arrange carrot, zucchini (courgette) and celery on a serving plate. Drizzle with dressing and sprinkle with sesame seeds.*
Makes 1 serving

Simple Green Salad

4 small lettuce leaves
6 slices cucumber
¹/₄ green capsicum (pepper), cut into thin strips
1 spring onion, finely chopped
1 teaspoon snipped fresh chives
1 teaspoon chopped fresh parsley
freshly ground black pepper
Basic Vinaigrette (page 483) or Low-oil Vinaigrette (page 484)

1 *Arrange lettuce, cucumber, green capsicum (pepper) and spring onion on a serving plate. Scatter with chives and parsley and black pepper to taste. Drizzle with vinaigrette and serve immediately.*
Note: *Always dress a lettuce salad as close to serving time as possible. The longer a dressing sits on the leaves, the less crisp they will be.*
Makes 1 serving

salads

Waldorf Salad

1 green or red apple, cored and sliced
1 teaspoon lemon juice
¹/₂ stalk celery, sliced
1 tablespoon roughly chopped walnuts
1¹/₂ tablespoons Mayonnaise (page 482)
or Yoghurt Dressing (page 483)
freshly ground black pepper

Place apple in a bowl, pour over lemon juice and toss to coat. Add celery, walnuts and mayonnaise or dressing and black pepper to taste and toss to combine.

Note: *Pecans or almonds are a tasty alternative to the walnuts in this easy salad.*

Makes 1 serving

Garden Salad

4 lettuce leaves, torn into pieces
4 cherry tomatoes or tomato wedges
4 button mushrooms, sliced
6 snow peas (mangetout)
or sugar snap peas
1 hard-boiled egg, cut into wedges
1 teaspoon chopped fresh parsley
1 teaspoon chopped fresh basil
2 teaspoons pine nuts, toasted
croûtons (see hint)
Mayonnaise (page 482) or
Yoghurt Dressing (page 483)

Arrange lettuce, tomatoes, mushrooms, snow peas (mangetout) or sugar snap peas and egg on a serving plate. Scatter with parsley, basil, pine nuts and croutons. Drizzle with a little mayonnaise or dressing and serve immediately.

Note: *To make croûtons, cut crusts from a slice of bread, then lightly brush with oil and cut into cubes. Place cubes on a baking tray and bake at 200°C/400°F/Gas 6 for 10-15 minutes or until croûtons are golden and crisp.*

Makes 1 serving.

vegetarian
delights

Vegetarian eating is a healthy alternative for today's lifestyle. Meals without meat, poultry or seafood are attractive, tasty and satisfying – as well as being good for you. The recipes in this book provide delectable dishes which can be combined, or can be enjoyed as a hearty meal on their own. Influenced by cuisines from around the world, there are easy-to-prepare dishes which have the wonderful texture and flavour of fresh vegetables, raw and cooked.

From an Asian-influenced soup to scrumptious desserts, this selection of satisfying and delicious recipes will enable you to prepare natural healthy food to suit every appetite and for every occasion, from a quick snack to a three-course dinner party.

Vegetable know-how

To make the most of your garden-fresh vegetables, we have put together these essential step-by-step preparation and cooking tips to help you create your own.

Ready

Easy cooking and preparation depends on having a few good basic pieces of equipment. To make life easier for you, it is worth investing a little time and money in some good equipment such as a large chopping board, a small sharp vegetable or paring knife, as well as several larger sharp knives for cutting and chopping, a grater, a vegetable peeler and a colander or large sieve. Remember to keep your knives sharp: either learn to sharpen them yourself or take them to a knife sharpener regularly. Sharp knives make preparation a breeze.

Set

Wash vegetables before preparing, but do not soak. Soaking tends to draw out the valuable water-soluble vitamins and you end up with vegetables with a lower nutrient content. As with every rule there are always exceptions and it may be necessary to soak very dirty vegetables to remove dirt and creepy-crawlies. If this is the case, always keep soaking times to a minimum.

- Vegetables that are left whole with their skins on have a higher nutrient and fibre content than those that are finely chopped and peeled. Many of the precious vitamins and minerals found in vegetables are stored just under the skin. Only peel vegetables if necessary.
- For maximum nutritional value, prepare vegetables just before cooking and serve as soon as they are cooked.
- The smaller the portion, the quicker the cooking time. For example, grated carrot will cook more quickly than carrot cut into slices.

Go

Here's how:
- To cube, cut into about 1cm pieces.
- To dice, cut into 0.5cm pieces.
- To mince, cut into 0.25cm pieces.
- To grate, use either a hand grater or a food processor with a grating attachment.
- To slice, cut either very thin to thick. You can also slice into rings. Another way to slice is to cut diagonally. This is a good way to prepare vegetables such as carrots, celery and zucchini for stir-frying.

Remember the three Ms
- Minimum water
- Minimum cooking
- Minimum cutting

Good for you

Health authorities recommend that we eat four serves of vegetables daily, at least one of which should be raw. The old adage of a white, a yellow and a green may be rarely taught these days, but it is a good reminder that the brightly coloured vegetables are usually the best source of vitamins. Most of the vitamin content lies just under the skin, so vegetables should be cooked and eaten with the skin on as often as possible.

Pantry planning

Try the following tips for no-fuss pantry planning.
- If you store herbs and spices in alphabetical order, they are easily located and you can quickly see when they need replacing.

- Growing a few herbs of your own such as basil, coriander, rosemary, mint, chives and parsley means that you always have these on hand. These fresh herbs are often the secret to delicate flavours in meals.
- Place all staples, such as sugar and flour, together. Store sauces and condiments according to favourite cuisines; just a glance in the cupboard will give you great ideas.
- Keep a good selection of frozen vegetables. Peas, beans, spinach and corn are great standbys and only take minutes to cook in the microwave.
- Keep a variety of breads and rolls in the freezer and defrost in the microwave for delicious instant sandwiches.
- Cooked pasta and rice freeze well; reheat in minutes in the microwave and save time on busy nights.
- Evaporated milk, available as full-cream or skim milk, is a terrific standby when there is no fresh cream. It can be used for sauces and quiches and it whips well when chilled. Store a few cans in the pantry for emergencies.

Fibre in vegetables

Vegetable	Serve	Fibre(g)*
Asparagus, boiled	6-8 spears (60g)	1.4
Beans, green, raw	1/2 cup (6g)	1.2
Bean sprouts	2 tablespoons (10g)	0.3
Beetroot, canned	2 slices (20g)	0.6
Broccoli, boiled	2/3 cup (100g)	3.9
Cabbage, white, boiled	1/2 cup (50g)	1.0
Capsicum, green, raw	1/4 capsicum (40g)	0.5
Carrot, peeled, boiled	1 carrot (100g)	2.9
Cauliflower, boiled	2/3 cup (100g)	2.0
Celery, raw	1 stalk (100g)	0.8
Chilli, raw	2 chillies (5g)	0.6
Cucumber, peeled, raw	4-5 slices (20g)	0.1
Eggplant, baked	1/2 small (75g)	2.7
Garlic, raw	2 cloves (10g)	1.7
Leek, boiled	1 leek (50g)	1.4
Lettuce, raw	2 leaves (20g)	0.1
Mushrooms, fried	4-6 mushrooms (75g)	1.4
Olives	3 green (20g)	0.8
Onion, peeled, fried	1 onion (80g)	2.2
Parsley	2 sprigs (2g)	0.1
Peas, green, boiled	1/3 cup (40g)	1.0
Potato, peeled, roasted	1 medium (120g)	2.4
Potato, unpeeled, boiled	1 medium (120g)	3.0
Pumpkin, peeled, boiled	1/2 cup (80g)	2.4
Radish, red, raw	2 radishes (10g)	0.1
Silverbeet, boiled	3 stalks (100g)	2.1
Sweet corn	1/2 cup kernels (70g)	3.5
Tomato, raw	1 medium (130g)	2.4
Zucchini, boiled	1 medium (110g)	1.5

* grams of dietary fibre per serve

Cubed **Diced** **Minced** **Grated** **Sliced**

Raw vegetables provide good health, vital energy and wellbeing. Many vegetables become valueless when overcooked so eat a variety of raw types whenever possible or as the season permits.
Raw vegetables will help supply your body with the essential vitamins, minerals, fibre and complex carbohydrates needed for your daily routine, however frantic. They are also generally low in fat and kilojoules and are a must for the diet-conscious. Don't forget to exercise daily to help maintain and support a healthy body.
Dark green and yellow vegetables are usually high in vitamin A. Leafy vegetables are rich in calcium, iron, magnesium, vitamin C and many of the B group. Skin and outer leaves of many vegetables should be retained wherever possible and thoroughly washed or scrubbed with a stiff brush. Raw vegetable juices are excellent, instant energy-givers as well as being a delicious and natural way to enhance your health. Juices can be digested and assimilated in minutes and will nourish your system while refreshing and invigorating it.

Raw energy salad

Serve this salad for a light spring lunch when all these vegetables are at their best. A combination of other young vegetables such as zucchini, shredded cabbage or baby beans can also be used for this salad.

1 parsnip, grated
2 small carrots, grated
1 small beetroot, grated
6 radishes, grated
Yoghurt dressing
¹/₂ cup/125g/4oz natural yoghurt
3 tablespoons olive oil
1 tablespoon finely chopped fresh dill
freshly ground black pepper

1 Arrange a separate mound of parsnip, carrots and beetroot on four serving plates. Position mounds on three points of the plate to form a triangle.

2 Place a radish mound in the centre of the triangle.
3 To make dressing, whisk together yoghurt, oil and dill in a small bowl. Season to taste with pepper. Serve with salad.

669 kilojoules	(169 calories)	per serve
Fat	16.3g	low
Cholesterol	5mg	low
Fibre	1.1g	low
Sodium	40mg	low

Serves 4

Carrots and apples

This delicious raw salad can be served as is or sprinkled with a little vinaigrette to give it extra zing.

2 green apples, cored and grated
juice 1 lemon
2 carrots, scrubbed and grated

1 Toss apples in lemon juice. Place in salad bowl and mix in carrots.

208 kilojoules	(49 calories)	per serve
Fat	0g	low
Cholesterol	0mg	low
Fibre	3.4 g	medium
Sodium	128mg	low

Serves 4

A feast of raw vegetables

A variety of vegetables can be used for this raw vegetable platter. The following are just a few suggestions. The important thing is to make it a feast for eyes and taste buds. Serve with one or more dressings from our section on final touches (pages 554).

3 stalks celery, cut into thin strips
4 small carrots, scrubbed and quartered
¹/₂ small cauliflower, cut into small florets
¹/₂ green capsicum (pepper), cut into strips
¹/₂ red capsicum (pepper), cut into strips
12 button mushrooms
12 cherry tomatoes
12 small radishes, tops attached
12 teardrop tomatoes
dressings of your choice

1 Choose a large platter or tray and arrange vegetables attractively on it. Serve with dressings in small bowls.

290 kilojoules	(67 calories)	per serve
Fat	0g	low
Cholesterol	0mg	low
Fibre	7.3g	high
Sodium	50mg	low

Serves 8

Early morning pick-up

½ cup/125mL/4oz tomato juice
3 tablespoons celery juice
3 tablespoons carrot juice
freshly ground black pepper
ice cubes
1 celery stick

1 Combine tomato, celery and carrot juices. Season to taste with pepper.
2 Place ice cubes in a serving glass. Pour over juice mixture and garnish with celery stick.

155 kilojoules	(37 calories)	per serve
Fat	0g	low
Cholesterol	0mg	low
Fibre	0 g	low
Sodium	79 mg	medium

Makes 1 cup/250 mL

Pink vegetable cocktail

½ cup/125mL/4oz beetroot juice
3 tablespoons cucumber juice
3 tablespoons orange juice
freshly ground black pepper
ice cubes
1 thin slice orange
strip cucumber skin

1 Combine beetroot, cucumber and orange juices. Season to taste with pepper.
2 Place ice cubes in a serving glass. Pour over juice mixture and garnish with orange slice and cucumber strip.

198 kilojoules	(48 calories)	per serve
Fat	0g	low
Cholesterol	0mg	low
Fibre	0.2g	low
Sodium	543mg	medium

Makes 1 cup/250mL

Just juices

You will need a juice extractor to make these juices. Follow our ideas to get you started then try some of your own. To get the most from your machine, read the manufacturer's instructions as they usually have some interesting suggestions for juice combinations. Serve juice immediately to ensure that it is at its best and that there is maximum vitamin retention. The time of year, age and maturity of vegetables will all affect the initial quality. After juicing you will have a quantity of pulp remaining. This can be pureed and used in casseroles, stews, stocks and soups.

Herbs can transform ordinary foods into culinary delights and have been used for centuries to promote good health. Every cuisine has its favourite herb and so does every cook. The amount used in cooking depends on individual taste and on the type of herb. Strongly flavoured herbs such as bay, sage, thyme, oregano and rosemary should be used sparingly. It is particularly important to chop fresh herbs at the last moment so that the full flavour of the aromatic oils is captured in the dish. Fresh herbs marry well with fresh vegetables and quite often herbs can be used as a seasoning instead of salt. Basil, coriander, dill, oregano, sage, tarragon and savory are a boon to people on low-salt diets. In most cases, fresh is best.

culinary herbs

Many fresh herbs such as caraway, chervil, lemon balm, salad burnet, savory and sorrel are not readily available from the local fruit and vegetable market. But all these can be grown easily and quickly in the home garden or in a trough on the kitchen windowsill. If dried herbs must be used as a substitute, remember that their flavour is rather concentrated and, as a general rule, about a third of the given quantity is sufficient.

Characteristics & uses of herbs

Basil:
(Ocimum basilicum): An annual growing to 60cm high with peppery, clove-scented leaves. Grow from seed in a sunny, moist but well-drained position sheltered from wind. Remove flower buds to encourage longer life.
Use: Use only fresh basil leaves as it loses its flavour when dried. Excellent with all tomato dishes and torn up in salads. It goes well with carrots, zucchini, pasta sauces and chicken.

Bay:
(Laurus nobilis): A slow-growing evergreen tree with aromatic leaves. Makes a good ornamental pot plant in a sunny sheltered position. Young plants need protection from frosts.
Use: Once established, the leaves can be harvested at any time of the year and used fresh. A bay leaf is one of the three herbs that make up the classic bouquet garni. Use with tomatoes and beetroot and to flavour soups, sauces and stews.

Caraway:
(Carum carvi): A handsome biennial to 60cm high with finely cut leaves and clusters of white flowers which produce aromatic seeds with a characteristic flavour. Sow seeds direct in spring or autumn. Needs a sunny, well-drained position protected from wind.
Use: Young leaves are used as a garnish for cooked vegetables. The seeds are used in dishes of cabbage, potatoes and parsnips. Also used in some cakes, biscuits and apple pie.

Chervil:
(Anthriscus cerefolium): A small spreading annual to 50cm. Fernlike leaves have a delicate aniseed flavour. Grow in a partially shaded position in a rich, moist soil.
Use: Chervil is used extensively in French cooking. Leaves are delicious with salad greens and spinach. Use in dressings, garnish for soups and with fish dishes.

Chives:
(Allium schoenoprasum): A perennial plant with hollow-onion flavoured leaves and attractive mauve flowers. Sow seeds in a sunny spot to form a clump. Provide a moist, rich soil. In cold climates, chives die back in winter.
Use: Use to flavour potatoes, any of the marrow family and in fresh salads. Good in most savoury dishes and excellent with eggs and cream.

Coriander:
(Coriandrum sativum): An attractive annual to 60 cm. Lacy foliage has a distinctive taste. Aromatic seeds follow pink and white flowers. Sow seeds direct in spring in a sunny position and water generously. Harvest seeds in autumn and dry in a light, airy position then transfer to an airtight container.
Use: Used in almost every Thai dish. Leaves are tasty in salads and as a garnish for pea soup. The seeds complement mushrooms, cauliflower, beetroot and celery. They are also used in curries, sausage-making and as a flavouring in cakes.

Dill:
(Anethum graveolens): A fast-growing, upright annual to 90 cm. Feathery leaves and clusters of yellow flowers, followed by sharp-tasting dill seeds. Sow seeds direct in a sunny, well-drained soil. The seeds can be harvested.
Use: Chopped dill leaves go well with potatoes. Fresh dill in salads can help you to digest raw vegetables. Seeds are used in chutneys, dill pickles and herb vinegar.

Fennel:
(Foeniculum vulgare): Fast-growing tall annual to 1.5m. It has bright green, feathery leaves and clusters of yellow flowers followed by aniseed-flavoured seeds. Grow in a well-drained, sunny position and provide plenty of water.
Use: The leaves are used in salads, relishes and as garnishes. Both leaves and seeds are traditionally used with fish. Seeds are used in soups, sauces and with lentils, rice and potatoes. Also used in breads and cakes.

Lemon balm:
(Melissa officinalis): A perennial to 90cm. Dark green, crinkled leaves that have a strong lemon scent. Grow in a rich, well-drained soil in full sun. Pinch back in early summer to encourage new growth.
Use: Use only fresh leaves sprinkled over vegetable or fruit salads. Leaves will give a light lemon flavour to cool drinks and make a good herbal tea.

Lemon grass:
(Cymbopogon citratus): A grass-like perennial to 3m high with strap-like leaves and a delicious lemon scent. It forms a large clump in a sunny, warm position with plenty of water, but good drainage.
Use: The fleshy white lower part of the leaves is used in South-East Asian dishes. It adds a tangy taste to salads and is a must for curries. The leaves are used to make a herbal tea.

Lovage:
(Levisticum officinale): A tall perennial plant to 2m high with a strong flavour of celery. Grow in a rich moist soil in full sun or part shade.
Use: The tender leaves add a celery-like flavour to potato salads, green salads and sauces. Delicious on tomato sandwiches. Use also to flavour soups and stews.

Marjoram:

(Origanum marjorana): A fragrant perennial plant to 70cm high with small oval leaves and clusters of white or mauve flowers. Grow in full sun in well-drained soil and keep trimmed to encourage fresh, compact growth.

Use: Fresh leaves are used in tomato dishes, with any of the cabbage family and green beans. Finely chop in salads and salad dressings. Use also to flavour soups, eggs and stuffings for meat dishes.

Mint:

(Mentha spp): There are many varieties of mint, but spearmint *(Mentha spicata)* and applemint *(Mentha suaveolens)* are the two most commonly used in cooking. They are fast-growing perennials which prefer a rich, moist soil and light shade.

Use: Freshly chopped and used with peas, new potatoes, zucchini and mixed green salad. Also good in fruit salads, cooling drinks, jellies, vinegar and lamb sauce.

Oregano:

(Origanum vulgare): A small spreading perennial to around 50cm. Small, pungent leaves and tiny white or mauve flowers. Grow in well-drained soil in a sunny position.

Use: The fresh leaves are used to season salads and many tomato dishes, especially tomato sauces used with pasta. It is also used with eggplant, beans, zucchini and cheese.

Parsley:

(Petroselinum crispum): A biennial plant to 60cm high with flat or curly leaves. Parsley is grown from seed which should be sown direct in spring and summer. Grow in a sunny position and keep up the water in dry weather.

Use: One of the best herbs of all with many uses in vegetable dishes, salads, soups, fish sauces, casseroles and omeletes. The fresh leaves are rich in vitamins A and C.

Rosemary:

(Rosmarinus officinalis): A Mediterranean evergreen shrub to around 1.6m high. It has shining aromatic leaves and pale blue flowers. Grow in full sun in a well-drained position protected from wind.

Use: Use finely chopped fresh leaves to flavour peas, spinach, baked pumpkin and potatoes. Also used to flavour roast lamb, chicken, stuffings and sauces.

Sage:

(Salvia officinalis): A small perennial shrub with soft, grey-green leaves and blue flowers during summer. Grow in a sunny, well-drained position. Trim regularly. An attractive border plant, it requires plenty of water during summer.

Use: Use chopped fresh leaves sparingly in salads, potato dishes and with cheese. Use with pork and veal and in seasoning.

Salad burnet:

(Sanquisorba minor): A low-spreading perennial with attractive lacy leaves set in pairs along the stems. Leaves have a slight cucumber taste. Crimson flowers in summer. Grow in a sunny or partially shaded position in a well-drained humus-enriched soil. Provide plenty of water during the growing season.

Use: Young, fresh leaves are used mostly in mixed green salads. Use to flavour vinegar, butter and herb butter.

Summer savory:

(Satureja hortensis): An annual to 60cm high with bronze-green leaves and white or pale pink flowers in summer. Grow in a sunny, well-drained position with plenty of organic matter added.

Use: Summer savory is traditionally served with broad beans, cooked green beans and green bean salad. Also good in stuffings, rice, soups, sauces and stews.

Winter savory:

(Satureja montana): A semi-prostrate perennial with narrow green leaves and pale blue flowers. Likes a sunny, well-drained position and plenty of compost.

Use: Particularly good when used in stuffings, rice, soups, sauces and stews.

Sorrel:

(Rumex acetosa): A perennial to 90cm tall with large bright green, arrow-shaped leaves that have a pronounced lemon taste and are rich in vitamin C. Prefers a well-drained, rich soil in sun or semi-shade.

Use: Young fresh leaves are excellent in a mixed green salad. A few leaves can be added when cooking spinach. Used in the classic French sorrel soup. Use also in sauces and vegetable purees.

Tarragon:

(Artemesia dracunculus): French tarragon is a bushy perennial to around 1m high. It has dark slender leaves with a slight anise flavour. Grow in a moderately rich, well-drained soil in a sunny spot. French tarragon can only be propagated by division.

Use: One of the four herbs in the "fines herbs" mixture. Use with fish, shellfish, chicken, turkey, game, veal, liver, kidneys and in egg dishes. Tarragon vinegar is an essential ingredient in Bernaise sauce.

Thyme:

(Thymus vulgaris): A strongly aromatic shrubby perennial to around 45cm high. It has tiny, oval leaves and bears pretty pastel-coloured flowers. There are many varieties including lemon thyme, caraway thyme and a pretty variegated type. All thymes like a sunny position with a light, well-drained soil.

Use: Use fresh leaves sparingly with most vegetables including beetroot, tomatoes and zucchini. Use in casseroles, meat dishes, pâtés and stuffings.

ripe red tomato soup

soups
&
starters

A first course based on vegetables

makes a light and healthy start to a meal. In this chapter you will find recipes such as curried lentil soup and paté mushroom which showcase tasty vegetables at their best.

felafels

Method:

1 Place chickpeas in a large bowl, cover with cold water and set aside to soak overnight. Drain. Place chickpeas in large saucepan, cover with water and bring to the boil. Boil for 10 minutes, then reduce heat and simmer for 45-60 minutes or until chickpeas are tender. Drain and set aside to cool.

2 Place chickpeas, garlic, onion, spring onions, coriander, parsley, cumin and turmeric in a food processor or blender and process to combine.

3 Heat oil in a large saucepan until a cube of bread dropped in browns in 50 seconds. Shape tablespoons of chickpea mixture into balls and deep-fry, a few at a time, for 3 minutes or until golden brown. Drain on absorbent kitchen paper.

ingredients

440g/14oz chickpeas
3 cloves garlic, crushed
1 small onion, chopped
4 spring onions, chopped
2 tablespoons chopped fresh coriander
2 tablespoons chopped fresh parsley
1 teaspoon ground cumin
1/2 teaspoon turmeric
vegetable oil, for deep frying

Note: To speed preparation, omit Step 1 and use canned chickpeas. You will need two 440g/14oz cans and the chickpeas should be drained and rinsed before making the felafel.
Serves 8

tzatziki

ingredients

Method:

1 *Place cucumber, yoghurt, mint, parsley, garlic and black pepper to taste in a bowl and mix to combine. Cover and refrigerate for at least 1 hour or until required.*

2 *To serve, accompany Tzatziki with broken or sliced bread for dipping.*

Note: *This easy dip makes a refreshing start to a meal and is also delicious served with raw vegetables.*

Serves 8

1 large cucumber, peeled and grated
500g/1 lb natural yoghurt
1 tablespoon chopped fresh mint
1 tablespoon chopped fresh parsley
2 cloves garlic, crushed
freshly ground black pepper
2 French breadsticks

summer
dip

ingredients

Method:

1 *Combine all ingredients in a bowl. Add more lemon juice if desired. Cover and chill until ready to serve.*

2 *Serve with crudite or crackers.*

Makes 1 ¼ cups

1 cup good quality egg mayonnaise
1 clove garlic, crushed
2 tblspn freshly squeezed lemon juice
2 tblspn chopped green olives
2 tblspn chopped gherkins
2 tblspn chopped capers

oriental
noodle soup

Photograph opposite

Method:

1 *Place stock and tamari in a large saucepan and bring to the boil. Reduce heat, add noodles, tofu, bok choy, lemon grass or lemon rind, spring onions, ginger, mushrooms, mint and coriander and simmer for 20 minutes.*
2 *To serve, divide bean sprouts between four warmed serving bowls and ladle over hot soup.*

Note: *Tamari is also called tamari shoyu or Japanese soy sauce. Made only from natural products, soya beans and salt, it contains no monosodium glutamate (MSG) which is often found in Chinese soy sauce. It is also lighter in flavour.*

Serves 4

ingredients

4 cups/1 litre/1³/₄pt vegetable stock
¹/₂ cup/125mL/4fl oz tamari
250g/8oz bean thread noodles
375g/12oz tofu, roughly chopped
155g/5oz bok choy, chopped
1 stalk fresh lemon grass, chopped, or
1 teaspoon dried lemon grass or
1 teaspoon finely grated lemon rind
3 spring onions, sliced diagonally
5cm/2in piece fresh ginger, sliced
200g/6¹/₂oz straw or button mushrooms
1 tablespoon chopped fresh mint
2 tablespoons chopped fresh coriander
100g/3¹/₂oz bean sprouts

carrot
& orange soup

Photograph opposite

Method:

1 *Heat oil in a large saucepan. Add leeks and cook over a medium heat, stirring, for 5 minutes or until golden.*
2 *Add carrots, curry powder, lemon rind and orange juice to pan, bring to the boil and simmer for 10 minutes or until carrots are soft.*
3 *Stir in coconut milk and stock and simmer for 10 minutes longer.*
4 *Remove pan from heat and set aside to cool slightly. Place soup mixture, in batches, in a food processor or blender and process until smooth.*
5 *Return soup to a clean saucepan and heat over a medium heat, stirring, for 4-5 minutes or until hot. Season to taste with black pepper. Serve soup topped with yoghurt, cashew nuts and mint.*

Note: *If commercially made coconut milk is unavailable, you can make it using desiccated coconut and water. To make coconut milk, place 500g/1 lb desiccated coconut in a bowl and pour over 3 cups/750mL/1¹/₄pt of boiling water. Leave to stand for 30 minutes, then strain, squeezing the coconut to extract as much liquid as possible. This will make a thick coconut milk. The coconut can be used again to make a weaker coconut milk.*

Serves 4

ingredients

1 tablespoon vegetable oil
2 leeks, thinly sliced
6 large carrots, sliced
2 tablespoons curry powder
1 tablespoon finely grated lemon rind
1 cup/250mL/8fl oz orange juice
1¹/₂ cups/375mL/12fl oz coconut milk
2 cups/500mL/16fl oz vegetable stock
freshly ground black pepper
¹/₃ cup/60g/2oz natural yoghurt
100g/3¹/₂oz cashew nuts, roasted and chopped
1 tablespoon chopped fresh mint

celery
and blue cheese soup

Photograph opposite

Method:
1 *Melt butter in a large saucepan. Add celery and onions and cook over a medium heat, stirring occasionally, for 4 minutes or until onions are soft but not browned.*
2 *Stir in flour and cook for 1 minute longer. Gradually stir in stock and mix until smooth. Bring to the boil, then reduce heat and simmer for 30 minutes, or until celery is very soft.*
3 *Stir in cheese and season to taste with black pepper. Ladle soup into warm bowls, sprinkle with chives and serve immediately.*
   Note: *There are several creamy blue cheeses available. Castello, Roquefort, Gorgonzola or a creamy Stilton are all suitable to use for this recipe.*

Serves 6

ingredients

**30g/1oz butter
1 bunch celery, finely chopped
2 onions, chopped
2 tablespoons flour
5 cups/1¼ litres/2pt vegetable stock
75g/2½oz strong creamy
blue cheese, mashed
freshly ground black pepper
2 tablespoons snipped fresh chives**

ripe
red tomato soup

Photograph opposite and page 494

Method:
1 *Heat oil in a large saucepan. Add garlic, chillies and red onions and cook over a medium heat, stirring, for 4 minutes or until onions are golden.*
2 *Add spring onions, thyme, sun-dried tomatoes, tomatoes, wine and stock. Bring to the boil, then reduce heat and simmer, covered, for 45 minutes.*
3 *Remove pan from heat and set aside to cool slightly. Place soup mixture, in batches, in a food processor or blender and process until smooth.*
4 *Return soup to a clean saucepan, add sugar, and cook over a medium heat, stirring, until hot. Serve soup topped with sour cream and basil.*

Serves 6

ingredients

**1 tablespoon vegetable oil
2 cloves garlic, crushed
2 fresh red chillies, finely chopped
2 red onions, chopped
4 spring onions, chopped
2 tablespoons chopped fresh thyme
or 1 teaspoon dried thyme
60g/2oz sun-dried tomatoes, chopped
1 kg/2 lb very ripe tomatoes,
peeled and chopped
1 cup/250mL/8fl oz dry white wine
4 cups/1 litre/1¾pt vegetable stock
2 teaspoons sugar
¼ cup/60g/2oz sour cream
2 tablespoons chopped fresh basil**

green minestrone
soup

Method:

1 Melt butter in a large saucepan, add asparagus stalks, broccoli, spring onions, broad beans and 185g/6oz peas and cook, stirring, for 5 minutes.

2 Stir in stock and bring to the boil. Reduce heat and simmer for 15 minutes or until vegetables are tender. Using a slotted spoon, transfer vegetables to a food processor or blender and process until smooth.

3 Return vegetable purée to stock mixture. Add reserved asparagus tips, green beans and remaining peas and bring to the boil. Reduce heat and simmer for 5 minutes or until vegetables are tender. Season to taste with black pepper.

Note: Most soups freeze well. When freezing any liquid leave a 5cm/2in space between the soup and lid of the container, as liquid expands during freezing.

Serves 4

ingredients

60g/2oz butter
250g/8oz asparagus, stalks chopped, tips reserved
250g/8oz broccoli, broken into florets
6 spring onions, chopped
250g/8oz fresh or frozen broad beans
250g/8oz fresh or frozen peas
4 cups/1 litre/1³/₄pt vegetable stock
250g/8oz green beans, cut into 2¹/₂cm/1in pieces
freshly ground black pepper

parsnip
and carrot bake

Method:

1 Melt butter in a large frypan. Cook garlic one minute. Add parsnip and carrot and cook over medium heat, stirring occasionally until almost cooked.
2 Season with rosemary, parsley and pepper.
3 Transfer to greased shallow ovenproof dish and pour over cream. Spinkle with breadcrumbs and cheese and dot with butter. Bake in a preheated 200°C/400°F oven for 35 minutes or until browned.

Serves 8

ingredients

60g/2oz butter
2 cloves garlic, crushed
500g/16oz parsnip, washed and grated
350g/11oz carrot, peeled and grated
300ml/10oz cream
ground black pepper to taste
1 1/2 cups/90g/3oz fresh breadcrumbs
3 tblspns/60g/2oz Parmesan cheese, grated
1 tspn dried rosemary leaves
1 tspn dried parsley flakes

Oven temperature 200°C, 400°F, Gas 6

spicy buckwheat noodles

fast food

If you have little time for preparation

and cooking, yet you want your meals to be interesting and delicious, the dishes in this chapter will be perfect for you.

bean sprout
omelette

Method:

1 To make filling, melt butter in a small frypan. Add ginger, bean sprouts and chives and cook for 1 minute. Remove from pan and keep warm.

2 To make omelette, melt butter in a small frypan. Lightly whisk together eggs and water and season with pepper. Pour into pan and cook over medium heat. Continually draw the edge of the omelette in with a fork during cooking until no liquid remains and the omelette is lightly set.

3 Sprinkle the bean sprout mixture over the omelette and fold in half. Slip onto a plate and serve immediately.

Serves 1

ingredients

Filling
30g/1oz butter
2 tablespoons grated fresh ginger
4 tablespoons bean sprouts
4 chives, finely chopped
Omelette
1 teaspoon butter
2 eggs
2 teaspoons water
freshly ground black pepper

spicy
buckwheat noodles

Photograph also appears on page 505

Method:

1 Cook noodles in boiling water in a large saucepan following packet directions. Drain, set aside and keep warm.

2 Heat oil in a frying pan. Add garlic and cook over a medium heat, stirring, for 1 minute. Add chillies, rocket and tomatoes and cook for 2 minutes longer or until rocket wilts. Toss vegetable mixture with noodles and serve immediately.

Note: If rocket is unavailable you can use watercress instead. For a complete meal, accompany with a tossed green salad and wholemeal bread rolls.

Serves 4

ingredients

500g/1 lb buckwheat noodles
1 tablespoon olive oil
3 cloves garlic, crushed
2 fresh red chillies, seeded and chopped
200g/6½oz rocket leaves removed and shredded
2 tomatoes, chopped

spinach
pancakes

Method:

1 To make pancakes, boil or microwave spinach or silverbeet until wilted. Drain and squeeze out as much liquid as possible.

2 Place flour in a bowl and make a well in the centre. Add eggs and a little of the milk and beat, working in all the flour. Beat in butter and remaining milk, then stir through spinach.

3 Pour 2-3 tablespoons of batter into a 20cm/8in nonstick frying pan and tilt pan so batter evenly covers base. Cook for 1 minute each side or until lightly browned. Set aside and keep warm. Repeat with remaining batter.

4 To make filling, heat oil in a frying pan, add garlic and cook over a medium heat, stirring, for 1 minute. Add spinach or silverbeet and cook for 3 minutes longer or until spinach or silverbeet wilts.

5 Stir in sour cream or yoghurt and black pepper to taste. Spread a spoonful of filling over each pancake. Fold pancakes into quarters and serve immediately.

Note: These wholesome pancakes envelop a delicious savoury filling and are best served immediately after cooking.

ingredients

8 spinach or silverbeet leaves, shredded
1 cup/125g/4oz flour
4 eggs, lightly beaten
155mL/5fl oz milk
30g/1oz butter, melted
<u>Spinach filling</u>
2 teaspoons vegetable oil
2 cloves garlic, crushed
12 spinach or silverbeet leaves, shredded
300g/9½oz sour cream or natural yoghurt
freshly ground black pepper

Serves 6

eggplant
(aubergine) kebabs

Method:

1 Place garlic, oil and cumin in a small bowl and whisk to combine. Brush oil mixture over cut sides of eggplant (aubergines).

2 Thread eggplant (aubergines) onto lightly oiled skewers and cook on a hot grill or under a preheated hot grill for 4 minutes each side or until tender.

3 To make sauce, place yoghurt, coriander and mint in a small bowl and mix to combine. Serve sauce with hot kebabs.

Note: For a complete meal, accompany this dish with pitta bread and a salad.

Serves 4

ingredients

2 cloves garlic, crushed
1 tablespoon vegetable oil
2 teaspoons ground cumin
8 baby eggplants (aubergines),
sliced in half lengthwise
<u>Yoghurt sauce</u>
3/4 cup/155g/5oz natural yoghurt
2 tablespoons chopped fresh coriander
2 tablespoons chopped fresh mint

Oven temperature 180°C, 350°F, Gas 4

super salad tubes

Method:

1 Spread pitta bread rounds with peanut butter. Top with carrot, beetroot, cheese, lettuce, cucumber and bean sprouts. Roll up pitta bread and wrap in greaseproof paper, then plastic food wrap.

Note: This pitta bread roll is simple to prepare and makes a complete meal in itself.

Makes 4 tubes

ingredients
4 large pitta bread rounds
3 tablespoons peanut butter
2 small carrots, grated
2 raw small beetroots, grated
60g/2oz tasty cheese
(mature Cheddar), grated
4 lettuce leaves, shredded
1/2 small cucumber, sliced
60g/2oz bean sprouts

cheese & date
sandwiches

Method:

1 Spread bread slices with cream cheese and drizzle with honey. Top 2 slices of bread with dates and snow pea sprouts or watercress then with remaining bread slices and wrap in plastic food wrap.

Makes 2 sandwiches

ingredients
4 slices bread of your choice
4 tablespoons cream cheese
1 tablespoon honey
8 dates, sliced
60g/2oz snow pea sprouts or watercress

watercress & brie
sandwiches

Method:

1 Place red capsicums (peppers) skin side up under a preheated hot grill and cook until skins blister and char. Place capsicums (peppers) in a paper or plastic food bag for 5-10 minutes, then remove skins.

2 Brush eggplant (aubergine) slices with oil and cook under preheated hot grill for 2-4 minutes each side or until golden.

3 Top half the bread slices or bases of rolls with watercress, red capsicums (peppers), eggplant (aubergine) slices, brie and black pepper to taste. Top with remaining bread slices or tops of rolls. Wrap in plastic food wrap.

Makes 4 sandwiches or rolls

ingredients
2 red capsicums (peppers), halved and seeded
1 eggplant (aubergine), sliced
1 tablespoon vegetable oil
8 slices bread or 4 bread rolls
1/2 bunch/125g/4oz watercress, stems removed
8 slices brie cheese
freshly ground black pepper

cheese
& basil sandwiches

Method:

I Spread 2 bread slices or bases of rolls with pesto. Top with mozzarella cheese, basil, tomato and black pepper to taste, then with remaining bread slices, or tops of rolls. Wrap in plastic food wrap.

Makes 2 sandwiches or rolls

ingredients

4 slices bread or 2 rolls of your choice
2 tablespoons ready-made pesto
6 slices mozzarella cheese
I tablespoon chopped fresh basil
I tomato, sliced
freshly ground black pepper

easy
vegetable stir-fry

Method:

1 *Place mushrooms in a bowl and cover with boiling water. Set aside to stand for 15-20 minutes or until mushrooms are tender. Drain, remove stalks if necessary and slice mushrooms.*

2 *Heat oil in a wok or frying pan, add garlic, ginger and onion and stir-fry over a medium heat for 3 minutes or until onion is soft.*

3 *Add red capsicum (pepper), carrots, broccoli and celery and stir-fry for 3 minutes longer.*

4 *Add mushrooms, sweet corn, tofu, chilli sauce, soy sauce and cashews and stir-fry for 1 minute longer. Serve immediately.*

Serves 4

ingredients

100g/3¹/₂oz dried mushrooms
2 teaspoons sesame oil
2 cloves garlic, crushed
1 tablespoon grated fresh ginger
1 large onion, sliced
1 red capsicum (pepper), cut into strips
2 carrots, sliced diagonally
250g/8oz broccoli, cut into florets
3 stalks celery, sliced diagonally
350g/11oz canned baby sweet corn, drained
200g/6¹/₂oz firm tofu, chopped
2 tablespoons sweet chilli sauce
2 tablespoons soy sauce
4 tablespoons cashew nuts

puff
mushroom pizza

Method:

1 Roll out pastry to fit a greased 26x32cm/
10½x12¾ in Swiss roll tin.

2 Sprinkle pastry with Parmesan cheese and
mozzarella cheese, then top with onion,
mushrooms, tomatoes and olives. Sprinkle
with oregano and thyme and bake for 30
minutes or until pastry is puffed and golden.
Serve hot, warm or cold.

Note: This quick pastry-based pizza is great
for weekend meals and leftovers are ideal for
packed lunches.

Serves 6

ingredients

375g/12oz prepared puff pastry
60g/2oz grated Parmesan cheese
125g/4oz grated mozzarella cheese
1 onion, thinly sliced
200g/6½oz mushrooms, sliced
3 tomatoes, cut into 1 cm/½ in slices
10 pitted black olives
2 teaspoons chopped fresh oregano
or ½ teaspoon dried oregano
2 teaspoons chopped fresh thyme
or ½ teaspoon dried thyme

kebabs
with broad bean purée

Photograph opposite

ingredients
250g/8oz cherry tomatoes
155g/5oz button mushrooms
3 zucchini (courgettes),
cut into thick rounds
1 yellow or green pepper, cut into chunks
250g/8oz marinated tofu, cut into
2cm/³/₄in cubes
1 red pepper, cut into chunks
<u>**Tangy citrus marinade**</u>
2 tablespoons lime or lemon juice
2 tablespoons honey
1 tablespoon reduced-salt soy sauce
1 tablespoon vegetable oil
<u>**Broad bean puree**</u>
250g/8oz shelled fresh or frozen
broad beans
¹/₂ cup/100g/3¹/₂oz natural yogurt
1 tablespoon chopped fresh thyme or
1 teaspoon dried thyme
2 teaspoons finely grated orange rind
freshly ground black pepper

Method:
1 *Thread tomatoes, mushrooms, zucchini (courgettes), yellow or green pepper, tofu and red pepper onto lightly oiled skewers.*
2 *To make marinade, combine lime or lemon juice, honey, soy sauce and oil. Brush over kebabs and marinate for 1 hour.*
3 *To make purée, bring a saucepan of water to the boil, add broad beans and cook for 10 minutes or until beans are tender. Drain and cool slightly. Place broad beans, yogurt, thyme, orange rind and black pepper to taste in a food processor or blender and process until smooth. Set aside.*

4 *Cook kebabs under a preheated hot grill, turning frequently, for 8 minutes or until tender. Serve with purée.*
Note: *Any cooked or canned beans can be used in this purée when broad beans are not available.*
Serves 4

endive & goat's cheese salad

super
salads

Salads have no special season.

*Quick to prepare they make a wonderful accompaniment
to a meal, serve as a perfect first course or can be a
complete meal in themselves at any time of the year.*

mediterranean
rocket salad

Photograph opposite

Method:
1 *Arrange rocket, endive, onion, chickpeas, tomatoes, feta cheese, olives, artichokes and pine nuts on a large serving platter.*
2 *Drizzle balsamic or red wine vinegar over salad and season with black pepper. Cover and chill salad until required.*
   Note: *If canned chickpeas are unavailable, use cold cooked chickpeas instead.*
   Serves 4

ingredients

100g/3¹/₂oz rocket
1 bunch curly endive, leaves separated
1 red onion, thinly sliced
440g/14oz canned chickpeas, drained
4 roma (egg or Italian) tomatoes, quartered
125g/4oz feta cheese, roughly chopped
250g/8oz black olives
8 marinated artichoke hearts, halved
4 tablespoons pine nuts, toasted
balsamic or red wine vinegar
freshly ground black pepper

watercress
& orange salad

Photograph opposite

Method:
1 *Place burghul (cracked wheat) in a bowl, cover with boiling water and allow to stand for 10-15 minutes or until soft. Drain.*
2 *Place burghul (cracked wheat), watercress, avocado, oranges, tomatoes and red pepper in a salad bowl.*
3 *To make dressing, place orange juice, poppy seeds and vinegar in a screwtop jar and shake well to combine. Spoon dressing over salad and toss to combine. Cover and chill until required.*
   Serves 4

ingredients

1 cup/185g/6oz burghul
(cracked wheat)
2 cups/500mL/16fl oz boiling water
1 bunch/250g/8oz watercress,
broken into sprigs
1 avocado, stoned,
peeled and chopped
2 oranges, white pith removed,
flesh chopped
250g/8oz cherry tomatoes, halved
1 red pepper, diced
Orange dressing
¹/₂ cup/125mL/4fl oz orange juice
1 tablespoon poppy seeds
2 tablespoons red wine vinegar

519

raw

mushroom salad

Method:

1 Place mushrooms in a bowl. To make marinade, combine oil, lemon juice, vinegar, garlic and chilli powder in a screwtop jar. Shake well and pour over mushrooms. Toss and leave to marinate for 2-3 hours, tossing from time to time.

2 Gently fold through chives, parsley and capsicum and serve.

Note: An all-time favourite, this mushroom salad is easy to make and delicious served as part of a salad buffet or with a barbecue.

Serves 6

ingredients

500g/1 lb button mushrooms, thinly sliced
1 tablespoon finely chopped
fresh chives
1 tablespoon finely chopped fresh
parsley
1/2 red capsicum (pepper), diced
Marinade
1/2 cup/125mL olive oil
3 tablespoons lemon juice
1 tablespoon white wine vinegar
1 clove garlic, crushed
1/4 teaspoon chilli powder

crunchy
snow pea (mangetout) salad

Method:

1 Blanch snow peas (mangetout) and refresh under cold running water and drain.
2 Line a salad bowl with mignonette lettuce. Arrange snow peas (mangtout), bean sprouts and tomato strips over lettuce.
3 To make dressing, place vegetable oil, sesame oil, soy, vinegar, ginger and pepper in a screwtop jar. Shake well to combine and pour over salad.

Note: Choose a variety of bean sprouts to give added flavour and texture to the salad. You might like to use alfalfa, mung bean sprouts or snow pea (mangetout) sprouts.

Serves 4

200g/6¹/₂oz prepared
snow peas (mangetout)
I mignonette lettuce
200g/6¹/₂oz mixed bean sprouts
I tomato peeled, seeded and
cut into strips
<u>**Dressing**</u>
3 tablespoons vegetable oil
¹/₂ teaspoon sesame oil
I tablespoon soy sauce
I tablespoon cider vinegar
I teaspoon grated fresh ginger
freshly ground black pepper

chickpea
& capsicum (pepper) salad

Photograph opposite

Method:
1 Heat oil in a large frying pan. Add red, green and yellow capsicums (peppers), garlic and spring onions and cook over a medium heat, stirring constantly, for 5 minutes or until capsicums (peppers) are soft. Remove pan from heat and set aside to cool.
2 Place chickpeas, pine nuts and capsicum (pepper) mixture in a salad bowl and toss to combine.
3 To make dressing, place pine nuts, oil, lemon juice, stock or water and coriander in a food processor or blender and process until smooth. Spoon dressing over salad, toss to combine, cover and chill until ready to serve.
Note: If yellow capsicums (peppers) are unavailable, use another red capsicum (pepper). If canned chickpeas are unavailable, use cold cooked chickpeas instead. To cook chickpeas, soak overnight in cold water. Drain. Place in a large saucepan, cover with cold water and bring to the boil over a medium heat. Reduce heat and simmer for 45-60 minutes or until chickpeas are tender. Drain and cool.

Serves 6

ingredients

2 teaspoons vegetable oil
1 red capsicum (pepper), roughly chopped
1 green capsicum (pepper), roughly chopped
1 yellow capsicum (pepper), roughly chopped
2 cloves garlic, crushed
4 spring onions, sliced diagonally
2 x 440g/14oz canned chickpeas, drained
4 tablespoons pine nuts, toasted
Pine nut dressing
4 tablespoons pine nuts, toasted
2 tablespoons olive oil
2 tablespoons lemon juice
3 tablespoons vegetable stock or water
1 tablespoon chopped fresh coriander

endive
& goat's cheese salad

Photograph opposite and page 517

Method:
1 Brush goat's cheese with oil and season with black pepper. Place under a preheated medium grill and cook for 3 minutes each side or until golden.
2 Arrange endive leaves, tomatoes, cucumber, toast and goat's cheese on a serving platter. Drizzle with vinegar and serve immediately.
Note: A simple yet delicious salad with a strong Mediterranean influence. Curly endive is a member of the chicory family and has a more bitter taste than lettuce.

Serves 4

ingredients

8 thick slices goat's cheese
1 tablespoon olive oil
freshly ground black pepper
300g/9¹/₂oz curly endive leaves
250g/8oz cherry tomatoes, halved
1 cucumber, sliced
1 small French stick, sliced and toasted
2 tablespoons white wine vinegar

523

nashi
& nut salad

Method:

1 *Arrange lettuce leaves, nashi pears, peaches, macadamia or brazil nuts and sesame seeds on a large serving platter.*

2 *To make dressing, place sesame and vegetable oils, chilli sauce and lemon juice in a screwtop jar and shake well to combine. Spoon dressing over salad and toss to combine. Cover and chill salad until required.*

Note: *Native to Australia, the macadamia nut has a very hard shell and a delicious rich buttery flavour. In most recipes that call for macadamia nuts, brazil nuts can be used instead. The nashi pear is also known as the Chinese pear and is originally from northern Asia. If nashis are unavailable, pears or apples are a delicious alternative for this salad.*

Serves 4

ingredients

300g/9¹/₂oz assorted lettuce leaves
2 nashi pears, cored and sliced
2 peaches, sliced
125g/4oz macadamia or brazil nuts
2 tablespoons sesame seeds, toasted
<u>Chilli-sesame dressing</u>
2 teaspoons sesame oil
1 tablespoon vegetable oil
1 tablespoon sweet chilli sauce
2 tablespoons lemon juice

mexican
salad

Method:

1 Place avocado and lime or lemon juice in a small bowl and toss to coat.

2 Arrange lettuce leaves, tomatoes, green capsicum (pepper), beans and avocado mixture attractively in two lunch boxes. Sprinkle with coriander and season to taste with black pepper. Cover and refrigerate until required.

Note: Tossing the avocado in lime or lemon juice helps prevent it from discolouring.

Serves 2

ingredients

1 avocado, stoned, peeled and chopped
1 tablespoon lime or lemon juice
lettuce leaves of your choice
2 tomatoes, cut into wedges
1 green capsicum (pepper), chopped
315g/10oz canned red kidney beans, drained
2 teaspoons chopped fresh coriander
freshly ground black pepper

coriander
vegetable salad

Method:

1 Place apple juice in a saucepan and bring to the boil over a medium heat. Remove pan from heat, stir in burghul (cracked wheat) and stand for 10 minutes or until liquid is absorbed.

2 Place burghul (cracked wheat), cabbage, beetroot, tomatoes, snow peas (mangetout), peanuts, coriander leaves and spring onions in a large bowl and toss to combine.

3 To make dressing, place mustard, honey, garlic and vinegar in a screwtop jar and shake well to combine. Spoon dressing over salad and toss.

Note: Red cherry tomatoes can be used in place of the yellow teardrop tomatoes. Most of the fat in this recipe comes from the peanuts. To reduce the fat content reduce the quantity of peanuts or omit them all together. If the peanuts are omitted the fat rating is reduced to low.

Serves 4

ingredients

¹/₂ cup/125mL/4fl oz apple juice
¹/₂ cup/90g/3oz burghul
(cracked wheat)
¹/₂ Chinese cabbage, shredded
2 large raw beetroot, peeled and grated
185g/6oz yellow teardrop tomatoes, halved
125g/4oz snow peas (mangetout),
cut into thin strips
155g/5oz peanuts, roasted
1 bunch fresh coriander
4 spring onions, sliced diagonally
<u>Mustard dressing</u>
1 tablespoon wholegrain mustard
1 tablespoon honey
1 clove garlic, crushed
¹/₄ cup/60mL/2fl oz balsamic vinegar

marinated
tofu salad

Method:

1 Place soy sauce, oil, ginger, lemon juice and wine in a small bowl. Add tofu and toss to coat. Cover and set aside to marinate for 10-15 minutes.

2 Place lettuce, tomatoes, snow pea (mangetout) sprouts or watercress and carrots in a bowl. Drain tofu and reserve marinade. Add tofu to salad, toss to combine and sprinkle with sesame seeds. Just prior to serving, drizzle with reserved marinade.

Note: An easy summer meal, this salad requires only wholegrain or rye bread to make it a complete meal.

Serves 4

ingredients

4 tablespoons soy sauce
2 teaspoons vegetable oil
1/2 teaspoon finely chopped fresh ginger
1 tablespoon lemon juice
2 teaspoons dry white wine
500g/1 lb tofu, cut into cubes
1 lettuce, leaves separated
2 tomatoes, cut into wedges
60g/2oz snow pea (mangetout) sprouts
or watercress
2 carrots, sliced
1 tablespoon sesame seeds, toasted

vegetable lasagne

main
meals

In this chapter you will find colourful

and tasty dishes that capture the flavours of a variety of international cuisines. All the dishes are substantial and delicious enough to be main meals in their own right, perhaps accompanied by a salad or steamed vegetables, or some crusty fresh bread.

tagiarini
with pistachios

Photograph opposite

ingredients

500g/1 lb fresh spinach tagliarini
45g/1¹/₂oz butter
60g/2oz pistachio nuts, shelled
4 tablespoons shredded
fresh basil leaves
250g/8oz cherry tomatoes, halved
1 tablespoon green peppercorns in
brine, drained

Method:

1 Cook tagliarini in boiling water in a large saucepan following packet directions. Drain, set aside and keep warm.

2 Melt butter in a frying pan, add pistachio nuts, basil, tomatoes and green peppercorns. Cook over a medium heat, stirring constantly, for 4-5 minutes or until heated through. Toss tomato mixture with pasta.

Note: Tagliarini is a flat ribbon pasta similar to tagliatelle but slightly narrower in width. If unavailable this dish is also delicious made with tagliatelle, fettuccine or spaghetti.

Serves 4

chilli
pasta bake

Photograph opposite

ingredients

375g/12oz penne pasta
300g/9¹/₂oz sour cream
125g/4oz tasty cheese
(mature Cheddar), grated
Chilli sauce
2 teaspoons vegetable oil
2 onions, chopped
1 teaspoon ground cumin
1 teaspoon ground coriander
¹/₂ teaspoon chilli powder
440g/14oz canned red
kidney beans, drained
440g/14oz canned tomato purée

Method:

1 Cook pasta in boiling water in a large saucepan following packet directions. Drain, stir in sour cream and spread over base of an ovenproof dish.

2 To make sauce, heat oil in a large saucepan. Add onions and cook over a medium heat, stirring, for 3 minutes or until onions are soft. Add cumin, coriander and chilli powder and cook, stirring constantly, for 1 minute longer. Stir in beans and tomato purée, bring to the boil and simmer for 5 minutes.

3 Pour sauce over pasta, sprinkle with cheese and bake for 15-20 minutes or until cheese melts and turns golden.

Note: Serve this tasty bake with steamed vegetables and Cheese and Basil Bread.

Serves 4

Oven temperature 180°C, 350°F, Gas 4

hummus
& vegetable terrine

Photograph opposite

ingredients

**500g/1 lb spinach,
stalks removed
4 zucchini (courgettes), sliced
4 carrots, sliced
2 avocados, stoned, peeled and mashed
3 tablespoons mayonnaise
1 tablespoon lemon juice
1 cup/220g/7oz rice, cooked
3 red capsicums
(peppers), halved,
roasted and skins
removed, chopped
200g/6¹/₂oz hummus**

1

2

3

Method:

1 Line an 11x21cm/4¹/₂x8¹/₂in loaf tin with plastic food wrap. Set aside.

2 Boil, steam or microwave spinach leaves until just wilted. Drain well. Line prepared loaf tin with overlapping spinach leaves. Allow leaves to overhang the sides of the tin.

3 Boil, steam or microwave zucchini (courgettes) and carrots, separately, until just tender. Drain and set aside.

4 Place avocados, mayonnaise and lemon juice in a bowl and mix to combine. Set aside.

5 Pack half the rice into spinach-lined loaf tin, pressing down well with the back of a spoon. Top with half the red capsicums (peppers), zucchini (courgettes), carrots and hummus.

Spread with avocado mixture, then top with remaining rice, red capsicums (peppers), zucchini (courgettes), carrots and, lastly, hummus.

6 Fold overhanging spinach leaves over filling. Place a heavy weight on terrine and refrigerate for at least 4 hours before serving. To serve, unmould and cut into slices.

Note: Hummus is a popular Middle Eastern dip made from a purée of cooked chickpeas and tahini (sesame paste). Hummus is available from delicatessens and some supermarkets, or you can make your own using the recipe on page 323.

Serves 6-8

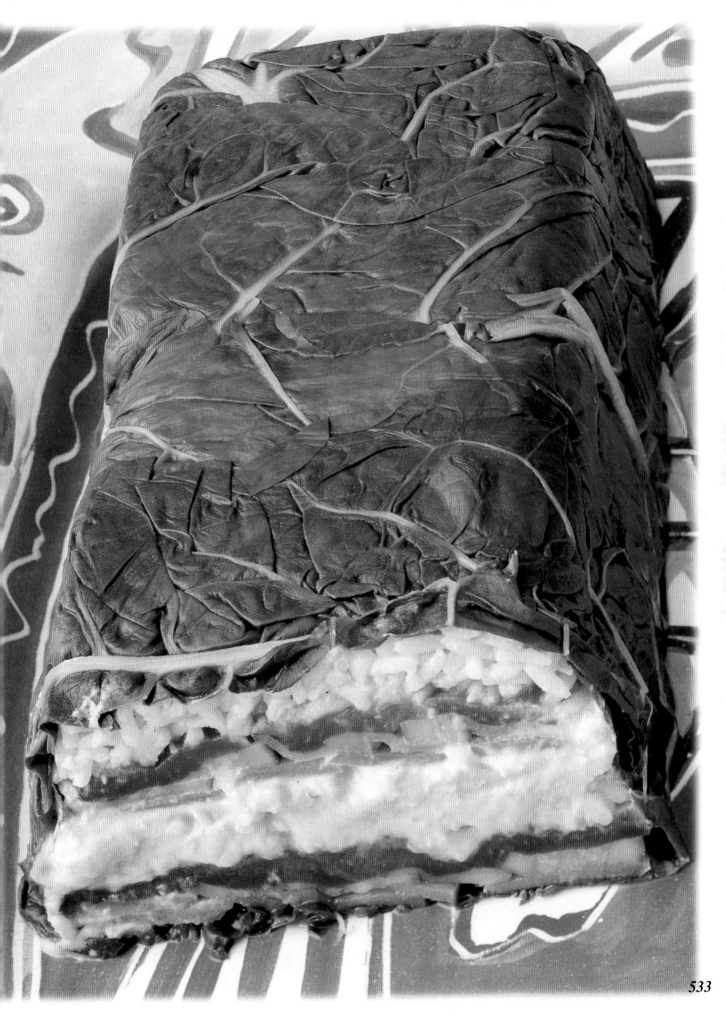

hearty bean
casserole

Method:

1 Place red kidney and black-eyed beans in a large bowl, cover with water and set aside to soak overnight. Drain. Bring a large saucepan of water to the boil, add beans and boil for 10 minutes. Reduce heat and simmer for 1 hour or until beans are tender. Drain and set aside.

2 Heat oil in a large saucepan over a medium heat, add garlic and onion and cook, stirring, for 3 minutes or until onion is soft and golden. Add tomatoes, cumin, mustard, golden syrup and tomato paste (purée) and bring to the boil. Reduce heat and simmer for 5 minutes.

3 Add cooked beans, carrots, zucchini (courgettes), butter beans, broad beans and oregano to pan and simmer for 30 minutes or until vegetables are tender.

Note: All types of beans adapt to a huge range of seasonings. The beans in this casserole can be varied to accommodate whatever you have available.

As an alternative, try a combination of haricot and butter beans with chickpeas, and substitute your favourite spices or dried herbs for the ground cumin and oregano.

Serves 4

ingredients

155g/oz dried red kidney beans
155g/5oz dried black-eyed beans
1 tablespoon vegetable oil
2 cloves garlic, crushed
1 red onion, chopped
440g/14oz canned peeled tomatoes, undrained and mashed
1 tablespoon ground cumin
1 tablespoon dry mustard
2 tablespoons golden syrup
1 tablespoon tomato paste (purée)
2 carrots, thickly sliced
3 zucchini (courgettes), thickly sliced
440g/14oz canned butter beans, rinsed and drained
100g/3¹/₂oz shelled fresh or frozen broad beans
2 tablespoons chopped fresh oregano or 1 teaspoon dried oregano

all-time
favourite vegetable pie

Method:

1 To make pastry, place flour and butter in a food processor and process until mixture resembles fine breadcrumbs. With machine running, slowly add egg and enough water to form a soft dough. Turn dough onto a lightly floured surface and knead briefly. Wrap dough in plastic food wrap and refrigerate for 30 minutes.

2 Roll out pastry to fit a deep 23cm/9in flan tin with a removable base. Line pastry case with nonstick baking paper, fill with uncooked rice and bake for 10 minutes. Remove rice and paper and bake for 10 minutes longer or until pastry is golden and crisp. Set aside to cool.

3 To make filling, heat oil in a large frying pan over a medium heat, add onion and leeks and cook, stirring, for 4 minutes or until onion is golden. Add pumpkin and potatoes and cook, stirring, for 10 minutes longer or until potatoes are just tender.

4 Add cauliflower, parsnip, broccoli, red capsicum (pepper), peas and stock to pan and bring to the boil. Reduce heat and simmer for 10 minutes or until vegetables are soft. Mix in basil. Set aside to cool.

5 Spoon cold filling into pastry case. Combine cheese and breadcrumbs, sprinkle over filling and bake for 20 minutes or until top is golden.

Serves 6

ingredients

125g/4oz grated tasty cheese
(mature Cheddar)
1 cup/60g/2oz breadcrumbs,
made from stale bread
Pastry
1 1/2 cups/185g/6oz flour
90g/3oz butter
1 egg, lightly beaten
1-2 tablespoons iced water
Vegetable filling
1 tablespoon vegetable oil
1 onion, sliced
2 leeks, sliced
250g/8oz pumpkin flesh, chopped
2 potatoes, chopped
1/4 cauliflower, broken into small florets
1 parsnip, chopped
1 small head broccoli, broken into
small florets
1 red pepper (capsicum), chopped
125g/4oz frozen peas
1/2 cup/125mL/4fl oz vegetable stock
2 tablespoons chopped fresh basil

Oven temperature 180°C, 350°F, Gas 4

535

italian
potato bake

ingredients

6 potatoes, sliced
¹/₂ cup/125g/4oz ready-made pesto
**2 yellow or green zucchini (courgettes),
sliced lengthwise**
¹/₂ cup/125g/4oz olive paste (pâté)
**6 baby eggplant (aubergines),
sliced lengthwise**
¹/₂ cup/125mL/4fl oz milk
¹/₂ cup/125g/4oz sour cream
60g/2oz grated Parmesan cheese
freshly ground black pepper

Method:

1 Arrange one-third of the potatoes over the base of a large ovenproof dish. Top with pesto, zucchini (courgettes) and half of the remaining potatoes.

2 Top potatoes with olive paste (pâté), eggplant (aubergines) and remaining potatoes.

3 Place milk and sour cream in a bowl, mix to combine and carefully pour over potatoes. Sprinkle with Parmesan cheese and black pepper to taste and bake for 50 minutes or until potatoes are tender.

Note: A hearty meal for a cold winter's night, it is delicious served with a tomato and onion salad or a stir-fry of mixed vegetables.

Serves 4

vegetable
lasagne

Photograph appears also on page 528

Method:

1 *Combine olive oil, black peppercorns and lemon juice and brush over eggplant (aubergine) slices. Cook eggplant (aubergine) under a preheated medium grill for 3-4 minutes each side or until golden. Set aside.*

2 *Place breadcrumbs and Parmesan cheese in a bowl, mix to combine and set aside.*

3 *Heat a nonstick frying pan, add onion, garlic and reserved tomato juice and cook over a medium heat, stirring, for 5 minutes or until onion is soft. Add tomatoes, tomato purée, wine, oregano, basil and cayenne pepper and cook for 5 minutes longer.*

4 *Spread one-third of the tomato mixture over base of a 15x25cm/6x10in ovenproof dish. Top with 3 lasagne sheets, half the breadcrumb mixture and cover with a layer of eggplant (aubergine). Top with half the ricotta cheese. Repeat layers, ending with a layer of tomato mixture. Sprinkle with mozzarella cheese and bake for 45 minutes.*
Note: *As an accompaniment to this hearty lasagne choose a light salad or steamed mixed vegetables.*

Serves 6

ingredients

1 tablespoon olive oil
1/2 teaspoon crushed black peppercorns
3 tablespoons lemon juice
1 large eggplant (aubergine), halved lengthwise and cut into 5mm/1/4in slices
1/2 cup/30g/1oz wholemeal breadcrumbs, made from stale bread
3 tablespoons grated Parmesan cheese
1 large onion, chopped
2 cloves garlic, crushed
440g/14oz canned tomatoes, drained, chopped and 1 tablespoon juice reserved
3/4 cup/185mL/6fl oz tomato purée
2 tablespoons white wine
1 teaspoon dried oregano
1 teaspoon dried basil
pinch cayenne pepper
6 sheets instant (no precooking required) wholemeal lasagne
185g/6oz ricotta cheese
3 tablespoons grated mozzarella cheese

Oven temperature 180°C, 350°F, Gas 4

537

spinach
& basil risotto

Method:

1 Place spinach and water in a saucepan, bring to the boil and cook for 1 minute or until spinach is tender. Remove from heat and set aside to cool.

2 Place spinach mixture in a food processor or blender and process until smooth. Set aside.

3 Melt butter in a saucepan, add onion and garlic and cook for 4-5 minutes or until onion is soft. Add rice to pan and stir to coat with butter mixture. Pour in wine and half the chicken stock. Cook over a medium heat, stirring occasionally, until almost all the liquid is absorbed. Stir in remaining stock with reserved spinach mixture and cook until almost all the liquid is absorbed.

4 Place basil, oil and 3 tablespoons pine nuts in food processor or blender and process until smooth. Stir into rice mixture. Sprinkle with remaining pine nuts and serve immediately.

Note: Risotto is an Italian favourite. Wonderful as a first course, main course or an accompaniment to meat, fish or poultry, it is nutritious and easy to make.

Serves 4

ingredients

500g/1 lb spinach, stalks removed and leaves chopped
1 cup/250mL/8fl oz water
60g/2oz butter
1 large onion, finely chopped
2 cloves garlic, crushed
2 cups/440g/14oz brown rice
1/2 cup/125mL/4fl oz white wine
5 cups/1.2 litres/2pt hot chicken stock
30g/1oz fresh basil leaves
2 tablespoons olive oil
4 tablespoons pine nuts, toasted

wholemeal
spinach quiche

Method:

1 Roll out pastry and line the base and sides of a lightly greased 23cm/9in flan tin. Trim edges of pastry and line base with baking paper. Fill with uncooked rice and bake for 15 minutes. Remove rice and paper and bake for 10 minutes longer. Remove from oven and set aside to cool slightly.

2 To make filling, melt butter in a frying pan, add onion and cook over a medium heat for 4-5 minutes or until soft. Stir in spinach and cook for 2-3 minutes longer or until spinach wilts. Remove pan from heat and set aside.

3 Place eggs, sour cream, cheese, nutmeg and black pepper to taste in a bowl and mix to combine. Spread spinach mixture over base of pastry case, then carefully spoon in egg mixture. Reduce oven temperature to 180°C/350°F/Gas 4 and bake for 30 minutes or until filling is firm.

Note: When making pastry, have all the utensils and ingredients as cold as possible. In hot weather, chill the utensils before using. Wash your hands in cold water and use only your fingertips for kneading.

Serves 6

ingredients

155g/5oz prepared wholemeal pastry
Spinach filling
30g/1oz butter
1 onion, finely chopped
1/2 bunch/250g/8oz spinach, stalks removed and leaves finely shredded
3 eggs, lightly beaten
300g/91/2oz sour cream
60g/2oz grated tasty cheese (mature Cheddar)
pinch ground nutmeg
freshly ground black pepper

Oven temperature 220°C, 425°F, Gas 7

mushroom
gougére

Method:

1 To make pastry, place water and butter in a saucepan, cover and cook until butter melts and mixture just boils. Remove pan from heat and add flour all at once. Stir vigorously with a wooden spoon over a low heat until mixture forms a ball and pulls away from sides of pan. Set aside to cool slightly.

2 Add eggs one at a time, beating well after each addition until mixture is smooth and glossy. Spread mixture around sides of a greased shallow 23cm/9in ovenproof dish.

3 To make filling, place mushrooms, eggs, sour cream, cream, flour, cheese, parsley, nutmeg and black pepper to taste in a bowl and mix to combine. Spoon filling into centre of pastry and bake for 35-40 minutes or until filling is firm and pastry is puffed and golden.

Note: Mushrooms should be stored in a brown paper bag or a cloth bag in the refrigerator. Stored in this way they will keep fresh for 5-7 days. Never store mushrooms in a plastic bag as this causes them to sweat and deteriorate very quickly.

Serves 4

ingredients

Choux pastry
1 cup/250mL/8fl oz water
90g/3oz butter
1 cup/125g/4oz flour, sifted
4 eggs
Mushroom filling
155g/5oz button mushrooms, sliced
3 eggs, lightly beaten
155g/5oz sour cream
1/2 cup/125mL/4fl oz thickened
(double) cream
1 tablespoon flour
125g/4oz grated tasty cheese
(mature Cheddar)
1 tablespoon chopped fresh parsley
pinch ground nutmeg
freshly ground black pepper

Oven temperature 200°C, 400°F, Gas 6

lentil
frittata

Method:

1 *Bring a large saucepan of water to the boil. Add lentils, reduce heat and simmer for 20 minutes or until tender. Drain and set aside.*

2 *Heat oil in a frying pan over a medium heat, add leeks and cook, stirring, for 4 minutes or until soft and golden. Add spinach, zucchini (courgettes) and smoked fish (if using) and cook for 3 minutes longer. Stir in lentils and mix to combine.*

3 *Place eggs, yogurt, chervil or parsley and black pepper to taste in a bowl and whisk to combine. Pour egg mixture over vegetables in pan and cook over a low heat for 6 minutes or until frittata is almost set. Place pan under a preheated hot grill and cook for 2 minutes or until top is golden.*

Note: *Don't be limited by the vegetables suggested in this recipe. A frittata is designed to use all kinds of fresh – and leftover cooked – vegetables, so choose the ones you like most from what is available.*

Serves 4

ingredients

155g/5oz red lentils
2 teaspoons vegetable oil
2 leeks, chopped
20 English spinach leaves, shredded
6 zucchini (courgettes), sliced
220g/7oz smoked cod or haddock, cooked
and flesh flaked (optional)
6 eggs, lightly beaten
¾ cup/155g/5oz natural yogurt
2 tablespoons chopped fresh chervil
or parsley
freshly ground black pepper

savoury
pumpkin flan

Method:

1 *Brush each sheet of pastry with oil and fold in half. Layer pastry, one folded piece on top of the other to give eight layers. Place an 18cm/ 7in flan dish upside down on layered pastry and cut around dish, making a circle 3cm/1 1/4in larger. Lift all layers of pastry into dish and roll edges.*

2 *Cook onion in a frying pan for 4-5 minutes or until onion is opague and soft. Place pumpkin or carrots, cheese, egg yolks, sour cream or yoghurt, chilli powder and black pepper to taste in a bowl and mix to combine.*

3 *Place egg whites in a bowl and beat until stiff peaks form. Fold egg white mixture into pumpkin mixture and spoon into pastry case. Sprinkle pumpkin mixture with parsley and bake for 30 minutes or until pastry is golden and cooked.*

Note: *When incorporating beaten egg whites into a mixture, first stir in 1 tablespoon of beaten egg white, then lightly fold remaining beaten egg white through, working as quickly as possible.*

Serves 4

ingredients

**4 sheets filo pastry
2 tablespoons vegetable oil
1 onion, chopped
250g/8oz pumpkin or carrots,
cooked and mashed
185g/6oz grated tasty cheese
(mature Cheddar)
2 eggs, separated
2 tablespoons sour cream
or natural yoghurt
pinch chilli powder
freshly ground black pepper
1 tablespoon chopped fresh parsley**

541

mushroom
risotto

Photograph opposite

ingredients

45g/1¹/₂oz butter
200g/6¹/₂oz flat mushrooms, thickly sliced
125g/4oz button mushrooms, halved
200g/6¹/₂oz shiitake mushrooms
200g/6¹/₂oz oyster mushrooms
2 cups/440g/14oz Arborio or risotto rice
4 cups/1 litre/1³/₄pt hot vegetable stock
4 tablespoons grated Parmesan cheese
freshly ground black pepper

Method:

1 *Melt 15g/¹/₂oz butter in a frying pan. Add flat, button, shiitake and oyster mushrooms and cook over a medium heat, stirring constantly, for 4-5 minutes or until mushrooms are soft. Remove pan from heat and set aside.*

2 *Melt remaining butter in a clean frying pan. Add rice and cook over a medium heat, stirring constantly, for 2 minutes. Pour 1 cup/250 mL/ 8fl oz hot stock into rice and cook over a medium heat, stirring constantly, until stock is absorbed. Continue cooking in this way until all the stock is used and rice is just tender.*

3 *Stir mushroom mixture, Parmesan cheese and black pepper to taste into rice mixture and cook for 2 minutes longer.*

Note: *Arborio or risotto rice is traditionally used for making risottos. It absorbs liquid without becoming soft and it is this special quality that makes it so suitable for risottos. If Arborio rice is unavailable, substitute short-grain rice. A risotto made in the traditional way, where liquid is added a little at a time as the rice cooks, will take 20-30 minutes to cook.*

Serves 4

tomato
risotto

Photograph opposite

ingredients

4 cups/1 litre/1³/₄pt vegetable stock
2 cups/500mL/16fl oz tomato juice
15g/¹/₂oz butter
2³/₄ cups/600g/1¹/₄lb Arborio or risotto rice
10 sun-dried tomatoes, sliced
2 tomatoes, chopped
125g/4oz pitted olives
freshly ground black pepper

Method:

1 *Place stock and tomato juice in a large saucepan and bring to the boil over a medium heat. Reduce heat and keep warm.*

2 *Melt butter in a large saucepan. Add rice and cook over a medium heat, stirring constantly, for 3 minutes. Pour 1 cup/250 mL/ 8fl oz stock mixture into rice and cook over a medium heat, stirring constantly, until stock is absorbed. Continue cooking in this way until all the stock is used and rice is tender.*

3 *Stir sun-dried tomatoes, tomatoes, olives and black pepper to taste into rice mixture and cook for 2 minutes longer.*

Note: *When serving a risotto, start with a salad and crusty bread and finish with fresh fruit or a dessert.*

Serves 6

vegetable
curry with chutney

Method:

1 To make chutney, place rhubarb, ginger, chilli, mustard seeds, sugar, vinegar and currants in a saucepan and cook over a medium heat, stirring occasionally, for 30 minutes or until mixture is soft and pulpy.

2 To make curry, heat oil in a large saucepan, add cumin, curry paste and onions and cook, stirring, for 3 minutes or until onions are soft. Add potatoes, cauliflower, broccoli, beans, red capsicum (pepper), zucchini (courgettes), coconut milk and stock and bring to the boil. Reduce heat and simmer, stirring occasionally, for 25-35 minutes or until vegetables are tender. Serve curry with Rhubarb chutney.

Note: Serve this curry with jasmine or basmati rice. Rhubarb chutney can be stored in sterilised airtight jars for several months.

Serves 4

ingredients

2 teaspoons vegetable oil
1 teaspoon ground cumin
1 tablespoon curry paste
2 onions, chopped
2 potatoes, finely chopped
200g/6¹/₂oz cauliflower, cut into florets
200g/6¹/₂oz broccoli, cut into florets
155g/5oz green beans, halved
1 red capsicum (pepper), chopped
2 zucchini (courgettes), chopped
200mL/6¹/₂fl oz coconut milk
200mL/6¹/₂fl oz vegetable stock
<u>Rhubarb chutney</u>
500g/1 lb rhubarb, chopped
1 tablespoon grated fresh ginger
1 fresh green chilli, chopped
1 tablespoon black mustard seeds
³/₄ cup/125g/4oz brown sugar
1 cup/250mL/8fl oz white vinegar
60g/2oz currants

soy burgers

Method:

1 To make dressing, place yoghurt, coriander, ginger, chilli sauce, garlic and black pepper to taste in a bowl and mix to combine.

2 To make burgers, place soy beans in a food processor or blender and process to roughly chop. Place chopped beans, breadcrumbs, onion, carrot, flour, mint, ginger and egg in a bowl and mix well to combine. Shape mixture into six burgers and roll each in sesame seeds.

3 Heat oil in a frying pan over a medium heat, add burgers and cook for 6 minutes each side or until heated through and golden.

4 Top bottom half of each roll with a lettuce leaf, a burger, a few alfalfa sprouts, tomato slices, beetroot, sunflower seeds, a spoonful of dressing and top half of roll. Serve immediately.

Note: Besan flour is made from chickpeas and is available from Asian and health food stores (you can substitute pea flour made from split peas, if desired). To make your own besan flour, place chickpeas on a baking tray and bake at 180°C/350°F/Gas 4 for 15-20 minutes or until roasted. Cool, then using a food processor or blender grind to make a fine flour.

Serves 6

ingredients

6 multigrain rolls, split and toasted
6 lettuce leaves of your choice
30g/1oz alfalfa sprouts
2 large tomatoes, sliced
1 raw beetroot, grated
4 tablespoons sunflower seeds, toasted
<u>Minted soy burgers</u>
440g/14oz canned soy beans,
rinsed and drained
1 cup/60g/2oz wholemeal breadcrumbs,
made from stale bread
1 red onion, finely chopped
1 carrot, grated
3 tablespoons besan flour
3 tablespoons chopped fresh mint
1 tablespoon finely grated fresh ginger
1 egg, lightly beaten
75g/2¹/₂oz sesame seeds
2 tablespoons vegetable oil
<u>Creamy dressing</u>
1 cup/200g/6¹/₂oz natural yoghurt
1 tablespoon chopped fresh coriander
1 tablespoon grated fresh ginger
2 tablespoons sweet chilli sauce
1 clove garlic, crushed
freshly ground black pepper

caramelised rice pudding

dreamy desserts

From light and refreshing fruit dishes

to heartier baked puddings, the desserts in this chapter
are a perfect ending to a nourishing and delicious meal.

quinces
with honey cream

Method:

1 Place water and sugar in a large saucepan and cook over a low heat, stirring constantly, until sugar dissolves.

2 Add lemon rind and quinces to syrup, bring to the boil and simmer for 40 minutes or until quinces are tender and change colour.

3 To serve, place quinces on serving plates, spoon over a little of the cooking liquid, accompany with cream and drizzle with honey.

Note: If quinces are unavailable, this recipe is also good when made with apples or pears. The cooking time will not be as long.

Serves 6

ingredients

6 cups/1¹/2 litres/2¹/2pt water
1¹/2 cups/375g/12oz sugar
4 strips lemon rind
6 quinces, peeled and quartered
³/4 cup/185mL/6fl oz thickened cream
(double), whipped
3 tablespoons honey

french
bread pudding

Method:

1 *To make filling, place figs, dates, orange juice, brandy and cinnamon stick in a saucepan and cook over a low heat, stirring, for 15-20 minutes or until fruit is soft and mixture thick. Remove cinnamon stick.*

2 *To assemble pudding, place one-third of the brioche slices in the base of a greased 11 x 21cm/ 4¹/₂x8¹/₂in loaf tin. Top with half the filling. Repeat layers, ending with a layer of brioche.*

3 *Place eggs, milk, vanilla essence and nutmeg in a bowl and whisk to combine. Carefully pour egg mixture over brioche and fruit and set aside to stand for 5 minutes. Place tin in a baking dish with enough boiling water to come halfway up the sides of the tin and bake for 45 minutes or until firm. Stand pudding in tin for 10 minutes before turning out and serving.*

Note: *This tempting dessert is best eaten cut into slices and served with cream shortly after it is turned out of the tin.*

Serves 6-8

ingredients

1 loaf brioche, sliced
6 eggs, lightly beaten
1¹/₂ cups/375mL/12fl oz milk
1 teaspoon vanilla essence
1 teaspoon ground nutmeg
<u>Fruit filling</u>
125g/4oz dried figs, chopped
**125g/4oz dried dates,
pitted and chopped**
¹/₂ cup/125mL/4fl oz orange juice
¹/₃ cup/90mL/3fl oz brandy
1 cinnamon stick

fruit
with passionfruit custard

Method:

1 Place quinces in a large saucepan. Add sugar, wine and enough water to cover. Bring to the boil, then reduce heat and simmer for 3 hours or until quinces are tender and a rich pink colour.

2 To make custard, place milk and vanilla essence in a saucepan and heat over a medium heat until almost boiling. Whisk in egg yolks and cook, stirring, until mixture thickens. Remove pan from heat and set aside to cool. Fold passionfruit pulp and cream into custard.

3 To serve, cut quinces into quarters and serve with custard.

Note: When quinces are unavailable peaches, nectarines or pears are all delicious alternatives. Just remember most other fruit will only require 15-30 minutes cooking.

The Passionfruit Custard is delicious served with any poached fruit. If fresh passionfruit is not available, canned passionfruit pulp may be used instead.

Serves 4

ingredients

2 quinces, peeled
¹/₂ cup/125g/4oz sugar
¹/₄ cup/60mL/2fl oz sweet dessert wine
water
Passionfruit custard
³/₄ cup/185mL/6fl oz milk
1 teaspoon vanilla essence
2 egg yolks
¹/₃ cup/90mL/3fl oz passion fruit pulp
¹/₂ cup/125mL/4fl oz thickened cream (double), whipped

baked apple
cheesecake

Method:

1. Roll out pastry to 3mm/⅛in thick and use to line a deep 23cm/9in flan tin with a removable base. Prick base and sides of pastry with a fork, line with nonstick baking paper and fill with uncooked rice. Bake for 10 minutes, then remove rice and paper and bake for 5-8 minutes longer or until lightly browned.

2. Melt butter in a frying pan, add apple slices and cook over a medium heat, stirring occasionally, until golden. Set aside to cool. Arrange apples evenly over base of pastry case.

3. To make filling, place all filling ingredients in a food processor and process until smooth.

4. Place egg whites in a separate bowl and beat until stiff peaks form. Fold egg white mixture into ricotta mixture. Carefully pour filling over apples.

5. Reduce oven temperature to 180°C/350°F/ Gas 4 and bake for 1¼ hours or until firm. Set aside to cool, then refrigerate overnight.

Serves 8

ingredients

200g/6½oz prepared
shortcrust pastry
30g/1oz butter
2 apples, cored, peeled and sliced
<u>**Ricotta filling**</u>
750g/1½lb ricotta cheese
4 eggs, separated
½ cup/170g/5½oz honey
1 tablespoon finely grated orange rind
3 tablespoons orange juice

Oven temperature 190°C, 375°F, Gas 5

caramelised
rice pudding

Photograph opposite and page 62

ingredients

1 cup/250g/8oz sugar
¹/₂ cup/125mL/4fl oz water
1 cup/220g/7oz short-grain rice
3¹/₂ cups/875mL/1¹/₂pt milk
1 teaspoon vanilla essence
4 egg yolks
¹/₂ cup/100g/3¹/₂oz caster sugar
**30g/1oz unsalted
butter**

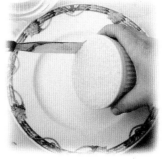

Method:

1 *Place sugar and water in a small saucepan and cook over a low heat, stirring constantly, until sugar dissolves. Bring to the boil and cook, without stirring, until lightly golden.*

2 *Pour toffee into four lightly greased 1 cup/ 250mL/8fl oz-capacity ramekins or moulds. Set aside to harden.*

3 *Place rice, milk and vanilla essence in a saucepan and cook over a medium heat, stirring, for 15 minutes or until rice is soft. Remove from heat and set aside to cool slightly.*

4 *Place egg yolks and sugar in a bowl and whisk to combine. Stir egg mixture and butter into rice mixture and mix well to combine.*

5 *Divide rice mixture between toffee-lined ramekins or moulds, cover and refrigerate overnight.*

6 *To serve, dip the base of ramekins or moulds in hot water, then invert onto serving plates.*
Note: *This luscious tasting version of an old favourite is sure to appeal, even to those who think they don't like rice pudding. Try it served with poached or fresh fruit.*
Serves 4

The final touch – dressings

A dressing or sauce should enhance a vegetable by bringing out its special flavour and texture and adding an appetising piquancy. Unless it has been used as a marinade, dress all salads and vegetable dishes just before serving. One serve is equivalent to 1 tablespoon.

Oriental mayonnaise

Serve as a dipping sauce for lightly cooked fresh vegetables such as asparagus spears, celery and carrot sticks, or spoon over hot vegetables.

1 clove garlic, crushed
2 teaspoons grated fresh ginger
4 tablespoons soy sauce
2 tablespoons cider vinegar
2 tablespoons brown sugar
1 teaspoon fennel seeds
2 egg yolks
1/2 teaspoon dry mustard powder
3/4 cup 190mL/6 oz vegetable oil
2 teaspoons sesame oil
1/2 teaspoon hot chilli sauce

1 *Place garlic, ginger, soy, vinegar, brown sugar and fennel seeds in a small saucepan and bring to the boil. Reduce heat and simmer, uncovered, for 10 minutes or until mixture reduces by half. Remove from heat and strain to remove fennel seeds. Set aside to cool.*
2 *Combine egg yolks and mustard powder in a bowl of food processor or blender. Process until just combined. With the machine running, pour in vegetable and sesame oils in a steady stream. Process until mayonnaise thickens.*
3 *Add soy mixture and process to combine. Mix in the chilli sauce to taste.*

479 kilojoules	(116 calories)	per serve
Fat	11.7g	low
Cholesterol	25mg	low
Fibre	0g	low
Sodium	255mg	low

Makes 1 1/2 cups/375mL

Yoghurt dressing

This dressing makes a great lower-calorie alternative to mayonnaise. Try it on potato salad, coleslaw or the Raw Energy Salad on page 6.

3/4 cup/190g/6oz unflavoured yoghurt
1 clove crushed garlic (optional)
2 tablespoons white wine vinegar
2 tablespoons chopped fresh chives

1 *Combine yoghurt, garlic, vinegar and chives in a bowl. Whisk well to combine. Serve with Raw Energy Salad.*

53 kilojoules	(13 calories)	per serve
Fat	0.6g	low
Cholesterol	3mg	low
Fibre	0g	low
Sodium	11mg	low

Makes 1 cup (250mL)

Vinaigrette

3/4 cup 190mL/6oz olive oil
3 tablespoons cider vinegar
1 tablespoon Dijon mustard
freshly ground black pepper

1 *Place oil, vinegar and mustard in screwtop jar. Season to taste with pepper. Shake well to combine.*

585 kilojoules	(142 calories)	per serve
Fat	15.8g	low
Cholesterol	0mg	low
Fibre	0g	low
Sodium	0mg	low

Variations

*Walnut or Hazelnut Dressing: Replace olive oil with 4 tablespoons walnut or hazelnut oil and 1 1/3 cup/335mL polyunsaturated vegetable oil.
Lemon Herb Vinaigrette: Replace vinegar with 3 tablespoons lemon juice, add 1/2 cup/60g mixed chopped fresh herbs. Suggested herbs include basil, parsley, chives, rosemary, thyme or tarragon.*

Makes 1 cup (250mL)

sauces

The following sauces can transform simple vegetables into wonderful meals. Our tomato sauce is perfect with pasta and also great with beans, capsicums (peppers), cauliflower, eggplant, fennel and zucchini.

White sauce

This classic sauce is the base to many sauces. Add ½ cup/60g grated cheese for a cheese sauce or 2 tablespoons finely chopped fresh parsley to make parsley sauce. Or make a curry sauce with 2 teaspoons curry powder and ½ onion, chopped. For mushroom sauce, simply add 50g sliced mushrooms cooked for about 5 minutes in butter.

15g butter
2 tablespoons plain flour
1 cup/250mL/8oz milk

1 Melt butter in a saucepan. Stir in flour and cook for 1 minute, stirring frequently during cooking.
2 Gradually stir in milk and cook over medium heat until sauce boils and thickens. Season to taste if desired.

122 kilojoules	(29 calories)	per serve
Fat	1.9g	low
Cholesterol	6mg	low
Fibre	0g	low
Sodium	21mg	low

Makes 1 cup/250mL

Fresh tomato sauce

Serve this sauce with any boiled, steamed or microwaved vegetables. Top with breadcrumbs and Parmesan cheese and place under a hot grill to create a tomato-flavoured gratin. Use six large fresh tomatoes in summer when they are plentiful. You may need to add a tablespoon of tomato purée for extra flavour.

1 tablespoon olive oil
1 onion, sliced
1 clove garlic, crushed
½ green capsicum (pepper), sliced
440g/14oz canned, peeled tomatoes, chopped

½ cup/125mL/4oz white wine
1 teaspoon dried mixed herbs
freshly ground black pepper

1 Heat oil in a saucepan and cook onion, garlic and capsicum (pepper) for 4-5 minutes until onion softens. Stir in tomatoes and wine and simmer for 5 minutes.
2 Add herbs and season to taste with pepper. Simmer for a further 20 minutes or until sauce reduces.

74 kilojoules	(18 calories)	per serve
Fat	0.9g	low
Cholesterol	0mg	low
Fibre	0.4g	low
Sodium	8mg	low

Makes 1½ cups/375mL

Camembert sauce

This creamy fondue-like sauce will dress up the plainest vegetable. Try it poured over zucchini, broccoli, potatoes or pumpkin. It is also a great way to use up that odd piece of Camembert or Brie left in the fridge.

15g/½ oz butter
1 tablespoon plain flour
½ cup/125mL/4oz milk
3 tablespoons white wine
75g/2½ oz Camembert or Brie cheese, rind removed
freshly ground black pepper

1 Melt butter in a small saucepan. Stir in flour and cook for 1 minute. Blend in milk and cook until sauce boils and thickens, stirring frequently during cooking.
2 Stir in wine and cheese. Season to taste with pepper, and cook over low heat until cheese melts.

232 kilojoules	(36 calories)	per serve
Fat	4.1g	low
Cholesterol	14mg	low
Fibre	0g	low
Sodium	76mg	low

Makes ¾ cup/190mL

vegetable
preparation

Vegetable	Preparation	Freezing
Artichokes	Place upside down in salted water to dislodge any hidden insects or earth. Trim stem and tough outer leaves. Snip sharp points from leaves. Brush any cut surfaces with lemon juice to prevent discolouration.	Remove tough outer leaves, trim and remove choke. Blanch 7 minutes in water with lemon juice. Drain upside down. Pack in rigid containers.
Asparagus	Bend lower end of stalk between thumb and forefinger to break off woody end.	Blanch 2-4 minutes, depending on thickness of stalk. Pack between sheets of freezer wrap.
Beans— green beans, runner beans	All beans need to be topped and tailed; some varieties, such as runner beans, will also need their strings removed. Beans can then be sliced in pieces or left whole.	Blanch 2-3 minutes, pack into freezer bags.
Beans— broad beans	Cooking times for broad beans are very dependent on age and size. If young and using whole, wash, cut off ends and remove strings. Older beans should be shelled.	Blanch 1-2 minutes, pack into freezer bags.
Beetroot	Trim tops, leaving 5cm/2in to prevent 'bleeding' during cooking. Scrub gently with a soft brush.	Blanch 5-10 minutes, peel and pack into freezer bags.
Broccoli	Trim tough woody stems, divide into florets. Rinse in cold water.	Blanch 3-4 minutes, pack in layers between sheets of freezer wrap.
Brussels sprouts	Trim base and tough outer leaves, do not trim too closely or the sprouts will fall apart during cooking.	Blanch 2-3 minutes, pack in freezer bags.
Cabbage	Trim tough and damaged outer leaves. Rinse, chop or shred.	Blanch 1 minute, pack into freezer bags.
Capsicums (Peppers)	Cut off top, remove seeds and core. Cube, dice or slice.	Halve, slice or dice, blanch halves 3 minutes, sliced or diced 1 1/2 minutes.
Carrots	Top, tail and scrub — young carrots do not require peeling. Slice, dice, or cut into julienne strips, leave young carrots whole.	Blanch 3-5 minutes, pack in freezer bags.
Cauliflower	Remove leaves, rinse, leave whole or cut into florets.	Blanch 3 minutes, pack into freezer bags or in rigid containers between sheets of freezer wrap.
Celery	Separate stalks, trim top and base. Some varieties will require the strings to be removed; this is easily done using a vegetable peeler.	Blanch 2 minutes, pack into freezer bags.
Eggplant (Aubergine)	Remove stem, halve, slice or dice; place in colander and sprinkle with salt, leave 20 minutes, rinse and pat dry.	Cut into slices, blanch 4 minutes, pack into rigid containers.

Cooking methods and times

Steam	Boil *Note: bring water to boil before adding vegetables*	Bake/roast	Microwave *Note: cook vegetables on high (100%) and always cover before microwaving*
45 minutes or until fork easily pierces just above the base	30-45 minutes or until a leaf pulls out easily	45 minutes-1 hour	4 artichokes 7-9 minutes (stand 3-4 minutes before serving)
15 minutes, tie in bundles and stand in 2cm/³/₄ in of water	8-10 minutes in boiling water		500g/1 lb 5-6 minutes (stand 3-4 minutes before serving)
15 minutes	8-10 minutes depending on age and size		500g/1 lb 8 minutes with ¹/₂ cup water (stand 3-4 minutes before serving)
20-30 minutes but cooking times depend on age and size	15-20 minutes		500g/1 lb 8-10 minutes with ¹/₄ cup water
	30-40 minutes	1-1¹/₂ hours, wrap in foil, cook at 200°C/400°F	500g/1 lb 15 minutes (stand 5 minutes before serving)
10-15 minutes	5-10 minutes		500g/1 lb 5 minutes
10-15 minutes	10 minutes		500g/1 lb 5-6 minutes
5-10 minutes	3-5 minutes		500g/1 lb 4-5 minutes
		When stuffed 30-45 minutes	
20-25 minutes	15-20 minutes		500g/1 lb 8-10 minutes
10-15 minutes	8-10 minutes		500g/1 lb 6-8 minutes
10-15 minutes	5 minutes		500g/1 lb 4-5 minutes
		45 minutes-1 hour	500g/1 lb 5-8 minutes

vegetable
preparation

Vegetable	Preparation	Freezing
Fennel	Trim root and top leaves, remove and discard any discoloured outer sheaths. Halve or slice.	Blanch 3 minutes, pack in rigid container in blanching water.
Leeks	Trim roots and tops. Rinse well to remove any earth between the leaves, leave whole or slice.	Slice finely, blanch 1-2 minutes, pack in freezer bags.
Marrow	Wash. Cut into chunks or slices. Remove seeds.	
Mushrooms	Wipe with a damp cloth. Wild mushrooms may need to lightly rinsed and peeled.	
Okra	Wash. Leave whole or slice.	
Onions	Remove skins and tough outer layers. Halve, quarter, dice or slice.	Chop, double wrap and pack in freezer bags.
Parsnips	Scrape or peel. Cut in half lengthwise, slice or cut into chunks.	Slice or dice, blanch 2 minutes, pack into freezer bags.
Peas	Shell and rinse.	Blanch 1 minute, pack into freezer bags.
Potatoes – new	Wash and scrape with a small vegetable knife.	Blanch 4 minutes, pack into freezer bags.
Potatoes – old	Wash, scrub and peel if desired. Leave whole, cut into halves or quarters.	Blanch 5 minutes, pack into freezer bags.
Pumpkin	Wash, cut into medium pieces. Remove seeds and skin if desired.	Cut into serving size pieces, pack into freezer bags.
Silverbeet	Separate white stem from green leaves. Shredded leaves and cut stems into pieces.	Remove stalks, blanch 2 minutes. Squeeze out as much liquid as possible, pack into freezer bags.
Snow peas (Mangetout)	Top and tail, remove strings.	Blanch 1 minute, pack into freezer bags.
Spinach	Cut off roots and stems. Remove any wilted or damaged leaves, wash well in several changes of water.	Blanch 2 minutes, squeeze out as much moisture as possible, pack into freezer bags.
Sweet corn	If leaving husks on for cooking. Gently pull back husk, remove silk, wash and pull husks back around the cob. Or husk can be completely removed before cooking.	Blanch 3-5 minutes, wrap individually and pack into freezer bags.
Witloof	Remove any damaged outer leaves, trim base.	
Zucchini/ courgette	Wash and trim ends. Leave whole, cut into halves or slices.	Cut into slices, blanch 2 minutes, pack into freezer bags.

Steam	Boil Note: bring water to boil before adding vegetables	Bake/roast	Microwave Note: cook vegetables on high (100%) and always cover before microwaving
15-20 minutes	10-15 minutes		500g/1 lb 5-6 minutes
15-20 minutes	10-15 minutes		500g/1 lb 5-6 minutes
	10-15 minutes	45 minutes-1 hour	500g/1 lb 5 minutes
			500g/1 lb 4-5 minutes
	10-15 minutes		500g/1 lb slices 4-5 minutes
20-30 minutes	20-30 minutes	45 minutes-1 hour	500g/1 lb 6-8 minutes
30-40 minutes	10-15 minutes	1-1 1/2 hours	500g/1 lb 8-10 minutes
15-20 minutes	10-15 minutes		500g/1 lb 4-5 minutes
25-30 minutes	15-25 minutes	30-45 minutes	500g/1 lb 8-10 minutes (stand 3-4 minutes before serving)
30-45 minutes	25-40 minutes	45 minutes-1 1/4 hours	500g/1 lb 10-12 minutes (stand 3-4 minutes before serving)
35-45 minutes	20-30 minutes	45 minutes-1 hour	500g/1 lb 10 minutes
10-15 minutes	5-10 minutes		500g/1 lb 4-5 minutes
5-10 minutes	3-5 minutes		500g/1 lb 3-4 minutes
10-15 minutes	5-10 minutes		500g/1 lb 4-5 minutes
	10-20 minutes		Each cob 2-3 minutes
		30 minutes	4 chicons 3-4 minutes
5-10 minutes	5-10 minutes		500g/1 lb 4-5 minutes

creamy
potato skins

ingredients

1.5kg/3 lb potatoes
90g/3oz butter, melted
salt
1 cup/250g/8oz sour cream
2 tablespoons snipped fresh chives

Oven temperature 200°C, 400°F, Gas 4

Method:

1 *Scrub potatoes, pierce with a fork and bake for 1 hour or until potatoes are tender.*

2 *Cut potatoes into quarters and carefully remove flesh, leaving a 5mm/¼in shell. Reserve the cooked potato for another use.*

3 *Increase oven temperature to 240°C/ 475°F/ Gas 8. Brush both surfaces of potato skins with melted butter, place on a baking tray, sprinkle with salt and bake for 10-15 minutes or until skins are crisp.*

4 *Place sour cream and chives in a small bowl and mix to combine. Serve with potato skins.*

Note: *Potato skins make a great snack or first course. You might like to try serving them with a yoghurt and mint dip or an avocado dip.*

Serves 6

ingredients

Making the most of **vegetables**

Health authorities recommend that we eat at least four serves of vegetables daily. Most of the vitamin content lies just under the skin, so vegetables should be cooked and eaten with the skin on as often as possible. Remember to also include raw vegetables regularly as these have the highest vitamin and nutrient content of all.

Equipment

All that you need to successfully prepare vegetables is a sharp vegetable or paring knife and a large chopping board. However to make life easier for you, it is worth investing a little time and money in a few other pieces of good equipment, such as several large sharp knives for cutting and chopping, a grater, a vegetable peeler and a colander or large sieve. Remember to keep your knives sharp and either learn to sharpen them yourself or take them to a knife sharpener regularly. Sharp knives make preparation a breeze.

Vegetable **preparation**

- Wash vegetables before preparing, but do not soak. Soaking tends to draw out the valuable water-soluble vitamins thereby decreasing the nutrient content. As with every rule there are always exceptions and it may be necessary to soak very dirty vegetables to remove dirt and creepy-crawlies. If this is the case, always keep soaking times to a minimum.
- Vegetables that are left whole with their skins on have a higher nutrient and fibre content than those that are finely chopped and peeled. Many of the precious vitamins and minerals found in vegetables are stored just under the skin. Only peel vegetables if necessary.
- For maximum nutritional value, prepare vegetables just before cooking and serve them as soon as they are cooked.
- Remember, the smaller you cut vegetables the quicker the cooking time. For example, grated carrot will cook more quickly than carrot cut into slices.
- As a general guide when preparing and cooking vegetables remember: minimum water, minimum cooking and minimum cutting. Following this guide, ensures that your vegetables retain maximum flavour, nutrients and vitamins. Vitamins such as vitamin C, folic acid and other B-group vitamins are destroyed by heat and exposure to air, and they dissolve readily in cooking water. Steaming or microwaving are ideal cooking methods for retaining vitamins, flavour and texture.

The right **size**

What is the difference between cubed and diced vegetables or grated and sliced? The picture below the following guide will ensure that you prepare your vegetables correctly and so achieve the best results.

Cube: Cut into about 1cm/¹/₂in pieces.

Dice: Cut into 5mm/¹/₄in pieces.

Mince: Cut into 3mm/¹/₈in pieces.

Grate: Use either a hand grater or a food processor with a grating attachment.

Slice: Cut from thin to thick. You can also slice into rings. Another way to slice is to cut diagonally. This is a good way to prepare vegetables such as carrots, celery and zucchini (courgettes) for stir-frying.

muffins
and quick breads

Nothing beats the taste of home-baked cakes and biscuits. Yet, today many people think of home-baked goodies as nothing more than a delightful memory. This need not be so. This book will show that not only is baking an easy and affordable way to fill lunch boxes and provide snacks for your family, but it is also fun. Here you will find a host of recipes that are easy to make and will bring those distant memories of freshly baked treats back to life.

Baking has never been simpler or more fun than with this selection of quick and easy cakes and bakes. A bowl, a beater and a few minutes in the kitchen is all it takes to fill the house with the homey warmth and aroma that only a homemade muffin, cake or batch of biscuits can provide. There's a recipe in these pages to please everyone and every occasion. So, discover the pleasure of home baking and watch your friends and family return for more.

Techniques

When adding fresh fruit to batter it is best to follow the following advice: Whole berries and chopped fresh fruit are less likely to sink to the bottom of muffins and other quick breads during baking if you dredge them in flour first. Then shake off the excess flour in a colander before adding them to the batter. Besides helping to suspend the fruit evenly throughout the batter, the flour coating keeps moist pieces of fruit from clumping together.

The basic ingredients in muffins – flour, flavourings, perhaps some leavening, and liquid – are the same ones used in almost a dozen other varieties of quick breads. Creating such amazing diversity from a few common staples is largely a matter of adjusting the proportions of dry and liquid ingredients. Use two parts dry to one part liquid ingredients and you get a thicker batter for baking muffins or loaves. Thicker still, with a ratio of dry to liquid ingredients approaching three to one, are soft doughs for cut biscuits and scones.

Muffins and most quick breads are at their best when eaten soon after baking. Those that contain fruit, nuts, vegetables or moderately high amounts of fat stay moist longer than those that are low in fat. If muffins are left over it is best to place in the freezer in an airtight container, where they will keep for up to twelve months.

To reheat, bake the frozen muffins, wrapped in foil, at 175°C/350°F for 15-20 minutes, or until heated through. You may also store quick breads and biscuits in the same manner.

classic blueberry muffins

muffins

The perfect muffin has a gently

rounded top and golden crust, moist finely grained crumb, an appealing aroma and a satisfying balance of flavour.

Muffins are mini-cakes for busy home bakers – freeze them for brunch treats, quick snacks and school lunch boxes, or when you need to stop and take a well-earned break.

apple
& bran muffins

Method:
1 Sift together flour, nutmeg and baking powder into a bowl. Add bran cereal and sugar and mix to combine.
2 Make a well in centre of flour mixture. Add apples, eggs, yoghurt and oil and mix until just combined.
3 Spoon mixture into twelve greased ½ cup/125mL/4fl oz muffin tins and bake for 15 minutes or until muffins are cooked when tested with a skewer.

Note: The secret to making great muffins is in the mixing – they should be mixed as little as possible. It doesn't matter if the mixture is lumpy, while overmixing the mixture will result in tough muffins.

Makes 12

ingredients

1½ cups/230g/7½oz wholemeal (wholewheat) flour
½ teaspoon ground nutmeg
1½ teaspoon baking powder
½ cup/30g/1oz bran cereal, toasted
⅓ cup/60g/2oz brown sugar
2 green apples, grated
2 eggs, lightly beaten
¼ cup/45g/1½oz low-fat natural yoghurt
1 tablespoon polyunsaturated vegetable oil

Oven temperature 180°C, 350°F, Gas 4

apricot
oat-bran muffins

Method:

1 Sift flour and baking powder together into a bowl. Add oat bran, apricots and sultanas, mix to combine and set aside.
2 Combine egg, milk, golden syrup and butter.
3 Add milk mixture to dry ingredients and mix until just combined. Spoon mixture into six greased 1 cup/250ml/8fl oz-capacity muffin tins and bake for 15-20 minutes or until muffins are cooked when tested with a skewer. Serve hot, warm or cold.

Note: Serve this muffin for breakfast or brunch fresh and warm from the oven, split and buttered and perhaps with a drizzle of honey.

Makes 6

2 cups/250g/8oz all purpose flour
2 teaspoons baking powder
1 cup/45g/1 1/2oz oat bran
60g/2oz dried apricots, chopped
60g/2oz sultanas
1 egg, lightly beaten
1 1/2 cups/325ml/12fl oz buttermilk
or milk
1/4 cup/60ml/2fl oz golden syrup
90g/3oz butter, melted

blackberry
spice muffins

Photograph opposite

Method:

1 Sift together wholemeal flour, flour, baking powder and allspice into a bowl. Return husks to bowl. Add sugar, almonds, blackberries and banana and mix to combine.
2 Place buttermilk, oil and egg in a bowl and whisk to combine. Stir milk mixture into dry ingredients and mix until just combined.
3 Spoon mixture into twelve nonstick ½ cup/ 125ml/4fl oz-capacity muffin tins and bake for 15-20 minutes or until muffins are cooked when tested with a skewer. Turn onto a wire rack to cool.

Note: If buttermilk is unavailable use equal parts of low-fat natural yoghurt and reduced-fat milk instead. This recipe will then make 12-15 muffins and the cooking time will be 12-15 minutes. Alternatively ramekins or small pudding basins can be used to make large muffins.

Makes 12

ingredients

½ cup/75g/2½oz wholemeal (wholewheat) flour
½ cup/60g/2oz all purpose flour
1½ teaspoon baking powder
½ teaspoon ground allspice
¼ cup/45g/1½oz brown sugar
60g/2oz ground almonds
185g/6oz blackberries
1 banana, mashed
1 cup/250ml/8fl oz buttermilk
⅓ cup/90ml/3fl oz vegetable oil
1 egg, lightly beaten

Oven temperature 190°C, 375°F, Gas 5

mango
bran muffins

Photograph opposite

Method:

1 Sift together flour, baking powder and cardamom into a bowl. Add bran, sugar and mango and mix to combine.
2 Place egg whites, milk and oil in a bowl and whisk to combine. Stir milk mixture into flour mixture and mix well to combine.
3 Spoon mixture into twelve nonstick ⅓ cup/ 90ml/3fl oz-capacity muffin tins and bake for 15-20 minutes or until muffins are cooked when tested with a skewer. Turn onto a wire rack to cool.

Note: When fresh mangoes are unavailable, drained, canned mangoes can be used instead.

Makes 12

ingredients

1 cup/125g/4oz all purpose flour
2½ teaspoons baking powder
1 teaspoon ground cardamom
1 cup/45g/1½oz oat bran
⅓ cup/60g/2 oz brown sugar
1 mango, chopped
2 egg whites
¾ cup/185ml/6fl oz reduced-fat milk
¼ cup/60ml/2fl oz vegetable oil

Oven temperature 190°C, 375°F, Gas 5

cornbread
muffins

Method:

1 Place flour, cornmeal flour (polenta), Parmesan cheese, baking powder, cumin and chilli powder in a bowl and mix to combine.

2 Make a well in centre of flour mixture, add milk, eggs and oil and mix until just combined.

3 Spoon mixture into twelve greased 1/3 cup/ 90mL/3fl oz muffin tins and bake for 30 minutes or until muffins are cooked when tested with a skewer.

Note: Cornmeal flour (polenta) is cooked yellow maize flour and is very popular in northern Italian and southern American cooking. It adds an interesting texture and flavour to baked products such as these muffins and is available from health-food stores and some supermarkets.

Makes 12

1 1/2 cups/185g/6oz all purpose flour
1 cup/170g/5 1/2oz cornmeal flour (polenta)
45g/1 1/2oz grated Parmesan cheese
2 1/2 teaspoon baking powder
1 teaspoon ground cumin
pinch chilli powder
2 cups/500ml/16fl oz buttermilk or low-fat milk
2 eggs, lightly beaten
1 tablespoon polyunsaturated vegetable oil

Oven temperature 190°C, 375°F, Gas 5

Oven temperature 180°C, 350°F, Gas 4

lemon-poppy
seed muffins

Method:
1 Place eggs, sour cream, milk, oil, honey, poppy seeds and lemon rind in a bowl and mix well to combine.
2 Add flour and baking powder to poppy seed mixture and mix until just combined.
3 Spoon mixture into six greased 1 cup/250ml/ 8fl oz-capacity muffin tins and bake for 25-30 minutes or until muffins are cooked when tested with a skewer. Turn onto wire racks to cool.
4 To make icing, place cream cheese, lemon juice and icing sugar in a food processor and process until smooth. Top cold muffins with icing.
Note: A simple glacé icing is another suitable topping for muffins. To make, sift 1 cup/ 155g/5oz icing sugar into a bowl, slowly stir in 3 teaspoons warm water and a few drops almond or vanilla essence to make a glaze of drizzling consistency. To vary the flavour, omit the essence and substitute the water with 3 teaspoons citrus juice or a favourite liqueur.
Makes 6

ingredients

2 eggs, lightly beaten
1 cup/250g/8oz sour cream
¹/₂ cup/125ml/4fl oz milk
¹/₄ cup/60ml/2fl oz oil
¹/₄ cup/90g/3oz honey
3 tablespoons poppy seeds
1 tablespoon grated lemon rind
2¹/₄ cups/280g/9oz all purpose flour, sifted
3 teaspoons baking powder
<u>Lemon cream-cheese icing</u>
60g/2oz cream cheese, softened
1 tablespoon lemon juice
³/₄ cup/125g/4oz icing sugar

choc-rough
muffins

Method:

1 Place butter and sugar in a bowl and beat until light and fluffy. Gradually beat in eggs.

2 Combine flour, baking flour and cocoa powder. Add flour mixture, chocolate chips, coconut and milk to butter mixture and mix until just combined.

3 Spoon mixture into six greased 1 cup/ 250ml/8fl oz-capacity muffin tins and bake for 35 minutes or until muffins are cooked when tested with a skewer.

Note: Muffin tins without a nonstick finish should be greased (and, if desired, also lined with paper baking cups) before use. Nonstick tins do not need lining but may need greasing; follow the manufacturer's instructions.

Makes 6

ingredients

125g/4oz butter, softened
1/2 cup/125g/4oz sugar
2 eggs, lightly beaten
2 cups/250g/8oz all purpose flour, sifted
2 1/4 teaspoons baking powder, sifted
1/4 cup/30g/1oz cocoa powder, sifted
155g/5oz chocolate chips
45g/1 1/2oz shredded coconut
3/4 cup/185ml/6fl oz buttermilk or milk

classic
blueberry muffins

Photograph also appears on page 569

Method:

1 Sift flour and baking powder together into a bowl, add sugar and mix to combine.

2 Combine eggs, milk and butter. Add egg mixture and blueberries to dry ingredients and mix until just combined.

3 Spoon mixture into six greased 1 cup/250ml/ 8fl oz-capacity muffin tins. Sprinkle with coffee sugar crystals and bake for 20-30 minutes or until muffins are cooked when tested with a skewer. Turn onto wire racks to cool.

Note: Finely shredded orange peel can be added to this mixture to enhance the flavour of the blueberries.

Coffee sugar crystals are coarse golden brown sugar grains. If unavailable, raw (muscovado) or demerara sugar can be used instead.

Makes 6

ingredients

2¹/₂ cups/315g/10oz all purpose flour
3 teaspoon baking powder
¹/₃ cup/90g/3oz sugar
2 eggs, lightly beaten
1 cup/250ml/8fl oz buttermilk or milk
60g/2oz butter, melted
125g/4oz blueberries
2 tablespoons coffee sugar crystals

Oven temperature 200°C, 400°F, Gas 6

potato
sour-cream muffins

Photograph opposite

ingredients

250g/8oz mashed potato
2 eggs, lightly beaten
1 cup/250ml/8fl oz milk
3/4 cup/185g/6oz sour cream
60g/2oz butter, melted
2 1/2 cups/315g/10oz all purpose flour
2 1/2 teaspoons baking powder
3 tablespoons snipped fresh chives

Oven temperature 180°C, 350°F, Gas 4

Method:

1 Place potato in a bowl. Add eggs, milk, sour cream and butter to the bowl and mix well to combine.

2 Combine sifted flour, baking powder and chives. Add to potato mixture and mix until just combined. Spoon mixture into six greased 1cup/250ml/8fl oz-capacity muffin tins and bake for 25-30 minutes or until muffins are cooked when tested with a skewer. Serve warm or cold.

Note: A properly cooked muffin should have risen well, be slightly domed in the middle (but not peaked!) and be evenly browned. It should also shrink slightly from the sides of the tin.

Makes 6

cheese
& bacon muffins

Photograph opposite

ingredients

4 rashers bacon, chopped
1 egg, lightly beaten
1 cup/250ml/8fl oz milk
1/4 cup/60ml/2fl oz vegetable oil
2 tablespoons chopped fresh parsley
2 cups/250g/8oz all purpose flour, sifted
2 1/2 teaspoons baking powder, sifted
90g/3oz grated tasty (mature Cheddar) cheese

Oven temperature 180°C, 350°F, Gas 4

Method:

1 Place bacon in a frying pan and cook over a medium heat, stirring, until crisp. Remove bacon from pan and drain on absorbent kitchen paper.

2 Place egg, milk, oil and parsley in a bowl and mix to combine. Combine sifted flour, baking powder and cheese. Add flour mixture and bacon to egg mixture and mix until combined.

3 Spoon mixture into twelve greased 1/2 cup/125mL/4 fl oz-capacity muffin tins and bake for 20-25 minutes or until muffins are cooked when tested with a skewer. Serve warm or cold.

Note: An accurate oven is essential for successful baking. It should be well insulated and draught-proof, as a discrepancy of a few degrees can ruin baked goods. Regular checking with an oven thermometer helps avoid baking failures.

Makes 12

mini sardine
muffins

Method:

1 Combine flour, lemon thyme and paprika in a bowl. In a separate dish mix, together the egg, oil and milk. Quickly and lightly combine the dry and liquid ingredients. Fold in the sardines. Spoon mixture into lightly greased muffin pans or patty pans. Bake in an oven at 200°C/400°F for 12-14 minutes or until golden. Serve warm.

Makes 24

1 ½ cups/185g/6oz all purpose flour
2 teaspoons baking powder
1 tablespoon lemon thyme
pinch paprika
1 egg
¼ cup/60ml/2fl oz canola oil
¾ cup/180ml/6fl oz milk
110g/4oz can sardines in tomato sauce, mashed

Oven temperature 200°C, 400°F, Gas 6

mushroom
muffins

Method:

1 Sift flour and baking powder into a large bowl. Mix in mushrooms, rice, cheese and herbs.

2 Make a well in the centre of the dry ingredients. Add the remaining ingredients. Mix until just combined (see note).

3 Spoon mixture into greased muffin tins until three quarters full. Bake in the oven 200°C / 400°F for 25 minutes. Remove from tin. Cool on a wire rack. Serve hot or cold.

Note: Don't worry if not all the flour is incorporated as this gives muffins their characteristic texture. Sixteen strokes is usually enough when mixing.

Makes about 12

ingredients

2 cups/250g/8oz all purpose flour
1 tablespoon baking powder
60g/2oz fresh mushrooms, chopped
1/2 cup/75g/2 1/2oz cooked brown rice
1/2 cup/60g/2oz shredded tasty (mature cheddar) cheese
1 tablespoon parsley flakes
2 teaspoons chives, chopped
125g/4oz margarine, melted
1 cup/250mL/8oz milk
1 egg, beaten

sweet-potato
muffins

Method:

1 Boil or microwave sweet potato until tender, drain well and mash. Set aside to cool.

2 Sift wholemeal (wholewheat) flour, all purpose flour, baking powder and sugar in a bowl and mix to combine. Make a well in centre of flour mixture. Add yoghurt, eggs, vanilla essence, currants and cinnamon and mix until just combined. Fold sweet potato into flour mixture.

3 Spoon mixture into twelve greased ¹/₂ cup/ 125ml/4fl oz-capacity muffin tins and bake for 35 minutes or until muffins are cooked when tested with a skewer.

Note: *Make muffins when you have time and freeze them to have on hand for quick snacks. If you take your lunch to work, simply take a muffin out of the freezer in the morning – by mid-morning or lunch time it will be thawed.*

Makes 12

ingredients

375g/12oz sweet potato,
peeled and chopped
¹/₂ cup/75g/2¹/₂oz wholemeal
(wholewheat) flour
1 cup/125g/ oz all purpose flour
2 teaspoons baking powder
¹/₃ cup/60g/2oz brown sugar
1 cup/200g/6¹/₂oz low-fat
natural yoghurt
2 eggs, lightly beaten
1 teaspoon vanilla essence
3 tablespoons currants
1 teaspoon ground cinnamon

Oven temperature 190°C, 370°F, Gas 5

Method:

1 Sift flour, bicarbonate of soda and cinnamon together into a bowl. Set aside.

2 Place sugar, butter and dates in a saucepan and heat over a low heat, stirring constantly, until butter melts. Pour date mixture into dry ingredients, add egg and milk. Mix until just combined.

3 Spoon mixture into six greased 1 cup/250ml/ 8fl oz-capacity muffin tins and bake for 30 minutes or until muffins are cooked when tested with a skewer.

4 To make sauce, place butter, sugar, golden syrup and brandy in a saucepan and heat over a low heat, stirring constantly, until sugar dissolves. Bring to the boil, then reduce heat and simmer for 3 minutes or until sauce is thick and syrupy. Serve with warm muffins.

Note: If 1 cup/250 ml/8 oz capacity muffin tins are unavailable, use the standard 1/2 cup/125ml/4fl oz-capacity tins and bake for approximately half the recommended time. The yield, of course, will be doubled.

These muffins make a delicious dessert treat, but are just as good in lunch boxes and for snacks without the sauce.

Makes 6

sticky
date muffins

ingredients

2 cups/250g/8oz all purpose flour
2 teaspoon baking powder
1 teaspoon bicarbonate of soda (baking soda)
1 teaspoon ground cinnamon
1/3 cup/60g/2oz brown sugar
90g/3oz butter
125g/4oz chopped dates
1 egg, lightly beaten
1 cup/250ml/8fl oz buttermilk or milk
<u>**Brandy sauce**</u>
100g/3 1/2oz butter
1/4 cup/45g/1 1/2oz brown sugar
1 tablespoon golden syrup
1 tablespoon brandy

Oven temperature 190°C, 370°F, Gas 5

banana
choc-chip muffins

Method:

I In a mixing bowl, mash the banana, add the milk, egg and melted margarine. Mix well. Stir the sifted flour, baking powder, sugar and choc bits into the banana mixture, mix only until the ingredients are combined. Spoon mixture into well-greased muffin tins. Bake in an oven 190°C/370°F for 20 minutes. Serve warm or cold.

Makes 12

ingredients

I large ripe banana
I cup/240ml/8fl oz milk
I egg
¼ cup/60ml/2fl oz margarine, melted
I½ cups/185g/6oz all purpose flour
I½ teaspoons baking powder
½ cup/120g/4oz caster sugar
¾ cup/120g/4oz choc bits

oat-bran
fruit muffins

Method:

1 Combine sifted flour, baking powder, oat bran and brown sugar. Beat oil and eggs together and stir in the dry ingredients along with the fruit medley and buttermilk. Mix until just combined, do not over mix.

2 Spoon mixture into lightly greased muffin tins. Bake in an oven 190°C/370°F for 25-30 minutes.

Makes 12

1 1/2 cups/185g/6oz all purpose flour
2 teaspoons baking powder
1/2 cup/60g/2oz oat bran
1/2 cup/75g/2 1/2oz brown sugar
1/2 cup/120ml/4fl oz canola oil
2 eggs
1/2 cup/90g/3oz fruit medley
1 cup buttermilk

Oven temperature 190°C, 370°F, Gas 5

olive soda bread

quick breads

Quick breads, true to their name,

are quick and easy to bake. They use baking powder or bicarbonate of soda (baking soda) instead of yeast as the rising agent. In this chapter, you will find recipes for such delicious quick breads as bacon-cornbread pots, herb rolls, and carrot and sesame muffins.

blue cheese
& walnut damper

Method:

1 Place sifted flour, baking powder, blue cheese, chives, paprika and 125g/4oz walnuts in a bowl and mix to combine.

2 Make a well in the centre of flour mixture, add milk and oil and mix to form a soft dough.

3 Turn dough onto a lightly floured surface and knead until smooth. Roll into a large ball, flatten slightly and place on a lightly greased baking tray. Sprinkle with Parmesan cheese and remaining walnuts and bake for 40 minutes or until damper is cooked.

Note: This loaf tastes wonderful served hot with hearty soups or at room temperature as part of a cheese and fruit board.

Makes 1 damper

ingredients

2¹/₂ cups/315g/10oz all purpose flour, sifted
2¹/₂ teaspoons baking powder
220 g/7 oz blue cheese, crumbled
1 tablespoon snipped fresh chives
1 teaspoon paprika
155g/5oz walnuts, chopped
1 cup/250ml/8fl oz buttermilk or milk
1 tablespoon walnut or vegetable oil
60g/2oz grated Parmesan cheese

Oven temperature 180°C, 350°F, Gas 4

cheesy
herb bread

Method:

1 Place flour, baking powder, salt, stock powder, rosemary, dill, chives, sage and 12g/4oz cheese in a bowl and mix to combine.

2 Combine egg, milk and butter. Add egg mixture to dry ingredients and mix to combine.

3 Spoon mixture into a greased and lined 11x21cm/4¹/₂inx8¹/₂in loaf tin, sprinkle with remaining cheese and bake for 45 minutes or until cooked when tested with a skewer. Turn onto a wire rack to cool.

Note: Another time, try combining the flavours of thyme, bay leaves and fennel seeds with the rosemary and sage for a loaf infused with the classic 'herbes de Provence'.

Makes one 11x21cm/4¹/₂x8¹/₂in loaf

ingredients

2 cups/250g/8oz all purpose flour, sifted
2 teaspoons baking powder
1 teaspoon salt
1 teaspoon chicken stock powder
2 tablespoons chopped fresh rosemary or
1 teaspoon dried rosemary
2 tablespoons chopped fresh dill
2 tablespoons snipped fresh chives
2 tablespoons chopped fresh sage or
1 teaspoon dried sage
185g/6oz grated tasty (mature Cheddar) cheese
1 egg, lightly beaten
155ml/5fl oz milk
30g/1oz butter, melted

olive
soda bread

Photograph on right and page 587

ingredients

125g/4oz butter, softened
¼ cup/60g/2oz sugar
1 egg
3 cups/470g/15oz wholemeal
(whole wheat) flour
3 teaspoons baking powder
1½ cups/185g/6oz flour
1½ teaspoons bicarbonate of soda
(baking soda)
1½ cups/375ml/12fl oz buttermilk
or milk
125g/4oz black olives, chopped
2 teaspoons fennel seeds
1 teaspoon coarse sea salt

Method:

1 *Place butter, sugar and egg in a food processor and process until smooth. Add wholemeal (wholewheat) flour, flour, bicarbonate of soda, baking powder and milk and process to form a soft dough.*

2 *Turn dough onto a lightly floured surface and knead in olives. Shape dough into a 20cm/ 8in-round and place on a lightly greased and floured baking tray. Using a sharp knife, cut a cross in the top. Sprinkle with fennel seeds and salt and bake for 45 minutes or until cooked.*

Note: *The famous Irish soda bread is influenced here by the Mediterranean flavours of fennel and olives. You may use one of the many types of marinated olives available, if you wish.*

Makes one 20cm/8in round loaf

basil-beer
bread

Photograph opposite

ingredients

3 cups/375g/12oz all purpose flour, sifted
3 teaspoons baking powder
¼ cup/60g/2oz sugar
6 tablespoons chopped fresh basil
1 teaspoon crushed black peppercorns
1½ cups/375ml/12fl oz beer, at room
temperature

Method:

1 *Place flour, baking soda, sugar, basil, peppercorns and beer in a bowl and mix to make a soft dough.*

2 *Place dough in a greased and lined 11x21cm/ 4½x8½in loaf tin and bake for 50 minutes or until bread is cooked when tested with a skewer.*

3 *Stand bread in tin for 5 minutes before turning onto a wire rack to cool. Serve warm or cold.*

Note: *This bread is delicious served spread with olive or sun-dried tomato paste. Any beer may be used here; you can experiment with light and dark ales and even stout to achieve different results.*

Makes one 11x21cm/4½x8½in loaf

shortbread

Method:

1 Place butter, sugar and vanilla essence in a bowl and beat until light and fluffy. Add flour and rice flour (ground rice) and mix to combine.

2 Roll out dough on a lightly floured surface to form a 2cm/³/₄in-thick circle.

3 Pinch edges or press dough into a large shortbread mould. Place on a lightly greased baking tray and bake for 25 minutes or until lightly browned.

Note: Butter shortbread originated in Scotland as a festive confection particularly for Christmas and Hogmanay.

Makes 1 large shortbread round

200g/6¹/₂oz butter, softened
¹/₂ cup/100g/3¹/₂oz caster sugar
1 teaspoon vanilla essence
2¹/₄ cups/280g/9oz flour, sifted
¹/₃ cup/60g/2oz rice flour
(ground rice), sifted

Oven temperature 160°C, 325°F, Gas 3

cornbread

Method:

1 Sift flour with baking powder and salt. Stir in sugar and cornmeal. Add eggs, milk and melted butter. Beat until just smooth.

2 Pour into a 23x23x5cm/9"x9"x2"in tin lined with baking paper and bake in 220°C/440°F oven for 20-25 minutes.

3 Remove from tin and cut into squares to serve with butter.

Serves 4

ingredients

125g/4oz sifted plain flour
4 teaspoons baking powder
³/₄ teaspoon salt
30g/1oz sugar
125g/4oz yellow cornmeal flour
2 eggs
1 cup/250ml/8oz milk
30g/1oz butter
butter, to serve

easy
berry bread

1

2

3

ingredients

Easy berry bread

3 cups/375g/12oz all purpose flour
1½ teaspoons ground mixed spice
4 teaspoon baking powder
1½ tablespoons sugar
30g/1oz butter
½ cup/170ml/5½ fl oz water
½ cup/125ml/4fl oz milk
200g/6½oz raspberries
1 tablespoon
caster sugar
4 teaspoons milk

Method:

1 Sift flour, mixed spice and baking powder together into a bowl. Add sugar then, using your fingertips, rub in butter until mixture resembles coarse breadcrumbs.

2 Make a well in the centre of flour mixture then, using a round-ended knife, mix in water and milk and mix to form a soft dough.

3 Turn dough onto a floured surface and knead lightly until smooth. Divide dough into two portions and flatten each into an 18cm/7in round.

4 Sprinkle raspberries and sugar over surface of one round leaving 2½cm/1in around edge. Brush edge with a little milk and place remaining round on top. Seal edges securely using fingertips.

5 Place on a greased and lightly floured baking tray. Brush surface of loaf with a little milk and bake for 10 minutes. Reduce oven temperature to 180°C/350°F/Gas 4 and bake for 20-25 minutes longer or until cooked.

Note: Butter absorbs other odours easily, so when keeping it in the refrigerator ensure that it is covered and away from foods such as onions and fish or you will have a strong-smelling butter that will affect the taste of baked goods.

Makes one 18cm/7in round

cheese
& bacon damper

Method:

1 Rub the margarine into the flour until mixture resembles coarse breadcrumbs.
2 Stir in parsley, chives, cheese and bacon, mix well.
3 Combine the egg and milk, stir into the dry ingredients and mix to a soft dough.
4 Turn dough onto a lightly floured board and knead lightly.
5 Shape into a cob, cut a deep cross in the centre of the cob and place on a sheet of baking paper on an oven tray.
6 Bake in the oven at 200°C/400°F for 30 minutes or until hollow-sounding when tapped underneath.
7 Serve hot with a crock of butter on a buffet table, cut into small pieces.

Serves 6-8

ingredients

3 tablespoons margarine or butter
2¹/₂ cups all purpose flour
3 teaspoons baking powder
2 teaspoons parsley flakes
1 teaspoon chopped chives
1 cup/125g/4oz grated tasty
(mature Cheddar) cheese
2 rashers cooked bacon,
finely chopped
1 egg
³/₄ cup/180ml/6fl oz milk

Oven temperature 200°C, 400°F, Gas 6

potato
scones

Method:

1 Sift the flour, baking powder and salt together, then rub in the margarine. Beat the eggs and milk together and add to flour mixture to make a firm dough.

2 Add finely mashed potatoes, spring onions and pepper. Stir through lightly. Turn onto a floured board or sheet of non-stick oven paper, knead, then roll out to 1cm/¹/₂ in thickness. Cut into rounds and bake in 230°C/450°F oven for 30 minutes. Split open while hot and spread with butter and serve.

Serves 6-8

ingredients

1¹/₂ cups/185g/6oz plain flour
1 teaspoon baking powder
¹/₂ teaspoon salt
¹/₂ cup/125g/4oz margarine
2 eggs, beaten
³/₈ cup/100ml/3oz milk
125g/4oz cold mashed potato
3 spring onions, finely chopped
ground black pepper
flour, for kneading
butter, for spreading

Oven temperature 230°C, 450°F, Gas 8

cheese
& onion scones

Method:

1 Sift flour, baking powder, salt and cayenne. Rub margarine or butter into flour. Add grated cheese, parsley and onion and mix well.

2 Make a well in the centre and add beaten egg and milk all at once, and mix quickly to a soft dough. Turn out on a floured board and knead just enough to make a smooth surface.

3 Roll to 1cm/¹/₂in thickness and cut into rounds. Place on a floured tray, glaze tops with milk or beaten egg and milk. Bake in a hot oven 230°C/450°F for 10-15 minutes or until scones are browned.

Serves 6

500g/1 lb all purpose flour
4 teaspoons baking powder
1 teaspoon salt
¹/₄ teaspoon cayenne pepper
60g/2oz margarine or butter
100g/3oz grated cheese
1 tablespoon finely chopped parsley
1 dessertspoon finely chopped onion
1 egg, beaten
1 ¹/₂ cups milk

scones

Method:

1 Sift together flour and baking powder into a large bowl. Stir in sugar, then rub in butter, using fingertips, until mixture resembles coarse breadcrumbs.

2 Whisk together egg and milk. Make a well in centre of flour mixture, pour in egg mixture and mix to form a soft dough. Turn onto a lightly floured surface and knead lightly.

3 Press dough out to a 2cm/³⁄₄in thickness, using palm of hand. Cut out scones using a floured 5cm/2in cutter. Avoid twisting the cutter, or the scones will rise unevenly.

4 Arrange scones close together on a greased and lightly floured baking tray or in a shallow 20cm/8in-round cake tin. Brush with a little milk and bake for 12-15 minutes or until golden.

ingredients

2 cups/250g/8oz all purpose flour
3 teaspoon baking powder
2 teaspoons sugar
45g/1¹⁄₂oz butter
1 egg
¹⁄₂ cup/125ml/4fl oz milk

Note: To grease and flour a cake tin or baking tray, lightly brush with melted butter or margarine, then sprinkle with flour and shake to coat evenly. Invert on work surface and tap gently to remove excess flour.

Makes 12

Oven temperature 220°C, 425°F, Gas 7

mini savoury
croissants

Photograph on right

ingredients

250g/8oz prepared puff pastry
1 egg, lightly beaten with
1 tablespoon water
<u>Asparagus and cheese filling</u>
60g/2oz Gruyère cheese, grated
4 stalks fresh asparagus, blanched and
finely chopped
1 paprika freshly ground
black pepper

1

2

3

Method:

1 To make filling, place cheese, asparagus, paprika and black pepper to taste in a bowl and mix to combine.

2 Roll out pastry to 0.3cm/⅛in thick and cut into 10cm/4in-wide strips. Cut each strip into triangles with 10cm/4in bases.

3 Place a little filling across the base of each triangle, roll up from the base and mould into a croissant shape. Brush with egg mixture.

4 Place croissants on greased baking trays andbake for 12-15 minutes or until puffed and golden. Serve hot or cold.

Ham and cheese croissants:

Melt 15g/½oz butter in a frying pan and cook 100g/3½oz finely chopped ham and 2 finely chopped spring onions over a medium heat for 3-4 minutes or until onions are soft. Remove from heat, stir in 2 teaspoons finely chopped parsley and black pepper to taste. Cool. Assemble, sprinkling filling with 45g/1½oz tasty (mature Cheddar) cheese and cook as directed.

Chocolate croissants:

Use 45g/1½oz grated milk or dark chocolate to fill triangles. Assemble and cook as directed.

Note: Puff pastry always gives a spectacular result and no more so than in these mini croissants. The secret with these savoury delights is in the shape. Follow the step-by-step instructions to make the quickest and tastiest treats ever.

Makes 12

simple
wholemeal loaf

Method:

1 Sift flour, then mix in the wholemeal flour. Make a well in the centre, crumble in the yeast, add the sugar and 3 tablespoons of the water. Stand in a warm place for 15 minutes.

2 Add the rest of the water and salt and make dough. Knead well on a floured board, place in a well-greased tin and stand in a warm place for 40 minutes to let rise.

3 Bake in a hot oven 220°C/440°F with decreasing heat and cook for 1 1/2 hours.

Serves 4

2cups/250g/8oz all purpose flour, sifted
2cups/250g/8oz wholemeal flour
15g/1/2 oz compressed yeast
1/2 teaspoon sugar
1 teaspoon salt
1 1/4 cups/310ml/10oz tepid water
extra flour, for kneading

Oven temperature 220°C, 425°F, Gas 7

banana bread

Method:

1 Cream the butter and sugar. Add the eggs, bananas and flour with salt and soda.

2 Place into a greased loaf tin and bake 45 minutes in a 180°C/350°F oven. Serve hot or cold, sliced and spread with butter.

Serves 4

Oven temperature 180°C, 350°F, Gas 4

125g/4oz butter
1/2 cup/125g/4oz caster sugar
2 eggs
3 mashed bananas
2cups/250g/8oz plain flour
1/4 teaspoon salt
3/4 teaspoon bicarbonate of soda
extra butter, for spreading

coffee rolls

Method:

1 Beat butter and sugar till creamy, add egg and milk. Sift the flour with the soda and cream of tartar and fold in. Roll out, cut into small squares, then roll each piece over 3 times.

2 Brush with the white of an egg or a little milk and bake in a hot oven 220°C/440°F until cooked.

Serves 4

1 heaped tablespoon butter
1 large tablespoon sugar
1 egg
1 cup/250ml/8oz milk
2cups/250g/8oz plain flour
1 teaspoon bicarbonate of soda
2 teaspoons cream of tartar

Oven temperature 220°C, 425°F, Gas 7

griddle cakes

Method:

1 Beat egg and sugar till creamy, sift the flour, baking powder and add salt. Stir in the milk until mixture drops easily from a spoon.
2 Heat a heavy frying pan, add a small knob of butter and when melted drop mixture by the spoonful. Turn when cooked on one side.

Serves 2

1 egg
2 teaspoons sugar
125g/4oz plain flour
1 teaspoon baking powder
pinch salt
3/4 cup/185ml/6oz milk
30g/1oz butter

rock cakes

Method:

1 Place flour, baking powder and sugar in a bowl. Rub in butter, using fingertips, until mixture resembles fine breadcrumbs. Stir in dried fruit, lemon rind and orange rind. Add egg and milk and mix to form a soft dough.
2 Place tablespoons of mixture on greased baking trays and spinkle lightly with cinnamon- sugar mixture. Bake for 12-15 minutes or until golden. Transfer to wire racks to cool.

Note: Do not sore different types of biscuits together as they will absorb flavours and moisture from each other.

Makes 30

2cups/250g/8oz plain flour, sifted
2 1/2 teaspoons baking powder
1/4 cup/60g/2oz caster sugar
90g/3oz butter
125g/4oz mixed dried fruit, chopped
1 teaspoon finely grated lemon rind
1 teaspoon finely grated orange rind
1 egg, lightly beaten
1/3 cup/90ml/3fl oz milk
1/2 teaspoon cinnamon mixed with
2 tablespoons caster sugar

Oven temperature 180°C, 350°F, Gas 4

soda bread

Photograph on page 606

Method:

1 Sift together flour, bicarbonate of soda and salt into a bowl. Rub in butter, using fingertips, until mixture resembles coarse breadcrumbs. Make a well in the centre of the flour mixture and pour in milk and, using a round-ended knife, mix to form a soft dough.

2 Turn dough onto a floured surface and knead lightly until smooth. Shape into an 18cm/7in round and place on a greased and floured baking tray. Score dough into eighths using a sharp knife. Dust lightly with flour and bake for 35-40 minutes or until loaf sounds hollow when tapped on the base.

Note: A loaf for when you need bread unexpectedly, Soda Bread is made with bicarbonate of soda rather than yeast so it requires no rising. It is best eaten slightly warm and is delicious with lashings of treacle or golden syrup.

Serves 8

ingredients

4 cups/500g/1 lb flour
1 teaspoon bicarbonate of soda
1 teaspoon salt
45g/1½oz butter
2 cups/500ml/16fl oz buttermilk
or milk

Oven temperature 200°C, 400°F, Gas 6

fig scones

Method:

1 Sift all dry ingredients together. Rub in the butter, add the figs and the slightly beaten egg. Stir with a fork until mixture forms a soft ball.

2 Roll out onto a lightly floured board about 1cm/½in thick and cut into triangles or rounds. Brush tops with a little milk, sprinkle with sugar and cinnamon and bake in a hot oven 200°C/400°F until golden brown, about 15 minutes.

Serves 3-4

ingredients

2cups/250g/8oz plain flour
2¼ teaspoons baking powder
65g/2oz sugar
¾ teaspoon salt
125g/4oz butter
65g/2oz finely chopped dried figs
2 eggs, slightly beaten
milk, for brushing
cinnamon and sugar, for glaze

Oven temperature 200°C, 400°F, Gas 6

chilli-soup
biscuits

Method:

1 Cook bacon in a nonstick frying pan over a medium-high heat for 3-4 minutes or until crisp. Remove from pan and drain on absorbent kitchen paper.

2 Sift together flour, baking powder and salt into a bowl. Rub in butter with fingertips until mixture resembles coarse breadcrumbs.

3 Stir bacon, cheese and chillies into flour mixture. Add milk and mix to form a soft dough. Turn onto a lightly floured surface and knead lightly with fingertips until smooth.

4 Using heel of hand, gently press dough out to 1cm/½in thickness. Cut out rounds using a 5cm/2in pastry cutter. Place on a greased baking tray and brush with melted butter. Bake for 12-15 minutes or until golden brown. Remove from tray and cool on a wire rack or serve warm spread with butter.

Makes 16

ingredients

2 rashers bacon, finely chopped
2 cups/250g/8oz flour
3 teaspoons baking powder
½ teaspoon salt
90g/3oz butter
90g/3oz grated tasty
(mature Cheddar) cheese
2 small fresh red chillies, seeded and finely chopped
²⁄₃ cup/170ml/5½fl oz milk
30g/1oz butter, melted

Oven temperature 220°C, 425°F, Gas 7

herb rolls

Method:

1 Melt butter in a frying pan and cook spring onions over a medium heat for 2-3 minutes or until soft. Remove from heat and set aside.

2 Sift together flour and self-raising flour, baking powder and bicarbonate of soda into a large bowl. Stir in sugar, parsley and basil. Combine milk, eggs and onion mixture and mix into flour mixture to form a firm dough.

3 Turn onto a floured surface and knead lightly until smooth. Divide dough into twelve equal portions, then roll each portion into a ball and place on greased and floured baking trays. Brush each roll with egg and oil mixture and bake for 30-35 minutes or until golden and cooked through.

Note: Spring onions and herbs have been added to this soda bread recipe. The dough is then formed into rolls to make the quickest herb-flavoured rolls ever.

Makes 12

ingredients

90g/3oz butter
8 spring onions, finely chopped
3½ cups/315g/10oz flour
4 teaspoons baking powder
½ teaspoon bicarbonate of soda
4 teaspoons sugar
1 tablespoon finely chopped fresh parsley
1 tablespoon finely chopped fresh basil
½ cup/125ml/4fl oz buttermilk or milk
3 eggs, lightly beaten
1 egg, beaten with 1½ tablespoons olive oil

Oven temperature 180°C, 350°F, Gas 4

herb
& cheese loaf

Method:

1 Place flour, baking powder, rolled oats, bran, tasty (mature Cheddar) cheese, Parmesan cheese, chives and parsley in a bowl and mix to combine. Make a well in the centre of the flour mixture, add milk and oil and mix well to combine.

2 Place egg whites in a clean bowl and beat until stiff peaks form. Fold egg whites into batter.

3 Spoon batter into a greased and lined 11x21cm/4^1/$_2$x8^1/$_2$in loaf tin and bake for 40 minutes or until cooked when tested with a skewer.

Note: This high-fibre loaf is terrific served warm.

Makes one 11x21cm/4^1/$_2$x8^1/$_2$in loaf

ingredients

1^1/$_4$ cups/185g/6oz wholemeal (wholewheat) flour
1^1/$_4$ teaspoon baking powder
1 cup/90g/3oz rolled oats
45g/1^1/$_2$oz unprocessed bran
60g/2oz grated tasty (mature Cheddar) cheese
1 tablespoon grated Parmesan cheese
2 tablespoons snipped fresh chives
2 tablespoons chopped fresh parsley
1 cup/250ml/8fl oz milk
^{1}/$_3$ cup/90ml/3fl oz vegetable oil
3 egg whites

Oven temperature 180°C, 350°F, Gas 4

carrot
& sesame muffins

Method:

1 Sift together flour, baking powder, bicarbonate of soda and mixed spice into a large bowl. Add sugar, carrot, sesame seeds and sultanas and mix to combine.

2 Place yoghurt, milk, butter and egg whites in a bowl and whisk to combine. Stir yoghurt mixture into flour mixture and mix until just combined. Spoon batter into lightly greased muffin tins and bake for 20 minutes or until golden and cooked.

Note: Delicious light muffins are perfect weekend fare. Any leftovers can be frozen and used when time is short.

Makes 24

ingredients

3 cups/375g/12oz all purpose flour
3^1/$_2$ teaspoons baking powder
^{1}/$_2$ teaspoon bicarbonate of soda (baking soda)
1 teaspoon ground mixed spice
^{1}/$_2$ cup/90g/3oz brown sugar
1 large carrot, grated
4 tablespoons toasted sesame seeds
170g/5^1/$_2$oz sultanas
1 cup/200g/6^1/$_2$oz natural yoghurt
1 cup/250ml/8fl oz milk
3 tablespoons melted butter
3 egg whites, lightly beaten

Oven temperature 200°C, 400°F, Gas 6

bacon cornbread pots

Method:

1 Cook bacon in a nonstick frying pan over a medium heat for 3-4 minutes or until crisp. Remove bacon from pan and drain on absorbent kitchen paper.

2 Place cornmeal flour (polenta), flour, baking powder, sugar, salt, Parmesan cheese and butter in a food processor and process until mixture resembles fine breadcrumbs.

3 Combine eggs and milk and, with machine running, pour into cornmeal (polenta) mixture and process until combined and batter is smooth. Take care not to overmix. Stir in bacon.

4 Spoon batter into three medium-sized terracotta flowerpots lined with well-greased aluminium foil. Place on a baking tray and bake for 25-30 minutes or until golden.

Note: Cooked in flowerpots these tasty cornbread loaves are a perfect accompaniment to soup or salad. Remember that the size of the flowerpots you use will determine the number of loaves you produce.

Serves 6
Makes 3 medium-sized flowerpot loaves

ingredients

4 rashers bacon, finely chopped
1 1/2 cups/250g/8oz fine cornmeal flour (polenta)
1 cup/125g/4oz flour
2 1/2 teaspoons baking powder
4 teaspoons sugar
1/2 teaspoon salt
60g/2oz grated Parmesan cheese
90g/3oz butter, chopped
2 eggs, lightly beaten
1 1/4 cups/315ml/10fl oz buttermilk or milk

Oven temperature 200°C, 400°F, Gas 6

609

monte carlo

cookies
and
biscuits

In this chapter you will find a wonderful

array of cookies and biscuits and other baked treats. It is easy to understand why this type of baked product is popular. Not only are they easy to make, but they come in a huge variety of flavours and textures. Best of all, they are just the right size for a snack.

coconut
cookies

Method:

1 *Place butter, sugar, vanilla essence, egg, flour, baking powder, rolled oats, coconut, lime rind and lime juice in a food processor and process until well combined.*

2 *Drop heaped teaspoons of mixture on greased baking trays and bake for 12-15 minutes or until lightly browned. Transfer to wire racks to cool.*

Note: *The tang of lime and the unique flavour and texture of coconut combine to make these wonderful cookies.*

Makes 35

125g/4oz butter, chopped
1 cup/170g/5¹/₂oz brown sugar
1 teaspoon vanilla essence
1 egg
1¹/₂ cup/125g/4oz flour
¹/₂ teaspoon baking powder
1 cup/90g/3oz rolled oats
45g/1¹/₂oz desiccated coconut
2 teaspoons finely grated lime rind
2 tablespoons lime juice

Oven temperature 180°C, 350°F, Gas 4

golden
oat biscuits

Method:

1 *Place rolled oats, flour, coconut and sugar in a large bowl. Combine golden syrup, butter, water and bicarbonate of soda.*

2 *Pour golden-syrup mixture into dry ingredients and mix well to combine. Drop teaspoons of mixture 3cm/1¹/₄in apart on greased baking trays and bake for 10-15 minutes or until biscuits are just firm. Stand on trays for 3 minutes before transferring to wire racks to cool.*

Note: *Biscuits should always be stored in an airtight container. Allow the biscuits to cool completely on wire cooling racks before storing.*

Makes 30

1 cup/90g/3oz rolled oats
1 cup/125g/4oz flour, sifted
90g/3oz desiccated coconut
1 cup/250g/8oz sugar
4 teaspoons golden syrup, warmed
125g/4oz butter, melted
2 tablespoons boiling water
1 teaspoon bicarbonate of soda

Oven temperature 180°C, 350°F, Gas 4

croissants

Method:

1 Sift flour onto a board and divide into four. Take one quarter and make a well in the centre. Place the yeast in this and mix with about 2-3 tablespoons warm milk-and-water mixture. The yeast must be dissolved and the dough soft.

2 Have ready a saucepan of warm water and drop the ball of yeast dough into this and set aside. Add the salt to the rest of the flour, make a well in the centre, add half the butter and work up, adding enough of the milk-and-water mixture to make a firm paste.

3 Beat on the board for about 5 minutes. Lift the yeast dough from the water – it should be spongy and well risen – mix into the paste thoroughly.

4 Turn into a floured bowl, cover with a plate and place in the refrigerator for 12 hours. Roll out the paste to a square, place the rest of the butter in the centre and fold up like a parcel.

5 Roll and fold the paste three times as for puff pastry, and a fourth if the butter is not completely absorbed. Rest the paste between every two turns and chill before shaping.

6 When ready for shaping, roll out very thinly to an oblong shape, divide into two lengthwise and cut each strip into triangles.

7 Roll up each one starting from the base and seal tip with beaten egg. Curl to form a crescent then set on a dampened baking tray. Let stand for about 10 minutes then brush with beaten egg. Bake in a hot oven 200°C/400°F for about 25 minutes.

Serves 4

375g/12oz flour
15g/¹/₂oz yeast
¹/₂ teaspoon salt
150ml/5oz warm milk and water
(half and half)
185g/6oz butter

Oven temperature 200°C, 400°F, Gas 6

coffee
kisses

ingredients

250g/8oz butter, softened
¹/₂ cup/100g/3¹/₂oz icing (powdered) sugar, sifted
2 teaspoons instant coffee powder dissolved in 1 tablespoon hot water, cooled
2 cups/250g/8oz flour, sifted
45g/1¹/₂oz dark chocolate, melted
icing (powdered) sugar

Method:

1 *Place butter and icing (powdered) sugar in a bowl and beat until light and fluffy. Stir in coffee mixture and flour.*

2 *Spoon mixture into a piping bag fitted with a medium star nozzle and pipe 2cm/³/₄in rounds of mixture 2cm/³/₄in apart on greased baking trays. Bake for 10-12 minutes or until lightly browned. Stand on trays for 5 minutes before removing to wire racks to cool completely.*

3 *Join biscuits with a little melted chocolate, then dust with icing sugar.*

Note: *These coffee-flavoured biscuits have a similar texture to shortbread – making the dough perfect for piping. For something different you can pipe 5cm/2in lengths instead of rounds. Rather than sandwiching the biscuits together with chocolate you might prefer to leave them plain and simply dusted with icing (powdered) sugar.*

Makes 25

afghan biscuits

Method:

1 Place butter and vanilla essence in a bowl and beat until light and fluffy. Gradually add sugar, beating well after each addition until mixture is creamy.

2 Sift together flour, baking powder and cocoa powder. Stir flour mixture into butter mixture, then fold in cornflakes and sultanas. Drop heaped teaspoons of mixture onto greased baking trays and bake for 12-15 minutes. Remove to wire racks to cool completely.

3 To make icing, place butter, cocoa powder and icing (powdered) sugar in a bowl and mix with enough water to make an icing of spreading consistency.

4 Place a little icing on each biscuit and sprinkle with almonds. Set aside until icing firms.

Note: Do not store different types of biscuits together as they absorb flavour and moisture from each other.

Makes 30

ingredients

200g/6¹/₂oz butter, softened
1 teaspoon vanilla essence
¹/₂ cup/100g/3¹/₂oz caster sugar
1¹/₂ cups/185g/6oz flour
1 teaspoon baking powder
1 tablespoon cocoa powder
90g/3oz cornflakes, crushed
2 tablespoons chopped sultanas
slivered almonds
Chocolate icing
15g/¹/₂oz butter, softened
1 tablespoon cocoa powder
1 cup/155g/5oz icing (powdered) sugar, sifted
1 tablespoon boiling water

Oven temperature 200°C, 400°F, Gas 6

melting moments

Method:

1 Place butter and icing (powdered) sugar in a bowl and beat until light and fluffy. Sift together cornflour and flour and stir into butter mixture.

2 Spoon mixture into a piping bag fitted with a large star nozzle and pipe small rosettes on greased baking trays, leaving space between each rosette. Bake for 15-20 minutes or until just golden. Allow biscuits to cool on trays.

3 To make filling, place butter in a bowl and beat until light and fluffy. Gradually add icing sugar and beat until creamy. Stir in lemon rind and lemon juice. Sandwich biscuits together with filling.

Note: Grease baking trays with a little vegetable oil. Biscuits should be of a uniform size; not only will they look more attractive but they will also cook more evenly.

Makes 24

ingredients

250g/8oz butter, softened
4 tablespoons icing sugar, sifted
1 cup/125g/4oz cornflour (cornstarch)
1 cup/125g/4oz flour
Lemon-cream filling
60g/2oz butter, softened
¹/₂ cup/75g/2¹/₂oz icing (powdered) sugar
2 teaspoons finely grated lemon rind
1 tablespoon lemon juice

Oven temperature 180°C, 350°F, Gas 4

ginger
snaps

Method:

1 Sift brown sugar, ginger and flour together into a bowl.

2 Place butter and golden syrup in a saucepan and cook over a low heat, stirring, until butter melts. Stir in bicarbonate of soda. Pour golden-syrup mixture into dry ingredients and mix until smooth.

3 Drop teaspoons of mixture onto greased baking trays and bake for 10-12 minutes or until golden. Remove from oven, loosen biscuits with a spatula and allow to cool on trays.

Note: As these biscuits cool, they become crisp.

Makes 45

1 cup/170g/5¹/₂oz brown sugar
3 teaspoons ground ginger
2 cups/250g/8oz flour
125g/4oz butter
1 cup/350g/11oz golden syrup
1 teaspoon bicarbonate of soda

Oven temperature 180°C, 350°F, Gas 4

617

christmas
cookies

Method:

1 Place butter and sugar in a bowl and beat until light and fluffy. Beat in egg, vanilla essence and milk and continue to beat until well combined.

2 Stir together flour and bicarbonate of soda and stir into butter mixture. Add hazelnuts, chocolate chips, coconut, sultanas and cherries and mix until well combined.

3 Drop tablespoons of mixture onto greased baking trays and bake for 15 minutes or until golden. Remove to wire racks to cool completely.

Note: Glacé fruits such as glacé cherries or pineapple should be rinsed and dried before using in cakes to remove the sugary coating. This will help to prevent the fruit from sinking to the bottom of the cake.

Makes 25

ingredients

125g/4oz butter
1 cup/220g/7oz caster sugar
1 egg, lightly beaten
2 teaspoons vanilla essence
¼ cup/60ml/2fl oz milk
1¼ cups/155g/5oz flour
½ teaspoon bicarbonate of soda
90g/3oz roasted hazelnuts, chopped
125g/4oz chocolate chips
90g/3oz shredded coconut
90g/3oz sultanas
90g/3oz glacé cherries, chopped

Oven temperature 180°C, 350°F, Gas 4

cinnamon
crisps

Method:

1 Place butter and ¾ cup/170g/5½oz sugar in a bowl and beat until light and fluffy. Add egg and beat well.

2 Sift together flour, baking powder and bicarbonate of soda and stir into butter mixture. Turn dough onto a floured surface and knead briefly. Wrap in plastic food wrap and refrigerate for 30 minutes or until firm.

3 Place cinnamon and remaining sugar in a small bowl and mix to combine. Roll dough into small balls, then roll balls in sugar mixture. Place 5cm/2in apart on lightly greased baking trays and bake for 8 minutes or until golden. Remove to wire racks to cool.

Note: Fat or shortening in whatever form makes a baked product tender and helps to improve its keeping quality. In most baked goods, top-quality margarine and butter are interchangeable.

Makes 25

ingredients

125g/4oz butter
1 cup/220g/7oz caster sugar
1 egg
1 cup/125g/4oz flour
½ teaspoon baking powder
½ teaspoon bicarbonate of soda
2 teaspoons ground cinnamon

cashew-nut
cookies

Photograph opposite

Method:

1 *Place butter and sugar in a bowl and beat until light and fluffy. Add vanilla essence and egg yolk and beat to combine.*

2 *Fold flour, baking powder and wheat germ into butter mixture. Turn dough onto a lightly floured surface and knead briefly. Shape into a log, wrap in plastic food wrap and refrigerate for 30 minutes or until firm.*

3 *Slice dough into 0.5cm/¼in slices and place on greased baking trays. Press a cashew nut into the top of each biscuit and bake for 10-12 minutes or until golden.*

Note: *Toasting nuts increases their flavour. To toast, place on a baking tray and cook at 180°C/350°F/Gas 4 for 5-10 minutes, shaking the tray from time to time. Take care that the nuts do not burn by removing them from the oven as soon as they are golden.*

Makes 48

ingredients

125g/4oz butter
⅓ cup/75g/2½ oz caster sugar
1 teaspoon vanilla essence
1 egg yolk
1 cup/185g/6oz flour, sifted
¾ teaspoon baking powder
2 tablespoons wheat germ
60g/2oz unsalted cashew nuts, toasted

Oven temperature 180°C, 350°F, Gas 4

chocolate-
almond balls

Photograph opposite

Method:

1 *Place cream and chocolate in a saucepan and cook over a low heat, stirring, until chocolate melts. Remove pan from heat and set aside to cool slightly. Stir in butter, cover and chill.*

2 *Using an electric mixer, beat chocolate mixture until soft peaks form. Return to the refrigerator until firm.*

3 *Place almonds and rice cereal in a bowl and mix to combine. Shape teaspoons of chocolate mixture into balls and roll in almond mixture. Store in an airtight container in the refrigerator.*

Note: *Served with coffee this uncooked biscuit makes a delicious after-dinner treat.*

Makes 24

ingredients

½ cup/125ml/4fl oz thickened
(double) cream
125g/4oz dark chocolate, chopped
15g½oz butter
60g/2oz almonds, finely
chopped, toasted
30g/1oz puffed rice cereal, crushed

Oven temperature 180°C, 350°F, Gas 4

triple choc-chip
cookies

Method:

1 Cream together sugars, margarine and vanilla essence. Add the egg and beat in well.
2 Sift the flour and baking powder together and add to the creamed mixture. Stir in the choc bits, milk bits and white bits.
3 Place teaspoonfuls of mixture onto lightly greased oven trays.
4 Bake in a 180°C/350°F oven for 15 minutes. Cool on tray 5 minutes before removing to wire tray to cool. Store in airtight container.

Makes 36

ingredients

½ cup/120g/4oz caster sugar
½ cup/75g/2½oz brown sugar
175g/6oz margarine
½ teaspoon vanilla essence
1 egg
1¾ cup/210g/7oz plain flour
1½ teaspoon baking powder
½ cup/75g/2½oz each choc bits, milk bits and white bits

Oven temperature 180°C, 350°F, Gas 4

peanut
cookies

Method:

1 *Cream peanut butter, butter and sugar together until light and fluffy. Add egg and vanilla and mix well. Stir flour and baking powder together and stir into the butter mixture. Mix to a stiff dough and, if necessary, add a little extra flour.*

2 *Take one rounded teaspoon of mixture and roll into a small ball. Repeat with remainder.*

3 *Cover the turntable with a sheet of non-stick baking paper cut to size. Place 10 balls around turntable 2cm/³/₄in in from the edge.*

4 *Flatten slightly with the back of a fork. Cook on high for 2 minutes. Re-press fork marks left on biscuits as soon as they are cooked if desired. Slide paper with biscuits onto a cake cooler and allow to cool before removing from paper. Cook remaining biscuits in the same manner.*

Makes 25-30 biscuits

ingredients

½ cup 120g/4oz peanut butter
90g/3oz butter
¾ cup/180g/6oz sugar
1 egg
½ teaspoon vanilla essence
1½ cups/180g/6oz flour
½ teaspoon baking powder

Oven temperature 180°C, 350°F, Gas 4

pecan
anzacs

Method:

1 *Melt margarine and golden syrup in a saucepan, and add the bicarbonate of soda dissolved in the boiling water.*

2 *Combine the oats, coconut, flour, sugar, and pecans. Pour the melted mixture over the dry ingredients and mix well. Place teaspoonfuls of the mixture onto greased oven trays allowing room for spreading.*

3 *Bake in an oven 160°C/330°C for 15 minutes or until golden. Cool biscuits a few minutes on tray before removing to a wire rack to cool completely.*

4 *Store in an airtight container.*

Makes approximately 48 biscuits

ingredients

125g/4oz margarine
1 tablespoon golden syrup
1 teaspoon of bicarbonate of soda
2 tablespoons boiling water
1 cup/90g/3oz rolled oats
³/₄ cup/65g/2oz desiccated coconut
1 cup/120g/4oz plain flour
1 cup/250g/8oz sugar
¹/₃ cup/75g/2¹/₂oz chopped pecans

prune & orange
cookies

Method:

1 Cream together margarine, icing sugar and orange rind, blend in the flour. Stir the prunes through the mixture.
2 Roll mixture into small balls and place on a lightly greased oven tray. Flatten with a fork.
3 Bake in an oven 180°C/350°F for 12-15 minutes.
4 Cool on a tray 5 minutes before removing to a wire rack to cool completely.
5 Decorate cookies with melted chocolate.

Makes 24

125g/4oz margarine
¹/₂ cup/75g/2¹/₃oz icing sugar
grated rind of 1 orange
1 cup/120g/4oz plain flour
¹/₂ cup/120g/4oz prunes, chopped
dark chocolate, melted

Oven temperature 180°C, 350°F, Gas 4

orange-
pistachio biscotti

Method:

1 Sift together flour, sugar, baking powder and salt into a bowl.

2 Place eggs, egg whites, orange rind and vanilla essence in a separate bowl and whisk to combine.

3 Stir egg mixture and pistachio nuts into flour mixture and mix to make a smooth dough. Turn dough onto a lightly floured surface and divide into two equal portions. Roll each portion into a log with a diameter of 5cm/2in. Flatten logs slightly and place 10cm/4in apart on a nonstick baking tray. Bake for 30 minutes. Remove from oven and set aside to cool.

4 Reduce oven temperature to 150°C/ 300°F/Gas 2.

5 Cut cooled logs into 1cm/½in thick slices, place on nonstick baking trays and bake for 10 minutes or until biscuits are crisp.

Makes 48

2 cups/250g/8oz flour
1 cup/250g/8oz sugar
1 teaspoon baking powder
pinch salt
2 eggs
2 egg whites
1 tablespoon finely grated orange rind
½ teaspoon vanilla essence
**75g/2½oz pistachios,
shelled and toasted**

Oven temperature 180°C, 350°F, Gas 4

sesame-pepper crackers

Method:

1 Place rice flour or flour, sesame seeds, sage and peppercorns in a bowl and mix to combine.

2 Combine mascarpone and tasty (mature Cheddar) cheese. Add cheese mixture to dry ingredients and mix to form a soft dough.

3 Turn dough onto a lightly floured surface, knead briefly and roll mixture into a sausage shape. Wrap in plastic food wrap and refrigerate for 40 minutes or until firm.

4 Cut into 1cm/½in-thick slices, place on lightly greased baking trays and brush with egg. Bake for 10 minutes or until biscuits are golden and crisp. Transfer to wire racks to cool.

Note: Mascarpone is made from cream. Unsalted and buttery with a fat content of 90 per cent, it is mostly used as a dessert cheese, either alone or as an ingredient. If it is unavailable, mix one part thick sour cream with three parts lightly whipped thickened (double) cream , or beat 250g/8oz ricotta cheese with 250ml/8fl oz pure (single) cream until the mixture is smooth and thick.

Makes 30

ingredients

1 cup/185g/6oz rice flour or
1 cup/125g/4oz flour, sifted
2 tablespoons sesame seeds, toasted
1 tablespoon chopped fresh sage or
1 teaspoon dried sage
2 teaspoons pink peppercorns, crushed
125g/4oz mascarpone
60g/2oz grated tasty (mature
Cheddar) cheese
1 egg, lightly beaten

mexican
cornbread

Method:

1 Place cornmeal flour (polenta), all-purpose flour and baking powder in a bowl. Add tasty (mature Cheddar) cheese , Parmesan cheese, olives, sun- dried tomatoes, sweet corn and green capsicums (peppers) in a bowl and mix to combine.

2 Combine eggs, milk, yoghurt and oil. Add egg mixture to dry ingredients and mix until just combined.

3 Pour mixture into a greased 20cm/8in springform pan and bake for 1 hour or until bread is cooked when tested with a skewer. Serve warm or cold.

Note: Split wedges of this loaf and layer with savoury fillings to create attractive sandwiches. This cornbread is also delicious served warm and topped with baked ricotta cheese.

Makes one 20cm/8in round loaf

ingredients

2 cups/350g/11oz cornmeal flour (polenta)
2 cups/250g/8oz all purpose flour, sifted
2¹/₂teaspoons baking powder
125g/4oz grated tasty
(mature Cheddar) cheese
60g/2oz grated Parmesan cheese
12 pitted black olives, sliced
12 sun-dried tomatoes, chopped
100g/3¹/₂oz canned sweet corn
kernels, drained
3 bottled green capsicums (peppers),
chopped finely
2 eggs, lightly beaten
1 cup/250ml/8fl oz milk
³/₄ cup/155g/5oz yoghurt
¹/₄ cup/60ml/2fl oz vegetable oil

Oven temperature 180°C, 350°F, Gas 4

Oven temperature 220°C, 425°F, Gas 7

ham-mustard
scrolls

Method:

1 *Place flour, baking powder and butter in a food processor and process until mixture resembles coarse breadcrumbs. With machine running, slowly add egg and milk and process to form a soft dough. Turn dough onto a lightly floured surface and press out to make a 1cm/¹/₂in-thick rectangle.*

2 *To make filling, place ham, ricotta cheese, tasty (mature Cheddar) cheese and mustard into a bowl and mix to combine. Spread filling over dough and roll up from short side.*

3 *Using a serrated edged knife, cut roll into 2cm/³/₄in thick slices and place on a lightly greased and floured baking tray. Bake for 15-20 minutes or until puffed and golden.*

Note: *These tangy scone pinwheels make an interesting accompaniment to egg dishes at breakfast or brunch. They can also be reheated briefly in the microwave oven for an afternoon snack.*

Makes 18

ingredients

2 cups/250g/8oz plain flour, sifted
2¹/₂ teaspoon baking powder, sifted
60g/2oz butter, chopped
1 egg, lightly beaten
¹/₂ cup/125ml/4fl oz milk
Ham and mustard filling
4 slices smoked ham, chopped
¹/₂ cup/125g/4oz ricotta cheese, drained
60g/2oz grated tasty
(mature Cheddar) cheese
2 tablespoons wholegrain mustard

thumbprint cookies

Method:
1 Place butter, icing sugar and vanilla essence in a bowl and beat until light and fluffy. Sift together flour, baking powder and custard powder. Fold flour mixture and milk, alternately, into butter mixture.
2 Roll tablespoons of mixture into balls and place on greased baking trays. Make a thumbprint in the centre of each cookie.
3 Fill thumbprint hole with a teaspoon of jam, lemon curd or chocolate. Bake for 12 minutes or until cookies are golden. Transfer to wire racks to cool.

Note: Wrap the dough in plastic food wrap and chill at least 30 minutes to make it easier to shape into balls. For a subtle toasty nut flavour, roll the balls in sesame seeds before making the thumbprint and filling.

Makes 30

ingredients

185g/6oz butter, softened
1/3 cup/45g/1 1/2oz icing sugar, sifted
1 teaspoon vanilla essence
1 teaspoon baking powder
1 1/2 cup/185g/6oz all purpose flour
1/2 cup/60g/2oz custard powder
1/4 cup/60ml/2fl oz milk
jam, lemon curd or chopped chocolate

Oven temperature 190°C, 375°F, Gas 5

---

monte carlo biscuits

Method:
1 Place butter, brown sugar and vanilla essence in a bowl and beat until light and fluffy. Add egg, flour, baking powder, coconut and rolled oats and mix well to combine.
2 Roll tablespoons of mixture into balls, place on greased baking trays and flatten slightly with a fork. Bake for 12 minutes or until biscuits are golden. Transfer to wire racks to cool.
3 To make Butter Cream, place butter, icing sugar and vanilla essence in a bowl and beat until light and fluffy. Spread half the biscuits with raspberry jam and top with Butter cream. Top with remaining biscuits.

Note: When shaping the biscuits ensure that all are of uniform size and appearance so that each pair is perfectly matched when sandwiched together.

Makes 20

ingredients

125g/4oz butter, softened
1 cup/170g/5 1/2oz brown sugar
2 teaspoons vanilla essence
1 egg, lightly beaten
1 1/2 cup/185g/6oz flour, sifted
1 teaspoon baking powder
90g/3oz desiccated coconut
3/4 cup/75g/2 1/2oz rolled oats
1/2 cup/155g/5oz raspberry jam
Butter cream
60g/2oz butter, softened
1/2 cup/75g/2 1/2oz icing sugar
1 teaspoon vanilla essence

Oven temperature 190°C, 375°F, Gas 5

pecan & cherry
bread

Method:

1 Beat egg whites until soft peaks form, gradually beat in sugar. Continue beating until mixture is firm and glossy. Fold through the sifted flour, pecans and cherries. Mix well. Spoon mixture into a grease 8cmx18cm/3x7in loaf pan

2 Bake in an oven 180°C/350°F for 30 minutes or until golden and firm to touch.

3 Cool cake in tin. Wrap in foil and refrigerate overnight. Next day cut the cake into thin slices and place on an ungreased baking tray. Bake in an oven 150°C/300°F until light and golden in colour. Cool. Store in an air tight container.

4 Serve with coffee or as a biscuit with ice cream.

3 egg whites
¹/₂ cup/120g/4oz castor sugar
1 cup/120g/4oz plain flour
³/₄ cup/90g/3oz pecan halves
¹/₂ cup/120g/4oz glacé cherries,
cut in half

Oven temperature 180°C, 350°F, Gas 4

gingerbread
people

Method:

1 Cream together the margarine and brown sugar, and beat in the egg yolk, mixing well. Sift in the flour, bicarbonate of soda and ginger and gradually blend into the creamed mixture, along with the golden syrup. Knead lightly to make a soft dough.

2 Divide the dough into small portions. Roll out each portion of dough to a thickness of ½ cm/¼in between two sheets of greaseproof paper. Cut into shapes using cutters.

3 Place on lightly greased oven trays. Bake in a 180°C/350°F oven for 10 minutes. Cool on trays.

Makes approximately 20 shapes (depending on size)

ingredients

125g/4oz margarine
½ cup/75g/2½oz brown sugar
1 egg yolk
2½ cups/300g/10oz plain flour
1 teaspoon bicarbonate of soda
3 teaspoons ginger ground
2½ tablespoons golden syrup

fig pinwheel
biscuits

1

2

3

ingredients

170g/5¹/₂oz butter
1 cup/170g/5¹/₂oz brown sugar
1 egg
¹/₂ teaspoon vanilla essence
3 cups/375g/12oz flour
¹/₂ teaspoon bicarbonate of soda
¹/₄ teaspoon ground cinnamon
¹/₄ teaspoon ground nutmeg
2 tablespoons milk
Fig and almond filling
250g/8oz dried figs,
finely chopped
¹/₄ cup/60g/2oz sugar
¹/₂ cup/125ml/4fl oz
water
¹/₄ teaspoon ground
mixed spice
30g/1oz almonds,
finely chopped

Method:

1. To make filling, place figs, sugar, water and mixed spice in a saucepan and bring to the boil. Reduce heat and cook, stirring, for 2-3 minutes or until mixture is thick. Remove pan from heat and stir in almonds. Set aside to cool.

2. Place butter in a bowl and beat until light and fluffy. Gradually add sugar, beating well after each addition until mixture is creamy. Beat in egg and vanilla essence.

3. Sift together flour, bicarbonate of soda, cinnamon and nutmeg. Beat milk and half the flour mixture into butter mixture. Stir in remaining flour mixture. Turn dough onto a lightly floured surface and knead briefly. Roll into a ball, wrap in plastic food wrap and refrigerate for 30 minutes.

4. Divide dough into two portions. Roll one portion out to a 20x28cm/8x11in rectangle and spread with half the filling. Roll up like a Swiss roll from the long side. Repeat with remaining dough and filling. Wrap rolls in plastic food wrap and refrigerate for 15 minutes or until you are ready to cook the biscuits.

5. Cut rolls into 1cm/¹/₂in-thick slices. Place slices on lightly greased baking trays and bake for 10-12 minutes. Stand biscuits on trays for 1 minute before removing to wire racks to cool completely.

Note: The uncooked rolls can be frozen if you wish. When you have unexpected guests, or the biscuit barrel is empty, these biscuits are great standbys.

Makes 50

palmiers

ingredients

170g/5¹/₂oz prepared puff pastry
15g/¹/₂oz butter, melted and cooled
3 tablespoons demerara sugar

1

2   3

Method:

1 Roll out pastry to make a 25cm/10in square, 3cm/1¹/₈in thick.
2 Brush with butter and sprinkle with a little sugar. Fold two opposite edges of pastry half way towards the centre.
3 Sprinkle with a little more sugar and fold, taking edges to the centre. Sprinkle with a more sugar and fold one half of pastry over the other half. Press lightly to join.
4 Cut pastry roll into 18 slices and place on a greased baking tray. Flatten slightly and bake for 10-15 minutes or until puffed and golden.

Pistachio Palmiers:
Combine 15g/¹/₂oz finely chopped unsalted pistachio nuts and 3 tablespoons soft brown sugar, and sprinkle over pastry in place of the demerara sugar.

Almond Palmiers:
Combine 3 tablespoons ground almonds, 2 tablespoons caster sugar and 1 teaspoon ground mixed spice and sprinkle over pastry in place of the demerara sugar.

Note: The secret to making these heart-shaped pastries is in the way that the pastry is folded. Palmiers are a great way to use left over puff pastry. Try sandwiching the palmierstogether with whipped cream. Delicious!

Makes 18

chocolate

sensations

Ah, chocolate!

From Aztec times people have enjoyed the tastes provided by the seeds of the tropical cocoa tree, called cocoa beans, which are the source of chocolate.

Advances in processing over the years have produced a variety of wonderful products, from unsweetened cocoa drink to milk chocolate. Cocoa pods are harvested and then broken open, removing the seeds and pulp. Seeds are then fermented for a period of two to ten days, to develop flavour; they are then dried, graded, packed and shipped to all corners of the world.

Chocolate manufacturers blend seeds from various areas to obtain a consistent style and flavour. The selected seeds are cleaned and blended then roasted to further develop flavour and aroma. After roasting and cooling, seeds are shelled, saving the meat, and the unwanted shells are normally sold off for animal feed. The meat (or nibs) which are about 50 percent cocoa butter, are then ground to produce chocolate liquor. The manufacturer will then use this ingredient alone, or blended with other ingredients to make specific types of chocolate or chocolate products.

Chocolate types

Chocolate-flavoured syrup:

Basically corn syrup and cocoa with preservatives , emulsifiers, and flavourings.

Commercial coating chocolate:

Used by professional confectioners who use coating chocolate for dipping and for making curls, ruffles and other garnishes. It has more cocoa butter than regular baking chocolate which allows it to melt and spread well.

Compound chocolate coating:

This is an imitation product and does not normally contain cocoa.

Eating chocolate:

Cocoa and sugar are added to chocolate liquor. Distinctions of bittersweet, semisweet and sweet do not correspond to any fixed degree of sweetness; the amount of sugar depends on the formula of the individual manufacturer.

Milk chocolate:

Dried milk solids are added to sweetened chocolate. Widely used for chocolate bars and confectionary, but rarely used for cooking.

Powdered cocoa:

Enough cocoa is pressed out of the chocolate liquor to leave a press cake with a content of between 10 to 25 percent cocoa butter.

Instant cocoa:

Contains lecithin, an emulsifier that makes cocoa easier to dissolve in cold liquids.

Solid unsweeted chocolate:

Generally poured into moulds and solidified. Used mainly in cooking.

White chocolate:

Lacks chocolate liquor, so is technically not real chocolate. Contains cocoa butter with added sugar, milk and flavourings. May contain lecithin and usually vanilla or vanillin. Should not be substituted for chocolate in recipes.

Whatever the occasion, chocolate is a celebration all of its own!

This collection of mouth-watering cakes, puddings and desserts is guaranteed to gladden the hearts and delight the taste buds of chocolate lovers everywhere. Luscious cakes and gateaux, creamy desserts and puddings, fresh fruit combinations, feather-light souffles and chocolate box treats, all are represented here. Whether you yearn for old favourites, chocolate home-bakes, or a spectacular centrepiece for that special celebration, these recipes are sure to satisfy the longings of even the most discerning chocoholics.

choc-almond biscotti

biscuit barrel

Reach into the barrel and pull out a

lusciously rich and sumptuous chocolate treat. Temptations in this chapter cover cookies, biscuits, brownies, biscotti, blondies, and macaroons.

mocha-
truffle cookies

Photograph on right

ingredients

125g/4oz butter, chopped
90g/3oz dark chocolate, broken into pieces
2 tablespoons instant espresso coffee powder
2¹/₂ cups/315g/10oz flour
¹/₂ cup/45g/1¹/₂oz cocoa powder
1 teaspoon baking powder
2 eggs, lightly beaten
1 cup/250g/8oz sugar
1 cup/170g/5¹/₂oz brown sugar
2 teaspoons vanilla essence
125g/4oz pecans, chopped

Oven temperature 180°C, 350°F, Gas 4

Method:

1 *Place butter, chocolate and coffee powder in a heatproof bowl. Set over a saucepan of simmering water and heat, stirring, until mixture is smooth. Remove bowl from pan and set aside to cool slightly.*

2 *Sift together flour, cocoa powder and baking powder into a bowl. Add eggs, sugar, brown sugar, vanilla essence and chocolate mixture and mix well to combine. Stir in pecans.*

3 *Drop tablespoons of mixture onto greased baking trays and bake for 12 minutes or until puffed. Stand cookies on trays for 2 minutes before transferring to wire racks to cool.*

Note: *This is the biscuit version of the traditional rich truffle confection and tastes delicious as an after-dinner treat with coffee.*

Makes 40

choc
layer biscuits

Photograph on right

ingredients

250g/8oz butter
1 cup/170g/5¹/₂oz brown sugar
³/₄ cup/185g/6oz sugar
2 teaspoons vanilla essence
1 egg
2³/₄ cups/350g/11oz flour
1 teaspoon baking powder
¹/₂ cup/45g/1¹/₂oz cocoa powder
¹/₂ cup/45g/1¹/₂oz malted milk powder

Oven temperature 180°C, 350°F, Gas 4

Method:

1 *Place butter, brown sugar, sugar and vanilla essence in a bowl and beat until light and fluffy. Add egg and beat well. Sift together flour and baking powder. Add flour mixture to butter mixture and mix to make a soft dough.*

2 *Divide dough into two equal portions. Knead cocoa powder into one portion and malted milk powder into the other.*

3 *Roll out each portion of dough separately on nonstick baking paper to make a 20x30cm/8x12in rectangle. Place chocolate dough on top of malt dough and press together.*

4 *Cut in half lengthwise and place one layer of dough on top of the other. You should now have four layers of dough in alternating colours. Place layered dough on a tray, cover with plastic food wrap and chill for 1 hour.*

5 *Cut dough into 1cm/¹/₂in-wide fingers and place on greased baking trays. Bake for 15 minutes or until biscuits are golden and crisp. Transfer to wire racks to cool.*

Note: *For a special occasion, dip the ends of cooled biscuits into melted white or dark chocolate and place on a wire rack until chocolate sets.*

Makes 40

original
choc-chip cookies

Method:

1 Place butter and sugar in a bowl and beat until light and fluffy. Beat in egg.
2 Add sifted flour and baking powder, coconut, chocolate chips and hazelnuts to butter mixture and mix to combine.
3 Drop tablespoons of mixture onto greased baking trays and bake for 12-15 minutes or until cookies are golden. Transfer to wire racks to cool.

Note: Everyone's favourite biscuit, it is full of the flavour of coconut, toasted hazelnuts and a generous portion of chocolate chips!

Makes 35

ingredients

250g/8oz butter, softened
1 cup/170g/5¹/₂oz brown sugar
1 egg
2 cups/250g/6oz plain flour
1¹/₄ teaspoons baking powder
45g/1¹/₂oz desiccated coconut
220g/7oz chocolate chips
185g/6oz hazelnuts, toasted, roughly chopped

Oven temperature 180°C, 350°F, Gas 4

double-choc
brownies

Method:

1 Place sugar, chocolate, oil, vanilla essence and eggs in a bowl and whisk to combine. Sift together flour and baking powder. Add flour mixture to chocolate mixture and mix well to combine.

2 Pour mixture into a greased and lined 20cm/ 8in-square cake tin and bake for 40 minutes or until firm to touch. Cool in tin, then cut into 5cm/2in squares and place on a wire rack.

3 To make glaze, place chocolate in a heatproof bowl set over a saucepan of simmering water and heat, stirring, until chocolate melts. Stir in oil. Spoon glaze over brownies and stand until set.

Note: These intensely chocolatey and tender treats will stay moist and delicious for several days if stored in an airtight container in a cool, dry place.

Makes 20

ingredients

1 ¹/₂ cups/375g/12oz sugar
200g/6¹/₂oz dark chocolate, melted
1 cup/250ml/8fl oz vegetable oil
2 teaspoons vanilla essence
4 eggs
1 ³/₄ cups/220g/7oz flour
1 teaspoon baking powder
<u>Chocolate glaze</u>
185g/6oz dark chocolate
2 teaspoons vegetable oil

Oven temperature 180°C, 350°F, Gas 4

chocky road
biscuits

Photograph on right

Method:

1 Place butter and sugar in a bowl and beat until light and fluffy. Gradually beat in eggs.

2 Sift together flour and cocoa powder. Add flour mixture, milk, chocolate, peanuts and chocolate chips to egg mixture and mix well to combine.

3 Drop tablespoons of mixture onto lightly greased baking trays and bake for 10 minutes or until biscuits are cooked. Transfer to wire racks to cool.

Note: Marshmallows, peanuts and chocolate chips must be the three most favourite additions to any biscuit designed for kids.

Makes 36

ingredients

250g/8oz butter, softened
1 cup/170g/5¹/2oz brown sugar
2 eggs, lightly beaten
3 cups/375g/12oz flour
1 cup/100g/3¹/2oz cocoa powder
1/4 cup/60ml/2fl oz buttermilk or milk
155g/5oz white chocolate, roughly chopped
90g/3oz dry roasted peanuts
185g/6oz chocolate chips

Oven temperature 180°C, 350°F, Gas 4

crazy
cookies

Photograph on right

Method:

1 Place chocolate in a heatproof bowl set over a saucepan of simmering water and heat, stirring, until smooth. Remove bowl from pan and set aside to cool slightly.

2 Place butter and sugar in a bowl and beat until light and fluffy. Add flour, and baking powder and chocolate to butter mixture and mix well to combine.

3 Roll tablespoons of mixture into balls and place on lightly greased baking trays. Flatten slightly and press a chocolate freckle or a caramel whirl into the centre of each cookie. Bake for 12 minutes or until cookies are firm. Transfer to wire racks to cool.

Note: A buttery shortbread-biscuit base is the perfect foil for sweet confectionery decorations.

Makes 36

ingredients

75g/2¹/2oz milk chocolate
220g/7oz butter, softened
1 cup/220g/7oz caster sugar
1¹/2 cups/185g/6oz plain flour
3/4 teaspoons baking powder
60g/2oz freckles (hundreds-and-thousands-coated chocolates)
60g/2oz caramel whirls

Oven temperature 180°C, 350°F, Gas 4

choc-almond
biscotti

Photograph also appears on Page 643

Method:

1 Sift together flour, cocoa powder and bicarbonate of soda into a bowl. Make a well in the centre of the flour mixture, add sugar, almonds and eggs and mix well to form a soft dough.

2 Turn dough onto a lightly floured surface and knead until smooth. Divide dough into four equal portions. Roll out each portion of dough to make a strip that is 5mm/^{1}/4in thick and 4cm/1^1/2in wide.

3 Place strips on a baking tray lined with nonstick baking paper. Brush with egg yolk and bake for 30 minutes or until lightly browned. Cut strips into 1cm/^{1}/2in slices, return to baking tray and bake for 10 minutes longer or until dry.

Note: Biscuits may be partially dipped into melted chocolate for a two-toned effect. Before the chocolate sets completely, dip into toasted crushed almonds.

Makes 35

ingredients

2 cups/250g/8oz flour
^{3}/4 cup/75g/2^1/2oz cocoa powder
1 teaspoon bicarbonate of soda
1 cup/250g/8oz sugar
200g/6^1/2oz blanched almonds
2 eggs
1 egg yolk

Oven temperature 180°C, 350°F, Gas 4

double-fudge
blondies

Method:

1 To make filling, place cream cheese, chocolate, maple syrup, egg and flour in a bowl and beat until smooth. Set aside.

2 Place butter, sugar and vanilla essence in a bowl and beat until light and fluffy. Gradually beat in eggs.

3 Sift together flour and baking powder over butter mixture. Add chocolate and mix well to combine.

4 Spread half the mixture over the base of a greased and lined 23cm/9in-square cake tin. Top with cream-cheese filling and then with remaining mixture. Bake for 40 minutes or until firm. Cool in tin, then cut into squares.

Note: These lusciously rich white brownies can double as a dinner party dessert if drizzled with melted white or dark chocolate and topped with toasted flaked almonds.

Makes 24

ingredients

250g/8oz butter, softened
1 1/2 cups/375g/12oz sugar
1 teaspoon vanilla essence
4 eggs, lightly beaten
1 3/4 cups/220g/7oz flour
1/2 teaspoon baking powder
185g/6oz white chocolate, melted
<u>Cream-cheese filling</u>
250g/8oz cream cheese, softened
60g/2oz white chocolate, melted
1/4 cup/60ml/2fl oz maple syrup
1 egg
1 tablespoon flour

Oven temperature 180°C, 350°F, Gas 4

night-sky cookies

Photograph on right

Method:

1 *Place butter, sugar and almond essence in a bowl and beat until light and fluffy. Gradually beat in egg.*
2 *Sift together flour and baking powder. Fold flour mixture and milk, alternately, into butter mixture and mix to form a soft dough.*
3 *Roll out dough on a lightly floured surface to 0.5cm/¹/₄in thick. Using a star and a moon-shaped cookie cutter, cut out cookies. Place cookies on lightly greased baking trays and bake for 10 minutes or until cookies are golden and cooked. Transfer to wire racks to cool.*
4 *Dip tops of moon-shaped cookies in white chocolate and tips of star-shaped cookies in dark chocolate. Place on wire racks to set.*
   Makes 24

ingredients

125g/4oz butter, softened
³/₄ cup/170g/5¹/₂oz caster sugar
¹/₂ teaspoon almond essence
1 egg, lightly beaten
2 cups/250g/8oz flour
¹/₂ teaspoon baking powder
¹/₄ cup/60ml/2fl oz milk
125g/4oz dark chocolate, melted
90g/3oz white chocolate, melted

Oven temperature 190°C, 375°F, Gas 5

chocolate macaroons

Photograph on right

Method:

1 *Place egg whites in a bowl and beat until stiff peaks form. Gradually beat in sugar and continue beating until mixture is thick and glossy.*
2 *Fold cocoa powder and coconut into egg whites. Drop tablespoons of mixture onto greased baking trays and bake for 15 minutes or until macaroons are firm. Transfer to wire racks to cool.*
   Note: *Avoid baking these on a humid day as moisture will affect their texture. Store macaroons in an airtight container in a cool, dry place.*
   Makes 20

ingredients

2 egg whites
³/₄ cup/170g/5¹/₂oz caster sugar
¹/₂ cup/45g/1¹/₂oz cocoa powder, sifted
1¹/₂ cups/140g/4¹/₂oz shredded coconut

Oven temperature 180°C, 350°F, Gas 4

chocolate-mocha cake

a
piece
of cake

Whether it be for a tempting snack,

a special treat or a formal afternoon tea, a freshly
baked cake is the most universally accepted offering.
Try cake cut in wedges with cream, or a rich buttery
cake served on its own or with a rich chocolate sauce.
The baked delights within this chapter include:
cheesecake, torte, mud cake, choc-meringue cake,
yoghurt cake, pound cake, gâteau and even
Grandma's favourite chocolate cake.

choc-meringue
cake

choc-meringue cake

ingredients

Hazelnut meringue
155g/5oz hazelnuts, ground
2 tablespoons cornstarch
1¼ cups 315g sugar
6 egg whites
Chocolate filling
220g/8oz unsalted butter
185g/6oz dark chocolate, melted
3 tablespoons caster sugar
2 cups/500ml/16fl oz cream
2 tablespoons brandy
125g/4oz hazelnuts, ground
Chocolate topping
155g/5oz dark chocolate
2 teaspoon vegetable oil
whipped cream, for decoration

Oven temperature 120°C, 250°F, Gas 1

Method:

1 To make meringue, mix together ground hazelnuts, cornstarch and ³/₄ cup/ 185g sugar. Beat egg whites until soft peaks form, add remaining sugar a little at a time and beat until thick and glossy. Fold into hazelnut mixture.

2 Mark three 20cm/8in squares on baking paper and place on baking trays. Place meringue mixture in a piping bag fitted with a small plain nozzle and pipe mixture to outline squares, then fill squares with piped lines of mixture. Bake for 40-50 minutes, or until crisp and dry.

3 To make filling, beat butter until soft. Add chocolate, caster sugar and cream and beat until thick. Fold in brandy and hazelnuts.

4 To make topping, place chocolate and oil in the top of a double saucepan and heat over simmering water, stirring until chocolate melts and mixture is smooth. Remove top pan and set aside to cool.

5 To assemble cake, place a layer of meringue on a serving plate and spread with half the filling. Top with another meringue layer and remaining filling. Cut remaining meringue into squares and position at angles on top of cake. Drizzle with topping and decorate with cream.

Serves 10

Oven temperature 190°C, 375°F, Gas 5

chocolate
pound cake

Method:

1 Place butter, sugar and vanilla essence in a bowl and beat until light and fluffy. Gradually beat in eggs.

2 Sift together baking powder, flour and cocoa powder. Fold flour mixture and milk, alternately, into butter mixture.

3 Pour mixture into a greased and lined 20cm/8in-square cake tin and bake for 55 minutes or until cake is cooked when tested with a skewer. Stand cake in tin for 10 minutes before turning onto a wire rack to cool.

Note: This rich buttery cake can be served plain, with a readymade chocolate sauce or with cream. A simple glacé icing drizzled over the top makes another delicious alternative.

Makes one 20cm/8in square cake

ingredients

185g/6oz butter, softened
1½ cups/330g/10½oz caster sugar
3 teaspoons vanilla essence
3 eggs, lightly beaten
2 cups/250g/8oz plain flour
2 teaspoons baking powder
½ cup/45g/1½oz cocoa powder
1¼ cups/315ml/10fl oz milk

grandma's
chocolate cake

Method:

1 *Place butter, caster sugar, eggs and vanilla essence in a bowl and beat until light and fluffy. Sift together baking powder, flour and cocoa powder.*

2 *Fold flour mixture and milk, alternately, into butter mixture. Divide mixture between four greased and lined 2cm/9in-round cake tins and bake for 25 minutes or until cakes are cooked when tested with a skewer. Turn cakes onto wire racks to cool.*

3 *To make filling, place chocolate and butter in a heatproof bowl set over a saucepan of simmering water and heat, stirring, until mixture is smooth. Remove bowl from pan. Add icing sugar and sour cream and mix until smooth.*

4 *To assemble cake, place one cake on a serving plate, spread with some jam and top with some filling. Top with a second cake, some more jam and filling. Repeat layers to use all cakes and jam. Finish with a layer of cake and spread remaining filling over top and sides of cake.*

Makes one 23cm/9in-round cake

ingredients

125g/4oz butter, softened
2 cups/440g/14oz caster sugar
2 eggs
2 teaspoons vanilla essence
1 3/4 cup/215g/7oz plain flour
2 teaspoons baking powder
3/4 cup/75g/2 1/2oz cocoa powder
1 cup/250ml/8fl oz buttermilk
<u>**Chocolate sour-cream filling**</u>
185g/6oz dark chocolate,
broken into pieces
125g/4oz butter, chopped
3 1/4 cups/500g/1 lb icing sugar, sifted
1/2 cup/125g/4oz sour cream
3/4 cup/235g/7 1/2oz raspberry jam

oven temperature 180°C, 350°F, Gas 4

659

chocolate-
espresso cheesecake

Photograph on right

Method:

1 To make base, place biscuit crumbs and butter in a bowl and mix to combine. Press mixture over the base of a lightly greased and lined 20cm/8in springform tin. Refrigerate until firm.

2 To make filling, place coffee powder and water in a bowl and mix until coffee powder dissolves. Set aside to cool slightly.

3 Place cream cheese, sour cream, eggs, sugar and coffee mixture in a bowl and beat until smooth.

4 Pour half the filling over prepared base. Drop 4 tablespoons of melted chocolate into filling and swirl with a skewer. Repeat with remaining filling and chocolate and bake for 40 minutes or until cheesecake is firm. Cool in tin.

5 To make glaze, place liqueur and rum into a saucepan and bring to simmering over a medium heat. Simmer, stirring occasionally, until mixture reduces by half. Add chocolate, butter and cream and cook, stirring, until mixture is smooth. Remove pan from heat and set aside until mixture thickens slightly. Spread glaze over cheesecake and allow to set.

Serves 10

ingredients

250g/8oz chocolate wafer biscuits, crushed
155g/5oz butter, melted
Chocolate-espresso filling
2 tablespoons instant espresso coffee powder
1 tablespoon hot water
250g/8oz cream cheese, softened
1 cup/250g/8oz sour cream
3 eggs, lightly beaten
1 cup/250g/8oz sugar
155g/5oz dark chocolate, melted
Coffee liqueur glaze
1/4 cup/60mL/2fl oz coffee-flavoured liqueur
1/4 cup/60ml/2fl oz rum
250g/8oz dark chocolate, broken into pieces
60g/2oz butter
1/2 cup/125ml/4fl oz thickened cream (double)

chocolate-
hazelnut torte

Photograph on right

Method:

1 Place chocolate in a heatproof bowl set over a saucepan of simmering water and heat, stirring, until chocolate melts. Remove bowl from pan and let cool slightly.

2 Place egg yolks and sugar in a bowl and beat until thick and pale. Fold chocolate, hazelnuts and rum into egg mixture.

3 Place egg whites into a clean bowl and beat until stiff peaks form. Fold egg whites into chocolate mixture. Pour mixture into a greased and lined 23cm/9in springform tin and bake for 50 minutes or until cake is cooked when tested with a skewer. Cool cake in tin. Dust cake with icing sugar just prior to serving.

Serves 8

ingredients

250g/8oz dark chocolate, broken into pieces
6 eggs, separated
1 cup/250g/8oz sugar
315g/10oz hazelnuts, toasted and roughly chopped
1 tablespoon rum
icing sugar, sifted

chocolate-pecan
gâteau

Method:

1 Place egg yolks, sugar and brandy in a bowl and beat until thick and pale. Place egg whites in a clean bowl and beat until stiff peaks form. Fold egg whites, pecans and flour into egg yolk mixture.

2 Pour mixture into a lightly greased and lined 23cm/9in springform tin and bake for 40 minutes or until cake is firm. Cool in tin.

3 To make glaze, place chocolate, coffee powder, cream and brandy in a heatproof bowl set over a saucepan of simmering water and heat, stirring, until mixture is smooth. Remove bowl from pan and set aside to cool slightly. Spread glaze over top and sides of cooled cake. Sprinkle pecans over top of cake and press into side of cake. Allow to set before serving.

Serves 8

ingredients

4 eggs, separated
³/₄ cup/170g/5³/₄oz caster sugar
2 tablespoons brandy
200g/6¹/₂oz pecans, roughly chopped
2 tablespoons flour
<u>Chocolate-brandy glaze</u>
315g/10oz milk chocolate
2 teaspoons instant coffee powder
¹/₃ cup/90ml/3fl oz thickened cream (double)
I tablespoon brandy
155g/5oz pecans, roughly chopped

Oven temperature 160°C, 325°F, Gas 3

simple
chocolate cake

Method:

1 Place butter, sugar and vanilla essence in a bowl and beat until light and fluffy. Gradually beat in eggs.

2 Sift flour, baking powder, cocoa powder and bicarbonate of soda together into a bowl. Fold flour mixture and milk alternately into egg mixture.

3 Pour mixture into a greased and lined 18cm/7in-square cake tin and bake for 40 minutes or until cake is cooked when tested with a skewer. Stand cake in tin for 5 minutes before turning onto a wire rack to cool.

4 To make icing, place chocolate, butter and cream in a heatproof bowl set over a saucepan of simmering water and heat, stirring constantly, until mixture is smooth. Remove bowl from pan and set aside to cool slightly. Spread top and sides of cake with icing and decorate with gold or silver dragees.

**Makes one
18cm/7in-square cake**

ingredients

125g/4oz butter, softened
1 cup/250g/8oz sugar
1 teaspoon vanilla essence
2 eggs, lightly beaten
1 1/4 cups/155g/5oz all purpose flour
1 1/2 teaspoons baking powder
1/2 cup/45g/1 1/2oz cocoa powder
1 teaspoon bicarbonate of soda
1 cup/250ml/8fl oz milk
gold or silver dragees
<u>Chocolate-butter icing</u>
125g/4oz dark chocolate
60g/2oz butter
1/4 cup/60ml/2fl oz thickened cream (double)

Oven temperature 180°C, 350°F, Gas 4

white chocolate-
yoghurt cake

Method:

1 Place chocolate in a heatproof bowl set over a saucepan of simmering water and heat, stirring, until smooth. Remove bowl from pan and cool slightly.

2 Place flour, baking powder, sugar, eggs, yogurt and butter in a bowl and beat for 5 minutes or until mixture is smooth. Add melted chocolate and mix well to combine.

3 Pour mixture into a greased 23cm/9in-ring tin and bake for 50 minutes or until cake is cooked when tested with a skewer. Stand cake in tin for 5 minutes before turning onto a wire rack to cool.

4 To make icing, place chocolate and cream in a heatproof bowl set over a saucepan of simmering water and heat, stirring, until mixture is smooth. Spread icing over top and sides of cake.

Makes one 23cm/9in-ring cake

ingredients

155g/5oz white chocolate, broken into pieces
2 cups/250g/8oz all purpose flour
2¼ teaspoons baking powder
1 cup/220g/7oz caster sugar
2 eggs, lightly beaten
200g/6½oz natural yoghurt
45g/1½oz butter, melted
<u>White chocolate icing</u>
75g/2½oz white chocolate
1 tablespoon thickened cream (double)

a piece of cake

Oven temperature 180°C, 350°F, Gas 4

the best
mud cake

Method:

1 Place chocolate, caster sugar and butter in a heatproof bowl set over a saucepan of simmering water and heat, stirring, until mixture is smooth. Remove bowl and set aside to cool slightly. Beat in egg yolks one at a time, beating well after each addition. Fold in flour.

2 Place egg whites in a clean bowl and beat until stiff peaks form. Fold egg whites into chocolate mixture. Pour mixture into a greased 23cm/9in springform tin and bake for 45 minutes or until cake is cooked when tested with a skewer. Cool cake in tin.

3 Just prior to serving dust cake with cocoa powder and icing sugar.

Makes one 23cm/9in-round cake

ingredients

**350g/11oz dark chocolate,
broken into pieces
³/4 cup/170g/5¹/2oz caster sugar
185g/6oz butter, chopped
5 eggs, separated
¹/3 cup/45g/1¹/2oz flour, sifted
cocoa powder, sifted
icing sugar, sifted**

devil's
food cake

Method:

1 Combine cocoa powder and water in a small bowl and mix until blended. Set aside to cool. Place butter and vanilla essence in a large mixing bowl and beat until light and fluffy. Gradually add sugar, beating well after each addition until mixture is creamy. Beat in eggs one at a time, beating well after each addition.

2 Sift together flour, cornflour, bicarbonate of soda and salt into a bowl. Fold flour mixture and cocoa mixture alternately into egg mixture.

3 Divide batter between three greased and lined 23cm/9in sandwich tins and bake for 20-25 minutes or until cakes are cooked when tested with a skewer. Stand in tins for 5 minutes before turning onto wire racks to cool completely.

4 To make icing, place butter in a mixing bowl and beat until light and fluffy. Mix in egg, egg yolks and icing sugar. Add chocolate and beat until icing is thick and creamy. Sandwich cakes together using whipped cream then cover top and sides with icing.

Serves 12

ingredients

1 cup/100g/3½ oz cocoa powder
1½ cups/375ml/12fl oz boiling water
375g/12oz unsalted butter, softened
1 teaspoon vanilla essence
1½ cups/315g/10oz caster sugar
4 eggs
2½ cups/315g/10oz flour
½ cup/60g/2oz cornflour
1 teaspoon bicarbonate of soda
1 teaspoon salt
½ cup/125ml/4fl oz thickened
double cream , whipped
Chocolate butter icing
250g/8oz butter, softened
1 egg and 2 egg yolks
1 cup/155g/5oz icing sugar, sifted
185g/6oz dark chocolate, melted & cooled

Oven temperature 180°C, 350°F, Gas 4

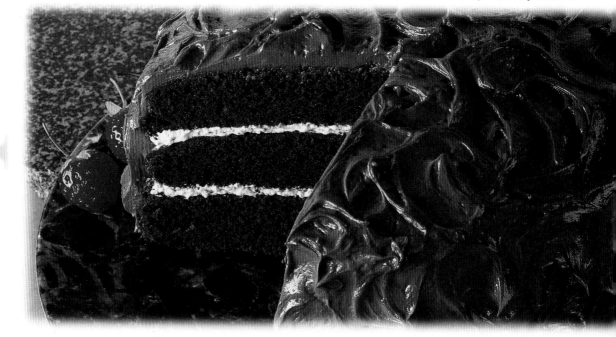

chocolate-
mocha cake

Photograph also appears on page 655

Method:

1 *Place chocolate in top of a double saucepan and heat over simmering water for 5 minutes, or until chocolate melts. Remove top pan from heat and stir until smooth. Set aside to cool.*

2 *Place egg yolks and sugar in a bowl and beat until pale and fluffy. Add butter and beat mixture until creamy. Add coffee and chocolate and continue beating mixture until creamy. Sift flour over mixture and fold in lightly.*

3 *Beat egg whites until soft peaks form. Lightly fold egg-white mixture into chocolate mixture. Pour into a greased and lined 20cm/8in-round cake tin and bake for 30 minutes, or until firm to touch. Turn off oven and cool cake in oven with door ajar. Remove from tin and refrigerate for 2 hours or overnight.*

4 *To make glaze, place chocolate, butter and water in top of a double saucepan and heat over simmering water until chocolate and butter melt. Remove top pan from heat and stir ingredients to combine. Set aside to cool.*

5 *Remove cake from refrigerator and place on a wire rack. Place on a tray and pour glaze over cake, smoothing it over edges and onto sides with a spatula. Leave until completely set. Transfer cake to a flat serving platter and cut into slices to serve.*

ingredients

**185g/6oz dark chocolate,
broken into small pieces
4 eggs, separated
1/2 cup/110g/3 1/2oz caster sugar
185g/6oz unsalted butter, softened
and cut into pieces
2 tablespoons strong black coffee
1/2 cup/60g/2oz plain flour, sifted**
<u>**Chocolate glaze**</u>
**200g/6 1/2oz dark chocolate,
broken into small pieces
100g/3 1/2oz unsalted butter
2 tablespoons water**

Variation: *For chocoholics, this cake can be made even more special by making two cakes, then sandwiching them together with whipped cream and decorating the top with chocolate caraques as photographed on page 655.*

Serves 8

Oven temperature 160°C, 325°F, Gas 3

the best
chocolate torte

the best chocolate torte

ingredients

155g/5oz dark chocolate, broken into pieces
1 cup/170g/5¹/₂oz brown sugar
¹/₂ cup/125ml/4fl oz thickened
cream (double)
2 egg yolks
200g/6¹/₂ oz butter, softened
1 cup/250g/8oz sugar
1 teaspoon vanilla essence
2 eggs, lightly beaten
1¹/₂ teaspoons baking powder
2 cup/250g/8oz cake flour
³/₄ cup/185ml/6fl oz milk
3 egg whites
Rich chocolate icing
³/₄ cup/185g/6oz sugar
³/₄ cup/185ml/6fl oz water
6 egg yolks
200g/6¹/₂oz dark chocolate, melted
250g/8oz butter, chopped
Decorations
90g/3oz flaked almonds, toasted
chocolate-drizzled strawberries

Method:

1 Place chocolate, brown sugar, cream and egg yolks in a heatproof bowl set over a saucepan of simmering water and cook, stirring constantly, until mixture is smooth. Remove bowl from pan and set aside to cool slightly.

2 Place butter, sugar and vanilla essence in a bowl and beat until light and fluffy. Gradually beat in eggs. Sift together flour and baking powder over butter mixture. Add chocolate mixture and milk and mix until well combined.

3 Place egg whites in a clean bowl and beat until stiff peaks form. Fold egg whites into chocolate mixture. Pour mixture into two greased and lined 23cm/9in round cake tins and bake for 40 minutes or until cakes are cooked when tested with a skewer. Stand cakes in tins for 5 minutes before turning onto wire racks to cool.

4 To make icing, place sugar and water in saucepan and heat over a low heat, stirring constantly, until sugar dissolves. Bring to the boil, then reduce heat and simmer for 4 minutes or until mixture is syrupy.

5 Place egg yolks in a bowl and beat until thick and pale. Gradually beat in sugar syrup and melted chocolate. Then gradually beat in butter and continue beating until mixture is thick. Cover and refrigerate until icing is of a spreadable consistency.

6 To assemble torte, split each cake horizontally. Place one layer of cake on a serving plate and spread with icing. Top with a second layer of cake and icing. Repeat layers to use remaining cake. Spread top and sides of cake with remaining icing. Press almonds into sides of torte and decorate top with chocolate-drizzled strawberries.

Note: To prepare the strawberries, wash, pat dry and place berries on a tray. Pipe thin lines of melted dark or white chocolate back and forth across the strawberries and let stand until set.

Serves 10-12

hazelnut snowballs

the choc box

Well, if you would like to try your hand

at petits fours, this is the chapter for you. Here are lots of little tidbits to elegantly tantalise the taste buds.

Try truffles, nougat hearts, panforte, tiny cups, little cakes or snowballs— all easy to make and a delight to taste.

pistachio
truffles

Photograph on right

ingredients

**315g/10oz dark chocolate,
broken into pieces
45g/1½oz butter, chopped
½ cup/125ml/4fl oz thickened
double cream
2 tablespoons sugar
2 tablespoons Galliano liqueur
125g/4oz chopped pistachio nuts**

Method:

1 *Place chocolate, butter, cream and sugar in a heatproof bowl set over a saucepan of simmering water and heat, stirring, until mixture is smooth. Add liqueur and half the pistachio nuts and mix well to combine. Chill mixture for 1 hour or until firm enough to roll into balls.*

2 *Roll tablespoons of mixture into balls, then roll in remaining pistachio nuts. Chill until required.*
   Note: *To bring out the bright green colour of the pistachios, blanch the shelled nuts in boiling water for 30 seconds, drain and vigorously rub in a clean towel to remove their skins.*
   Serves 4

caramel-
walnut petits fours

Photograph on right

ingredients

**1 cup/250g/8oz sugar
½ cup/90g/3oz brown sugar
2 cups/500ml/16fl oz thickened
double cream
1 cup/250ml/8fl oz light corn or
golden syrup
60g/2oz butter, chopped
½ teaspoon bicarbonate of soda
155g/5oz chopped walnuts
1 tablespoon vanilla essence
Chocolate icing
375g/12oz dark or
milk chocolate, melted
2 teaspoons vegetable oil**

Method:

1 *Place sugar, brown sugar, cream, corn or golden syrup and butter in a saucepan and heat over a low heat, stirring constantly, until sugar dissolves. As sugar crystals form on sides of pan, brush with a wet pastry brush.*

2 *Bring syrup to the boil and stir in bicarbonate of soda. Reduce heat and simmer until syrup reaches the hard-ball stage or 120°C/250°F on a sugar thermometer.*

3 *Stir in walnuts and vanilla essence and pour mixture into a greased and foil-lined 20cm/8in -square cake tin. Set aside at room temperature for 5 hours or until caramel sets.*

4 *Remove caramel from tin and cut into 2cm/³⁄₄in-squares.*

5 *To make icing, combine chocolate and oil. Half dip caramels in melted chocolate, place on greaseproof paper and leave to set.*
   Note: *For easy removal of the caramel from the tin, allow the foil lining to overhang the tin on two opposite sides to form handles for lifting.*
   Makes 40

chocolate
nougat hearts

Method:

1 Place chocolate, butter and cream in a heatproof bowl set over a saucepan of simmering water and heat, stirring, until mixture is smooth.

2 Add nougat and almonds and mix well to combine. Pour mixture into a greased and lined 18x28cm/7x11in shallow cake tin. Refrigerate for 2 hours or until set.

3 Using a heart-shaped cutter, cut out hearts from set mixture.

Note: Dip cutter into warm water and dry on a clean towel between each cut to achieve evenly straight edges.

Makes 40

ingredients

375g/12oz milk chocolate, broken into pieces
45g/1¹/₂oz butter, chopped
¹/₂ cup/125ml/4fl oz thickened double cream
200g/6¹/₂oz nougat, chopped
100g/3¹/₂oz almonds, toasted & chopped

chocolate
panforte

Method:

1 Place honey and sugar in a small saucepan and heat, stirring constantly, over a low heat until sugar dissolves. Bring to the boil, then reduce heat and simmer, stirring constantly, for 5 minutes or until mixture thickens.

2 Place almonds, hazelnuts, apricots, peaches, mixed peel, flour, cocoa powder and cinnamon in a bowl and mix to combine. Stir in honey syrup. Add chocolate and mix well to combine.

3 Line an 18x2cm/7x11in shallow cake tin with rice paper. Pour mixture into tin and bake for 20 minutes. Turn onto a wire rack to cool, then cut into small pieces.

Makes 32

ingredients

1 cup/250ml/8fl oz liquid honey
1 cup/250g/8oz sugar
250g/8oz almonds, toasted, chopped
250g/8oz hazelnuts, toasted, chopped
125g/4oz glacé apricots, chopped
125g/4oz glacé peaches, chopped
100g/3½oz candied mixed peel
1½ cups/185g/6oz flour, sifted
⅓ cup/45g/1½oz cocoa powder, sifted
2 teaspoons ground cinnamon
155g/5oz dark chocolate,
melted rice paper

tiny fudge cakes

Method:

1 Place dark chocolate and butter in a heatproof bowl set over a saucepan of simmering water and heat, stirring, until mixture is smooth. Remove bowl from pan and set aside to cool slightly.

2 Place egg yolks and sugar in a bowl and beat until thick and pale. Fold flour into egg mixture. Add chocolate mixture to egg mixture and stir to combine.

3 Place egg whites into a clean bowl and beat until stiff peaks form. Fold egg whites into chocolate mixture.

4 Spoon mixture into greased mini-cupcake tins or small paper cupcake cases and bake for 10 minutes. Remove cakes from tins and cool on wire racks.

5 To make icing, place white chocolate and cream in a heatproof bowl set over a saucepan of simmering water and heat, stirring, until

ingredients

100g/3¹/₂oz dark chocolate
60g/2oz butter
3 eggs, separated
¹/₂ cup/100g/3¹/₂oz caster sugar
¹/₄ cup/30g/1oz flour, sifted
White chocolate icing
100g/3¹/₂oz white chocolate, chopped
2 tablespoons thickened double cream
sugared violets

mixture is smooth. Remove bowl from pan and set aside until mixture thickens slightly. Spread icing over cakes and decorate with sugared violets.

Makes 20

Oven temperature 180°C, 350°F, Gas 4

tuile cups
with white chocolate

Photograph on right

Method:

1 To make tuiles, place butter, egg whites, milk, flour and sugar in a bowl and beat until smooth.

2 Place 2 teaspoons of mixture on a lightly greased baking tray and spread out to make a 10cm/4in round. Repeat with remaining mixture leaving 10cm/4in between each tuile. Sprinkle with almonds and bake for 3-5 minutes or until edges of tuiles are golden. Using a spatula, carefully remove tuiles from trays and place over a small upturned strainer. Press gently to shape, then allow to cool and harden before removing from strainer.

3 To make filling, place chocolate, butter and cream in a heatproof bowl set over a saucepan of simmering water and heat, stirring, until mixture is smooth. Remove bowl from pan and set aside until mixture thickens slightly. Beat mixture until light and thick. Spoon mixture into a piping bag and pipe into tuile cups.

Makes 28

ingredients

125g/4oz butter, melted
4 egg whites
2 tablespoons milk
1 cup/125g/4oz flour
²/₃ cup/140g/4¹/₂oz caster sugar
60g/2oz flaked almonds
White chocolate filling
250g/8oz white chocolate, broken into pieces
60g/2oz butter, chopped
¹/₄ cup/60ml/2fl oz cream (double)

Oven temperature 160°C, 325°F, Gas 3

hazelnut
snowballs

Method:

1 *Place chocolate, butter, cream and liqueur, if using, in a heatproof bowl set over a saucepan of simmering water and heat, stirring, until mixture is smooth. Remove bowl from pan and set aside to cool slightly.*

2 *Stir chocolate mixture until thick and pliable. Roll tablespoons of mixture into balls. Press a hazelnut into the centre of each ball and roll to enclose nut. Roll balls in coconut and refrigerate for 1 hour or until firm.*

Makes 40

ingredients

200g/6¹/₂oz white chocolate, broken into pieces
45g/1¹/₂oz butter, chopped
¹/₄ cup/60ml/2fl oz thickened double cream
1 tablespoon hazelnut-flavoured liqueur (optional)
125g/4oz hazelnuts, toasted with skins removed
60g/2oz desiccated coconut

chocolate-
fig truffles

Method:

1 Place chocolate, butter, cream, corn or golden syrup and cognac or brandy in a heatproof bowl set over a saucepan of simmering water and heat, stirring, until mixture is smooth. Remove bowl from pan.

2 Add figs and slivered almonds to chocolate mixture and mix well to combine. Chill mixture for 1 hour or until firm enough to roll into balls.

3 Take 3 teaspoons of mixture and roll into balls, then roll in flaked almonds. Place on nonstick baking paper and chill until required.

Note: If preferred, chopped soft dried prunes or dates may be used in place of the figs.

Makes 24

ingredients

**185g/6oz milk chocolate,
broken into pieces
90g/3oz butter, chopped
1/2 cup/125ml/4fl oz thickened
double cream
1/4 cup/60ml/2fl oz light corn syrup or
golden syrup
1 tablespoon cognac or brandy
75g/2 1/2oz chopped dried figs
45g/1 1/2oz slivered almonds, toasted
60g/2oz flaked almonds, toasted**

truffle easter eggs

something special

Without doubt, chocolate is always

acceptable for that special occasion. Make your own
and tempt your friends with great special cakes such
as black forest gâteau, chocolate mascarpone roulade
or a blissful chocolate bombe.

black forest
gâteau

Method:

1 Place chocolate in a heatproof bowl set over a saucepan of simmering water and heat, stirring, until chocolate melts. Remove bowl from pan and set aside to cool slightly.

2 Sift together flour, sugar and cocoa powder into a bowl. Add milk, eggs and butter and beat for 5 minutes or until mixture is smooth. Beat in chocolate until mixture is well combined.

3 Pour mixture into a greased, deep 23cm/9in-round cake tin and bake for 60 minutes or until cake is cooked when tested with a skewer. Stand cake in tin for 5 minutes before turning onto a wire rack to cool.

4 To make filling, place cream and sugar in a bowl and beat until soft peaks form. Divide cream into two portions. Fold cherries into one portion.

5 To assemble cake, use a serrated edged knife to cut cake into three even layers. Sprinkle each layer with cherry brandy. Place one layer of cake on a serving plate, spread with half the cherry cream and top with a second layer of cake. Spread with remaining cherry cream and top with remaining layer of cake. Spread top and sides of cake with cream. Decorate top of cake with chocolate curls.

Note: For even more sumptuous results, soak the cherries in extra cherry brandy or Kirsch overnight. Reserve a few cherries to decorate the top of the gâteau, then sprinkle all with a dusting of icing sugar just before serving.

Serves 6-8

ingredients

200g/6¹/₂oz dark chocolate, chopped
3 cups/375g/12oz cake flour
2¹/₂ teaspoons baking powder
1 cup/220g/7oz caster sugar
¹/₄ cup/30g/1oz cocoa powder
1¹/₂ cups/375ml/12fl oz milk
3 eggs, lightly beaten
185g/6oz butter, softened
2 tablespoons cherry brandy
chocolate curls
<u>Cherry Cream Filling</u>
2 cups/500ml/16fl oz thickened double cream
¹/₃ cup/75g/2¹/₂ oz caster sugar
440g/14oz canned pitted cherries, well-drained

Oven temperature 180°C, 350°F, Gas 4

chocolate-
mascarpone roulade

Method:

1 Place chocolate and coffee in a heatproof bowl set over a saucepan of simmering water and heat, stirring, until mixture is smooth. Cool slightly.

2 Beat egg yolks until thick and pale. Gradually beat in caster sugar. Fold chocolate mixture and flour into egg yolks.

3 Beat egg whites until stiff peaks form. Fold into chocolate mixture. Pour mixture into a greased and lined 26x32cm/10¹/₂ x 12³/₄in Swiss roll tin and bake for 20 minutes or until firm. Cool in tin.

4 To make filling, beat mascarpone, icing sugar and brandy in a bowl.

5 Turn roulade onto a clean teatowel sprinkled with caster sugar. Spread with chocolate hazelnut spread and half the filling and roll up. Spread with remaining filling and decorate with frosted rose petals.

Serves 8-10

ingredients

185g/6oz dark chocolate
¹/₄ cup/60ml/2fl oz strong black coffee
5 eggs, separated
¹/₂ cup/100g/3¹/₂oz caster sugar
2 tablespoons plain flour, sifted
frosted rose petals
<u>Mascarpone filling</u>
375g/12oz mascarpone
2 tablespoons icing sugar
2 tablespoons brandy
¹/₂ cup/125g/4oz chocolate-hazelnut spread

black-and-white
tart

Photograph on right

black-and-white tart

ingredients

Macaroon shell
2 egg whites
1/2 cup/100g/3 1/2oz caster sugar
220g/7oz desiccated coconut
1/4 cup/30g/1oz flour, sifted
<u>**Chocolate sour cream filling**</u>
2 egg yolks
**3/4 cup/185ml6fl oz thickened
double cream**
185g/6oz dark chocolate
2 tablespoons cognac or brandy
185g/6oz white chocolate
2/3 cup/155g/5oz sour cream
<u>**Raspberry coulis**</u>
250g/8oz raspberries
1 tablespoon icing sugar

Oven temperature 180°C, 350°F, Gas 4

Method:

1 *Place egg whites in a bowl and beat until soft peaks form. Gradually beat in caster sugar. Fold in coconut and flour. Press mixture over base and up sides of a greased and lined 23cm/9in round flan tin with a removable base. Bake for 20-25 minutes or until golden. Stand in tin for 5 minutes then remove and place on a wire rack to cool.*

2 *To make filling, place egg yolks and cream in a heatproof bowl set over a saucepan of simmering water and beat until thick and pale. Stir in dark chocolate and cognac or brandy and continue stirring until chocolate melts. Remove bowl from pan and set aside to cool.*

3 *Place white chocolate and sour cream in a heatproof bowl set over a saucepan of simmering water and heat, stirring, until mixture is smooth. Remove bowl from pan and set aside to cool.*

4 *Place alternating spoonfuls of dark and white mixtures in macaroon shell and, using a skewer, swirl mixtures to give a marbled effect. Chill for 2 hours or until filling is firm.*

5 *To make coulis, place raspberries in a food processor or blender and process to make a purée. Press purée through a sieve to remove seeds, then stir in icing sugar. Serve with tart.*

Note: *This dessert is best served the day it is made as the macaroon shell may absorb too much moisture on standing and lose its crispness.*

Serves 8

truffle
easter eggs

Photograph also appears on page 681

Method:

1 Place a spoonful of dark chocolate in a small easter egg mould and use a small paintbrush to evenly coat. Freeze for 2 minutes or until chocolate sets. Repeat with remaining chocolate to make 32 shells.

2 To make filling, place cream in a saucepan and bring to the boil. Remove pan from heat, add milk chocolate and stir until smooth. Stir in golden syrup and chill for 20 minutes or until mixture is thick enough to pipe.

3 Spoon filling into a piping bag fitted with a star-shaped nozzle and pipe filling into chocolate shells.

Note: Eggs can be moulded and filled several hours in advance. Store in a covered container in a cool, dry place.

Makes 32

ingredients

Truffle easter eggs
125g/4oz dark chocolate, melted
Truffle filling
¹/₂ cup/125ml/4fl oz thickened double cream
250g/8oz milk chocolate
1 tablespoon golden syrup

ice-cream
christmas pudding

Method:

1 Place ice cream, apricots, cherries, pears, sultanas, raisins and rum in a bowl and mix to combine. Pour into an oiled and lined 6 cup/1½ litre/2½ pt-capacity pudding basin.

2 Freeze for 3 hours or until firm. To serve, slice pudding and serve with rum custard.

Note: To help unmould the pudding, briefly hold a wram damp teatowel around the outside of the mould. To serve, slice pudding and serve with rum custard.

Serves 8

ingredients

1 litre/1¾pt chocolate ice cream, softened
125g/4oz glacé apricots, chopped
125g/4oz glacé cherries, chopped
125g/4oz glacé pears, chopped
90g/3oz sultanas
75g/2½oz raisins, chopped
2 tablespoons rum

yule log

Photograph on right

yule log

ingredients

5 eggs, separated
¹/₄ cup/60g/2oz caster sugar
100g/3¹/₂oz dark chocolate,
melted and cooled
2 tablespoons self-raising flour, sifted
2 tablespoons cocoa powder, sifted
chocolate shavings
<u>White chocolate filling</u>
60g/2oz white chocolate
²/₃ cup/170ml/5¹/₂fl oz thickened
double cream
<u>Chocolate icing</u>
200g/6¹/₂oz dark chocolate, melted
60g/2oz butter, melted

Oven temperature 180°C, 350°F, Gas 4

Method:

1. Place egg yolks and sugar in a bowl and beat until thick and pale. Stir in chocolate, flour and cocoa powder.
2. Place egg whites in a clean bowl and beat until stiff peaks form. Fold egg whites into chocolate mixture.
3. Pour mixture into a greased and lined 26x 32cm/10¹/₂x12³/₄in-Swiss roll tin and bake for 15 minutes or until firm. Turn cake onto a teatowel sprinkled with caster sugar and roll up from short end. Set aside to cool.
4. To make filling, place white chocolate in a heatproof bowl set over a saucepan of simmering water and heat, stirring, until smooth. Add cream and stir until combined. Cover and chill until thickened and of a spreadable consistency.

5. Unroll cake and spread with filling leaving a 1cm/¹/₂in border. Re-roll cake.
6. To make icing, combine chocolate and butter and mix until combined. Spread icing over roll then, using a fork, roughly texture the icing. Decorate with chocolate shavings.

Note: Keep this dessert refrigerated until served. Dust log with icing sugar to create 'snow' just before serving.

Serves 8

blissful
chocolate bombe

ingredients

Vanilla ice cream
1 cup/220g caster sugar
8 egg yolks
2²/₃ cups/660ml/1pt cream
1 vanilla bean
1¹/₂ cups/375ml/12fl oz thickened
double cream
Chocolate mousse
175g/5¹/₂oz dark chocolate, chopped
3 tablespoons strong black coffee
4 eggs, separated
15g/¹/₂oz butter, softened
1 tablespoon brandy
3 tablespoons caster sugar
¹/₂ cup/125ml/8fl oz double cream, whipped

Method:

1 To make ice cream, place sugar and egg yolks in a bowl and beat until thick and creamy. Place cream and vanilla bean in a heavy-based saucepan and simmer for 3 minutes. Cool slightly, then remove vanilla bean.

2 Gradually add 1 cup/250mL/16fl oz of warm cream to egg mixture, beating well. Add egg mixture to remaining cream, stirring over low heat until mixture coats the back of a spoon. Set aside to cool.

3 Stir through cream mixture, pour into a freezerproof tray lined with plastic food wrap, and freeze until almost set. Break up mixture with a fork and place in food processor. Process until mixture is thick and creamy. Pour ice cream into a chilled mould (9 cup/2.25 litre capacity) lined with plastic food wrap. Push a smaller mould, covered with plastic food wrap, into centre of ice cream, forcing ice cream up around the sides of the mould. Freeze until firm.

4 To make chocolate mousse, place chocolate and coffee in a bowl and melt over hot water, stirring until smooth. Remove from heat and beat in egg yolks one at a time. Continue beating and add butter and brandy. Allow mixture to cool.

5 Beat egg whites until soft peaks form, then beat in sugar. Fold egg whites and cream through chocolate mixture. Remove smaller mould from ice cream. Spoon mousse into centre of ice cream and return to freezer until set.

Serves 12

pink-and-white
mousse

Method:

1. Place berries in a food processor or blender and process to make a purée. Press purée through a sieve into a saucepan. Stir in $^1/_3$ cup/90g/3oz sugar and liqueur and bring to simmering over a low heat. Simmer, stirring occasionally, until mixture reduces to 1 cup/25mL/8fl oz. Remove pan from heat and set aside.

2. Place water, egg yolks and remaining sugar in a heatproof bowl set over a saucepan of simmering water and beat for 8 minutes or until mixture is light and creamy.
   Remove bowl from pan. Add chocolate and vanilla essence and beat until mixture cools. Fold whipped cream into chocolate mixture. Divide mixture into two portions.

3. Stir berry purée into one portion of mixture and leave one portion plain. Drop alternate spoonfuls of berry and plain mixtures into serving glasses. Using a skewer swirl mixtures to give a ripple effect. Refrigerate until firm. Just prior to serving decorate with chocolate curls.
   Note: Garnish with additional fresh berries or red and white currants when available.

Serves 8

ingredients

500g/1 lb mixed berries of your choice
1 cup/250g/8oz sugar
1 tablespoon orange-flavoured liqueur
$^1/_4$ cup/60ml/2fl oz water
6 egg yolks
200g/6$^1/_2$oz white chocolate, melted
2 teaspoons vanilla essence
1$^2/_3$ cup/410ml/13fl oz double
thickened cream, whipped
white chocolate curls

the ultimate chocolate sundae

delightful
desserts

The best way to finish off a great meal

is with a delightful dessert. In this chapter we offer some of the most luscious desserts imaginable. From the ultimate chocolate sundae to chocolate self-saucing pudding, you are sure to find something to really delight the taste buds and give your meal the final touch.

chocolate
self-saucing pudding

Method:

1 Sift together flour, baking fpowder and cocoa powder in a bowl. Add caster sugar and mix to combine. Make a well in the centre of the dry ingredients, add milk and butter and mix well to combine. Pour mixture into a greased 4 cup/1 litre/1³/₄pt-capacity ovenproof dish.

2 To make sauce, place brown sugar and cocoa powder in a bowl. Gradually add water and mix until smooth. Carefully pour sauce over mixture in dish and bake for 40 minutes or until cake is cooked when tested with a skewer. Serve scoops of pudding with some of the sauce from the base of the dish and top with a scoop of vanilla or chocolate ice cream.

Serves 6

ingredients

1 cup/125g/4oz all purpose flour
³/₄ teaspoon baking powder
¹/₄ cup/30g/1oz cocoa powder
³/₄ cup/170g/5¹/₂oz caster sugar
¹/₂ cup/125ml/4fl oz milk
45g/1¹/₂oz butter, melted
<u>Chocolate sauce</u>
³/₄ cup/125g/4oz brown sugar
¹/₄ cup/30g/1oz cocoa powder, sifted
1¹/₄ cups/315ml/10fl oz hot water

Oven temperature 180°C, 350°F, Gas 4

chocolate
soufflé

Method:

1 Place chocolate and half the cream in a heatproof bowl set over a saucepan of simmering water and heat, stirring constantly, until mixture is smooth. Remove bowl from pan and set aside to cool slightly.

2 Place egg yolks and caster sugar in a clean bowl and beat until thick and pale. Gradually beat in flour and remaining cream and beat until combined.

3 Transfer egg-yolk mixture to a saucepan and cook over a medium heat, stirring constantly, for 5 minutes or until mixture thickens. Remove pan from heat and stir in chocolate mixture.

4 Place egg whites in a clean bowl and beat until stiff peaks form. Fold egg whites into chocolate mixture. Divide mixture evenly between six buttered and sugared 1 cup/250mL/8fl oz-capacity soufflé dishes and bake for 25 minutes or until soufflésare puffed. Dust with icing sugar, if desired, and serve immediately.

ingredients

250g/8oz dark chocolate, broken into pieces
1 cup/250ml/8fl oz thickened double cream
6 eggs, separated
1 cup/220g/7oz caster sugar
1/4 cup/30g/1oz flour
icing sugar, sifted (optional)

Note: To prepare soufflé dishes, brush interior of each with melted unsalted butter, coating lightly and evenly, then sprinkle lightly with caster sugar to coat.

Serves 6

695

chocolate
profiteroles

Method:

1 To make pastry, place water and butter in a saucepan and slowly bring to the boil. As soon as the mixture boils, quickly stir in flour, using a wooden spoon. Cook over a low heat, stirring constantly, for 2 minutes or until mixture is smooth and leaves sides of pan.

2 Beat in eggs one at a time, beating well after each addition and until mixture is light and glossy.

3 Place heaped tablespoons of mixture on greased baking trays and bake for 10 minutes. Reduce oven temperature to 180°C/350°F/ Gas 4 and cook for 10 minutes longer or until pastries are golden and crisp. Pierce a small hole in the base of each pastry and transfer to wire racks to cool.

4 To make filling, place sugar and egg yolks in a bowl and beat until thick and pale. Add flour and beat until combined.

5 Place milk, chocolate and liqueur in a saucepan and heat over a medium heat, stirring constantly, until mixture is smooth. Remove pan from heat and slowly stir in egg-yolk mixture. Return pan to heat and cook over medium heat, stirring constantly, until mixture thickens. Remove pan from heat, cover and set aside to cool.

6 Place filling in a piping bag fitted with a small, plain nozzle and pipe filling through hole in base of profiteroles. Dip tops of profiteroles in melted chocolate and place on a wire rack to set.

Note: Serve with whipped cream and fresh fruit. The pastry puffs can be baked in advance, cooled completely and stored in an airtight container at room temperature overnight or, for longer storage, in the freezer for up to six weeks before filling.

Serves 6-8

ingredients

185g/6oz dark chocolate, melted
<u>**Choux pastry**</u>
1 cup/250ml/8fl oz water
90g/3oz butter
1 cup/125g/4oz flour
3 eggs
<u>**Chocolate liqueur filling**</u>
1/2 cup/125g/4oz sugar
3 egg yolks
2 tablespoons flour
1 cup/250ml/8fl oz milk
60g/2oz dark chocolate, broken into pieces
1 tablespoon orange-flavoured liqueur

Oven temperature 200°C, 400°F, Gas 6

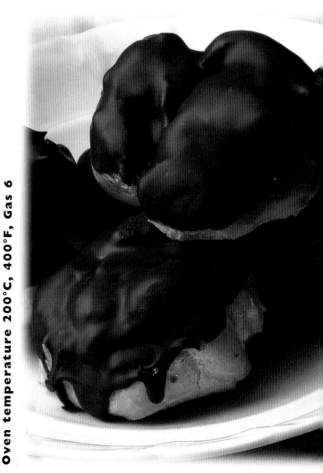

cassata
alla siciliana

ingredients

4 eggs
¹/₂ cup/100g/3¹/₂oz caster sugar
³/₄ cup/90g/3oz plain flour, sifted
¹/₂ teaspoon baking powder
¹/₃ cup/90ml/3fl oz brandy
Cassata filling
¹/₂ cup/125g/4oz sugar
4 teaspoons water
375g/12oz ricotta cheese
**¹/₂ cup/125ml/4fl oz thickened
double cream, whipped**
60g/2oz mixed peel, chopped
**100g/3¹/₂oz dark chocolate,
finely chopped**
60g/2oz glacé cherries, quartered
45g/1¹/₂oz unsalted pistachio nuts, chopped
Chocolate topping
315g/10oz dark chocolate
90g/3oz butter

Method:

1 Place eggs in a large mixing bowl and beat until light and fluffy. Gradually add sugar, beating well after each addition until mixture is creamy. Fold in flour and baking powder. Pour batter into a greased and lined 26x32cm/10¹/₂x12³/₄in Swiss roll-tin and bake for 10-12 minutes or until cooked when tested with a skewer. Turn onto a wire rack to cool.

2 To make filling, place sugar and water in a saucepan and cook over a low heat, stirring constantly, until sugar dissolves. Remove from heat and set aside to cool. Place ricotta cheese in a food processor or blender and process until smooth. Transfer to a bowl and mix in sugar syrup, cream, mixed peel, chocolate, cherries and nuts.

3 Line an 11x21cm/4¹/₂x8¹/₂in loaf dish with plastic food wrap. Cut cake into slices and sprinkle with brandy. Line base and sides of prepared dish with cake. Spoon filling into loaf dish and top with a final layer of cake. Cover and freeze until solid.

4 To make topping, place chocolate and butter in a saucepan and cook, stirring, over a low heat until melted and mixture is well blended. Allow to cool slightly.

5 Turn cassata onto a wire rack and cover with topping. Return to freezer until chocolate sets.
Serving Suggestion: Decorate with glacé fruits and serve with whipped cream.

Serves 10

sacher torte

sacher torte

ingredients

250g/8oz butter, softened
1 1/2 cups/265g/8 1/2oz brown sugar
2 teaspoons vanilla essence
2 eggs, lightly beaten
1 1/2 cups/185g/6oz flour
2/3 cup/60g/2oz cocoa powder
3/4 teaspoon baking powder
1 1/2 cups/375ml/8fl oz buttermilk
1/2 cup/155g/5oz apricot jam
<u>Dark chocolate icing</u>
185g/6oz dark chocolate,
broken into pieces
185g/6oz butter, chopped

Oven temperature 180°C, 350°F, Gas 4

Method:

1 *Place butter, sugar and vanilla essence in a bowl and beat until light and fluffy. Gradually beat in eggs.*

2 *Sift together flour, cocoa powder and baking powder over butter mixture. Add buttermilk and mix well to combine.*

3 *Pour mixture into two greased and lined 23cm/ 9in cake tins and bake for 25 minutes or until cakes are cooked when tested with a skewer. Stand cakes in tins for 5 minutes before turning onto wire racks to cool.*

4 *To make icing, place chocolate and butter in a heatproof bowl set over a saucepan of simmering water and heat, stirring, until mixture is smooth. Remove bowl from pan and set aside to cool until mixture thickens and has a spreadable consistency.*

5 *To assemble cake, place one cake on a serving plate and spread with jam. Top with remaining cake and spread top and sides with icing. Place remaining icing in a piping bag and pipe swirls around edge of cake.*

Note: *This Austrian favourite comes complete with a hidden layer of apricot jam. The words 'Sacher Torte' piped onto the top of the cake in chocolate adds a touch of authenticity to the decoration.*

Serves 8-10

the ultimate
chocolate sundae

Photograph on right

Method:

1. To make base, place butter, eggs, caster sugar and vanilla essence in a bowl and beat to combine. Add flour, cocoa powder, dates and pecans and mix well to combine.

2. Pour mixture into a greased and lined 20cm/ 8in-square cake tin and bake for 30 minutes or until firm to touch, but still fudgey in the centre. Cool in tin, then cut into six squares.

3. To make sauce, place brown sugar, cocoa powder, cream and butter in a saucepan and cook over a low heat, stirring constantly, until sugar dissolves. Bring to the boil, then reduce heat and simmer for 5 minutes or until sauce thickens slightly.

4. To assemble sundaes, top each brownie square with a scoop of vanilla, chocolate and choc-chip ice cream. Drizzle with hot sauce and serve.

Note: *Extra fudge sauce can be stored in an airtight container in the refrigerator.*

Serves 6

ingredients

6 scoops vanilla ice cream
6 scoops chocolate ice cream
6 scoops choc-chip ice cream
<u>Brownie base</u>
250g/8oz butter, melted
4 eggs, lightly beaten
1 1/2 cups/330g/10 1/2oz caster sugar
2 teaspoons vanilla essence
3/4 cup/90g/3oz flour, sifted
1/4 cup/30g/1oz cocoa powder, sifted
60g/2oz chopped dates
45g/1 1/2oz chopped pecans
<u>Fudge sauce</u>
2 cups/350g/11oz brown sugar
1/4 cup/30g/1oz cocoa powder, sifted
1 cup/250ml/8fl oz thickened double cream
2 tablespoons butter

chocolate
mousse

Method:

1. Place chocolate in a heatproof bowl set over a saucepan of simmering water and heat, stirring, until chocolate melts. Remove bowl from pan and set aside to cool slightly.

2. Gradually beat egg yolks into chocolate. Add butter and beat until smooth. Fold in cream and brandy.

3. Place egg whites into a clean bowl and beat until soft peaks form. Gradually beat in sugar and continue beating until stiff peaks form. Fold egg white mixture into chocolate mixture.

4. Spoon mousse mixture into six dessert glasses and refrigerate until set. Decorate with chocolate curls, if desired.

Note: *To make chocolate curls, see instructions on page 712.*

Serves 6

ingredients

300g/9 1/2oz dark chocolate, broken into pieces
4 eggs, separated
100g/3 1/2oz butter, softened
1 cup/250ml/8fl oz thickened double cream, whipped
1 tablespoon brandy
1 tablespoon sugar
white chocolate curls (optional)

raspberry-choc
truffle cakes

Photograph on right

1

2

ingredients

¹/₂ **cup/60g/2oz cocoa powder, sifted**
I cup/250ml/8fl oz boiling water
125g/4oz butter
I³/₄ cups/390g/12¹/₂oz caster sugar
I¹/₂ tablespoons raspberry jam
2 eggs
I²/₃ cups/200g/6¹/₂oz plain flour, sifted
I teaspoon baking powder
410g/13oz dark chocolate, melted
raspberries for garnishing
<u>Raspberry cream</u>
125g/4oz raspberries, puréed and sieved
¹/₂ **cup/125ml/4fl oz thickened**
double cream, whipped
<u>Chocolate sauce</u>
125g/4oz dark chocolate
¹/₂ **cup/125ml/4fl oz water**
¹/₄ **cup/60g/2oz caster sugar**
I teaspoon brandy (optional)

Method:

1 *Combine cocoa powder and boiling water. Mix to dissolve and set aside to cool.*

2 *Place butter, sugar and jam in a bowl and beat until light and fluffy. Beat in eggs one at a time, adding a little flour with each egg. Fold remaining flour, baking powder and cocoa mixture, alternately, into creamed mixture.*

3 *Spoon mixture into eight lightly greased ¹/₂ cup/125mL/4fl oz capacity ramekins or large muffin tins. Bake for 20-25 minutes or until cakes are cooked when tested with a skewer. Cool for 5 minutes then turn onto wire racks to cool. Turn cakes upside down and scoop out centre leaving a Icm/¹/₂in shell. Spread each cake with chocolate to cover top and sides, then place right way up on a wire rack.*

4 *To make cream, fold raspberry purée into cream. Spoon cream into a piping bag fitted with a large nozzle. Carefully turn cakes upside down and pipe in cream to fill cavity. Place right way up on individual serving plates.*

5 *To make sauce, place chocolate and water in a small saucepan and cook over a low heat for 4-5 minutes or until chocolate melts. Add sugar and continue cooking, stirring constantly, until sugar dissolves. Bring just to the boil, then reduce heat and simmer, stirring, for 2 minutes. Set aside to cool for 5 minutes, then stir in brandy, if using. Cool sauce to room temperature.*

To serve: *Decorate plates with sauce.*

Note: *These rich little chocolate cakes filled with a raspberry cream and served with a bittersweet chocolate sauce are a perfect finale to any dinner party. Follow the step-by-step instructions and you will see just how easy this spectacular dessert is.*

Serves 8

frozen maple-
nut parfait

Photograph on right

Method:

1 *Place egg yolks in a bowl and beat until thick and pale. Place sugar and water in a saucepan and heat over a low heat, stirring, until sugar dissolves. Bring mixture to the boil and boil until mixture thickens and reaches soft-ball stage or 118°C/244°F on a sugar thermometer.*

2 *Gradually beat sugar syrup and maple syrup into egg yolks and continue beating until mixture cools. Place cream in a bowl and beat until soft peaks form. Fold cream, macadamia nuts and chocolate into egg mixture.*

3 *Pour mixture into an aluminium foil-lined 15x25cm/6x10in loaf tin and freeze for 5 hours or until firm.*

4 *Turn parfait onto a serving plate, remove foil, cut into slices and drizzle with maple syrup.*
   Note: *This light and luscious frozen Italian meringue is the perfect partner for a garnish of fresh fruit and perhaps some almond-flavoured biscotti.*
   Serves 8

ingredients

6 egg yolks
I cup/220g/7oz caster sugar
1/2 cup/125ml/4fl oz water
1/2 cup/125ml/4fl oz maple syrup
600ml/Ipt thickened
double cream
100g/3 1/2oz macadamia nuts,
finely chopped
100g/3 1/2oz white chcolate,
chopped extra maple syrup

banana
mousse

Photograph on right

Method:

1 *Place gelatine and boiling water in a bowl and stir until gelatine dissolves. Set aside to cool.*

2 *Place bananas, sugar and lemon juice in a food processor and process until smooth. Stir gelatine mixture into banana mixture.*

3 *Place cream and coconut milk in a bowl and beat until soft peaks form. Fold cream mixture into banana mixture.*

4 *Spoon mousse into six serving glasses. Divide melted chocolate between glasses and swirl with a skewer. Refrigerate for 2 hours or until set.*
   Note: *When available, dried banana chips make an attractive garnish with fresh mint leaves.*
   Serves 6

ingredients

I tablespoon powdered gelatine
1/4 cup/60ml/2fl oz boiling water
500g/I lb ripe bananas
1/4 cup/60g/2oz sugar
I tablespoon lemon juice
220ml/7fl oz thickened
double cream
100ml/3 1/2fl oz coconut milk
100g/3 1/2oz dark chocolate, melted

techniques

techniques

The source of chocolate, the cacao tree, was one of the greatest discoveries made on the American continent. Chocolate's scientific name is Theobroma cacao – theobroma means 'food of the gods'.

Storing chocolate

Chocolate should be stored in a dry, airy place at a temperature of about 16°C/60°F. If stored in unsuitable conditions, the cocoa butter in chocolate may rise to the surface, leaving a white film. A similar discoloration occurs when water condenses on the surface. This often happens to refrigerated chocolates that are too loosely wrapped. Chocolate affected in this way is still suitable for melting, but not for grating.

Melting chocolate

Chocolate melts more rapidly if broken into small pieces. The melting process should occur slowly since chocolate scorches if overheated. To melt chocolate, place the chocolate in the top of a double saucepan or in a bowl set over a saucepan of simmering water and heat, stirring, until chocolate melts and becomes smooth. Alternatively, chocolate can be melted in the microwave. To melt 375g/12oz chocolate, break it into small pieces and place in a microwavable glass or ceramic bowl or jug and cook on HIGH (100%) for 1 1/2-2 minutes. Stir. If the chocolate is not completely melted cook for 30-45 seconds longer. When melting chocolate in the microwave you should be aware that it holds its shape and it is important to stir it frequently so that it does not burn.

- The container in which the chocolate is being melted should be kept uncovered and completely dry. Covering could cause condensation and just one drop of water will ruin the chocolate.
- Chocolate 'seizes' if it is overheated, or if it comes into contact with water or steam. Seizing results in the chocolate tightening and becoming a thick mass that will not melt. To rescue seized chocolate, stir in a little cream or vegetable oil, until the chocolate becomes smooth again.

Tempering chocolate

Coarsely chop chocolate to be tempered. Also finely grate a few grams/ounces, of unmelted semisweet or bittersweet coating chocolate. You will need 1 tablespoon grated chocolate for every 125g/4oz of coarsely chopped chocolate. Melt chopped chocolate in a dry bowl set over hot water; stir until smooth. Do not allow chocolate to exceed 46°C/115°F – test with an instant read thermometer. Remove bowl from hot water and set firmly on bench (on a towel is best). Gradually stir in grated chocolate, a spoonful at a time, stirring until melted before adding another spoonful. If the dipping chocolate is semisweet or bittersweet, cool to 30-32°C/86-90°F ; if milk chocolate, cool to 28-31°C/83-88°F. Keep temperature at constant temperature by returning it to the warm water, if temperature drops too much mixture will be too thick to coat properly. Similarly, if temperature rises too high above 32°C/90°F, it will have to be retempered.

choc-o-holic

Watchpoints

- *Do not melt chocolate over a direct flame.*
- *The container in which the chocolate is being melted should be kept uncovered and completely dry. Covering could cause condensation and just one drop of water will ruin the chocolate.*
- *Chocolate 'seizes' if it is over-heated, or if it comes into contact with water or steam. Seizing results in the chocolate tightening and becoming a thick mass that will not melt. To rescue seized chocolate, stir in a little cream or vegetable oil, until the chocolate becomes smooth again.*

Compound chocolate

Compound chocolate, also called chocolate coating, is designed to replace couverture chocolate for coating. It can be purchased in block form or as round discs. Both forms are available in milk or dark chocolate. Compound chocolate is made from a vegetable oil base with sugar, milk solids and flavouring. It contains cocoa powder, but not cocoa butter and is easy to melt. It does not require tempering and is the easiest form for beginners to work with.

Chocolate decorations

Compound caraques

Pour melted chocolate over a cool work surface such as marble, ceramic or granite. Spread the chocolate as smoothly as possible, using a flexible metal spatula, in a layer about .15cm/ $^1/_{16}$ in thick; do not leave any holes. If the chocolate is too thick it will not roll. Allow chocolate to set at room temperature. Holding a long sharp knife at a 45° angle, pull gently over the surface of the chocolate to form scrolls.

Chocolate curls and shavings

Chocolate curls are made from chocolate that is at room temperature. To make shavings, chill the chocolate first. Using a vegetable peeler, shave the sides of the chocolate. Curls or shavings will form depending on the temperature of the chocolate.

Chocolate leaves

Use stiff, fresh, non-poisonous leaves such as rose or lemon leaves. Keep as much stem as possible to hold onto. Wash and dry leaves, brush the shiny surface of the leaf with a thin layer of melted, cooled chocolate. Allow to set at room temperature then carefully peel away leaf.

Piping chocolate

Chocolate can be piped into fancy shapes for decorating desserts or cakes. Trace a simple design on a thin piece of paper. Tape a sheet of baking paper to the work surface and slide the drawing under the sheet of paper. Pipe over outline with melted chocolate. Set aside to firm at room temperature, then remove carefully with a metal spatula and use as desired.

Chocolates cases: Quarter-fill mould with melted chocolate and tap to remove any air bubbles. Brush chocolate evenly up sides of mould to make a shell, then freeze for 2 minutes or until set. Larger chocolate cases to hold desserts can also be made in this way using foil-lined individual metal flan tins, brioche or muffin pans as moulds. When set, remove from tins and fill with a dessert filling such as mousse or a flavoured cream.

marbled
shells

1

2

3

ingredients

200g/6¹/₂oz dark chocolate, melted
200g/6¹/₂oz white chocolate, melted
<u>**Creamy chocolate filling**</u>
200g/6¹/₂oz milk chocolate
**¹/₂ cup/125mL/4fl oz thickened
double cream**
**2 tablespoons coffee-flavoured or
hazelnut-flavoured
liqueur**

Method:

1 *To make filling, place milk chocolate, cream and liqueur in a heatproof bowl set over a saucepan of simmering water and heat, stirring, until mixture is smooth. Remove bowl from pan and set aside until mixture cools and thickens.*

2 *Place a teaspoon of dark chocolate and a teaspoon of white chocolate in a shell-shaped chocolate mould. Swirl with a skewer to marble chocolate and using a small brush, brush chocolate evenly over mould. Tap mould gently on work surface to remove any air bubbles. Repeat with remaining chocolate to make 30 moulds. Freeze for 2 minutes or until chocolate sets.*

3 *Place a small spoonful of filling in each chocolate shell. Spoon equal quantities of the remaining dark and white chocolate over*

filling to fill mould. Using a skewer, carefully swirl chocolate to give marbled effect. Tap mould gently on work surface. Freeze for 3 minutes or until chocolate sets. Tap moulds gently to remove chocolates.

Note: *Do not overmix the white and dark chocolates or the marbled effect will diminish. Make sure the first coating sets completely before adding the filling so that the first coating does not crack.*

Makes 30

Chocolate leaves

Choose non-poisonous, fresh, stiff leaves with raised veins. Retain as much stem as possible. Wash leaves, then dry well on absorbent kitchen paper. Brush the underside of the leaves with melted chocolate and allow to set at room temperature. When set, carefully peel away leaf. Use one leaf to decorate an individual dessert, or a make a bunch and use to decorate a large dessert or cake.

Piped chocolate decorations

These are quick and easy to make. Trace a simple design onto a sheet of paper. Tape a sheet of baking or greaseproof paper to your work surface and slide the drawings under the paper. Place melted chocolate into a paper or material piping bag and, following the tracings, pipe thin lines. Allow to set at room temperature and then carefully remove, using a metal spatula. If you are not going to use these decorations immediately, store them in an airtight container in a cool place.

Chocolate cases

To make chocolate cases, quarter-fill the mould with melted chocolate and tap to remove any air bubbles. Brush chocolate evenly up sides of mould to make a shell, then freeze for 2 minutes or until set. Larger chocolate cases to hold desserts can also be made in this way using foil-lined individual metal flan tins, brioche or muffin tins as moulds. When set, remove from tins and fill with dessert filling such as mousse or a flavoured cream.

Chocolate caraques

These are made by spreading a layer of melted chocolate over a marble, granite or ceramic work surface. Allow the chocolate to set at room temperature. Then, holding a metal pastry scraper or a large knife at a 45° angle slowly push it along the work surface away from you to form the chocolate into cylinders. If chocolate shavings form, then it is too cold and it is best to start again.

Chocolate curls or shavings

Chocolate curls are made from chocolate that is at room temperature. To make shavings, chill the chocolate first. Using a vegetable peeler, shave the sides of the chocolate. Whether curls or shavings form depends on the temperature of the chocolate.

Making a paper piping bag

1 Cut a 25cm/10in square of greaseproof paper.

2 Cut square in half digonally to form two triangles.

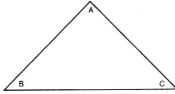

3 To make piping bag, place paper triangles on top of each other and mark the three corners A, B and C.

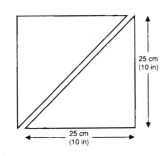

4 Fold corner B around and inside corner A.

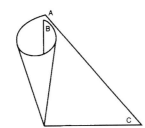

5 Bring corner C around the outside of the bag until it fits exactly behind corner A. At this stage all three corners should be together and point closed.

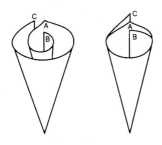

6 Fold corner A over two or three times to hold the bag together.

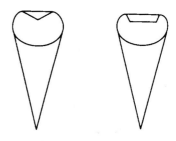

7 Snip the point off the bag and drop in icing nozzle. The piping bag can also be used without a nozzle for writing and outlines, in which case only the very tip of the point should be snipped off the bag.

To fill the piping bag: Spoon chocolate or icing into the bag to half fill. Fold the top over about 1cm/$\frac{1}{2}$in then fold over again. Fold the tips towards the centre and press with your thumb on the join to force the chocolate or icing out.

Holding the piping bag: To hold the piping bag correctly, grip the bag near the top with the folded or twisted end held between the thumb and fingers. Guide the bag with your free hand. Right-handed people should decorate from left to right, while left-handers will decorate from right to left, the exception being when piping writing.

The appearance of your piping will be directly affected by how you squeeze and relax your grip on the piping bag, that is, the pressure that you apply and the steadiness of that pressure. The pressure should be so consistent that you can move the bag in a free and easy glide with just the right amount of chocolate or icing flowing from the nozzle. A little practice will soon have you feeling confident.

ice cream

and frozen desserts

introduction

Who Invented Ice Cream?

A popular legend attributes the invention of ice cream to the Roman emperor Nero, who in the first century A.D. sent runners to fetch snow from the top of nearby mountains and then had it flavoured with wine and fruit juices. In truth, historical records suggest that ice cream originated much earlier. There is evidence that the ancient Chinese were already making water ices at the beginning of recorded history, and they were probably doing so well before. From China frozen desserts spread to Arabia, India and Persia.

Marco Polo encountered flavoured ices on his journeys to the East and was responsible for introducing them to Italy. The dessert he introduced was probably the forerunner of what we would call a milk ice (rather than a water ice, or sherbet), goat's milk probably having been added to the original Chinese water ices by the Arabians. The art of making frozen desserts in Italy was refined with the discovery of salt as an aid to freezing. Ice cream (along with another Italian innovation, the dinner fork) was introduced to France in the sixteenth century by Catherine de Medici. From there it quickly spread to England and then to the rest of Europe.

The dessert we now know as ice cream - at first called cream ice - was introduced by a French chef to King Charles I of England early in the seventeenth century. Initially it was available only to royalty and court nobility, but by the end of the seventeenth century, commoners too were indulging in frozen desserts. By 1676 there were 250 shops selling ice cream and ices in Paris alone, and the French government gave ice cream vendors official status as a trade guild. Despite the rapid spread of ices and ice cream throughout Europe, the enormous and widespread popularity that ice cream enjoys today is a relatively modern, and largely American, phenomenon, attributable in no small way to the development of reliable refrigeration in the twentieth century. The familiar hand-cranked ice cream churn was invented in 1846 by an American woman named Nancy Johnson (about whom little else is known). The first ice cream cone evidently was sold at the St. Louis World Exposition of 1904, when an ice cream vendor ran out of dishes and started substituting rolled-up wafers from a neighbouring concessionaire. During the 1920s a variety of frozen desserts were invented in rapid succession, including the Eskimo pie, the Good Humour bar, and the Popsicle. In 1939 a machine for making soft ice cream, by incorporating a great deal of air into the mixture, was perfected and fast-food businesses serving ice cream or ice milk quickly proliferated. Unfortunately, as the manufacture of ice cream became big business in the United States, quality often suffered. Gelatin and milk were introduced into sherbets; flour and whole eggs were added to ice cream, and the amount of fresh cream was drastically reduced.

Today ice cream and frozen desserts continue to gain in popularity, and many commercial manufacturers are returning to stricter quality standards. A new generation of home ice cream freezers - smaller, easier to use, and more efficient than earlier versions - are inspiring ice cream enthusiasts to make homemade frozen desserts on a regular basis, not just for the occasional special party. Thousands of electric ice cream machines and pre-chilled canisters now stand ready to swing into action at a moment's notice.

basic
knowledge

Sweet Freeze: A Primer

From icy poles to Peach Melba, frozen specialties run the gamut from simple to sophisticated. Gelato, glace, ice cream, nieve, granita, helado, ice milk, sherbet, sorbet, sorbetto, frozen yoghurt, water ice - names and distinctions for these icy delights blur across cultural boundaries, reflecting their enormous popularity worldwide. Here are some broad definitions to help sort it all out:

Ice Cream

Made from either a cooked custard or uncooked base. Ice cream made with eggs and cream is higher in fat than ice "cream" made with skim milk (low-fat or nonfat). As a rule, the higher the fat content of the base mixture, the creamier the texture; incorporating gelatin, egg substitutes, or lecithin (an emulsifier made from soybeans) into mixtures made with skim milk makes the texture creamier.

Granita

A type of water ice (sherbet) with a slightly grainy texture, the result of freezing without constant churning. Granita is traditionally served slightly thawed and slushy, but if you like a smoother texture similar to a churn-frozen sherbet, purée it in a food processor shortly before serving.

Ice

A generic term for a sherbet, milk ice is sherbet to which a small amount of milk or cream has been added.

Sorbet, Sherbet and Sorbetto

A water ice usually made with fruit (or fruit juice) and sugar syrup. Other names for this product include ice, water ice, Italian ice, and fruit ice. To further complicate the issue, sometimes "sherbet" is the name for milk ice; "sorbet" is water ice. A small serving of wine - or citrus-flavoured sorbet - a palate cleanser - is sometimes served between courses to freshen the taste buds.

Frozen yoghurt

Has a smooth texture similar to ice cream and a slightly acidic taste that complements fruit particularly well.

Dream Machines

For anyone who loves frozen desserts, the new generation of ice cream freezers is pure dreamery, making it easier than ever before to enjoy your favourite frozen specialties at home anytime you like, not just on special occasions. Compact, convenient, and highly efficient, these machines stand ready to crank out icy pleasures at a moment's notice.

Although a few recipes in this book are made by still-freezing the base mixture in the freezer compartment of a refrigerator, most employ churn-freezing, using one of the following types of hand or electric-powered ice cream makers:

Salt and Ice Bucket Freezer

Licking the dasher after hand cranking the ice cream churn is a sweet childhood memory for many ice cream enthusiasts. This type of machine features a bucket fitted with a lidded metal canister that holds the base mixture. Powered by a hand crank or electric motor, the canister rotates continuously, surrounded by ice and rock salt, causing the contents of the canister to freeze as it is churned by a stationary dasher. This machine requires about 20-30 minutes of cranking for each batch. The slower the freezing process, the finer the texture while fast freezing yields an icy, coarse texture. One variation on this type of machine needs no salt or ice because it operates inside the freezer compartment of a refrigerator, with the power cord snaking out through the closed door.

Prechilled Canister Freezer

This type of machine features a coolant sealed in a hollow metal canister. After the canister has chilled in the freezer compartment of a refrigerator for at least 8 hours, the base mixture is poured into the center of the canister, and the dasher assembly and lid are fitted into place. Hand-powered models have a crank that is rotated every 2 or 3 minutes until the mixture freezes (usually in about 15 minutes). Electric models require about the same amount of time.

Self-Contained Refrigerated Freezer

The Maserati of ice cream makers, this Italian design boasts a countertop unit with built-in refrigeration and motorized dasher. It is the easiest to use (and the most expensive), producing the smoothest texture of any machine for home use.

basic
ingredients

For ice cream to have a smooth, creamy texture, both the water molecules and the fat globules in the mixture must be suspended evenly, so that the ice crystals that form during freezing are very small. The basic ice cream ingredients, in addition to contributing flavour, help that to happen.

Many commercial ice cream manufacturers use emulsifiers and stabilizers to improve the texture of their product, mask or compensate for inferior ingredients or achieve an extended shelf life. Such artificial ingredients are never needed in ice cream made in small quantities at home with fresh, wholesome ingredients. There are also homemade ice cream recipes that call for such ingredients as cornstarch, instant vanilla pudding, gelatin, and flour in an attempt to simulate the texture produced by more expensive ingredients. Anyone who has tasted good homemade ice cream, made with pure, high quality ingredients, will find it hard to offer such pseudo-flavours to family and guests.

Cream

The butterfat in cream is primarily responsible for providing the rich, smooth texture of ice cream. In general, the higher the proportion of butterfat, the richer and smoother the ice cream. However, resist the temptation to substitute whipping cream for the half and half or milk in an ice cream recipe. Too much cream greatly increases the chance of producing ice cream flecked with butter. As a general rule, do not exceed a ratio of 75 percent cream to 25 percent milk.

Eggs

Egg yolks are cooked to form the custard base used in many ice cream recipes. They act as emulsifiers; that is, they keep the fat globules in milk and cream from clumping together. Use large eggs for all the recipes in this book. Yolks are most easily separated from whites when eggs are cold, but egg whites at room temperature provide more volume when whisked. Egg whites may be frozen until needed, then thawed in the refrigerator.

Fruit

Most fruits used to flavour ice cream contain naturally occurring pectin and a certain amount of fiber. Both of these substances help to keep milk fat and water molecules in an even suspension as they freeze.

Milk

Milk fat forms small globules in the ice cream mixture that help to keep the water molecules dispersed. The emulsifying action of cooked egg yolks helps keep these small fat globules from clumping together as they are churned. If they do form clumps, they will produce butter.

Sugar

Water in which sugar has been dissolved has a freezing point below 0°C/32°F. Because of the sugar present, not all the water in ice cream freezes. Sugar thus helps keep ice cream from becoming a solid block of ice.

nectarine sorbet

sorbets and sherbets

Let your taste buds delight in the flavour

of cool Nectarine Sorbet, Melon Sherbet or a Strawberry Ice. You can frolic guiltlessly through this chilly wonderland because the recipes in this section are not only sinfully delicious, they contain less than 1 gram of fat per serving.

melon
sherbet

Photograph opposite

melon sherbet

ingredients

1pt/600ml/20fl oz water
³/4 cup/180g/6oz caster sugar
1 tablespoon lemon juice
1kg/2 lb honeydew melon or
rockmelon
grated orange rind
1 teaspoon ginger essence
2 egg whites
4 drops food colour (optional)

Method:

1 *Put water, sugar and lemon juice in a heavy based saucepan and heat gently until sugar has dissolved. Increase heat and cook rapidly fo 5 minutes. Allow to cool.*

2 *Scoop flesh from the melon, remove pips and using a food processor or blender, purée.*

3 *Stir into sugar syrup the orange rind and ginger essence.*

4 *Beat egg whites until soft peaks form and fold into melon mixture.*

5 *Pour into ice cream maker, add colour if desired. Churn approximately 30 minutes or until blades stop.*

Note: *This looks great served in tiny halved melon skins (that have been reserved) as individual serving portions.*

Makes approximately
4 cups/1 litre/1³/4pints

strawberry
and rhubarb sorbet

Method:

1 In a heavy based saucepan combine rhubarb and water. Bring to a boil over medium heat and simmer, covered, until rhubarb is tender (approximately 5 minutes). Stir in sugar until dissolved.

2 Using a food processor or blender, purée the rhubarb. Place into a bowl.

3 Purée strawberries and stir into rhubarb mixture.

4 Pour into ice cream maker and churn approximately 20 minutes or until blades stop.

**Makes approximately
6cups/1 1/2 litres/2 1/2 pts**

**4 cups/500g/1 lb fresh rhubarb, cut
into 2 1/2cm/1 in lengths
1/4 cup/60ml/2fl oz water
1 1/2 cups/375g/12 1/2oz sugar
2 punnets/500g/1 lb fresh strawberries**

kiwi
fruit sorbet

Method:

1 Put the water, lemon juice and caster sugar into a heavy based saucepan. Heat gently until the sugar has dissolved. Increase the heat and cook rapidly for 5 minutes. Allow to cool.

2 Using a food processor or blender, purée the kiwifruit and stir into the sugar syrup.

3 Beat the egg whites to soft peaks and fold into the mixture.

4 Pour into ice cream maker and churn approximately 30 minutes or until blades stop.

Makes approximately 6 cups/ 1 1/2 litres/2 1/2pts

ingredients

2 1/2cups/600ml/1 pt water
2 tablespoons lemon juice
100g/3oz caster sugar
8-10 kiwifruit, peeled
2 egg whites

watermelon
sherbet

Method:

1 Sprinkle sugar and salt over melon chunks and mix well. Once the sugar has dissolved, taste melon for sweetness; add more sugar if desired.

2 Purée melon, any juice it has released and egg whites in a blender or food processor. Chill well. Transfer to an ice cream machine and freeze according to manufacturer's instructions.

Note: Any of your favourite melons can be substituted for watermelon in this recipe. Be sure to reserve any juice that is released when you cut the melon into chunks.

**Makes approximately
4 cups/900ml/8fl oz**

¹/₄ **cup/60g/2oz sugar**
¹/₄ **teaspoon salt**
**900ml/1 quart chilled watermelon
chunks, seeds removed
(about one 2kg/4lb melon)
2 egg whites**

wine
sorbet

Method:

1 A day ahead, in a saucepan combine 1 cup/ 250mL/8fl oz water, sugar, and half the wine. Stir to dissolve sugar; bring to a boil. Reduce heat and simmer 3 minutes. Allow syrup to cool.

2 Add remaining wine to syrup. Pour into a shallow container and freeze overnight.

3 Two to four hours before serving remove frozen mixture from freezer. Transfer to a food processor and process until smooth, about 20-30 seconds. Return mixture to freezer container or individual serving glasses and freeze to set.

4 Remove sorbet from the freezer 5-10 minutes before serving to soften slightly.

Note: This delicate palate refresher can be made from just about any table wine except a really tannic red. You can also use a sweet wine, but reduce the sugar in the syrup by a tablespoon. Riesling or White Zinfandel would be good wines to start with, but feel free to experiment with various whites, roses and reds.

ingredients

¹/₂ **cup/125g/4oz sugar**
**1 cup/250ml/8fl oz dry or slightly
sweet table wine**

Alcohol affects the freezing process, so don't omit the step of boiling half the wine with the syrup one day before you plan to serve the sorbet. This procedure removes some, but not all, of the alcohol, giving the sorbet just the right texture and flavour. The sorbet does not keep well, as it tends to separate in the freezer.

**Make approximately
1 ¹/₂ cups/375ml/12 ¹/₂fl oz**

watermelon
and strawberry sorbet

Method:

1 *Combine water and sugar in a saucepan and bring to the boil. Remove from heat and allow to cool completely.*

2 *In a food processor or blender puree watermelon flesh and strawberries.*

3 *Mix puree into sugar mixture and freeze in a stainless steel bowl. Whisk from time to time during freezing to give a smooth even texture. To serve, spoon into elegant glasses and at the last minute pour a tablespoon of champagne into each glass.*

Serves 8

ingredients

**1 cup/250ml/8fl oz water
2 tablespoons caster sugar
300g/10oz watermelon, skinned, seeds removed and chopped
250g/8oz strawberries, hulled
3/4 cup/190ml/6fl oz dry champagne (optional)**

fresh
apple sorbet

ingredients

6 small tart green apples,
cored and peeled
1 cup/250ml/8fl oz simple sugar syrup
(see page 786)
1 tablespoon lemon juice

Method:

1 *Blend apples in a blender or food processor with syrup and lemon juice until completely smooth.*

2 *Transfer to an ice cream machine and freeze according to manufacturer's instructions.*

Note: *The flavour of this sorbet will vary with the variety of apple you choose.*

Makes approximately
4cups/1 litre/1³/₄ pints

ruby
grapefruit sorbet

Photograph opposite

ingredients

1 cup/250g/8oz sugar
1 tablespoon finely grated ruby
grapefruit rind
4 cups/1 litre/1³/₄pt ruby red
grapefruit juice
¹/₂ cup/125ml/4fl oz champagne or
sparkling white wine

Method:

1 *Place sugar, grapefruit rind and 1 cup/250ml/ 8fl oz juice in a non-reactive saucepan and cook, stirring, over a low heat until sugar dissolves.*

2 *Combine sugar syrup, wine and remaining juice, pour into an ice cream maker and freeze following manufacturer's instructions. Alternately, pour mixture into a shallow freezerproof container and freeze until ice crystals start to form around the edges. Using a fork, stir to break up ice crystals. Repeat the process once more then freeze until firm.*

Note: *Serve sorbet in scoops with slices of peach or nectarine. For this recipe, Ocean Spray ruby red grapefruit juice was used. It is available from supermarkets.*

Serves 8

lemon
sherbet

ingredients

2¹/₂ cups/625g/1¹/₄lb sugar
3 cups/750ml/1¹/₄pt water
2 cups/500ml/16fl oz lemon juice

Method:

1 *Place sugar and water in a saucepan over a low heat and cook, stirring, until sugar dissolves. Bring to the boil and boil for 30 seconds. Pour syrup into a heatproof bowl and chill.*

2 *Combine sugar syrup and lemon juice, pour into an ice-cream maker and freeze following manufacturer's instructions. Alternatively, pour mixture into a shallow freezerproof container and freeze until ice crystals start to form around the edges. Using a fork, stir to break up ice crystals. Repeat the process once more then freeze until firm.*

Serves 6

mango
sherbet

ingredients

2¹/₂ cups/625g/1¹/₄lb sugar
2 cups/500ml/16fl oz water
1¹/₂kg/3 lb fresh mango flesh

Method:

1 *Place sugar and water in a saucepan over a low heat and cook, stirring, until sugar dissolves. Bring to the boil and boil for 30 seconds. Pour syrup into a heatproof bowl and chill.*

2 *Place mango in a food processor and process until smooth. Push puréed mango through a fine sieve, then stir in syrup. Pour mango mixture into a ice-cream maker and freeze following manufacturer's instructions. Alternatively, pour mixture into a shallow freezerproof container and freeze until ice crystals start to form around the edges. Using a fork, stir to break up ice crystals. Repeat the process once more then freeze until firm.*

Serves 6

strawberry
ice

Method:

1 *Purée melon, strawberries, lemon juice, sugar and water in a blender or food processor.*

2 *Pour mixture into an ice cream maker and chill according to instructions. Alternatively, freeze in ice trays. When semi-frozen, beat the mixture to break up any large ice crystals. Repeat the process twice more, then freeze in a suitable container until solid.*

Serves 6

ingredients

315g/10oz cantaloupe melon flesh, chopped
185g/6oz strawberries, hulled
2 tablespoon lemon juice
60g/2oz sugar
125ml/4fl oz water

---

tangy
lemon ice

Method:

1 *Combine water and sugar in a heavy saucepan and bring to the boil, stirring until sugar dissolves. Then simmer for 1-2 minutes or until a syrup forms. Remove from heat, stir in lemon juice and set aside to cool completely.*

2 *Pour mixture into a freezer container and freeze, beating occasionally with an electric mixer or whisk, until solid, or use an ice cream maker.*

Makes approximately
4cups/1 litre/1 ³/₄ pints

ingredients

2 cups/500ml/16fl oz water
315g/10oz sugar
2 cups/500ml/16fl oz strained fresh lemon juice

pineapple
and mint sherbet

Photograph opposite

Method:

1 Remove the skin and core from the pineapple. Finely chop $1/3$ of the flesh and set aside.

2 Using a food processor or blender, purée remaining pineapple with the icing sugar and yoghurt.

3 Beat the egg whites until soft peaks form and fold into the pineapple together with chopped mint.

4 Pour into ice cream maker and churn approximately 30 minutes or until blades stop.

Note: For a party, serve large scooped out pineapple shell with diced fresh pineapple and chopped mint. Chill. Just before serving top with pineapple sherbet and decorate.

**Makes approximately
4 cups/1 litre/1 3/4 pints**

ingredients

**1 small pineapple or 750g/1 1/2 lb can
pineapple pieces, drained
60g/2oz icing sugar
300ml/10oz plain unsweetened yoghurt
1 tablespoon chopped fresh mint
2 egg whites**

orange
sherbet

Method:

1 Place zest in a fine strainer and pour boiling water over it. Drain, reserving zest.

2 In a saucepan over high heat, bring orange juice, sugar, 2 cups/500ml/16fl oz water, and lemon juice to a boil, stirring occasionally. Boil for 5 minutes. Remove from heat and let cool. Add orange zest.

3 Transfer to an ice cream machine and freeze according to manufacturer's instructions.

Note: For an unusual and attractive presentation, pipe the sherbet through a pastry bag into chilled glass dishes or champagne glasses and refreeze until serving time. For a creamier texture, you can substitute skim milk for up to half of the juice.

**Makes approximately
4 cups/1 litre/1 3/4 pints**

ingredients

**2 teaspoons orange zest
1 cup/250ml/8fl oz boiling water
4 cups/900ml/1 1/2pt freshly squeezed
orange juice
2 3/4 cups/650g/22oz sugar
3 tablespoons lemon juice**

pear
sorbet

ingredients

2 tablespoons lemon juice
1 1/4 kg/2 1/2lb fully ripe pears
4 cups/900ml/1 1/2pts water
3 cups/750g/1 1/2pts sugar
1/2 lemon, sliced
1 vanilla bean, split in half lengthwise
1-2 tablespoons lemon juice extra

Method:

1 Stir the 2 tablespoons lemon juice into a bowl of cold water. Peel and core pears; place in lemon water.

2 Combine 3 1/2 cups/800ml/1 1/3pts water and 2 1/2 cups/600ml/1pt of the sugar in a large saucepan. Stir over medium heat until sugar dissolves and syrup come to a boil. Reduce heat and add lemon, vanilla bean and pears. Cover and simmer 5 minutes. Turn pears over and simmer until tender (5-10 minutes, depending on ripeness of pears).

3 Drain pears, reserving poaching syrup. Let cool. Purée in food processor. Chill 1 cup /250ml/8fl oz of the poaching syrup, reserving any remaining syrup for another use.

4 Combine 1/3 cup/85ml/3fl oz water and the remaining sugar in a saucepan; stir over medium heat until syrup comes to the boil. Cool to room temperature; refrigerate until cold.

5 Combine the 1 cup/250ml/8fl oz reserved poaching syrup, the 1 tablespoon lemon juice, and pear purée. Then add half the cold sugar syrup. Taste and add more syrup if mixture is not sweet enough or more lemon juice if needed.

6 Freeze in ice cream machine according to manufacturer's instructions. Cover and store in freezer for up to 2 weeks.

**Makes approximately
4 cups/900ml/8fl oz**

celery
and tomato sorbet

Method:

1 Using a food processor or blender, purée half of the tomato and celery. Place into a bowl. Purée remaining half together with the dill. Add to bowl.
2 Add vinegar, salt and pepper and stir to combine.
3 Whisk egg white until thick. Fold into tomato mixture.
4 Pour into ice cream maker and churn approximately 30 minutes or until blades stop. **Note:** Looks very attractive when served in hollowed out tomatoes.

**Makes approximately
4 cups/1 litre/1 ³/₄ pints**

ingredients

6 large tomatoes, peeled and quartered
4 stalks celery, strings removed and roughly chopped
1 tablespoon fresh chopped dill
1 tablespoon wine vinegar
1 tablespoon salt
¹/₄ teaspoon pepper
1 egg white
parsley sprigs for garnish

nectarine

sorbet

Photograph opposite

ingredients

**4 cups/900g/1 1/2pts nectarines,
sliced and peeled
1/2 cup/125ml/4fl oz freshly squeezed
orange juice
sugar to taste
pinch salt
mint leaves, for garnish as needed**

nectarine sorbet

Method:

1 *Spread sliced nectarines in one layer on a baking sheet. Freeze, uncovered, until frozen solid.*

2 *Place frozen nectarines and orange juice in a blender or food processor. Process until smooth, stopping to scrape work bowl as necessary. If your machine struggles to process the frozen nectarines, let fruit stand 10-15 minutes at room temperature to thaw slightly. Depending on the size of your blender or food processor, you may have to process nectarines in several batches.*

3 *Add sugar to taste and salt. Mix thoroughly by hand or in food processor. Serve at once, garnished with mint leaves, or return to freezer for up to 1 hour.*

Note: *For a cool refreshing end to any meal, serve this tangy dessert garnished with fresh mint leaves.*

**Makes approximately
3 cups/750ml/24fl oz**

chocolate ice cream

ice creams

I scream, you scream, we all scream

for ice cream. As children we delighted in ice cream cones and sandwiches, sundaes and banana splits. As adults we still do. Ice Cream is a universal treat; travel just about anywhere and you can enjoy it with the natives. Birthday parties and afternoons at the beach absolutely demand it. Dinner party guests adore it. Whether it's shaped into an elaborate bombe, set aflame with brandy, topped with sauce, or just scooped into a cone, ice cream is a tasty, refreshing, happy dessert. With so many inexpensive, simple to operate and mess free ice cream machines now on the market, any home kitchen can be a first-class ice cream parlour, every dessert loving cook an ice cream pro.

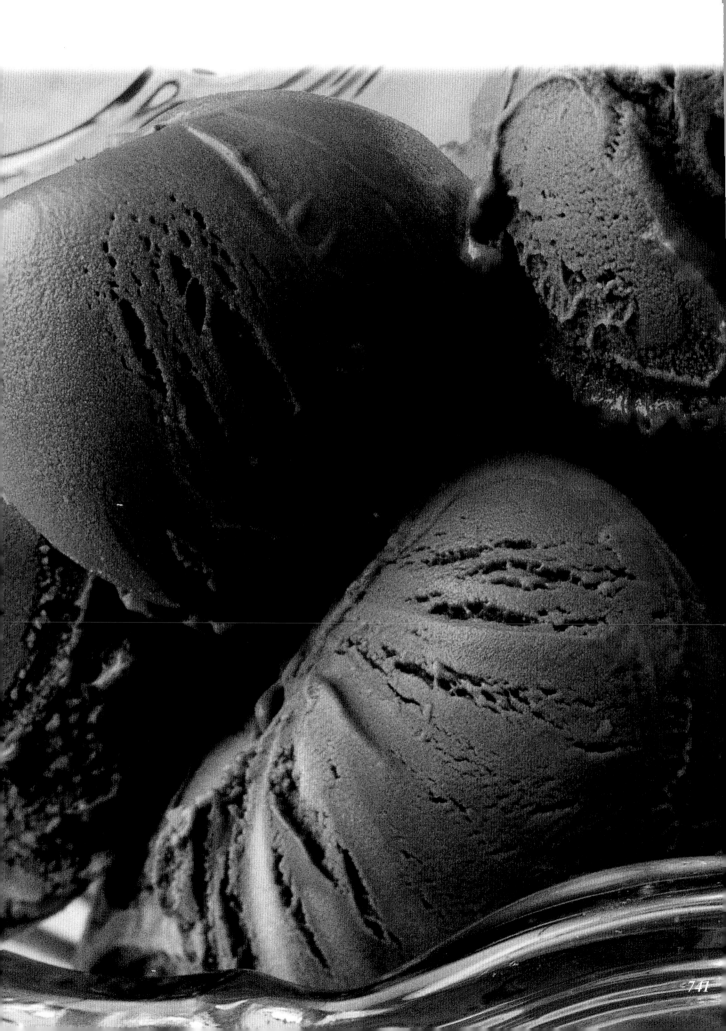

fresh
peach ice cream

Photograph opposite

ingredients

3 fresh peaches, white or yellow
2 cups/500ml/16fl oz smoothy
(see page 784 for recipe)
1/2 cup/120g/4oz sugar
1/2 teaspoon lemon juice
almond flavouring

Method:

1 *Peel the peaches after dipping into boiling water. Cut into small pieces. Add the sugar and leave to mature at room temperature for*

2 *Mix 1 cup of peaches and 1 cup of smoothy and blend until smooth. Fold into the remaining peach pieces and smoothy with the lemon juice and almond flavouring and chill.*

3 *Either churn or set by the freeze/beat method. Cover and ripen for one to two hours in the freezer, or until firm.*

Note: *Blending half the peaches helps to spread the flavour and adds colour, while the other half being left in pieces adds to the texture. Lemon juice is usually used with peaches to prevent them from browning. In this case, it is added later so that some discolouration takes place, because it is attractive in the ice cream.*

**Makes approximately
4 cups/900ml/8fl oz**

vanilla
ice cream

ingredients

4 cups/1 litre/35fl oz smoothy
(see page 784 for recipe)
1 1/4 cups/300g/10oz sugar
vanilla flavouring

Method:

1 *Mix all ingredients together and chill for one to two hours in the refrigerator.*

2 *Churn or set by the freeze/beat method and ripen, covered, in the freezer for two hours or until firm, before serving.*

Serves 8

rich
vanilla
ice cream

Method:

1 Beat the yolks and sugar until pale and frothy.

2 Heat smoothy in a medium-sized saucepan and stir constantly until custard thickens and coats the back of a wooden spoon. Add vanilla and leave to cool. Place a circle of greaseproof paper directly on top of the custard.

3 Whip the cream until it forms soft peaks, and fold into the thoroughly cooled custard. Pour into a wetted 3 cup/750ml/24fl oz mould and leave to set.

Note: Because this ice cream is so rich, it is not necessary to beat halfway through the setting period. This custard-based ice cream is a neutral base which can be used in a number of ways and flavoured in many different ways as well. If wanting to unmould this ice cream, first rinse the mould out with cold water, before pouring in the ice cream and freezing it.

To Unmould: Dip the mould into tepid water, invert over a serving dish and shake until the ice cream slips out. Return to the freezer to firm before garnishing and presenting.

Makes approximately 3 cups/750mL/24fl oz

ingredients

4 egg yolks
²/₃ cup/160g/5oz sugar
1 cup/250ml/8fl oz smoothy
(see page 72 for recipe)
1¼cup/300ml/10fl oz thickened cream
vanilla flavouring

white chocolate
and raspberry ice cream

Method:

1 *Place sugar and water in a small saucepan and cook over a low heat, stirring constantly until sugar dissolves. Bring to the boil, then reduce heat and simmer for 5 minutes or until syrup reduces by half.*

2 *Place egg yolks in a large mixing bowl and beat until thick and creamy. Continue beating, adding syrup in a thin stream. Add vanilla essence and chocolate and beat until mixture thickens and is cool.*

3 *Fold cream and raspberries into chocolate mixture. Place in a large freezerproof container, cover and freeze until firm.*

Makes approximately 7cups/1750ml/3pts

ingredients

1¼ cups/315g/10oz sugar
½ cup/125ml/4fl oz water
6 egg yolks
1 teaspoon vanilla essence
250g/8oz white chocolate, melted
2 cups/500ml/16fl oz cream
(double), whipped
500g/1lb raspberries, roughly chopped

chocolate
ice cream

Photograph opposite

ingredients

1 cup/220g/7oz caster sugar
9 egg yolks
¹/₂ cup/45g/1¹/₂oz cocoa powder, sifted
2 cups/500ml/16fl oz milk
2¹/₂ cups/600ml/1pt thickened cream
125g/4oz milk chocolate, melted

chocolate ice cream

Method:

1 *Place sugar and egg yolks in a bowl and beat until thick and pale.*
2 *Place cocoa powder in a saucepan. Gradually stir in milk and cream and heat over a medium heat, stirring constantly, until mixture is almost boiling. Stir in chocolate.*
3 *Remove pan from heat and whisk hot milk mixture into egg mixture. Set aside to cool.*
4 *Pour mixture into a freezerproof container and freeze for 30 minutes, or until mixture begins to freeze around edges. Beat mixture until even in texture. Return to freezer and repeat beating process two more times. Freeze until solid. Alternatively, place mixture in an ice cream maker and freeze according to manufacturer's instructions.*
Note: *For true chocoholics, chopped chocolate or chocolate bits can be folded into the mixture before it freezes solid. Serve in scoops with vanilla tuiles or raspberries.*
Makes approximately 7cups/1750ml/3pts

hazelnut
ice cream

Method:

1 Bring milk to the boil in a saucepan. Stir in hazelnuts, cream and vanilla; lower the heat so the mixture is just simmer.

2 Beat egg yolks with sugar until pale and creamy. Gradually add two thirds of the milk mixture, beating constantly.

3 Pour the contents of the mixing bowl into the remaining milk mixture in the pan. Cook over moderate heat, stirring constantly, until the mixture thickens enough to coat the back of a spoon. Cool.

4 Pour mixture into an ice cream maker and freeze according to instructions. Alternatively, freeze in ice trays. When semi-frozen, beat the mixture to break up any large ice crystals. Repeat the process twice more, then freeze in a suitable container until solid.

Serves 6

ingredients

500ml/16fl oz milk
110g/3¹/₂oz hazelnuts, ground
250ml/8fl oz double cream
2 teaspoon vanilla essence
6 egg yolks
185g/6oz soft brown sugar

mocha
ice cream

Method:

1 Combine the first 5 ingredients in the top of a double saucepan.

2 Stir over simmering water until chocolate has melted, cool.

3 Fold in evaporated milk and cream. Pour into ice cream machine. Churn until firm and blades stop turning. Approximately 40 minutes. Serve immediately or spoon into a container and freeze.

Note: If larger quantity required, double the ingredients listed above.

Makes approximately 3cups/³/₄ litre/1¹/₄pts

ingredients

4 egg yolks
¹/₂ cup/120ml/4oz caster sugar
2 tablespoons coffee liqueur
1 tablespoon instant coffee powder
100g/3¹/₂oz dark chocolate, chopped
375ml/12¹/₂oz canned evaporated milk, chilled
1 cup/250ml/8fl oz cream, whipped

rich
chocolate ice cream

Method:

1 Combine the first 4 ingredients in the top of a double saucepan.
2 Whisk over simmering water until chocolate has melted. Cool.
3 Whip evaporated milk until thick and fold into mixture with cream.
4 Pour into ice cream machine. Churn until firm and blades stop turning. (Approximately 40 minutes) Serve immediately or spoon into a container and freeze.

**Makes approximately
3 cups/750ml/1 1/4pts**

ingredients

**4 egg yolks, lightly beaten
1/2 cup/120g/4oz castor sugar
2 tablespoons chocolate liqueur
200g/7oz dark chocolate, chopped
375ml/12 1/2oz can evaporated milk, chilled
1 cup/250ml/8fl oz cream, whipped**

mango
ice cream

Photograph opposite

ingredients

**2 x 440g/14oz cans sliced mangoes,
drained
4 tablespoon lemon juice
185g/6oz caster sugar
2 eggs, separated
300ml/10fl oz double cream, whipped**

Method:

1 *Set aside a few mango slices for decoration. Purée mango with lemon juice and caster sugar in a blender or food processor. Transfer to a bowl. Cover. Refrigerate.*

2 *Using an electric mixer, beat egg yolks until pale and creamy. In a separate bowl, beat egg whites until stiff.*

3 *Fold egg yolks into cream, then fold in mango purée. Finally, fold in stiffly beaten egg whites.*

4 *Spoon mixture into an ice cream maker and chill according to instructions. Alternatively, freeze in ice trays. When semi-frozen, beat the mixture to break up any large ice crystals. Repeat the process once more, then freeze in a suitable container until solid.*

5 *Soften slightly before serving, decorated with strawberries and the reserved mango slices.*

**Makes approximately
4cups/1 litre/1 3/4 pts**

pistachio
ice cream

ingredients

**2 teaspoons gelatine
2 tablespoons boiling water
375ml/12 1/2 fl oz can evaporated milk, chilled
60g/2oz sugar
2 tablespoons Galliano
250g/8oz pistachio nuts, shelled,
husked and chopped**

Method:

1 *Dissolve gelatine in water. Whip evaporated milk, sugar, dissolved gelatine and Galliano until thick and frothy.*

2 *Stir in pistachio nuts. Pour into ice cream machine. Churn until firm and blades stop turning. (Approximately 40 minutes) Spoon into a container and freeze.*

**Makes approximately
4cups/1 litre/1 3/4 pints**

crunchy
caramel apricot sundae

ingredients

4 large scoops vanilla ice cream
440g/14oz canned apricots, drained

Crunchy caramel topping
30g/1oz unsalted butter
2 tablespoons brown sugar
60g/2oz toasted muesli
2 tablespoons walnuts, chopped
1 tablespoon shredded coconut

Method:
1 To make topping, place butter and sugar in a saucepan and cook, stirring, over a medium heat for 2-3 minutes or until sugar dissolves and mixture bubbles. Stir in muesli, nuts and coconut, mix well and remove pan from heat.
2 Place a scoop of ice cream in each serving dish, top with a few apricots and sprinkle with topping. Serve immediately.
Note: Any canned fruit can be used to make this easy dessert. The cooled topping will keep in an airtight container for several days.
Serves 4

rocky
road ice cream

Method:
1 Place ice cream in a large mixing bowl. Fold in Turkish Delight, pink and white marshmallows, red and green cherries, coconut and peanut bars. Spoon mixture into a freezerproof container, cover and freeze until firm.

Note: Serving suggestion: Place scoops of ice cream into bowls and serve with wafers.

Makes approximately
6 cups/1 ½ litre/2 ½pts

ingredients

1 litre/1 ³/₄pt vanilla
ice cream, softened
2 x 60g/2oz chocolate-coated Turkish
Delight bars, chopped
10 pink marshmallows, chopped
5 white marshmallows, chopped
6 red glacé cherries, chopped
6 green glacé cherries, chopped
4 tablespoons shredded
coconut, toasted
2 x 45g/1 ½oz chocolate-coated
scorched peanut bars, chopped

strawberry
and cream ice cream

Photograph opposite

Method:

1 *Beat egg yolks and sugar until thick. Heat evaporated milk gently and then combine with egg yolk mixture.*
2 *Whisk over simmering water until slightly thickened. Cool.*
3 *Fold in remaining ingredients and pour into ice cream machine. Churn until firm and blades stop turning*

Makes approximately 4 cups/1 litre/1 ¾ pts

ingredients

3 egg yolks
¼ cup/60g/2oz castor sugar
375ml/12½fl oz can evaporated milk
1 teaspoon vanilla essence
1 cup/250ml/8fl oz cream, whipped
1 punnet strawberries, hulled and quartered
4 tablespoons strawberry topping

boysenberry
swirl ice cream

Method:

1 *Beat egg yolks and sugar together.*
2 *Gently heat evaporated milk and combine with egg yolk mixture in the top of a double saucepan.*
3 *Whisk over simmering water until slightly thickened. Cool.*
4 *Add vanilla, half the boysenberries and cream.*
5 *Pour into ice cream machine. Churn until firm and blades stop turning.*
6 *Using a food processor or blender, purée remaining boysenberries with the dissolved gelatine. Spoon ice cream into a container and lightly fold in puréed boysenberries to give swirled appearance. Serve immediately or place in freezer.*

Makes approximately 4 cups/1 litre/1 ¾ pts

ingredients

4 egg yolks
½ cup caster sugar
375ml/13oz can evaporated milk
1 teaspoon vanilla essence
425g/14oz can boysenberries, drained
1 cup/250ml/8oz cream
1 teaspoon gelatine, dissolved in 1 tablespoon boiling water

1 In a large heatproof bowl, melt milk chocolate with the chocolate and hazelnut spread. Cool slightly, stir in Tia Maria and egg yolks. Whip half the cream until soft peaks form. Fold into chocolate mixture.

2 Beat egg whites in a bowl until soft peaks form. Gradually add sugar, beating until mixture is stiff.

3 Melt dark chocolate; fold half into creamy chocolate mixture, then fold in the egg whites. Keep remaining chocolate warm over hot water.

4 Spoon mixture into a large loaf tin lined with cling film. Freeze until firm.

5 Make sauce by adding the remaining cream to the reserved chocolate. Stir over low heat until smooth. Serve with the sliced terrine.

Serves 12

frozen
nutty choc terrine

ingredients

300g/9¹/₂oz milk chocolate
250g/8oz chocolate and hazelnut spread
60ml/2fl oz Tia Maria
6 eggs, separated
600ml/1pt double cream
3 tblspn caster sugar
250g/8oz dark chocolate

cinnamon
ice cream

Method:

1 Combine milk, cream, cinnamon stick and ground cinnamon in a heavy saucepan and heat over a very low heat, without boiling, for 15 minutes. Cover and cool to room temperature. Discard cinnamon stick.

2 Dissolve sugar in water over low heat, bring to the boil and boil rapidly until syrup reaches 120°C/250°F when tested with a sugar thermometer, or until a little syrup dropped into cold water will form a hard ball.

3 Beat egg yolks until thick and creamy then gradually add boiling syrup in a thin, steady stream, beating constantly until mixture is cold, thick and fluffy. Add cinnamon liquid and mix well.

4 Pour mixture into a freezer container and freeze, stirring or whisking mixture several times, until solid, or use an ice cream maker. **Note:** Serve with hot peaches either poached or gently fried in a little butter with sugar.

Makes approximately 4cups/1 litre/1 ³/₄ pts

ingredients

**315ml/10fl oz milk
200ml/6¹/₂ fl oz double cream
1 stick cinnamon
1 tablespoon freshly ground cinnamon
125g/4oz sugar
200ml/6¹/₂ fl oz water
6 egg yolks**

coconut
ice cream

Method:

1 Combine cream, milk and coconut in a saucepan and heat over a very low heat, without boiling, for 15 minutes. Cover and cool to room temperature. Blend mixture briefly in a food processor then strain through a sieve, rubbing to extract as much liquid as possible from the coconut. Discard coconut pulp.

2 Beat eggs, egg yolks, sugar and salt in a heatproof bowl until thick. Place over simmering water, add coconut liquid and cook, stirring, until slightly thickened. Remove from heat, place over a pan of iced water and allow to cool, stirring occasionally.

3 Pour mixture into a freezer container, cover and freeze until firm. Scoop into bowls and decorate with lightly toasted shredded coconut.

Makes approximately 4 cups/1 litre /1 ³/₄ pt

ingredients

**375ml/12fl oz double cream
375ml/12fl oz milk
90g/3oz desiccated coconut
2 eggs
2 egg yolks
125g/4oz sugar
pinch salt
toasted shredded coconut for serving**

creamy
honey ice cream

Photograph opposite

Method:
1 Combine egg yolks and egg in the top of a double saucepan. Beat until light and fluffy.
2 Heat evaporated milk in a separate saucepan until lukewarm.
3 Stir in honey and gradually whisk into egg mixture. Stir constantly over simmering heat.
4 Remove from heat and cool. Fold through whipped cream.
5 Pour into ice cream machine. Churn until firm and blades stop turning. Approximately 40 minutes. Serve immediately or spoon into a container and freeze.

Makes approximately 4 cups/1 litre/1³/₄ pts

ingredients

**3 egg yolks
1 egg
375ml/13oz can evaporated milk
200ml/7oz honey
300ml/10fl oz cream, whipped**

caramel
ice cream

Method:
1 Whip evaporated milk and caramel sauce together until thick and frothy.
2 Fold in crushed toffee.
3 Pour into ice cream machine. Churn until firm and blades stop turning (approximately 30 minutes). Spoon into a container and freeze.
Note: If larger quantity required, double the ingredients listed above.

Makes approximately 2 cups/¹/₂ litre/16fl oz

ingredients

**375ml/13oz can evaporated milk
¹/₂ cup/120ml/4oz caramel sauce
¹/₂ cup/90g/3oz crushed toffee**

pernod
and peach ice cream

Method:

1 *Put peaches in a bowl and cover with boiling water. Drain after 15 seconds and remove the skins.*

2 *Cut the peaches into quarters, discarding the stones.*

3 *Put the sugar and water into a heavy based saucepan and heat gently until sugar dissolves. Increase the heat and cook rapidly for 5 minutes.*

4 *Purée the peaches together with the syrup and stir in the Pernod and yoghurt.*

5 *Beat the cream until soft peaks form and fold into fruit mixture.*

6 *Pour into ice cream maker and churn approximately 30 minutes or until blades stop.*

Makes 4cups/1 litre/1 ³/₄ pts

ingredients

4-5 fresh peaches
¹/₂ cup/125g/4oz caster sugar
300ml/10fl oz water
2 tablespoons Pernod
300ml/10fl oz plain unsweetened yoghurt
150ml/5fl oz thickened cream

morello
cherry ice cream

Method:

1 Chop the cherries (medium fine) and stir all ingredients together, making sure the sugar is dissolved. Chill.

2 Either churn or set by the freeze/beat method. Cover and ripen in the freezer until firm.

**Makes approximately
3 ½ cups/900ml/1 ½pts**

ingredients

**2 cups/500ml/16fl oz smoothy
(see page 784 for recipe)
²/₃ cup/150g/5oz pitted Morello
cherries, drained
¹/₂ cup/120ml/4fl oz syrup from cherries
2 tablespoons cherry brandy, optional
¹/₃ cup/80g/3oz sugar
few drops red food colouring**

fresh
fig ice cream

Photograph opposite.

ingredients

200g/7oz fresh ripe figs, white or purple
1/2 cup/120g/4oz sugar
2 cups/500ml/16fl oz smoothy
(see page 784 for recipe)

Method:
1 *Peel and chop figs roughly, cook slowly with sugar for 10 minutes, stirring from time to time to dissolve sugar and prevent catching.*
2 *Purée in blender of food processor and cool.*
3 *Add to smoothy and mix well. Chill.*
4 *Either churn or set by the freeze/beat method. Cover and ripen in freezer for one to two hours or until firm. Garnish with chocolate curls or grated chocolate.*

**Makes approximately
3 1/2 cups/900ml/1 1/2pts**

apple-pie
ice cream

ingredients

2 cups/500ml/16fl oz smoothy
(see page 784 for recipe)
3/4 cup/180g/6oz bottled apple sauce
sugar, optional
150ml/5fl oz thickened cream
pinch ground cloves
1/8 teaspoon cinnamon
1/2 teaspoon green food colouring

Method:
1 *Mix all ingredients together and chill.*
2 *Either churn or set by the freeze/beat method. Cover and ripen in the freezer for one hour, or until firm.*
3 *Before serving, rest in the bottom of the refrigerator if too firm.*

**Makes approximately
3 1/2 cups/850ml/1 1/3pts**

chocolate
brandy ice cream

Photograph opposite

1 Combine the cream, milk, chocolate and coffee in a large saucepan over moderate heat. Stir until the chocolate melts, do not allow mixture to boil.

2 Meanwhile, using an electric mixer, beat egg yolks with sugar until pale and thick. Continue to beat while adding hot mocha cream. Return mixture to a clean pan and stir constantly over moderate heat until mixture thickens slightly. Stir in brandy. Set aside until cool.

3 Pour mixture into an ice cream maker and chill according to instructions. Alternatively, freeze in ice trays. When semi-frozen, beat mixture to break up any large ice crystals. Repeat the process twice more, then freeze in a suitable container until solid.

Serves 12

ingredients

750ml/1¼pt double cream
250ml/8fl oz milk
155g/5oz dark chocolate, grated
2 teaspoon instant coffee powder
5 egg yolks
185g/6oz caster sugar
2 tablespoon brandy

quick
chocolate chip ice cream

Method:

1 Whip cream with Kahlua until soft peaks form; fold mixture into ice cream. Spoon into a freezerproof container and freeze until semi-frozen.

2 Beat mixture to break up any large ice crystals. Stir in chocolate chips and nuts. Freeze until solid.

Serves 12

ingredients

Chop the nuts very finely.
A food processor,
250ml/8fl oz double cream
3 tblspn Kahlua
2 litres/3½pt good quality vanilla ice cream, softened
250g/8oz chocolate chips
125g/4oz almonds, chopped

chocolate pear bombe

special treats

Frozen desserts always seem special.

For adults, ice cream desserts, especially those laced with luscious liqueurs, are the perfect endings for stylish dinnerparties or romantic evenings. Frozen drinks are refreshing on lazy summer afternoons, bringing with them memories - or dreams - of vacations in exotic, tropical places. For children, frozen treats mean birthday parties, days at the beach and the ice cream truck coming down the street at last. Ice cream has a way of adding sparkle to any occasion. What could be more fun to eat than birthday cake and ice cream?

watermelon
bombe

Photograph opposite

watermelon bombe

ingredients

**French vanilla ice milk base
(see page 784)
¹/₄ cup/60ml miniature semisweet
chocolate chips
900ml/1 quart purchased raspberry
sherbet, slightly softened
green food colouring, as needed**

Method:

1 *Chill a 1⁴/₅ litre/2 quart melon-shaped mold in the freezer for at least 1 hour.*

2 *Line inside of mold with a layer of Vanilla Ice Milk. Cover with plastic film, pressing against the ice milk to seal it tightly and fill any air pockets. Return mold to freezer for at least 4 hours.*

3 *Stir chocolate chips into raspberry sherbet to simulate watermelon seeds. Remove plastic wrap from mold and fill cavity with sherbet. Top with plastic film and freeze until firm.*

4 *To unmold, dip mold quickly in lukewarm water and invert onto a chilled platter. Return to freezer to set.*

5 *Paint outside of molded ice milk with green food colouring. Cover well and return to freezer. Slice to serve.*

Note: *This molded dessert looks like a miniature watermelon. It's a treat for the eyes as well as the palate. The bombe must freeze in stages, so preparation must begin early on the day it will be served, or even the day before.*

Serves 10

coffee
granita

**500ml/16fl oz hot strong black coffee
sugar to taste
freshly whipped double cream,
sweetened to taste**

Method:

1 *While the coffee is still piping hot, stir in sugar until dissolved. Cool completely, then chill thoroughly.*
2 *Pour mixture into a freezer container and freeze, beating with an electric mixer or processing mixture several times, until solid, or use an ice cream maker.*
3 *For easier serving, break up granita, place in a food processor and process to a fine textured soft ice. Spoon into chilled goblets and garnish with cream.*

**Makes approximately
2 ¹/₂ cups/600ml/1 pint**

macadamia
nut ice cream

ingredients

**2 cups/500ml/16fl oz smoothy
(see page 784 for recipe)
1 ¹/₂ cups/180g/6oz shelled macadamia nuts
¹/₃ cup/80g/3oz sugar
few grains salt
almond flavouring, optional**

Method:

1 *Chop the nuts very finely. A food processor, blender or nut mill are the most efficient. Otherwise, using a large board, a large knife and lots of patience, chop the nuts and add to the smoothy in a medium-sized saucepan and bring very slowly to the boil. Turn off the heat, put on lid and infuse for five minutes.*
2 *Stir in sugar and salt, optional flavouring and cool. Chill.*
3 *Either churn or set by the freeze/beat method. Cover and ripen in the freezer for one to two hours before serving.*

Serves 5-6

ice cream
christmas pudding

Method:

1 *Place ice cream, apricots, cherries, pears, sultanas, raisins and rum in a bowl and mix to combine. Pour into an oiled and lined 6 cup/1 ½ litre/2½pt capacity pudding basin.*

2 *Freeze for 3 hours or until firm.*

Note: *To help unmould the pudding, briefly hold a warm, damp teatowel around the outside of the mould. Slice pudding and serve with rum custard.*

Serves 8

ingredients

1 litre/1¾ pt chocolate ice cream, softened
125g/4oz glacé apricots, chopped
125g/4oz glacé cherries, chopped
125g/4oz glacé pears, chopped
90g/3oz sultanas
75g/2½oz raisins, chopped
2 tablespoons rum

chocolate-
pear bombe

Photograph opposite

chocolate-pear bombe

ingredients

<u>Pear Ice Milk</u>
⅓ cup/85ml/3oz sugar
2 tablespoons lemon juice
I tablespoon pear-flavoured liqueur
I tablespoon grated lemon zest
**850ml/29oz can pear halves,
packed in natural juice or water,
drained, puréed and chilled**

500ml/I pint Chocolate ice milk
**I ½ litre/I ½ quarts Vanilla ice milk
whipped light cream and chocolate
shavings, for garnish (optional)
as needed**

Method:

I In a saucepan heat sugar with ⅓ cup/85ml water until sugar melts. Remove from heat and cool. Add lemon juice, liqueur, and lemon zest. Chill. Stir sugar syrup into chilled pear purée. Transfer to an ice cream machine and freeze according to manufacturer's instructions. Let ice milk "ripen" in freezer for several hours.

2 Chill a I ½ litre/I ½ quart mold in the freezer for several hours or overnight. Press three quarters of the chocolate ice milk into the mold, evenly covering the sides and bottom. Cover with plastic film, pressing against the ice milk to seal it tightly and fill any air pockets. Freeze until firm.

3 Press the Vanilla Ice Milk into an even layer over the Chocolate Ice Milk. Cover and freeze until very firm.

4 Fill in the centre of the bombe with the Pear Ice Milk. Freeze until very firm.

5 Cover the top surface with the remaining Chocolate Ice Milk. Cover with plastic film and freeze overnight or until ice milk is very firm.

6 To unmold, dip mold quickly in lukewarm water and invert onto a chilled serving plate. Return to freezer to set. Before serving, decorate the bombe with whipped cream and chocolate shavings, if used.

Note: This elegant bombe boasts two luscious ice-milk layers surrounding a creamy pear sorbet centre.

Serves I0

tia maria
and chocolate ice cream

Method:

1 *Heat fresh cream and vanilla. Add ¹/₂ grated chocolate to mixture and melt.*

2 *Whisk egg yolks and sugar together - pour on chocolate cream and beat - reheat until thickened. Cool.*

3 *Add remainder of chocolate, Tia Maria, thickened cream and grated orange rind. Pour into ice cream maker and churn, approximately 30 minutes or until blades stop.*

**Makes approximately
4cups/1 litre /1³/₄pt**

**45ml/1¹/₂oz standard fresh cream
3 drops vanilla essence
3 egg yolks
100g/3¹/₃oz castor sugar
1 cup/120g/4oz grated cooking
chocolate
2 tablespoons Tia Maria
150ml/5fl oz thickened cream
1 teaspoon grated orange rind**

grand
marnier and cream

Method:

1 *In a heavy-based saucepan combine sugar, orange juice, water and peel. Stir constantly over a medium heat until mixture comes to a boil. Cook rapidly for 5 minutes. Set aside.*

2 *Beat egg yolks until fluffy and pale lemon coloured. Beating constantly, pour hot syrup over beaten egg yolks. Continue beating and cook over hot water until mixture is very thick; then cool.*

3 *Fold in Grand Marnier liqueur.*

4 *Whip cream until soft peaks form and fold into egg mixture. Pour into ice cream maker and churn approximately 30 minutes or until blades stop.*

Makes 4 cups/1 litre/1 ³/₄ pts

ingredients

¹/₂ cup/125g/4oz sugar
¹/₄ cup/60ml/2 fl oz orange juice
¹/₂ cup/125ml/4oz water
1 teaspoon grated orange peel
8 egg yolks
¹/₄ cup/60ml/2 fl oz Grand Marnier liqueur
1 cup/250ml/8oz whipping cream

party friend
ice creams

Method:

1 Cut through the cones where the cup joins the cornet "handle" and place the cup upside down on a baking tray covered with foil.
2 Place a scoop of firm ice cream on the inverted cup. Scatter over chocolate nonpareilles or coconut to make hair. Using a small rose piping tube, pipe cream around the base of the ice cream or leave plain.
3 To make the hats, dip the base of the cornet into glace icing or melted chocolate, turning to coat approximately 2½cm/1in, up the cone. Then dip into chocolate nonpareilles, or leave plain.
4 When the cornet is dry, decorate by sticking a row of three Smarties down one side using melted chocolate or very stiff glace icing. Place cornet on ice cream at a jaunty angle and form faces with jubes, etc.
5 Place tray in the freezer until ready to serve.

Make 1 party friend per child

ingredients

**scoops of vanilla, chocolate and
strawberry ice cream
cornet ice cream cones
Smarties
chocolate nonpareilles
multi-coloured nonpareilles
desiccated coconut
life savers
coloured jubes
cooking chocolate, melted
glace icing (icing sugar mixed with
thickened cream)
thickened cream, whipped**

chocolate
hazelnut meringue baskets

Method:

1 *Preheat oven to 150°C/300°F/Gas 2. Cut 2 pieces of nonstick baking parchment to fit two baking sheets. Invert the baking parchment and draw four circles on each piece, each measuring 7¹/₂cm/3in in diameter. Replace the parchment, pencilled side down.*

2 *In a large heatproof bowl, whisk egg whites with salt until stiff. Whisk in icing sugar, 1 tablespoon at a time. Place the bowl over a saucepan of gently simmering water; continue to whisk for about 5 minutes until meringue is stiff.*

3 *Spoon meringue into a piping bag fitted with a fluted nozzle and, starting in the centre of each circle, pipe 6 individual meringue baskets, using a spiral action and making the sides three spirals high.*

4 *Bake meringue baskets for 1¹/₄-1¹/₂ hours. Cool on a wire rack, then store in an airtight tin.*

5 *Make ice cream. Combine sugar, milk and cream in a saucepan. Bring to the boil, stirring to dissolve the sugar. Remove from the heat. In a bowl, beat egg yolks lightly. Add scalded cream mixture in a thin stream, beating constantly to make a light foamy mixture. Transfer to the top of a double boiler (or a heatproof bowl) and place over simmering water. Stir until custard coats the back of a spoon, then pour into a clean bowl and chill in a larger bowl filled with ice. As soon as custard is cool, cover it closely and refrigerate for 2 hours.*

6 *Fold in ground hazelnuts. Pour into an ice cream maker and chill according to instructions, adding the chopped nuts and chocolate chips when churning is almost complete. Alternatively, freeze in ice trays. When semi-frozen, beat mixture to break up any large ice crystals. Repeat theprocess twice more, adding the chopped hazelnuts and chocolate chips during the final beating. Freeze in a suitable container until ice cream is solid.*

7 *About 30 minutes before serving, transfer the ice cream to the refrigerator to*

soften slightly. Make the chocolate sauce. Melt chocolate with butter in a heavy-based saucepan. Gradually beat in cream and warm through, stirring constantly.

8 *Arrange the meringue baskets on individual plates. Place 2 scoops of ice cream in each basket, then top each scoop of ice cream with hot chocolate sauce. Serve at once.*

Kitchen tips:

For a quick cheat's pudding use a good quality bought ice cream (coffee is delicious). Don't be tempted to use bought meringue baskets, however, unless you have access to a good baker. The super-sweet, dry meringues sold in packs in supermarkets are not suitable. Make a plain vanilla ice cream by omitting the hazelnuts and adding 2 teaspoons natural vanilla essence. Before scooping it into the meringue baskets, fill them with strawberrries or raspberries for a summer treat.

Serves 6

ingredients

4 egg whites
pinch salt
280g/9oz icing sugar

Ice cream
125g/4oz caster sugar
300ml/10fl oz milk
600ml/1pt double cream
8 egg yolks
155g/5oz ground hazelnuts
60g/2oz toasted hazelnuts, chopped
90g/3oz chocolate chips

Chocolate sauce
185g/6oz plain chocolate
60g/2oz butter
185ml/6fl oz double cream
vanilla essence (optional)

cassata
layers

ingredients

Method:

1 To make filling place ice cream, cream, apricots, pineapple, cherries, raisins, chocolate and pistachio nuts in a bowl and mix to combine.

2 Split sponge horizontally into three even layers. Place one layer of sponge in the base of a lined 20cm/8in springform tin and sprinkle with 1 tablespoon of liqueur. Top with one-third of the filling. Repeat layers to use all ingredients ending with a layer of filling. Freeze for 5 hours or until firm. Remove from freezer 1 hour before serving and place in refrigerator.

3 Just prior to serving, decorate with chocolate curls.

Note: Use the best quality ice cream you can afford. To retain maximum volume and creamy texture, keep the cassata filling mixture well chilled until the cassata is finally assembled.

Serves 10

1 x 20cm/8in sponge cake
¼ cup/60ml/2fl oz almond-flavoured liqueur
chocolate curls
Cassata filling
1 litre/1¾pt vanilla ice cream, softened
1 cup/250ml/8fl oz cream (double)
125g/4oz glacé apricots, chopped
125g/4oz glacé pineapple, chopped
60g/2oz glacé cherries, chopped
60g/2oz raisins, halved
125g/4oz dark chocolate, grated
125g/4oz pistachio nuts, chopped

nougat
tartufo

Method:

1 Place nougat, hazelnuts, almonds, chocolate, ice cream and honey in a bowl and mix carefully to combine.

2 Spoon ice cream mixture into eight 1 cup/250ml/ 8fl oz capacity chilled aluminium moulds lined with plastic food wrap and freeze for 1 hour.

3 Remove moulds from freezer and unmould. Roll ice cream in coconut. Place on a tray lined with plastic food wrap, cover and freeze until required.

Note: To toast nuts, place them in a single layer on a baking tray or in a shallow ovenproof dish and bake at 180°C/350°F/ Gas 4 for 10-15 minutes or until they are golden. Turn them several times during cooking. Set aside to cool.

Serves 8

ingredients

¹/₂ cup/125g/4oz sugar
200g/6¹/₂oz nougat, chopped
60g/2oz hazelnuts,
toasted and chopped
6g/2oz slivered almonds, toasted
200g/6¹/₂oz dark or milk
chocolate, chopped
2 litres/3¹/₂pt vanilla ice
cream, softened
3 tablespoons honey
¹/₂ cup/45g/1¹/₂oz shredded
coconut, toasted

cassata
log

Photograph opposite

ingredients

¹/₂ cup/100g/3¹/₂oz caster sugar
2 tablespoons water
315g/10oz ricotta cheese, drained
90g/3oz dark chocolate, chopped
45g/1¹/₂oz mixed glacé cherries
2 tablespoons chopped candied
mixed peel
2 tablespoons crushed nuts
2 tablespoons sweet sherry
1¹/₂ cups/375mL/12fl oz cream
(double), whipped

cassata log

Method:

1 Place sugar and water in a saucepan and bring to the boil over a medium heat, stirring until sugar dissolves. Reduce heat and simmer, without stirring, for 2 minutes. Remove pan from heat and set aside to cool slightly.

2 Push ricotta cheese through a fine sieve into a large bowl. Slowly stir sugar syrup into cheese, mixing well to combine. Add chocolate, cherries, mixed peel, nuts and sherry and mix to combine. Fold in cream.

3 Spoon mixture into a foil-lined 11x21cm/4¹/₂x8¹/₂in loaf tin. Cover with foil and freeze overnight. To serve, unmould and cut into slices.

Note: Delicious served with thick cream and savoiardi biscuits (sponge fingers) or topped with purchased chocolate topping.

Serves 6

apricot
yoghurt ice cream

Method:

1 *Place the first 7 ingredients into a saucepan. Stir over heat until sugar dissolves. Bring to the boil. Simmer 20 minutes, or until apricots are tender. Cool.*
2 *Strain, reserving 1 cup of liquid. Discard cloves and cinnamon stick.*
3 *Using a food processor or blender, purée apricots and liquid together.*
4 *Stir in yoghurt and evaporated milk.*
5 *Pour into ice cream machine. Churn until firm and blades stop turning. (Approximately 40 minutes) Serve immediately or spoon into a container and freeze.*

**Makes approximately
4cups/1 litre/1 ³/₄pt**

ingredients

**375g/13oz dried apricots
1 cinnamon stick
¹/₂ teaspoon grated nutmeg
3 cloves
1 cup/155g/5oz brown sugar
¹/₃ cup/100g/3oz honey
2 cups/500ml/16oz water
1 cup/250ml/8oz natural yoghurt
375ml/13oz evaporated milk, chilled**

yoghurt
passionfruit ice cream

Method:

1 *Combine the honey and yoghurt in a bowl; mix well. Dissolve the gelatine in the water. Cool slightly, then stir into the yoghurt mixture. Freeze in ice trays until firm.*

2 *Transfer the frozen yoghurt mixture to a large bowl. Using a hand-held electric mixer, beat until the mixture doubles in bulk.*

3 *Beat the egg white in a grease-free bowl until stiff peaks form. Fold into the yoghurt mixture with the passionfruit pulp. Freeze in a freezerproof container until firm. Decorate with passionfruit pulp.*

Serves 4

ingredients

2 tablespoons clear honey
215ml/7fl oz natural low fat yoghurt
1 teaspoon powdered gelatine
2 tablespoons water
1 egg white
pulp of 1 passionfruit, plus extra to decorate

yoghurt
orange ice cream

Method:

1 *Combine the honey and yoghurt in a large bowl; mix well. Dissolve gelatine in the water. Cool slightly, then stir into yoghurt mixture.*

2 *Line a loaf tin with cling film. Spoon yoghurt mixture into the tin, cover and freeze for 3 hours.*

3 *Beat the frozen mixture in a large bowl until doubled in bulk. Beat in the vanilla, orange rind and juice.*

4 *Whisk the egg whites to soft peaks in a separate, grease-free bowl. Fold into the yoghurt ice, return the mixture to the loaf tin, cover and freeze until solid. Soften slightly before serving- with fresh fruit.*

Serves 6-8

ingredients

4 tablespoons clear honey
375ml/12fl oz orange-flavoured yoghurt
1 tablespoon powdered gelatine
60ml/2fl oz water
1 teaspoon vanilla essence
2 teaspoon finely grated orange rind
2 tablespoons freshly squeezed orange juice
2 egg whites

french
vanilla ice milk base

Photograph opposite

Method:

1 In a heavy-based saucepan, heat milk, sugar, and vanilla bean. (If you are using vanilla extract, do not add it until step 4). Stir occasionally until sugar is dissolved and the mixture is hot but not boiling.

2 Whisk egg yolks together in a bowl. Continue whisking and very slowly pour in approximately 1 cup/250ml/8oz of the milk mixture. When smooth, pour back into the pan.

3 Whisk constantly over low heat until the mixture thickens slightly and coats the back of a spoon (about 5 minutes). Take care that the mixture doesn't boil, or it will curdle. Draw your finger across the back of the coated spoon. If the line you make remains, the custard is done.

4 Remove vanilla bean; or, if you're using vanilla extract, add it at this stage.

5 Strain into a clean bowl and cool thoroughly.

6 Transfer to an ice cream machine and freeze according to manufacturer's instructions.

ingredients

4 1/4 cups/960ml/32 fl oz skim milk
3/4 cup/185g/6oz sugar
2 vanilla beans or
2 tablespoons vanilla extract
2 egg yolks

Note: *Increase vanilla in the above recipe to 2 vanilla beans or 2 tablespoons vanilla extract. This recipe is recommended as the foundation for some of the ice creams in this book. It produces consistently excellent flavour and texture. The same ingredients combined in different proportions give somewhat different results. Experiment to find which combination of ingredients is most appealing to your palate. Vanilla beans will give a richer flavour than extract.*

**Makes approximately
4 cups/900ml/32fl oz**

smoothy
base

Method:

1 Dissolve the skim milk powder in the milk and then gently blend the cream into the mixture.

2 The mixture should be chilled and well stirred before use in ice cream making.

ingredients

750ml/25oz milk
225ml/7fl oz thickened (double) cream
30g/1oz instant skim milk powder

simple
sugar syrup

ingredients

2 cups/500g/16oz sugar
1 cup/250ml/8oz water

Method:

1 In a medium sized saucepan, cook sugar and the water over high heat, stirring constantly, until sugar dissolves and mixture reaches a full, rolling boil.

2 Immediately remove from heat and cool to room temperature. Strain through a fine sieve into a jar or bowl. Cover and refrigerate until needed. Sugar syrup should always be well cooled to about 4°C/40°F before being used.

Makes about 3 cups

The Stages of Cooked Sugar Syrup

Simple **syrup -** The sugar has dissolved. The syrup is clear and registers about 104°C /215°F on a candy thermometer.

Soft-ball **stage -** 120°C/234°- 240°F. A small spoonful of syrup dropped into ice water then rubbed between finger and thumb forms a soft ball.

Caramel **stage -** 180°C/320°to355°F. The syrup turns golden brown.

Note: This traditional syrup falls somewhere between French and Italian. It may be stored in the refrigerator for several weeks.

simple syrup

soft-ball stage

caramel stage

make your own
ice cream cones

ingredients

I cup/250g/8oz unsalted butter
6 eggs
I ½ cups/375g/12oz sugar
2 tablespoons vanilla extract
3 ½ cups/440g/14oz flour
4 teaspoons baking powder

Method:

I *Melt butter over low heat; let cool. Beat eggs with an electric mixer. While beating, add sugar in a steady stream; continue beating until smooth. Add cooled butter and vanilla extract, then mix in flour and baking powder.*

2 *Bake in pizzelle iron according to manufacturer's instructions.*

3 *Lift the edges of the hot pizzelle with a knife and carefully peel it from the iron.*

4 *Roll one side toward the centre to begin forming a cone.*

5 *Wrap the opposite side around to complete the cone shape. Pinch the overlapping edges together.*

Makes approximately 50

fresh
fruit sauces

Colourful and refreshing, low-fat dessert sauces are a welcome change from rich toppings and gooey syrups laden with butter or cream. Made with a variety of fresh seasonal or frozen fruits and a few other simple ingredients you probably already have on hand in your refrigerator or pantry, these sauces are ideal for impromptu entertaining or a quiet night at home. They take only minutes to make in a blender or food processor; they complement most any ice cream, sherbet, sorbet, or ice; and best of all, you can make them as sweet or tart, as thick or thin as you like.

Melon-Berry Sauce

2 chilled cantaloupes
1 cup/250g/8oz fresh strawberries
1 teaspoon freshly squeezed lemon or lime juice
1/8 teaspoon grated nutmeg or freshly grated ginger
light sour cream or yoghurt, for garnish (optional) as needed

1 Halve and seed melons. Scoop out flesh, discarding shells. Using a blender or food processor and working in batches, purée melon and strawberries until smooth.
2 Add lemon juice and nutmeg and stir briefly to blend. Pour into serving dish and garnish with sour cream, if desired. Serve at once or refrigerate, covered, for up to 4 hours before serving.
Makes 3 cups/700ml/23fl oz 4 servings

Just-a-Bowl-of-Cherries Sauce

3 cups/700ml pitted sweet red cherries
1/2 cup/125ml fresh or bottled pomegranate juice
honey or sugar (optional) to taste
1/2 teaspoon almond or vanilla extract
light sour cream or non-fat yoghurt, for garnish (optional) as needed

1 Using a blender and working in batches, purée cherries with pomegranate juice until smooth.
2 Sweeten mixture with honey or sugar to taste, if desired; add almond extract and blend briefly to mix well. Pour into serving dish and garnish with sour cream, if desired. Serve at once or refrigerate, covered, for up to 4 hours before serving.
Makes 3 cups/700mL/23fl oz 4 servings

Kiwi-Nectarine Sauce

2 1/2 cups/600ml peeled, chopped kiwifruit
1 nectarine or peach, pitted and quartered
currant or mint jelly to taste
light sour cream or non-fat yoghurt (optional) as needed

1 Using a blender and working in batches, purée kiwifruit with nectarine or peach until smooth.
2 Stir in jelly to taste and blend briefly to mix well. Pour into serving dish and garnish with sour cream, if desired. Serve at once or refrigerate, covered, for up to 4 hours before serving.
Makes 3 cups/700ml/23fl oz 4 servings

Cooking is not an exact science: one does not require finely calibrated scales, pipettes and scientific equipment to cook, yet the conversion to metric measures in some countries and its interpretations must have intimidated many a good cook.

Weights are given in the recipes only for ingredients such as meats, fish, poultry and some vegetables. Though a few grams/ounces one way or another will not affect the success of your dish.

Though recipes have been tested using the Australian Standard 250mL cup, 20mL tablespoon and 5mL teaspoon, they will work just as well with the US and Canadian 8fl oz cup, or the UK 300mL cup. We have used graduated cup measures in preference to tablespoon measures so that proportions are always the same. Where tablespoon measures have been given, these are not crucial measures, so using the smaller tablespoon of the US or UK will not affect the recipe's success. At least we all agree on the teaspoon size.

For breads, cakes and pastries, the only area which might cause concern is where eggs are used, as proportions will then vary. If working with a 250mL or 300mL cup, use large eggs (60g/2oz), adding a little more liquid to the recipe for 300mL cup measures if it seems necessary. Use the medium-sized eggs (55g/1^1/4oz) with 8fl oz cup measure. A graduated set of measuring cups and spoons is recommended, the cups in particular for measuring dry ingredients. Remember to level such ingredients to ensure their accuracy.

English measures

All measurements are similar to Australian with two exceptions: the English cup measures 300mL/10fl oz, whereas the Australian cup measure 250mL/8fl oz. The English tablespoon (the Australian dessertspoon) measures 14.8mL/^{1}/2fl oz against the Australian tablespoon of 20mL/^{3}/4fl oz.

American measures

The American reputed pint is 16fl oz, a quart is equal to 32fl oz and the American gallon, 128fl oz. The Imperial measurement is 20fl oz to the pint, 40fl oz a quart and 160fl oz one gallon.

The American tablespoon is equal to 14.8mL/^{1}/2fl oz, the teaspoon is 5mL/^{1}/6fl oz. The cup measure is 250mL/8fl oz, the same as Australia.

Dry measures

All the measures are level, so when you have filled a cup or spoon, level it off with the edge of a knife. The scale below is the "cook's equivalent"; it is not an exact conversion of metric to imperial measurement. To calculate the exact metric equivalent yourself, use 2.2046 lb = 1 kg or 1 lb = 0.45359kg

Metric		Imperial	
g = grams		oz = ounces	
kg = kilograms		lb = pound	
15g		^{1}/2oz	
20g		^{2}/3oz	
30g		1oz	
60g		2oz	
90g		3oz	
125g		4oz	^{1}/4 lb
155g		5oz	
185g		6oz	
220g		7oz	
250g		8oz	^{1}/2 lb
280g		9oz	
315g		10oz	
345g		11oz	
375g		12oz	^{3}/4 lb
410g		13oz	
440g		14oz	
470g		15oz	
1,000g	1kg	35.2oz	2.2 lb
	1.5kg		3.3 lb

Oven temperatures

The Celsius temperatures given here are not exact; they have been rounded off and are given as a guide only. Follow the manufacturer's temperature guide, relating it to oven description given in the recipe. Remember gas ovens are hottest at the top, electric ovens at the bottom and convection-fan forced ovens are usually even throughout. We included Regulo numbers for gas cookers which may assist. To convert °C to °F multiply °C by 9 and divide by 5 then add 32.

Oven temperatures

	C°	F°	Regulo
Very slow	120	250	1
Slow	150	300	2
Moderately slow	150	325	3
Moderate	180	350	4
Moderately hot	190-200	370-400	5-6
Hot	210-220	410-440	6-7
Very hot	230	450	8
Super hot	250-290	475-500	9-10

Cake dish sizes

Metric	Imperial
15cm	6in
18cm	7in
20cm	8in
23cm	9in

Loaf dish sizes

Metric	Imperial
23x12cm	9x5in
25x8cm	10x3in
28x18cm	11x7in

Liquid measures

Metric	Imperial	Cup & Spoon
mL	fl oz	
millilitres	fluid ounce	
5mL	$^1/_6$fl oz	1 teaspoon
20mL	$^2/_3$fl oz	1 tablespoon
30mL	1fl oz	1 tablespoon plus 2 teaspoons
60mL	2fl oz	$^1/_4$ cup
85mL	2$^1/_2$fl oz	$^1/_3$ cup
100mL	3fl oz	$^3/_8$ cup
125mL	4fl oz	$^1/_2$ cup
150mL	5fl oz	$^1/_4$ pint, 1 gill
250mL	8fl oz	1 cup
300mL	10fl oz	$^1/_2$ pint)
360mL	12fl oz	1$^1/_2$ cups
420mL	14fl oz	1$^3/_4$ cups
500mL	16fl oz	2 cups
600mL	20fl oz 1 pint,	2$^1/_2$ cups
1 litre	35fl oz 1 $^3/_4$ pints,	4 cups

Cup measurements

One cup is equal to the following weights.

	Metric	Imperial
Almonds, flaked	90g	3oz
Almonds, slivered, ground	125g	4oz
Almonds, kernel	155g	5oz
Apples, dried, chopped	125g	4oz
Apricots, dried, chopped	190g	6oz
Breadcrumbs, packet	125g	4oz

	Metric	Imperial
Breadcrumbs, soft	60g	2oz
Cheese, grated	125g	4oz
Choc bits	155g	5oz
Coconut, desiccated	90g	3oz
Cornflakes	30g	1oz
Currants	155g	5oz
Flour	125g	4oz
Fruit, dried (mixed, sultanas etc)	185g	6oz
Ginger, crystallised, glace	250g	8oz
Honey, treacle, golden syrup	315g	10oz
Mixed peel	220g	7oz
Nuts, chopped	125g	4oz
Prunes, chopped	220g	7oz
Rice, cooked	155g	5oz
Rice, uncooked	220g	7oz
Rolled oats	90g	3oz
Sesame seeds	125g	4oz
Shortening (butter, margarine)	250g	8oz
Sugar, brown	155g	5oz
Sugar, granulated or caster	250g	8oz
Sugar, sifted icing	155g	5oz
Wheatgerm	60g	2oz

Length

Some of us still have trouble converting imperial length to metric. In this scale, measures have been rounded off to the easiest-to-use and most acceptable figures.

To obtain the exact metric equivalent in converting inches to centimetres, multiply inches by 2.54 whereby 1 inch equals 25.4 millimetres and 1 millimetre equals 0.03937 inches.

Metric	Imperial
mm=millimetres	in = inches
cm=centimetres	ft = feet
5mm, 0.5cm	$^1/_4$in
10mm, 1.0cm	$^1/_2$in
20mm, 2.0cm	$^3/_4$in
2.5cm	1in
5cm	2in
8cm	3in
10cm	4in
12cm	5in
15cm	6in
18cm	7in
20cm	8in
23cm	9in
25cm	10in
28cm	11in
30cm	1 ft, 12in

acidulated water: water with added acid, such as lemon juice or vinegar, which prevents discoloration of ingredients, particularly fruit or vegetables. The proportion of acid to water is 1 teaspoon per 300ml.

al dente: Italian cooking term for ingredients that are cooked until tender but still firm to the bite; usually applied to pasta.

americaine: method of serving seafood - usually lobster and monkfish - in a sauce flavoured with olive oil, aromatic herbs, tomatoes, white wine, fish stock, brandy and tarragon.

anglaise: cooking style for simple cooked dishes such as boiled vegetables. Assiette anglaise is a plate of cold cooked meats.

antipasto: Italian for "before the meal", it denotes an assortment of cold meats, vegetables and cheeses, often marinated, served as an hors d'oeuvre. A typical antipasto might include salami, prosciutto, marinated artichoke hearts, anchovy fillets, olives, tuna fish and Provolone cheese.

au gratin: food sprinkled with breadcrumbs, often covered with cheese sauce and browned until a crisp coating forms.

balsamic vinegar: a mild, extremely fragrant, wine-based vinegar made in northern Italy. Traditionally, the vinegar is aged for at least seven years in a series of casks made of various woods.

baste: to moisten food while it is cooking by spooning or brushing on liquid or fat.

baine marie: a saucepan standing in a large pan which is filled with boiling water to keep liquids at simmering point. A double boiler will do the same job.

beat: to stir thoroughly and vigorously.

beurre manie: equal quantities of butter and flour kneaded together and added a little at a time to thicken a stew or casserole.

blanc: a cooking liquid made by adding flour and lemon juice to water in order to keep certain vegetables from discolouring as they cook.

blanch: to plunge into boiling water and then, in some cases, into cold water. Fruits and nuts are blanched to remove skin easily.

blanquette: a white stew of lamb, veal or chicken, bound with egg yolks and cream and accompanied by onion and mushrooms.

blend: to mix thoroughly.

bonne femme: dishes cooked in the traditional French "housewife" style. Chicken and pork bonne femme are garnished with bacon, potatoes and baby onion; fish bonne femme with mushrooms in a white wine sauce.

bouquet garni: a bunch of herbs, usually consisting of sprigs of parsley, thyme, marjoram, rosemary, a bay leaf, peppercorns and cloves, tied in muslin and used to flavour stews and casseroles.

braise: to cook whole or large pieces of poultry, game, fish, meat or vegetables in a small amount of wine, stock or other liquid in a closed pot. Often the main ingredient is first browned in fat and then cooked in a low oven or very slowly on top of the stove. Braising suits tough meats and older birds and produces a mellow, rich sauce.

broil: The American term for grilling food.

brown: cook in a small amount of fat until brown.

burghul (also bulgur): a type of cracked wheat, where the kernels are steamed and dried before being crushed.

buttered: to spread with softened or melted butter.

butterfly: to slit a piece of food in half horizontally, cutting it almost through so that when opened it resembles butterfly wings. Chops, large prawns and thick fish fillets are often butterflied so that they cook more quickly.

buttermilk: a tangy, low-fat cultured milk product whose slight acidity makes it an ideal marinade base for poultry.

calzone: a semicircular pocket of pizza dough, stuffed with meat or vegetables, sealed and baked.

caramelise: to melt sugar until it is a golden brown syrup.

champignons: small mushrooms, usually canned.

chasseur: (hunter) a French cooking style in which meat and chicken dishes are cooked with mushrooms, shallots, white wine, and often tomato. See also cacciatora.

clarify: to melt butter and drain the oil off the sediment.

coat: to cover with a thin layer of flour, sugar, nuts,

crumbs, poppy or sesame seeds, cinnamon sugar or a few of the ground spices.

concasser: to chop coarsely, usually tomatoes.

confit: from the French verb confire, meaning to preserve. Food that is made into a preserve by cooking very slowly and thoroughly until tender. In the case of meat, such as duck or goose, it is cooked in its own fat, and covered with it so that it does not come into contact with the air. Vegetables such as onions are good in confit.

consomme: a clear soup usually made from beef.

coulis: a thin puree, usually of fresh or cooked fruit or vegetables, which is soft enough to pour (couler means 'to run'). A coulis may be rough-textured or very smooth.

court bouillon: the liquid in which fish, poultry or meat is cooked. It usually consists of water with bay leaf, onion, carrots and salt and freshly ground black pepper to taste. Other additives can include wine, vinegar, stock, garlic or spring onions (scallions).

couscous: cereal processed from semolina into pellets, traditionally steamed and served with meat and vegetables in the classic North African stew of the same name.

cruciferous vegetables: certain members of the mustard, cabbage and turnip families with cross-shaped flowers and strong aromas and flavours.

cream: to make soft, smooth and creamy by rubbing with back of spoon or by beating with mixer. Usually applied to fat and sugar.

croutons: small toasted or fried cubes of bread.

crudites: raw vegetables, whether cut in slices or sticks to nibble plain or with a dipping sauce, or shredded and tossed as salad with a simple dressing.

cube: to cut into small pieces with six equal sides.

curdle: to cause milk or sauce to separate into solid and liquid. Example, overcooked egg mixtures.

daikon radish: (also called mooli): a long white Japanese radish. dark sesame oil (also called Oriental sesame oil): dark polyunsaturated oil with a low burning point, used for seasoning. Do not replace with lighter sesame oil.

deglaze: to dissolve congealed cooking juices or glaze on the bottom of a pan by adding a liquid, then scraping and stirring vigorously whilst bringing the liquid to the boil. Juices may be used to make gravy or to add to sauce.

degrease: to skim grease from the surface of liquid. If possible the liquid should be chilled so the fat solidifies. If not, skim off most of the fat with a large metal spoon, then trail strips of paper towel on the surface of the liquid to remove any remaining globules.

devilled: a dish or sauce that is highly seasoned with a hot ingredient such as mustard, Worcestershire sauce or cayenne pepper.

dice: to cut into small cubes.

dissolve: mix a dry ingredient with liquid until absorbed.

dredge: to coat with a dry ingredient, as flour or sugar.

drizzle: to pour in a fine thread-like stream over a surface.

dust: to sprinkle or coat lightly with flour or icing sugar.

emulsion: a mixture of two liquids that are not mutually soluble- for example, oil and water.

entree: in Europe, the "entry" or hors d'oeuvre; in North America entree means the main course.

fillet: special cut of beef, lamb, pork or veal; breast of poultry and game; fish cut of the bone lengthways.

flake: to break into small pieces with a fork.

flame: to ignite warmed alcohol over food.

fold in: a gentle, careful combining of a light or delicate mixture with a heavier mixture using a metal spoon.

fricassee: a dish in which poultry, fish or vegetables are bound together with a white or veloute sauce. In Britain and the United States, the name applies to an old-fashioned dish of chicken in a creamy sauce.

galette: sweet or savoury mixture shaped as a flat round.

garnish: to decorate food, usually with something edible.

gastrique: caramelized sugar deglazed with vinegar and used in fruit-flavoured savoury sauces, in such dishes as duck with orange.

glaze: a thin coating of beaten egg, syrup or aspic which is brushed over pastry, fruits or cooked meats.

gluten: a protein in flour that is developed when dough

is kneaded, making it elastic.

gratin: a dish cooked in the oven or under the grill so that it develops a brown crust. Breadcrumbs or cheese may be sprinkled on top first. Shallow gratin dishes ensure a maximum area of crust.

grease: to rub or brush lightly with oil or fat.

joint: to cut poultry, game or small animals into serving pieces by dividing at the joint.

julienne: to cut food into match-like strips.

knead: to work dough using heel of hand with a pressing motion, while stretching and folding the dough.

line: to cover the inside of a container with paper, to protect or aid in removing mixture.

infuse: to immerse herbs, spices or other flavourings in hot liquid to flavour it. Infusion takes from two to five minutes depending on the flavouring. The liquid should be very hot but not boiling.

macerate: to soak food in liquid to soften.

marinade: a seasoned liquid, usually an oil and acid mixture, in which meats or other foods are soaked to soften and give more flavour.

marinara: Italian "sailor's style" cooking that does not apply to any particular combination of ingredients. Marinara tomato sauce for pasta is most familiar.

marinate: to let food stand in a marinade to season and tenderize.

mask: to cover cooked food with sauce.

melt: to heat until liquified.

mince: to grind into very small pieces.

mix: to combine ingredients by stirring.

monounsaturated fats: one of three types of fats found in foods. Are believed not to raise the level of cholesterol in the blood.

nicoise: a garnish of tomatoes, garlic and black olives; a salad with anchovy, tuna and French beans is typical.

non-reactive pan: a cooking pan whose surface does not chemically react with food. Materials used include stainless steel, enamel, glass and some alloys.

noisette: small "nut" of lamb cut from boned loin or rack that is rolled, tied and cut in neat slices. Noisette also means flavoured with hazelnuts, or butter cooked to a nut brown colour.

olive oil: various grades of oil extract from olives. Extra virgin olive oil has a full, fruity flavour and the lowest acidity. Virgin olive oil is slightly higher in acidity and lighter in flavour. Pure olive oil is a processed blend of olive oils and has the highest acidity and lightest taste.

papillote: to cook food in oiled or buttered greasepoof paper or aluminium foil. Also a decorative frill to cover bone ends of chops and poultry drumsticks.

parboil: to boil or simmer until part cooked (i.e. cooked further than when blanching).

pare: to cut away outside covering.

pate: a paste of meat or seafood used as a spread for toast or crackers.

paupiette: a thin slice of meat, poultry or fish spread with a savoury stuffing and rolled. In the United States this is also called "bird" and in Britain an "olive".

peel: to strip away outside covering.

plump: to soak in liquid or moisten thoroughly until full and round.

poach: to simmer gently in enough hot liquid to cover, using care to retain shape of food.

polyunsaturated fat: one of the three types of fats found in food. These exist in large quantities in such vegetable oils as safflower, sunflower, corn and soya bean. These fats lower the level of cholesterol in the blood.

puree: a smooth paste, usually of vegetables or fruits, made by putting foods through a sieve, food mill or liquefying in a blender or food processor.

ragout: traditionally a well-seasoned, rich stew containing meat, vegetables and wine. Nowadays, a term applied to any stewed mixture.

ramekins: small oval or round individual baking dishes.

reconstitute: to put moisture back into dehydrated foods by soaking in liquid.

reduce: to cook over a very high heat, uncovered, until the liquid is reduced by evaporation.

refresh: to cool hot food quickly, either under running water or by plunging it into iced water, to stop it cooking. Particularly for vegetables and occasionally for shellfish.

rice vinegar: mild, fragrant vinegar that is less sweet than cider vinegar and not as harsh as distilled malt vinegar. Japanese rice vinegar is milder than the Chinese variety.

roulade: a piece of meat, usually pork or veal, that is spread with stuffing, rolled and often braised or poached. A roulade may also be a sweet or savoury mixture that is baked in a Swiss roll tin or paper case, filled with a contrasting filling, and rolled.

rubbing-in: a method of incorporating fat into flour, by use of fingertips only. Also incorporates air into mixture.

safflower oil: the vegetable oil that contains the highest proportion of polyunsaturated fats.

salsa: a juice derived from the main ingredient being cooked or a sauce added to a dish to enhance its flavour. In Italy the term is often used for pasta sauces; in Mexico the name usually applies to uncooked sauces served as an accompaniment, especially to corn chips.

saturated fats: one of the three types of fats found in foods. These exist in large quantities in animal products, coconut and palm oils; they raise the level of cholesterol in the blood. As high cholesterol levels may cause heart disease, saturated fat consumption is recommended to be less than 15% of kilojoules provided by the daily diet.

sauté: to cook or brown in small amount of hot fat.

score: to mark food with cuts, notches of lines to prevent curling or to make food more attractive.

scald: to bring just to boiling point, usually for milk. Also to rinse with boiling water.

sear: to brown surface quickly over high heat in hot dish. seasoned flour: flour with salt and pepper added.

sift: to shake a dry, powdered substance through a sieve or sifter to remove any lumps and give lightness.

simmer: to cook food gently in liquid that bubbles steadily just below boiling point so that the food cooks in even heat without breaking up.

singe: to quickly flame poultry to remove all traces of feathers after plucking.

skim: to remove a surface layer (often of impurities and scum) from a liquid with a metal spoon or small ladle.

slivered: sliced in long, thin pieces, usually refers to nuts, especially almonds.

soften: ie: gelatine - sprinkle over cold water and allow to gel (soften) then dissolve and liquefy.

souse: to cover food, particularly fish, in wine vinegar and spices and cook slowly; the food is cooled in the same liquid. Sousing gives food a pickled flavour.

steep: to soak in warm or cold liquid in order to soften food and draw out strong flavours or impurities.

stir-fry: to cook thin slices of meat and vegetable over a high heat in a small amount of oil, stirring constantly to even cooking in a short time. Traditionally cooked in a wok, however a heavy based frying pan may be used.

stock: a liquid containing flavours, extracts and nutrients of bones, meat, fish or vegetables.

sweat: to cook vegetables over heat until only juices run.

sugo: an Italian sauce made from the liquid or juice extracted from meat during cooking.

sweat: to cook sliced or chopped food, usually vegetables, in a little fat and no liquid over very low heat. Foil is pressed on top so that the food steams in its own juices, usually before being added to other dishes.

thicken: to make a thin, smooth paste by mixing together arrowroot, cornflour or flour with an equal amount of cold water; stir into hot liquid, cook, stirring until thickened.

toss: to gently mix ingredients with two forks or fork and spoon.

total fat: the individual daily intake of all three fats previously described in this glossary. Nutritionists recommend that fats provide no more than 35% of the energy in the diet.

whip: to beat rapidly, incorporate air and produce expansion.

zest: thin outer layer of citrus fruits containing the aromatic citrus oil. It is usually thinly pared with a vegetable peeler, or grated with a zester or grater to separate it from the bitter white pith underneath.

notes